DOING THE TRUTH IN CHARITY

DOING THE TRUTH IN CHARITY

Statements of Pope Paul VI,
Popes John Paul I, John Paul II,
and the Secretariat for
Promoting Christian Unity
1964–1980

edited by
Thomas F. Stransky, C.S.P.
and
John B. Sheerin, C.S.P.

Preface by John Cardinal Willebrands

PAULIST PRESS • *New York/Ramsey*

Library of Congress
Catalog Card Number: 81-85384

ISBN: 0-8091-2398-3

Published by Paulist Press
545 Island Road, Ramsey, N.J. 07446

Printed and bound in the
United States of America

Contents

Preface

For just over the two decades which span the preparatory period of the Second Vatican Council, the Council itself and the following years, the Secretariat for Promoting Christian Unity has been the official organ for the stimulation and coordination of the Roman Catholic Church's contribution to the ecumenical movement. The Secretariat's aims and history are here sketched by Father Stransky. During these twenty years the Secretariat has been responsible for or contributed to numerous documents which clarify and develop the Catholic understanding and practice of ecumenism. These statements of the Holy See can of course be discovered by those who are disposed to search through the back numbers of its many official publications. But these documents are not themselves "back numbers." Any Catholic who is laboring for Christian unity, indeed any Christian who shares such work with Catholics, will frequently need to refer to these texts. The two Paulist editors and the Paulist Press have therefore done a generous service by gathering all these texts in a handy reference volume, which I hope will find a place on the desk of every ecumenist.

But documents, with their stated principles, laws and guidelines, are not the sum of ecumenism. They are, so to speak, a skeleton that has to be fleshed out. As Pope John Paul II reminds us, "The experience of the [Second Vatican] Council and the texts in which this experience was expressed remain a source of ever relevant inspiration. They are rich in guidelines, in requirements that still have to be discovered and put into practice in the concrete life of the people of God" (Address to the Unity Secretariat plenary, February 8, 1980). In such ecumenical developments successive Popes have given a continuous lead, both in their teaching and catechesis to Catholics, and in their correspondence and meetings with leaders of other Churches, whether in Rome or in the course of their travels. The editors have increased the value of this book by including a very ample collection of extracts from the speeches and letters of Popes Paul VI and John Paul II, and from the documentation concerned with more important exchanges of visits with Church leaders, many of which have led to common declarations.

These texts are but milestones on the way to the restoration of unity among Christians, and should encourage and guide those who are ministering for the same cause at the regional, national and local levels. The Secretariat's 1975 document on ecumenical collaboration recognizes these levels as facing their own specific needs and situations with their own resources: "Ecumenism on the local level ... has an initiative of its own and its task is a wider one than merely implementing worldwide ecumenical directives on a small scale." This volume both contains those worldwide directives and provides authoritative material that can stimulate such local initiatives.

The Secretariat, as the historical sketch here records, is also responsible for the Commission for Religious Relations with the Jews. The pertinent documents and some striking excerpts from papal addresses are also found in this useful volume.

During these entire two decades Fr. Tom Stransky has been a close and generous collaborator of the Secretariat, first as a staff member during its first ten years, and more recently as an official consultor. The compilation of this book is one more evidence of his tireless work for Christian unity. I thank him warmly, and with him I thank his Paulist collaborators and publishers for a book that will surely be welcomed by all who have the cause of Christian unity at heart.

> John Cardinal Willebrands
> President
> Secretariat for Promoting Christian Unity

Week of Prayer for Christian Unity
January 1982

General Introduction

The sixteen years since the Second Vatican Council's promulgation of the *Decree on Ecumenism* (Nov. 1964) have witnessed a steady stream of Roman Catholic ecumenical documents on the international, regional and national levels. Some are internal to the Church, addressed to Catholics but welcoming others looking over their shoulders. Other documents have been the results of multilateral or bilateral dialogues, and are addressed to the partner church communities, including the Roman Catholic.

These statements, of course, have already been published. They are usually scattered in various brochures or isolated in past issues of journals and newspapers. The demand increases for easy access to a broad sweep of such documents, selective and comprehensive. The question "Where can I find them?" is not uncommon. Even those who, more than the average committed Christian, spend time and energy on ecumenical pastoral concerns are hard put to keep up with the flow. An indication of the serious need: in 1978 the Vatican Secretariat for Promoting Christian Unity's plenary session of 24 cardinals and bishops pressed for an easily available, systematic publication for themselves and others; and in 1979, the same demand came from the SPCU's meeting of 64 delegates, from 58 countries, of national ecumenical commissions.

Paulist Press now intends to meet the demand by the *Ecumenical Documents* series. The first volume, this one, collects the significant official documents and statements from the Roman Curia, especially from the Unity Secretariat (SPCU), and from the popes, 1964–1981. The second volume, edited by Harding Meyer and Lukas Vischer, brings together the more important interconfessional doctrinal agreements reached in the international dialogues. The third, edited by John B. Sheerin and John Hotchkin, republishes agreements in the national dialogues, especially in the United States. We hope a future fourth volume will bring up to date the intentions of the first three.

1

For the use of this first volume we offer a few reminders:

1. Editorial judgment intrudes in the very selection of the texts. Some editors would have been more inclusive. We have not, for example, included all papal addresses to other Christian leaders because we judge several are over-repetitious in the same context: John Paul II's talk to Christian leaders in Zaire is not here, for the same was said more forcefully four days later in Kenya (May 7, 1980); or for the same reason, not all the popes' informal talks on ecumenism to the Catholic faithful are here. Other editors would have been more exclusive because of the repetitious content. But we judge that the different context often provides different emphasis, e.g., the "papacy-and-ecumenism" theme in papal addresses to the SPCU plenary meeting, to the World Council of Churches, and to the Taizé ecumenical community of youth. Nevertheless, in both our selections and our introductions to them, we try to avoid those pro and con interpretations and criticisms which we and others may have done elsewhere. We do hope that many readers, now that they have a comprehensive fifteen-year array of official texts under one cover, will more easily and accurately offer such evaluations.

2. Many curial documents and papal statements which do not mention "ecumenism" or "Christian unity" do have ecumenical implications. Because of the theological and pastoral relationship within the triadic unity/mission/renewal, almost any official utterance from the Holy See has ecumenical repercussions, even though the authors may not have explicitly intended that—for example, concerning human rights and evangelization, marriage and the family, abortion and birth control, priesthood and women's ordination, and liturgical expressions in the two-thirds world (one could list at least 300 post-Vatican Council II documents from the Holy See). Such ecumenical analyses and interpretations of official church statements and practices are, literally, voluminous.

3. Not all texts have the same authority. A papal encyclical which refines, enlarges and deepens the discussions and conclusions of a Bishops' Synod—e.g., Paul VI's *Evangelization in the Modern World* (Dec. 8, 1975) and John Paul II's *Catechetics* (Oct. 25, 1979)—carry far more inner authority than a normal Wednesday general audience talk, and the Council's declaration concerning the Jews is of far greater import than a pope's Good Friday sermon. As for SPCU documents, one should note the carefully intended ways by which they were promulgated. Example: the Directory, Parts One (1967) and Two (1969), is "approved and confirmed by the authority of Paul VI," who "ordered that they be published"; it is intended to be normative. But the SPCU reflections on the ecumenical dialogue (1970) is only advisory: "its authority rests uniquely in the fact that it is a result of prolonged reflection on many levels." Authority is qualitative, and is distorted if quantity scales are used. Here again, analy-

ses and interpretations by others have already been varied, even contradictory.

4. This fifteen-year coverage does not imply a static repetition with no development in contents and emphases. For example, there is a marked development in ecclesiological understanding between the Church of Rome and its separated "Sister Churches" of the East; and compared with Paul VI's thoughts, John Paul II places stronger emphasis on common witness in order to lessen the scandal of divisions in Christian mission.

5. These statements have been influenced by a whole range of ecumenical activities and converging dialogue streams. Popes and curial offices are not only teachers. They too engage, consciously or implicitly, in that common "searching and finding, finding and searching" into the unfathomable riches of Christ (cf. *Decree on Ecumenism,* n. 11; the Augustinian expression is often quoted by Paul VI). The ecumenical movement, both theologically understood and historically developed, has no sole teaching center with only pupil satellites.

Our main sources are the *Acta Apostolicae Sedis,* the official Vatican journal of records; and *L'Osservatore Romano,* the daily Vatican newspaper in Italian, and its weekly English edition. But the most ample source of information for our purposes is the *Information Service (IS)* of the Secretariat for Promoting Christian Unity.* Since its first number in 1967, *IS* has brought readers up to date on SPCU activities—relations with other churches, the WCC and other forums, bilateral dialogues, staff travel, etc. Its editors also keep an eagle-eye on significant statements from the popes and other curial departments, and republish many of them in *IS.* We are most grateful to Msgr. Eric Salzmann, the SPCU archivist since 1962, for providing us with materials for our consideration.

The title of this volume, *Doing the Truth in Charity,* from the Latin Vulgate version of Ephesians 3:14, was the favorite "ecumenical motto" of Augustin Cardinal Bea, the first SPCU president.

We dedicate our efforts here to our Paulist confrere, John Keating. From 1966 he was general secretary of the Canadian Bishops' Ecumenical Commission until, in mid-1974, the Paulists elected him their vice-president. Inflicted by a cancerous blood system, he spent much of his remaining strength in putting together such a volume as his last service for the cause he so untiringly cherished and for the Church he so deeply loved. He died on November 20, 1975.

The Editors
Pentecost Sunday 1981

---

* Issues three times a year in French and in English editions: *Information Service,* Secretariat for Promoting Christian Unity, 00120 Vatican City State, Europe. As of 1980, U.S. $6.50 per year.

An Historical Sketch
THE SECRETARIAT FOR PROMOTING CHRISTIAN UNITY

Three months after Angelo Roncalli, the seventy-eight-year-old ex-patriarch of Venice, began his pontificate as John XXIII, he announced his intention to convoke an "Ecumenical Council for the Universal Church" (Jan. 25, 1959). He contemplated a Council that would be of service "not only for the spiritual good and joy of the Christian people but also an invitation to the separated communities to seek again that unity for which many souls are longing in these days throughout the world."[1] The Pope later described his decision: "The idea of the Council did not come as the slowly ripening fruit of long deliberation but was like the sudden flowering of an unexpected spring."[2]

The announcement stunned Roman Catholics and perplexed other Christians. Was this a papal attempt to reunite all Christians in the fashion of the Councils of Lyons (1274) and of Florence (1438–1442)—a common table at which "reunion formulae" could and would be forged?

Six months later John XXIII clarified his intention, perhaps even to himself. His first encyclical, *Ad Petram cathedram* (June 29, 1959), specified that only bishops in communion with the See of Rome would gather to discuss those pressing topics which concern "the development of the Catholic faith, the revival of Christian standards of living, and the bringing of ecclesiastical discipline into closer accord with the needs and conditions of our times." The Council's ecumenical significance? The gathering of over 2,100 bishops would "surely provide the outstanding example of truth, unity and love. May those who are separated from this Apostolic See, beholding this manifestation of unity, derive from it the gentle invitation to seek that unity for which Jesus Christ prayed so ardently to his heavenly Father."[3] If in 1870 the First Vatican Council had declared the Church to be its own apologetic, its own "sign of credibility,"[4] then in the 1960s the Second Vatican could induce a sweeping renewal of the

5

Church that would enhance that sign. If the coming Council and its aftermath could "eliminate as much as possible the human obstacles which prevent a true view of the Church," then "we shall point to the Church in all its splendor, 'without stain or wrinkle' (Eph. 5:27), and say to all those who are separated from us, Orthodox, Protestant and the rest: Look, brethren, this is the Church of Christ. We have striven to be true to it, to ask the Lord for grace that it may remain forever what he willed. Come, here the way lies open for meeting and for homecoming. Come, take, or resume, that place which is yours, which for many was your fathers' place."[5]

John XXIII thus shifted attention from a reunion Council to one of renewal, from other Christians' joining the Catholic leaders for debate and, one hopes, eventual consensus, to their watching at a distance the Roman Catholic Church being "renewed" through its own exclusive gathering.

But could there not be a middle way for the Council's role in the restoration of unity among Christians? In early 1960 Cardinal Lorenz Jaeger of Paderborn, Germany's foremost leader in ecumenical discussions, approached Augustin Bea, then, as he described himself, a retired, quietly working, praying cardinal in Rome.[6] Would this fellow German petition Pope John for a "commission for the union of Christians"? Such a commission would be an explicit instrument in guiding the Council's ecumenical dimensions of Church renewal and in facilitating communications with other Christians. On March 11, 1960, Bea transmitted to John XXIII a more elaborated request. To Bea's surprise, two days later he received the Pope's "agreement in principle." In late May, again to Bea's surprise, the Pope told him of his coming appointment as president of the new office, to be called not a "commission" but a "secretariat"; the low-keyed title would offer "more freedom of movement."[7]

On Pentecost Sunday (June 5, 1960), John XXIII instituted, among the twelve preparatory conciliar bodies, the *Secretariatus ad Christianorum Unitatem fovendam* (literally, the Secretariat for Promoting the Unity of Christians, but it would call itself in English, the Secretariat for Promoting Christian Unity—SPCU). It would enable "those who bear the name of Christians but are separated from this Apostolic See . . . to follow the work of the Council and to find more easily the path by which they may arrive at that unity for which Christ prayed."[8] Catholics and other Christians immediately saw the new secretariat an active symbol of Pope John's loving concern for Christian unity. In August 1960 the executive committee of the World Council of Churches stated that the SPCU was "an important development in the Roman Catholic Church. . . . It would no longer leave all initiative (in ecumenical conversation) to individual Roman Catholics, but begin to speak and set itself in relation to other Churches and to ecumenical organizations."[9] In the words of the WCC general secretary, Dr. Wilhelm Visser 't Hooft, "We finally have a friendly address in Rome."

During the summer of 1960, the Pope appointed the SPCU secretary, Johannes G. M. Willebrands, then representative of the Dutch hierarchy for ecumensim and secretary of the International Catholic Conference for Ecumenical Questions.[10] Two other staff members were added.[11] The foursome entered their small offices on the Via dei Corridori in October. In mid-November took place the first plenary session of seventeen episcopal voting members and their twenty consultors.

So began, in hindsight, the official entrance of the Roman Catholic Church into the one ecumenical movement, four years later to be chartered by the *Decree on Ecumenism* (Nov. 22, 1964).

In July of that same 1960 summer, the French Jew, Jules Isaac, visited John XXIII and asked if the coming Council could counteract anti-semitism and further Jewish-Catholic understanding. Listening sympathetically, the Pope urged the renowned scholar to discuss the same concerns with Cardinal Bea. On September 18 John XXIII commissioned the SPCU president to prepare a conciliar draft on the Church and the Jews. So began that delicate, often twisted path[12] which led to the charter five years later—the long section on the Jews in the *Declaration on the Relation of the Church to Non-Christian Religions* (Oct. 28, 1965).

* * *

The immediate purpose of the SPCU, 1960–1965, directly concerned Vatican Council II. But besides eventually presenting and defending its own drafts on the Council floor, the SPCU immediately began in 1960 to contact other Christian leaders and organizations. It informed them of the Council's purposes and work, received their wishes and suggestions, and, if necessary, used these in its own draft work or passed them on to other commissions. The SPCU broke through the old walls of distance and suspicion by arranging visits of Christian leaders with the Pope. The first tête-à-tête of a Pope with the head of another communion since the Reformation was John XXIII with the Archbishop of Canterbury, Geoffrey Fisher (Dec. 3, 1960). What was then an historic breakthrough now has become normal in post-Vatican II courtesies or acts of Christian charity among Church heads.

In November 1961 the Central Preparatory Commission approved SPCU proposals for non-Catholic Christian delegated observers and guests to participate in all the Council phases, including the closed general sessions.[13] After informal, confidential explorations, the SPCU in June 1962 sent out invitations to the "world confessional bodies," e.g., Lambeth Conference of Bishops (Anglicans), World Methodist Council, Lutheran

World Federation, etc., and to the Eastern Orthodox and other separated Eastern Churches. During the Council these observers had the opportunity to submit suggestions for improving each of the eventual sixteen promulgated documents. They were especially close to the SPCU's own drafting work on ecumenism, on religious freedom, on relations with non-Christian religions, and on divine revelation (for this last declaration the SPCU was an equal partner with the Theological Commission). At the Council's conclusion, Paul VI touchingly confided to the observers, "Your departure produces a solitude around us unknown before the Council and which now saddens us. We would like to see you with us always."[14] These contacts initiated the personal and organizational relations which in the post-conciliar years led to the active presence of SPCU-delegated observers at confessional and interconfessional gatherings, to a variegated series of international and national bilateral dialogues with Orthodox, Anglicans and Protestants, and to ongoing collaboration with the World Council of Churches.

Of special import during 1960–1965 were the first official contacts of the Holy See, through the SPCU, with the Orthodox Churches of the USSR and of Eastern Europe. And the initial relations with the Greek Orthodox led to the embrace of Pope Paul VI and Patriarch Athenagoras in the Holy City of Jerusalem (Jan. 1964) and to the mutual lifting of the anathemas between the Sees of Rome and Constantinople (Dec. 14, 1965).

Shortly after the closing session of Vatican II (Dec. 8, 1965), Paul VI confirmed the SPCU as a permanent organ of the Holy See, on the same occasion as his worldwide vision also created the secretariats for Non-Christians and for Non-Believers.[15] The SPCU retained its working structure of bishop-members and consultors, and of its office with president, secretary and two under-secretaries—one for the Eastern Churches, the other for Anglicans and Protestants. The competence of the SPCU was more officially specified in Paul VI's constitution on the Roman Curia reform (Aug. 15, 1967): it shall foster relations with Christians of other Churches, execute those Vatican decrees which bear on ecumenism, see to the right interpretation and carrying out of ecumenical principles, establish or encourage and coordinate national and international Catholic ecumenical organizations, institute official dialogues with other Churches and Christian communities, and delegate official Catholic observers to Christian meetings, while also inviting non-Catholic observers to Catholic meetings. The SPCU also has juridical competence in Catholic-Jewish relations "from the religious aspect."[16]

* * *

During 1965–1970, the SPCU vigorously gave flesh to the Council's spirit and principles in four major ways.

First, in answer to many requests from the bishops for more detailed guidelines for ecumenical action, the SPCU followed a general working procedure: a series of guidelines on specific topics to be issued at intervals rather than a thick book of directives at one time. The *Directory, Part One* (1967), concerned the setting up of diocesan and national ecumenical commissions, the validity of baptisms conferred in other Christian communions, the fostering of "spiritual ecumenism" within the Catholic Church, and the sharing of spiritual activities, including liturgical worship. *Part Two* (1969) outlined ecumenical principles and practices at the university and seminary levels. In 1970 the SPCU offered its experienced reflections and suggestions concerning the ecumenical dialogue in general. The SPCU officers also were consulted for the new norms in mixed marriages (1970). And in a project very close to Cardinal Bea's biblical heart, in 1968 were published with the United Bible Societies guiding principles for interconfessional cooperation in translating, producing and distributing the Bible; for facilitating this work, the SPCU had a special desk, and helped establish the independent World Catholic Federation for the Biblical Apostolate (1969).

Second, in the conviction that standing dialogue structures should be erected before the immediate post-Vatican II enthusiasm waned and an inevitable but temporary lull in mood set in, the SPCU, with papal approval and that of the other churches' authorities, established joint dialogue commissions with the Lutheran World Federation (1965), the Anglican Communion (1966), the World Methodist Council (1966), and the World Alliance of Reformed Churches (1968). In a unique category was the dialogue with some of the Old Catholic Churches of the Union of Utrecht. This dialogue began in 1966, and within a few years passed from the SPCU level to some bishops' conferences (Switzerland, Netherlands, Germany, and France).

Already in 1965, before Vatican II's final session, the WCC and the Holy See agreed to establish a joint working group (JWG) which would recommend to the parent bodies both the agenda and means of collaboration in studies and action. The JWG's first annual meeting was held in 1966.

Slowly and firmly collaboration developed with the WCC. The annual preparations for the Week of Prayer for Christian Unity; the role of the laity and its grass-roots education in the ecumenical movement; realistic collaboration in emergency relief, development aid and medical work; the common Christian dialogue with people of other religious faiths; the approach to the phenomenon of unbelief—these became normal areas of mutual reflection and programs. Raw issues, such as religious freedom in some countries, mixed marriages as a pastoral concern, and distorted methods of evangelism and church-growth, also appeared on the JWG agenda. Structured improvements emerged. Twelve Roman Catholic theologians became full members of the Faith and Order Commission. Consultors were assigned to the Commission for World Mission and Evangelism and to the Church and Society Commission. In 1969 a joint committee on society, development and peace (SODEPAX) was set up. Already in 1968 at the WCC general assembly in Uppsala, the question was raised: Should and could the Roman Catholic Church become a member of the WCC? The JWG, which already had been discussing the question, now worked more intensively on it.

Third, in order to foster official relations with the separated Eastern Churches in a "dialogue of love," the SPCU negotiated visits of their leaders with Paul VI, most often during which common declarations of intent were promulgated—for example, with heads of the Byzantine Orthodox Church (Athenagoras, 1967) and of the Armenian Orthodox Church (Koren I, 1967; Vasken I, 1968). In a more quiet style, Paul VI kept up a continual correspondence with the leaders of the separated Eastern "sister Churches," especially on the occasion of the great feast days—for example, with Patriarch Alexis (Russian Orthodox) and Amba Shenouda III (Coptic Orthodox).

Fourth, the SPCU's enlarged staff devoted considerable time and energy in travel, away from its Vatican offices: first-hand relations with emerging national and regional Catholic ecumenical commissions; participation as members of official observer teams to conferences of the WCC and of world confessional bodies; contacts with Christian leaders at meetings of regional organizations—for example, the Christian Conference of Asia, the All Africa Conference of Churches, and the European Conference of Churches; conducting seminars for Catholics and other Christians, clergy and laity, in Japan, the Philippines, India, New Zealand, Ghana and Nigeria, South Africa and Kenya, the U.S.A. and Canada, almost every country in western Europe, Poland and Lebanon, Mexico and Madagascar, Brazil and Peru.

During the three years before Cardinal Bea's death (1965–1968), already in his mid-eighties, the ailing SPCU president harnessed his remaining strength for Rome itself, harmonizing the SPCU's increasing, varied activities.[17] Bea died on November 16, 1968. In April 1969, Paul VI appointed the cardinal's faithful collaborator as the new SPCU president, Johannes Willebrands. Willebrands continued his predecessor's mixture of office responsibilities and frequent travel for personal contacts, lectures and seminars.[18]

* * *

The ecumenical decade of the 1970s presented the SPCU with bewildering, shifting moods, attitudes and practices in the local churches of six continents. Alongside the gloom of those physicians who proclaimed ecumenism dead, at least atrophied or overly tired, was the patient joy of others who saw the first steps of a healthy child stumbling into adolescence. Ecumenism was burdened by what faced clerical (including episcopal) and lay Catholics in every sphere of communal and personal renewal as called for by the Second Vatican Council: the *future* Church and its demands became *present* too quickly for too many—a "future shock" or disorientation of the individual and collective psyche to the premature arrival of the future. Resulting insecurities and "polarizations" affected ecumenical renewal. And too many generalizations of the world situation were shaped through narrow local experiences. The SPCU inevitably was often caught in the middle of contradictory complaints: "You dreamers are too far ahead of us" versus "You bureaucrats are lagging behind where ecumenism is really at."

Nevertheless, in the 1970s the general movement was forward. Paul VI, in so many addresses and more official documents, pressed Catholics to be faithful to the ecumenical commitment of the Church; and to the careful reader, John Paul II (October 1978–) has been using even stronger language from the Vatican and on his travels. A new "tradition" of activities in all six continents was growing. These were described in the SPCU 1975 Report *Ecumenical Collaboration at the Regional, National and Local Levels.* An updated outline is found in the *Common Witness* document which the WCC/RCC joint working group issued in 1981.[19]

The SPCU sees its primary tasks within the Roman Catholic Church as international, worldwide. Well aware that "Christian unity can come about only by a process of people growing together where they live together—in local churches," the SPCU also knows that "the process eventually transcends the local situation; hence there must be coordination of local processes . . . not regimentation but cross-fertilization."[20] SPCU's contacts with bishops, clergy and lay people help foster this coordination. Within the Roman Curia itself, informal and formally structured relations exist. The SPCU president is a member of other curial congregations, viz., For the Doctrine of the Faith, For the Evangelization of Peoples, For the Sacraments and Divine Worship, For the Eastern Churches, and For the Revision of Canon Law. Also the SPCU secretary, helped by his staff, acts as consultor to other congregations of the Roman Curia.

During the 1970s the SPCU stubbornly continued the patient international dialogues. By the 1980s the official theological conversations with the Anglicans, the Lutherans, the Methodists, the Presbyterians, the Pentecostals (begun in 1972), and the Disciples of Christ (in 1978) began to turn in their results on those classical themes provoked by the Protestant Reformation and the Catholic Counter-Reformation: e.g., Scripture and tradition; baptism, ministry and ordination; the Eucharist; authority in and of the Church. The Faith and Order Commission, with full Roman Catholic membership since 1968, was completing multilateral studies on baptism/Eucharist/ministry, and on a common confession of faith. By the decade's end, the question was no longer primarily the contents of such dialogues and the consensus among their immediate participants but the awareness and reception of such dialogues by all levels of the participating churches. As Cardinal Willebrands explained to the 1980 Bishops' Synod, for the first time in its history the Church is faced with texts drawn up by officially commissioned representatives who will be asking the Church: "Have we done what you expect of us? Do you recognize your faith, the faith of all ages, in this exposition of the faith?"[21]

Collaboration with the World Council of Churches continued. The optimistic "yes" to Roman Catholic membership in the WCC glowed in the post-Uppsala Assembly air. But after the JWG study, Cardinal Willebrands announced in May 1972 that for the immediate future, the answer is "no"; nevertheless, the two partners would work out, indeed intensify, the positive relationship in a non-membership atmosphere.[22] In 1979 John Paul II asked the JWG "to find ways of ensuring increased collaboration . . . in all fields in which this is now possible."[23]

In its task of bearing the Holy See's competence for Jewish religious concerns, the SPCU helped form, with the International Jewish Committee for Interreligious Consultations, the Catholic/Jewish International Liaison Committee. This group has met annually since 1970. In October 1974 Paul VI set up the Commission for Religious Relations with the Jews, with Cardinal Willebrands as its president, and the SPCU as vice-president. Under the name of this commission was promulgated in January 1975 *Guidelines and Suggestions* for implementing the Vatican Council's statement on the Jews (*Nostra aetate*, n. 4).

Other formal dialogues on the world level were just commencing at the decade's turn. Although for over fifteen years there had been numerous contacts with leaders of the separated Eastern Churches and significant declarations between their leaders and the Popes, only in June 1980 at Patmos and Rhodes did the first meeting of the official Roman Catholic/Orthodox dialogue take place.

On the other hand, by the mid-1970s the SPCU recognized that in many ways the main gap within the Christian community was no longer a simple Roman Catholic versus Protestant/Orthodox, but between the mainstream Protestant/Roman Catholic/Orthodox and the commonly called "conservative Evangelicals," most of whom have a bias against "conciliar ecumenism." In April 1977 an ad hoc Evangelical/Roman Catholic dialogue on mission (ERCDOM) was held between the SPCU and leaders within the Lausanne Committee for World Evangelization. Between then and a second ad hoc meeting in March 1982 (Cambridge, England), organized conversations on some regional levels took place, e.g., the North American, at Maryknoll, New York (November 1981).

* * *

This sketch of the structure, aims and activities of the SPCU during its first twenty years is all too brief. One still awaits a far more detailed, if not definitive, history.

A personal note concludes. I was one of the original foursome who opened the doors of the SPCU in the autumn of 1960, remained on the staff during the Vatican Council and five years afterward, and am now one of its official consultors. Its former and present staff, members and consultors are more than names from afar; indeed, some I cherish as the closest of friends. I have shared most of their highest moments of joyful, forward strides, and so many of their quiet frustrations and holy headaches. In short, I have been humbly privileged to have grown up with the Secretariat, that effective symbol of the Catholic Church's commitment to restore unity among all Christians for the sake of the saving Lord's mission to humankind.

Two decades form but a brief series on the continuum of two millennia. If asked for the lessons I have learned, I would answer, above all: the gift of real assent to the understanding that ecumenism is measured in God's time, not ours. As a mission of hope which "transcends human powers and gifts,"[24] ecumenism, experienced between 1960–1980, leads one daily to affirm the Vatican Council's hope that the initiatives of the sons and daughters of the Catholic Church, joined to those of other Christian Communions, "will go forward, without obstructing the ways of divine Providence, and without prejudicing the future inspirations of the Holy Spirit."[25]

Thomas F. Stransky
Paulist Fathers

Notes

1. *Acta Apostolicae Sedis* (AAS) 51 (1959), p. 69.

2. "Address to Italian Catholic Action Presidents," *Osservatore Romano,* August 11, 1959. The idea was "an inspiration the spontaneity of which hit Us as a sudden and unforeseen blow, in the humility of Our soul." Letter to the Clergy of Venice, April 21, 1959. *AAS* 51 (1959), p. 379.

3. *AAS* 51 (1959), p. 511.

4. *Constitution on Catholic Faith* (April 24, 1870): *Conciliorum Oecumenicorum Decreta,* ed. Instituto per le Scienze Religiose, Bologna (Herder: Basil, 1962), p. 783.

5. Address to Italian Catholic Action Presidents, *op. cit.*

6. *Spiritual Profile: Diary Notes,* ed. Stjepan Schmidt, SJ (London: Chap-

man, 1971), cf. chap. 4. Born in the village of Riedböhringen at the edge of Germany's Black Forest, Bea was educated as a Jesuit in the Netherlands, Austria and Germany. Ordained a priest in 1912, he studied Oriental philology under Protestant scholars at Berlin University. After a three-year term as Jesuit provincial in Munich (1921–24), he was called to Rome to supervise Jesuits who specialized in philosophy and theology and to teach biblical theology and exegesis. From 1930–49 he was rector of the Pontifical Biblical Institute, as well as consultor to several Roman Curia congregations. Although John XXIII had met Bea only once and briefly, he created him a cardinal in December 1959, one surmises, out of traditional respect for John's predecessor; Bea had been a close advisor to Pius XII and, since 1945, that Pope's confessor. Cardinal Bea and Pope John quickly became confidants. A few weeks before death, John XXIII remarked to a lay friend, "Imagine what a grace the Lord has given in making me discover Cardinal Bea!"

7. Cf. Bea's "Il Segretariato per l'Unione dei Christiani," *La Rivista del Clero Italiano,* November 1965, pp. 4–5.

8. *Superno Dei nutu: AAS* 52 (1960), p. 436.

9. *Ecumenical Review,* October 1960, p. 46.

10. Born in 1909 in Bovenkarspel and ordained in 1934, Willebrands went to Rome for a doctoral study on John Henry Newman. He returned to The Netherlands for three years of parish work in Amsterdam, then taught philosophy at the Warmond, and later became its rector. In 1946 he was named president of the Association of St. Willibrord, the national Catholic organization for ecumenism. In 1951 he helped organize the Catholic Conference for Ecumenical Questions, an unofficial group of leading Catholic theologians, most of them from Europe; they met annually until 1963.

11. Jean-Francois Arrighi, from Corsica, who is still on the staff, and the American, Thomas F. Stransky, who left in 1970 after his election as president of the Paulist Fathers.

12. Such difficult beginnings were foreseen. Bea communicated to the first SPCU meeting, November 1960, that by John XXIII's request even the fact of initial discussion and drafting be *sub secreto.*

13. Already John XXIII had accepted the World Council of Churches' invitation to delegate, through the SPCU, five observers to the third general assembly in New Delhi (November 1961).

14. At the prayer service for Christian unity, St. Paul's Basilica, Dec. 4, 1965. *Osservateurs-Délegués et Hôtes du Secrétariat pour l'Unité des Chrétiens au Deuxième Concile Oecuménique du Vatican* (Vatican Polyglot Press, 1965), p. 59. Oscar Cullmann, a SPCU guest at all four sessions, commented during the first: "Our presence . . . is really a miracle. When I look about every morning at the places we occupy, places of honor facing the Cardinals, when the secretary of the Council proclaims the 'Exeant omnes' (All should leave) every morning, while we remain in our places, I consider the manner and mode with which we are welcomed to the Council a never-ending miracle . . . above all when we call to mind what Councils have meant in the past for Christians who are not Catholics." Quoted by Cardinal Willebrands in an address at Assumption College, Worcester, Mass., August 18, 1980.

15. *Finis concilio,* Jan. 3, 1966: *AAS* 58 (1966), p. 40.

16. *Regimini Ecclesiae universae: AAS* 59 (1967), pp. 918–919.

17. During this slowdown of three years, Bea managed to write, besides several articles, five books!

18. The new secretary was the Dominican Jerôme Hamer, until he was succeeded in 1973 by the Louvain scholar, Charles Moeller. Willebrands became Archbishop of Utrecht in December 1973, while remaining the SPCU president. To cover the SPCU offices full time, Paul VI appointed (Dec. 1975) as vice-president Bishop Ramon Torella Cascante (1923–   ). In 1970 the Pope has already called to Rome this auxiliary bishop of Barcelona to become the vice-president of both the Council for the Laity and the Commission for Justice and Peace.

19. *Common Witness* is the first of a series on current mission topics published by the WCC Commission on World Mission and Evangelism (WCC, 150 route de Ferney, CH-1211 Geneva 20, Switzerland). The entire JWG text is found also in SPCU *IS* 44 (1980), pp. 142–162.

20. SPCU Report to the meeting of national ecumenical commission representatives (Rome, Nov. 1972). SPCU *IS* 20 (1973), p. 12.

21. Report to the Synod on some aspects of SPCU activities, 1977–1980. SPCU *IS* 44 (1980), pp. 119–120. Cf. the Meyer-Vischer second volume of this *Ecumenical Documents* series, esp. the introduction. The participating world confessional communions, including the Catholic Church, have held three forums on their bilateral conversations, giving special attention to "consensus" and "reception." The conclusions of these meetings (April 1978; June 1979; Nov. 1980) can be obtained from Faith and Order.

22. Cf. SPCU *IS* 19 (1973), p. 13.

23. Letter addressed to Bishop Torrella on the occasion of the Feb. 26-March 2, 1979 JWG meeting. SPCU *IS* 40 (1979), p. 15. The JWG regularly publishes official reports to its two authorities—the Pope and the WCC central committee or general assembly: Report I (SPCU *IS* 1 [1967]; II, 3 [1967]; III, 14 [1971]; IV, 30 [1976].

24. *Decree on Ecumenism*, concluding paragraph (n. 24).

25. *Ibid.*

Chapter One
THE DECREE ON ECUMENISM
AND OTHER CONCILIAR TEXTS

Introduction

At their first session in the autumn of 1962, the Fathers of the Second Vatican Council hesitated to discuss ecumenism as such because three preparatory commissions—the commissions for Theology, for the Eastern Churches, and for Christian Unity—had separate texts on the theme. The Council postponed discussion of the subject by voting for a single document on Church Unity which would combine the contents of the former three. The SPCU submitted the draft *On Ecumenism* for discussion and written comments during the second session (1963). Revised during that session and the interim, this draft at the third session was overwhelmingly approved by the Bishops: 2,137 votes in favor, only 11 in opposition. On November 21, 1964, Pope Paul VI, "together with the Fathers of the Sacred Council", promulgated the Decree *Unitatis Redintegratio*—the official title from the first two Latin words. Text: *AAS* 57 (1965), pp. 90–97. Translation by John Long, S.J. and Thomas F. Stransky, C.S.P., published by the Vatican Polyglot Press, 1965.

Several other of the fifteen promulgated Council documents also contained ecumenical statements of theological and pastoral significance. The various drafting commissions had received suggestions from the SPCU and from official observers delegated by other Churches and Communities.*

---

* During each session representatives from Church bodies observed the plenary meetings, had direct access to the official drafts and other documents, and were given the opportunity directly to react to the unfinished drafts in progress. Over the four sessions 186 official observers attended, for longer or shorter periods or were present at one or another of every session. They were delegated by: The Patriarchates of Constantinople, of Alexandria, of Moscow; the Serbian Orthodox Church; the Orthodox Church of Georgia; the Orthodox Church of Bulgaria; the Russian Orthodox Church Outside of Russia; the Coptic Orthodox

I

DECREE ON ECUMENISM

Introduction

1. The RESTORATION OF UNITY among all Christians is one of the principal concerns of the Second Vatican Council. Christ the Lord founded one Church and one Church only. However, many christian Communions present themselves to men as the true inheritors of Jesus Christ; all indeed profess to be followers of the Lord but they differ in mind and go different ways, as if Christ Himself were divided (Cf. 1 Cor. 1, 13). Certainly, such division openly contradicts the will of Christ, scandalizes the world, and damages that most holy cause, the preaching of the Gospel to every creature.

The Lord of Ages nevertheless wisely and patiently follows out the plan of His grace on our behalf, sinners that we are. In recent times He has begun to bestow more generously upon divided Christians remorse over their divisions and longing for unity.

Everywhere large numbers have felt the impulse of this grace, and among our separated brethren also there increases from day to day a movement, fostered by the grace of the Holy Spirit, for the restoration of unity among all Christians. Taking part in this movement, which is called ecumenical, are those who invoke the Triune God and confess Jesus as Lord and Savior. They do this not merely as individuals but also as members of the corporate groups in which they have heard the Gospel, and which each regards as his Church and indeed, God's. And yet, almost everyone, though in different ways, longs for the one visible Church of God, a Church truly universal and sent forth to the whole world that the world may be converted to the Gospel and so be saved, to the glory of God.

Church; the Orthodox Church of Syria; the Armenian Orthodox Church of Etchmiadzin; the Armenian Orthodox Church of Cilicia; the Orthodox Church of Ethiopia; the Syrian Orthodox Church of India; the Old Catholic Church; the Syrian Church of Mar Tomas of Malabar; the Anglican Communion; the Lutheran World Federation; the World Presbyterian Alliance; the Evangelical Church of Germany; the World Methodist Council; the International Council of Congregationalists; the World Convention of Disciples of Christ; the World Committee of Friends; the International Association of Liberal Christianity and Religious Freedom; the Church of South India; the United Church of Christ in Japan; the Protestant Federation of France; the World Council of Churches; the Australian Council of Churches.

With less official titles: Guests of the Unity Secretariat from the Orthodox Theology Institute of St. Serge (Paris), the Orthodox Seminary of St. Vladimir (New York), the Taizé Community, the Missouri Synod (Lutheran), the National Council of Churches, U.S.A., and others.

For details and all names, cf. *Observateurs-Délégués et Hôtes du Secrétariat pour l'Unité des Chrétiens au Deuxième Concile Oecuménique du Vatican* (Vatican Polyglot Press, 1965).

The sacred Council gladly notes all this. It has already declared its teaching on the Church, and now, moved by a desire for the restoration of unity among all the followers of Christ, it wishes to set before all Catholics guidelines, helps and methods, by which they too can respond to the grace of this divine call.

1. Catholic Principles on Ecumenism

2. What has revealed the love of God among us is that the only-begotten Son of God has been sent by the Father into the world, so that, being made man, He might by His redemption of the entire human race give new life to it and unify it (Cf. 1 Jn. 4, 9; Col. 1, 18–20; Jn. 11, 52). Before offering Himself up as a spotless victim upon the altar of the cross, He prayed to His Father for those who believe: "that they all may be one; even as thou, Father, art in me, and I in thee, that they also may be one in us, so that the world may believe that thou hast sent me" (Jn. 17, 21). In His Church He instituted the wonderful sacrament of the Eucharist by which the unity of the Church is both signified and brought about. He gave His followers a new commandment to love one another (Cf. Jn. 13, 34), and promised the Spirit, their Advocate (Cf. Jn. 16,7), who, as Lord and life-giver, should remain with them forever.

After being lifted up on the cross and glorified, the Lord Jesus poured forth the Spirit whom He had promised, and through whom He has called and gathered together the people of the New Covenant, which is the Church, into a unity of faith, hope and charity, as the Apostle teaches us: "There is one body and one Spirit, just as you were called to the one hope of your calling; one Lord, one faith, one baptism" (Eph. 4, 4–5). For "all you who have been baptized into Christ have put on Christ . . . for you are all one in Christ Jesus" (Gal. 3, 27–28). It is the Holy Spirit, dwelling in those who believe and pervading and ruling over the entire Church, who brings about that wonderful communion of the faithful and joins them together so intimately in Christ that He is the principle of the Church's unity. By distributing various kinds of spiritual gifts and ministries (Cf. 1 Cor. 12, 4–11), He enriches the Church of Jesus Christ with different functions "in order to equip the saints for the work of service, so as to build up the body of Christ" (Eph. 4, 12).

In order to establish this His holy Church everywhere in the world till the end of time, Christ entrusted to the College of the Twelve the task of teaching, ruling and sanctifying (Cf. Mt. 28, 18–20, in conjunction with Jn. 20, 21–23). Among their number He chose Peter. And after his confession of faith, He determined that on him He would build His Church; to him He promised the keys of the kingdom of heaven (Cf. Mt. 16, 19, in conjunction with Mt. 18, 18), and after his profession of love, entrusted all His sheep to him to be confirmed in faith (Cf. Lk. 22, 32) and shepherded in perfect unity (Cf. Jn. 21, 15–18), with Himself, Christ Jesus, forever remaining the chief cornerstone (Cf. Eph. 2, 20) and shepherd of our souls (Cf. 1 Pet. 2, 25; 1 Vatican Council, Sess. IV [1870], The Constitution *Pastor Aeternus:* Coll. Lac. 7, 482 a).

It is through the faithful preaching of the Gospel by the Apostles and their successors—the bishops with Peter's successor at their head—through their administering the sacraments, and through their governing in love, that Jesus Christ wishes His people to increase, under the action of the Holy Spirit; and He perfects its fellowship in unity: in the confession of one faith, in the common celebration of divine worship, and in the fraternal harmony of the family of God.

The Church, then, God's only flock, like a standard high lifted for the nations to see it (Cf. Is. 11, 10–12), ministers the Gospel of peace to all mankind (Cf. Eph. 2, 17–18, in conjunction with Mk. 16, 15), as it makes its pilgrim way in hope toward its goal, the fatherland above (Cf. 1 Pet. 1, 3–9).

This is the sacred mystery of the unity of the Church, in Christ and through Christ, with the Holy Spirit energizing its various functions. The highest exemplar and source of this mystery is the unity, in the Trinity of Persons, of one God, the Father and the Son in the Holy Spirit.

3. In this one and only Church of God from its very beginnings there arose certain rifts (Cf. 1 Cor. 11, 18–19; Gal. 1, 6–9; 1 Jn. 2, 18–19), which the Apostle strongly censures as damnable (Cf. 1 Cor. 1, 11 ff.; 11, 22). But in subsequent centuries much more serious dissensions appeared and quite large Communities became separated from full communion with the Catholic Church—for which, often enough, men of both sides were to blame. However, one cannot charge with the sin of the separation those who at present are born into these Communities and in them are brought up in the faith of Christ, and the Catholic Church accepts them with respect and affection as brothers. For men who believe in Christ and have been properly baptized are brought into certain, though imperfect, communion with the Catholic Church. Without doubt, the differences that exist in varying degrees between them and the Catholic Church—whether in doctrine and sometimes in discipline, or concerning the structure of the Church—do indeed create many obstacles, sometimes serious ones, to full eccesiastical communion. The ecumenical movement is striving to overcome these obstacles. But even in spite of them it remains true that all who have been justified by faith in baptism are incorporated into Christ (Cf. Council of Florence, Sess. VIII [1439], The Decree *Exultate Deo:* Mansi 31, 1055 A); they therefore have a right to be called Christians, and with good reason are accepted as brothers by the children of the Catholic Church (Cf. St. Augustine, *In Ps. 32, Enarr. II, 29: PL* 36, 299).

Moreover, some, even very many of the most significant elements and endowments, which together go to build up and give life to the Church itself, can exist outside the visible boundaries of the Catholic Church: the written Word of God; the life of grace; faith, hope and charity, with the other interior gifts of the Holy Spirit, as well as visible elements. All of these, which come from Christ and lead back to Him, belong by right to the one Church of Christ.

The brethren divided from us also carry out many liturgical actions of the christian religion. In ways that vary according to the condition of each Church or Community, these most certainly can truly engender a life of grace, and, one must say, can aptly give access to the communion of salvation.

It follows that the separated Churches (Cf. IV Lateran Council [1215], Constitution IV: Mansi 22, 990; II Council of Lyons [1274], Profession of faith of Michael Palaeologos: Mansi 24, 71 E; Council of Florence, Sess. VI [1439], Definition *Laetentur caeli:* Mansi 31, 1026 E) and Communities as such, though we believe they suffer from defects already mentioned, have been by no means deprived of significance and importance in the mystery of salvation. For the Spirit of Christ has not refrained from using them as means of salvation which derive their efficacy from the very fullness of grace and truth entrusted to the Catholic Church.

Nevertheless, our separated brethren, whether considered as individuals or as Communities and Churches, are not blessed with that unity which Jesus Christ wished to bestow on all those to whom He has given new birth into one body, and whom He has quickened to newness of life—that unity which the Holy Scriptures and the ancient Tradition of the Church proclaim. For it is through Christ's Catholic Church alone, which is the all-embracing means of salvation, that the fullness of the means of salvation can be obtained. It was to the apostolic college alone, of which Peter is the head, that we believe that our Lord entrusted all the blessings of the New Covenant, in order to establish on earth the one Body of Christ into which all those should be fully incorporated who belong in any way to the people of God. During its pilgrimage on earth, this people, though still in its members liable to sin, is growing in Christ and is guided by God's gentle wisdom, according to His hidden designs, until it shall happily arrive at the fullness of eternal glory in the heavenly Jerusalem.

4. Today, in many parts of the world, under the inspiring grace of the Holy Spirit, many efforts are being made in prayer, word and action to attain that fullness of unity which Jesus Christ desires. The sacred Council exhorts, therefore, all the Catholic faithful to recognize the signs of the times and to take an active and intelligent part in the work of ecumenism.

The term "ecumenical movement" indicates the initiatives and activities encouraged and organized, according to the various needs of the Church and as opportunities offer, to promote christian unity. These are: first, every effort to avoid expressions, judgments and actions which do not represent the condition of our separated brethren with truth and fairness and so make mutual relations with them more difficult. Then, "dialogue" between competent experts from different Churches and Communities; in their meetings, which are organized in a religious spirit, each explains the teaching of his Communion in greater depth and brings out clearly its distinctive features. Through such dialogue everyone gains a truer knowledge and more just appreciation of the teaching and religious life of both Communions. In addition, these Communions engage in that more intensive cooperation in carrying out any duties for the common good of humanity which are demanded by every christian conscience. They also come together for common prayer, where this is permitted. Finally, all are led to examine their own faithfulness to Christ's will for the Church and, wherever necessary, undertake with vigor the task of renewal and reform.

Such actions, when they are carried out by the Catholic faithful with prudent patience and under the attentive guidance of their bishops, promote justice and truth, concord and collaboration, as well as the spirit of brotherly love and unity. The result will be that, little by little, as the obstacles to perfect ecclesiastical communion are overcome, all Christians will be gathered, in a common celebration of the Eucharist, into the unity of the one and only Church, which Christ bestowed on His Church from the beginning. This unity, we believe, subsists in the Catholic Church as something she can never lose, and we hope that it will continue to increase until the end of time.

However, it is evident that the work of preparing and reconciling those individuals who wish for full Catholic communion is of its nature distinct from ecumenical action. But there is no opposition between the two, since both proceed from the marvelous ways of God.

In ecumenical work, Catholics must assuredly be concerned for their separated brethren, praying for them, keeping them informed about the Church, making the first approaches toward them. But their primary duty is to make a careful and honest appraisal of whatever needs to be renewed and done in the Catholic household itself, in order that its life may bear witness more clearly and faithfully to the teachings and institutions which have been handed down from Christ through the Apostles.

For although the Catholic Church has been endowed with all divinely revealed truth and with all means of grace, yet its members fail to live by them with all the fervor that they should. As a result the radiance of the face shines less brightly in the eyes of our separated brethren and of the world at large, and the growth of God's kingdom is retarded. Every Catholic must therefore aim at christian perfection (Cf. James 1, 4; Rom. 12, 1–2) and, each according to his station, play his part that the Church, which bears in her own body the humility and dying of Jesus (Cf. 2 Cor. 4, 10; Phil. 2, 5–8), may daily be more purified and renewed, against the day when Christ will present her to Himself in all her glory without spot or wrinkle (Cf. Eph. 5, 27).

While preserving unity in essentials, let everyone in the Church, according to the office entrusted to him, preserve a proper freedom in the various forms of spiritual life and discipline, in the variety of liturgical rites, and even in the theological elaborations of revealed truth. In all things let charity prevail. If they are true to this course of action, they will be giving ever richer expression to the authentic catholicity of the Church.

On the other hand, Catholics must gladly acknowledge and esteem the truly christian endowments from our common heritage which are to be found among our separated brethren. It is right and salutary to recognize the riches of Christ and virtuous works in the lives of others who are bearing witness to Christ, sometimes even to the shedding of their blood. For God is always wonderful in His works and worthy of all praise.

Nor should we forget that anything wrought by the grace of the Holy Spirit in the hearts of our separated brethren can contribute to our own edification. Whatever is truly christian is never contrary to what genuinely belongs to the faith; indeed, it can always bring a more perfect realization of the very mystery of Christ and the Church.

Nevertheless, the divisions among Christians prevent the Church from realizing the fullness of catholicity proper to her in those of her sons who, though joined to her by baptism, are yet separated from full communion with her. Furthermore, the Church herself finds it more difficult to express in actual life her full catholicity in all its aspects.

This sacred Council is gratified to note that the participation by the Catholic faithful in ecumenical work is growing daily. It commends this work to the bishops everywhere in the world for their diligent promotion and prudent guidance.

2. The Practice of Ecumenism

5. The concern for restoring unity involves the whole Church, faithful and clergy alike. It extends to everyone, according to the talent of each, whether it be exercised in daily christian living or in theological and historical studies. This concern itself already reveals to some extent the bond of brotherhood existing among all Christians and it leads toward full and perfect unity, in accordance with what God in His kindness wills.

6. Every renewal of the Church (Cf. V Lateran Council, Sess. XII [1517], Constitution *Constituti:* Mansi 32, 988 B-C) essentially consists in an increase of fidelity to her own calling. Undoubtedly this explains the dynamism of the movement toward unity.

Christ summons the Church, as she goes her pilgrim way, to that continual reformation of which she always has need, insofar as she is an institution of men here on earth. Consequently, if, in various times and circumstances, there have been deficiencies in moral conduct or in church discipline, or even in the way that church teaching has been formulated— to be carefully distinguished from the deposit of faith itself—these should be set right at the opportune moment and in the proper way.

Church renewal therefore has notable ecumenical importance. Already this renewal is taking place in various spheres of the Church's life: the biblical and liturgical movements, the preaching of the Word of God and catechetics, the apostolate of the laity, new forms of religious life and the spirituality of married life, and the Church's social teaching and activity. All these should be considered as promises and guarantees for the future progress of ecumenism.

7. There can be no ecumenism worthy of the name without interior conversion. For it is from newness of attitudes of mind (Cf. Eph. 4, 23), from self-denial and unstinted love, that desires of unity take their rise and develop in a mature way. We should therefore pray to the Holy Spirit for the grace to be genuinely self-denying, humble, gentle in the service of others and to have an attitude of brotherly generosity toward them. The Apostle of the Gentiles says: "I, therefore, a prisoner for the Lord, beg you to lead a life worthy of the calling to which you have been called, with all humility and meekness, with patience, forbearing one another in love, eager to maintain the unity of the spirit in the bond of peace" (Eph. 4, 1– 3). This exhortation is directed especially to those raised to sacred orders in order that the mission of Christ may be continued. He came among us "not to be served but to serve" (Mt. 20, 28).

St. John has testified: "if we say we have not sinned, we make Him a liar, and His word is not in us" (1 Jn. 1, 10). This holds good for sins against unity. Thus, in humble prayer we beg pardon of God and of our separated brethren, just as we forgive them that trespass against us.

The faithful should remember that they are better promoting union among Christians, indeed living it better, the more they strive to live holier according to the Gospel. For the closer their union with the Father, the Word, and the Spirit, the more deeply and easily will they be able to grow in mutual brotherly love.

8. This change of heart and holiness of life, along with public and private prayer for the unity of Christians, should be regarded as the soul of the whole ecumenical movement, and merits the name, "spiritual ecumenism."

It is a recognized custom for Catholics to meet for frequent recourse to that prayer for the unity of the Church with which the Savior Himself on the eve of His death so fervently appealed to His Father: "That they may all be one" (Jn. 17, 20).

In certain special circumstances, such as in prayer services "for unity" and during ecumenical gatherings, it is allowable, indeed desirable that Catholics should join in prayer with their separated brethren. Such prayers in common are certainly a very effective means of petitioning for the grace of unity, and they are a genuine expression of the ties which still bind Catholics to their separated brethren. "For where two or three are gathered together in my name, there am I in the midst of them" (Mt. 18, 20).

Yet worship in common *(communicatio in sacris)* is not to be considered as a means to be used indiscriminately for the restoration of unity among Christians. There are two main principles upon which the practice of such common worship depends: first, that of the unity of the Church which ought to be expressed; and second, that of the sharing in means of grace. The expression of unity very generally forbids common worship. Grace to be obtained sometimes commends it. The concrete course to be adopted, when due regard has been given to all the circumstances of time, place and persons, is left to the prudent decision of the local episcopal authority, unless the Bishops' Conference according to its own statutes, or the Holy See, has determined otherwise.

9. We must get to know the outlook of our separated brethren. Study is absolutely required for this, and it should be pursued in fidelity to truth and with a spirit of good will. Catholics, who already have a proper grounding, need to acquire a more adequate understanding of the respective doctrines of our separated brethren, their history, their spiritual and liturgical life, their religious psychology and cultural background. Most valuable for this purpose are meetings of the two sides—especially for discussion of theological problems—where each can treat with the other on an equal footing, provided that those who take part in them under the guidance of the authorities are truly competent. From such dialogue will emerge still more clearly what the situation of the Catholic Church really is. In this way, too, we will better understand the outlook of our separated brethren and more aptly present our own belief.

10. Sacred theology and other branches of knowledge, especially those of an historical nature, must be taught with due regard also for the ecumenical point of view, so that they may correspond as exactly as possible with the facts.

It is important that future pastors and priests should have mastered a theology that has been carefully worked out in this way and not polemically, especially with regard to those aspects which concern the relations of separated brethren with the Catholic Church. For it is the formation which priests receive upon which so largely depends the necessary instruction and spiritual formation of the faithful and of religious.

Moreover, Catholics engaged in missionary work in the same territories as other Christians ought to know, particularly in these times, the problems and the benefits which affect their apostolate because of the ecumenical movement.

11. The manner and order in which Catholic belief is expressed should in no way become an obstacle to dialogue with our brethren. It is,

of course, essential that the doctrine be clearly presented in its entirety. Nothing is so foreign to the spirit of ecumenism as a false irenicism which harms the purity of Catholic doctrine and obscures its assured genuine meaning.

At the same time, Catholic belief must be explained more profoundly and precisely, in such a way and in such terms as our separated brethren can also really understand it.

Furthermore, in ecumenical dialogue, Catholic theologians, standing fast by the teaching of the Church yet searching together with separated brethren into the divine mysteries, should do so with love for the truth, with charity, and with humility. When comparing doctrines with one another, they should remember that in Catholic doctrine there exists an order or "hierarchy" of truths, since they vary in their relation to the foundation of the christian faith. Thus the way will be opened whereby this kind of "fraternal rivalry" will incite all to a deeper realization and a clearer expression of the unfathomable riches of Christ (Cf. Eph. 3, 8).

12. Before the whole world let all Christians confess their faith in God, one and three, in the incarnate Son of God, our Redeemer and Lord. United in their efforts, and with mutual respect, let them bear witness to our common hope which does not play us false. Since cooperation in social matters is so widespread today, all men without exception are called to work together; with much greater reason are all those who believe in God, but most of all, all Christians in that they bear the seal of Christ's name. Cooperation among Christians vividly expresses that bond which already unites them, and it sets in clearer relief the features of Christ the Servant. Such cooperation, which has already begun in many countries, should be developed more and more, particularly in regions where a social and technical evolution is taking place. It should contribute to a just appreciation of the dignity of the human person, to the promotion of the blessings of peace, the application of Gospel principles to social life, and the advancement of the arts and sciences in a truly christian spirit. It should also be intensified in the use of every possible means to relieve the afflictions of our times, such as famine and natural disasters, illiteracy and poverty, lack of housing, and the unequal distribution of wealth. Through such cooperation, all believers in Christ are able to learn easily how they can understand each other better and esteem each other more, and how the road to the unity of Christians may be made smooth.

3. Churches and Ecclesial Communities Separated
from the Roman Apostolic See

13. We now turn our attention to the two principal types of division which affect the seamless robe of Christ.

The first divisions occurred in the East, either because of the dispute over the dogmatic formulae of the Councils of Ephesus and Chalcedon, or later by the dissolving of ecclesiastical communion between the Eastern Patriarchates and the Roman See.

Still other divisions arose in the West more than four centuries later. These stemmed from the events which are commonly referred to as the Reformation. As a result, many Communions, national or confessional, were separated from the Roman See. Among those in which Catholic traditions and institutions in part continue to exist, the Anglican Communion occupies a special place.

These various divisions, however, differ greatly from one another not only by reason of their origin, place and time, but still more by reason of the nature and seriousness of questions concerning faith and church order. Therefore, without minimizing the differences between the various christian bodies, and without overlooking the bonds which continue to exist among them in spite of the division, the Council has decided to propose the following considerations for prudent ecumenical action.

1. The Special Position of the Eastern Churches
14. For many centuries the Churches of the East and of the West went their own ways, though a brotherly communion of faith and sacramental life bound them together. If disagreements in faith and discipline arose among them, the Roman See acted by common consent as moderator.

This Council gladly reminds everyone of one highly significant fact among others: in the East there flourish many particular or local Churches; among them the Patriarchal Churches hold first place, and of them many glory in taking their origins from the Apostles themselves. Hence, of primary concern and care among the Orientals has been, and still is, the preservation in a communion of faith and charity of those family ties which ought to exist between local Churches, as between sisters.

From their very origins the Churches of the East have had a treasury from which the Church of the West has drawn largely for its liturgy, spiritual tradition and jurisprudence. Nor must we underestimate the fact that the basic dogmas of the christian faith concerning the Trinity and the Word of God made flesh from the Virgin Mary were defined in Ecumenical Councils held in the East. To preserve this faith, these Churches have suffered, and still suffer much.

However, the heritage handed down by the Apostles was received in different forms and ways, so that from the very beginnings of the Church it had a varied development here and there, owing also to diverse mentalities and conditions of life. These reasons, plus external causes as well as the lack of charity and mutual understanding, lay the way open to divisions.

For this reason the Council urges all, but especially those who commit themselves to the work for the restoration of the full communion that is desired between the Eastern Churches and the Catholic Church, to give due consideration to this special feature of the origin and growth of the Churches of the East, and to the character of the relations which obtained between them and the Roman See before the separation, and to form for themselves a correct evaluation of these facts. The careful observation of this will greatly contribute to the dialogue in view.

15. Everyone knows with what love the Eastern Christians celebrate the Sacred Liturgy, especially the eucharistic mystery, source of' the Church's life and pledge of future glory. In this mystery the faithful, united with their bishop, have access to God the Father through the Son, the Word made flesh who suffered and was glorified, in the outpouring of the Holy Spirit. And so, made "sharers of the divine nature" (2 Pet. 1, 4), they enter into communion with the most holy Trinity. Hence, through the celebration of the Eucharist of the Lord in each of these Churches, the Church of God is built up and grows in stature (Cf. St. John Chrysostom, *In Ioannem Homelia XLVI,* PG 59, 260–262), and through concelebration, their communion with one another is made manifest.

In this liturgical worship, the Eastern Christians pay high tribute, in beautiful hymns of praise, to Mary ever Virgin, whom the ecumenical Synod of Ephesus solemnly proclaimed to be the holy Mother of God in order that Christ might be truly and properly acknowledged as Son of God and Son of Man, according to the Scriptures. They also give homage to the saints, among them Fathers of the universal Church.

These Churches, although separated from us, yet possess true sacraments, above all—by apostolic succession—the priesthood and the Eucharist, whereby they are still joined to us in closest intimacy. Therefore some worship in common *(communicatio in sacris),* given suitable circumstances and the approval of church authority, is not merely possible but is encouraged.

Moreover, in the East are to be found the riches of those spiritual traditions which are given expression especially in monastic life. From the glorious times of the holy Fathers, that monastic spirituality flourished in the East which later flowed over into the Western world, and there provided a source from which Latin monastic life took its rise and has often drawn fresh vigor ever since. Therefore, it is earnestly recommended that Catholics avail themselves more often of the spiritual riches of the Eastern Fathers which lift up the whole man to the contemplation of divine mysteries.

Everyone should realize that it is of supreme importance to understand, venerate, preserve and foster the rich liturgical and spiritual heritage of the Eastern Churches in order faithfully to preserve the fullness of christian tradition, and to bring about reconciliation between Eastern and Western Christians.

16. From the earliest times the Churches of the East followed their own disciplines, sanctioned by the holy Fathers, by Synods, and even by Ecumenical Councils. Far from being an obstacle to the Church's unity, such diversity of customs and observances only adds to her comeliness, and contributes greatly to carrying out her mission, as has already been stated. To remove all shadow of doubt, then, this holy Synod solemnly declares that the Churches of the East, while keeping in mind the necessary unity of the whole Church, have the power to govern themselves according to their own disciplines, since these are better suited to the character of their faithful and better adapted to foster the good of souls. The perfect observance of this traditional principle—which indeed has not always been observed—is a prerequisite for any restoration of union.

17. What has already been said about legitimate variety we are pleased to apply to differences in theological expressions of doctrine. In the study of revealed truth East and West have used different methods and approaches in understanding and confessing divine things. It is hardly surprising, then, if sometimes one tradition has come nearer to a full appreciation of some aspects of a mystery of revelation than the other, or has expressed them in a better manner. In such cases, these various theological formulations are to be considered often as complementary rather than conflicting. With regard to the authentic theological traditions of the Orientals, we must recognize that they are rooted in an admirable way in Holy Scripture, fostered and given expression in liturgical life, and nourished by the living tradition of the Apostles and by the works of the Fathers and spiritual writers of the East; they are directed toward a right ordering of life, indeed, toward a full contemplation of christian truth.

This sacred Council, while thanking God that many Eastern children of the Catholic Church, who are preserving this heritage and wish to express it more faithfully and completely in their lives, are already living in full communion with their brethren who follow the tradition of the West, declares that this entire heritage of spirituality and liturgy, of discipline and theology, in their various traditions, belongs to the full catholic and apostolic character of the Church.

18. After taking all these factors into consideration, this sacred Council confirms what previous Councils and Roman Pontiffs have proclaimed: in order to restore communion and unity or preserve them, one must "impose no burden beyond what is indispensable" (Acts 15, 28). It is the Council's urgent desire that every effort should be made toward the gradual realization of this unity in the various organizations and living activities of the Church, especially by prayer and by fraternal dialogue on points of doctrine and the more pressing pastoral problems of our time. Similarly, to the pastors and faithful of the Catholic Church, it commends close relations with those no longer living in the East but far from their

homeland, so that friendly collaboration with them may increase in a spirit of love, without bickering or rivalry. If this task is carried on wholeheartedly, the Council hopes that with the removal of the wall dividing the Eastern and Western Church at last there may be but the one dwelling, firmly established on the cornerstone, Christ Jesus, who will make both one (Cf. Council of Florence, Sess. VI [1439], Definition *Laetentur caeli:* Mansi 31, 1026 E).

2. *The Separated Churches and Ecclesial Communities in the West*

19. The Churches and ecclesial Communities which were separated from the Apostolic See of Rome during the grave crisis that began in the West at the end of the Middle Ages or in later times, are bound to the Catholic Church by a specially close relationship as a result of the long span of earlier centuries when the christian people had lived in communion.

But since these Churches and ecclesial Communities differ considerably not only from us, but also among themselves, due to their different origins and convictions in doctrine and spiritual life, the task of describing them adequately is extremely difficult; we do not propose to do it here.

Although the ecumenical movement and the desire for peace with the Catholic Church have not yet taken hold everywhere, it is nevertheless our hope that the ecumenical spirit and mutual esteem will gradually increase among all men.

At the same time, however, one should recognize that between these Churches and ecclesial Communities on the one hand, and the Catholic Church on the other, there are very weighty differences not only of an historical, sociological, psychological and cultural character, but especially in the interpretation of revealed truth. To facilitate entering into the ecumenical dialogue in spite of those differences, we wish to set down in what follows some considerations which can, and indeed should serve as a basis and encouragement for such dialogue.

20. Our thoughts are concerned first of all with those Christians who openly confess Jesus Christ as God and Lord and as the only mediator between God and man for the glory of the one God, the Father, the Son and the Holy Spirit. We are indeed aware that there exist considerable differences from the doctrine of the Catholic Church even concerning Christ the Word of God made flesh and the work of redemption, and thus concerning the mystery and ministry of the Church and the role of Mary in the work of salvation. But we rejoice that our separated brethren look to Christ as the source and center of ecclesiastical communion. Their longing for union with Christ impels them ever more to seek unity, and also to bear witness to their faith among the peoples of the earth.

21. A love and reverence—almost a cult—of Holy Scripture leads our brethren to a constant and diligent study of the sacred text. For the Gospel

"is the power of God for salvation to everyone who has faith, to the Jew first and then to the Greek" (Rom. 1, 16).

While invoking the Holy Spirit, they seek in these very Scriptures God as He speaks to them in Christ, the One whom the prophets foretold, the Word of God made flesh for us. In the Scriptures they contemplate the life of Christ, as well as the teachings and the actions of the Divine Master for the salvation of men, in particular the mysteries of His death and resurrection.

But when Christians separated from us affirm the divine authority of the Sacred Books, they think differently from us—different ones in different ways—about the relationship between the Scriptures and the Church. For in the Church, according to Catholic belief, its authentic teaching office has a special place in expounding and preaching the written Word of God.

Nevertheless, in the dialogue itself, the Sacred Word is a precious instrument in the mighty hand of God for attaining to that unity which the Savior holds out to all men.

22. By the sacrament of baptism, whenever it is properly conferred in the way the Lord determined and received with the proper dispositions of soul, man becomes truly incorporated into the crucified and glorified Christ and is reborn to a sharing of the divine life, as the Apostle says: "For you were buried together with Him in baptism, and in Him also rose again through faith in the working of God who raised Him from the dead" (Col. 2, 12; cf. Rom. 6, 4).

Baptism, therefore, constitutes the sacramental bond of unity existing among all who through it are reborn. But baptism, of itself, is only a beginning, a point of departure, for it is wholly directed toward the acquiring of fullness of life in Christ. Baptism is thus ordained toward a complete profession of faith, a complete incorporation into the system of salvation such as Christ Himself willed it to be, and finally, toward a complete integration into eucharistic communion.

Although the ecclesial Communities separated from us lack the fullness of unity with us which flows from baptism, and although we believe they have not preserved the proper reality of the eucharistic mystery in its fullness, especially because of a deficiency of the sacrament of Order, nevertheless when they commemorate the Lord's death and resurrection in the Holy Supper, they profess that it signifies life in communion with Christ and await His coming in glory. For these reasons, the doctrine about the Lord's Supper, about the other sacraments, worship, and ministry in the Church, should form subjects of dialogue.

23. The christian way of life of these brethren is nourished by faith in Christ. It is strengthened by the grace of baptism and the hearing of the Word of God. This way of life expresses itself in private prayer, in meditation of the Scriptures, in the life of a christian family, and in the

worship of the community gathered together to praise God. Furthermore, their worship sometimes displays notable features of a liturgy once shared in common.

The faith by which they believe in Christ bears fruit in praise and thanksgiving for the benefits received from the hands of God. Joined to it is a lively sense of justice and a true charity toward others. This active faith has been responsible for many organizations for the relief of spiritual and material distress, the furtherance of education of youth, the improvement of social conditions of life, and the promotion of peace throughout the world.

And if in moral matters there are many Christians who do not always understand the Gospel in the same way as Catholics, and do not admit the same solutions for the more difficult problems of modern society, they nevertheless want to cling to Christ's word as the source of christian virtue and to obey the command of the Apostle: "Whatever you do in word or in work, do all in the name of the Lord Jesus, giving thanks to God the Father through Him" (Col. 3, 17). Hence, the ecumenical dialogue could start with the moral application of the Gospel.

24. Now, after this brief exposition of the conditions under which ecumenical activity may be practiced, and of the principles by which it is to be guided, we confidently look to the future. This sacred Council urges the faithful to abstain from any frivolousness or imprudent zeal, for these can cause harm to true progress toward unity. Their ecumenical activity cannot be other than fully and sincerely catholic, that is, loyal to the truth we have received from the Apostles and the Fathers, and in harmony with the faith which the Catholic Church has always professed, and at the same time tending toward that fullness in which Our Lord wants His Body to grow in the course of time.

This sacred Council firmly hopes that the initiatives of the sons of the Catholic Church joined with those of the separated brethren will go forward, without obstructing the ways of divine Providence, and without prejudging the future inspirations of the Holy Spirit. Further, this Council declares that it realizes that this holy objective—the reconciliation of all Christians in the unity of the one and only Church of Christ—transcends human powers and gifts. It therefore places its hope entirely in the prayer of Christ for the Church, in the love of the Father for us, and in the power of the Holy Spirit. "And hope does not disappoint, because God's love has been poured forth in our hearts through the Holy Spirit who has been given to us" (Rom. 5, 5).

*   *   *

The entire text and all the individual elements which have been set forth in this Decree have pleased the Fathers. And by the Apostolic power conferred on Us by Christ, We, together with the Venerable Fathers, in the Holy Spirit, approve, decree and enact them; and We order that what has been thus enacted in Council be promulgated, to the glory of God.

Rome, at St. Peter's, November 21, 1964.

I, PAUL, Bishop of the Catholic Church

There follow the signatures of the Fathers.

II
OTHER RELATED VATICAN II TEXTS*

1. From: *Constitution on the Church (Lumen Gentium,* **Nov. 21, 1964)**
a.N.8. This is the unique Church of Christ which in the Creed we profess as one, holy, catholic and apostolic. After His Resurrection our Savior handed it over to Peter to be shepherded (Jn. 21:17) and He commissioned him and the other apostles to extend and govern it (cf. Mt. 28:18 ff.). This Church He raised up for all ages as "the pillar and bulwark of the truth" (1 Tim. 3:15). This Church, constituted and organized in this world as a society, subsists in the Catholic Church, which is governed by the successor of Peter and by the bishops in communion with him. Although many elements of sanctification and of truth are found outside its visible boundaries, these elements, as gifts which belong to the Church of Christ, impel towards Catholic unity.
b.N.13. All men and women are called to form the new People of God. . . . All are called to this catholic unity of the People of God, a unity which prefigures and fosters universal peace. And to this unity, in various ways, belong or are related: the Catholic faithful, other believers in Christ, and indeed all humankind. For all are called by God's grace to salvation.
c.N.15. The Church recognizes that in many ways it is joined to the baptized who are honored by the name of Christian but do not profess the faith in its entirety or do not preserve unity or communion under the successor of Peter. For there are many who honor sacred Scripture as a norm of believing and of living; who show a sincere religious zeal; who lovingly believe in God the Father Almighty and in Christ, the Son of God and the Savior; who are sealed by baptism, through which they are united with Christ; and who recognize and receive other sacraments in their own Churches or ecclesiastical communities. Many of them enjoy the episcopate, celebrate the Holy Eucharist, and cultivate devotion toward the Virgin Mother of God. There is, furthermore, a communion they also

* Translated from the Latin by Thomas F. Stransky, C.S.P.

share with us in prayer and other spiritual resources; these Christians are indeed in some real way joined to us in the Holy Spirit, for, by His gifts and graces, His sanctifying power is also operative in them. Some indeed He has strengthened even to the shedding of their blood. And so the Spirit stirs up desire and action in all of Christ's disciples in order that all may be peacefully united, as Christ ordained, in one flock under one shepherd, and He prompts them to pursue this goal. Mother Church never ceases to pray, hope and work that this may come about. She exhorts her children to purify and renew themselves so that the sign of Christ may shine more brightly over the face of the Church.

d.N.67. In careful study of Sacred Scripture, the Fathers and the Doctors and the liturgy of the Church, and under the guidance of the Church's magisterium, let [theologians and preachers of the word of God] rightly illustrate the gifts, functions and privileges of the Blessed Virgin which always refer to Christ, the source of all truth, sanctity and devotion. Let them carefully guard against any word or deed which might lead the separated brethren or any others into error about the true doctrine of the Church.

e.N.69. It gives great joy and comfort to this most Holy Synod that there are also among the separated brethren those who give due honor to the Mother of our Lord and Savior. This is especially so among the Eastern Christians who with ardent emotion and devout mind concur in reverencing the Mother of God, ever virgin.

2. From: *Decree on the Eastern Catholic Churches (Orientalium Ecclesiarum,*
   Nov. 21, 1964)

N.24. The Eastern Churches in communion with the Apostolic See of Rome have the special duty of promoting the unity of all Christians, particularly the Eastern Christians, according to the principles of this sacred Synod's *Decree on Ecumenism:* first of all, by prayer, then by their example, by religious fidelity to ancient Eastern traditions, by better mutual understanding, by collaboration, and by a brotherly respect for persons and things.

N.25. Nothing more should be required of separated Eastern Christians who, under the influence of the grace of the Holy Spirit, come to Catholic unity than what the simple profession of the Catholic faith demands. And since a valid priesthood is preserved among Eastern clerics, those who come to Catholic unity have the faculties to exercise their own Orders in accordance with the norms laid down by the competent authority.

N.26. Divine Law forbids sharing in liturgical worship *(communicatio in sacris)* which damages the unity of the Church, or involves formal acceptance of error, or the danger of deviation in the faith, of scandal and of indifferentism. At the same time, with respect to our Eastern brethren, pastoral experience shows that various circumstances affecting individuals can and ought to be taken into consideration where the unity of the Church is not jeopardized nor intolerable dangers involved, but where the need of salvation itself and the spiritual good of souls are urgently at issue. Therefore, by reason of circumstances of time, place and persons, the Catholic Church has often adopted and still follows a less rigorous policy, offering to all the means of salvation and a witness to charity among Christians through participation in the sacraments and in other sacred functions and things. In view of this, "lest we be an obstacle to those who seek salvation because of harsh judgement", and in order to foster closer union with the Eastern Churches separated from us, this sacred Synod lays down the following policy:

N.27. In view of the principles recalled above, Eastern Christians who are separated in good faith from the Catholic Church, if they ask of their own accord and are rightly disposed, may be given the sacraments of Penance, the Eucharist, and the Anointing of the Sick. Furthermore, Catholics also may ask for these sacraments from those non-Catholic ministers in whose Churches there are valid sacraments, as often as necessity or a genuine spiritual benefit recommends such action, and when access to a Catholic priest is physically or morally impossible.

N.28. Further, in view of these same principles, Catholics may for a just cause join with their separated brethren in sacred functions, things and places.

N.29. This more lenient policy with regard to sharing in sacred things *(communicatio in sacris)* with our brethren of the separated Eastern Churches is entrusted to the vigilant control of the local Ordinaries so that, by consulting among themselves and, if circumstances warrant, after consultation also with the Ordinaries of the separated Churches, they may so govern relations between Christians by timely and effective precepts and norms.

3. From: *Decree on the Pastoral Office of Bishops (Christus Domini,* **Oct. 28, 1965)**

a.N.13. Since it is the mission of the Church to converse with the human society in which it lives, above all the bishops have the duty to approach people and to seek to foster dialogue with them. These conversations on salvation should be marked by clarity of expression, by humility and gentleness, so that truth may always be joined with charity, and understanding with love. Likewise, the discussions should be characterized by due prudence allied, however, with that trustfulness which fosters friendship and thus is conducive to a union of minds.

b.N.16. Bishops should deal lovingly with the separated brethren and should urge the faithful also to exercise all kindness and charity in their regard, fostering ecumenism as it is understood by the Church.

4. From: *Decree on the Up-to-Date Renewal of Religious Life (Perfectae caritatis,* Oct. 28, 1965)

N.2. All religious institutes should share in the life of the Church. According to its individual character, each institute should make its own and foster to the best of its ability the initiatives and objectives of the Church in such fields as these: the scriptural, liturgical, doctrinal, pastoral, ecumenical, missionary, and social.

5. From: *Decree on the Training of Priests (Optatam totius,* Oct. 28, 1965)

N.16. According to an opportune evaluation of the conditions of various regions, seminarians should be introduced to a more adequate understanding of the Churches and Ecclesial Communities which are separated from the Roman Apostolic See, so that they can contribute to the promoting of the restoration of unity among all Christians, according to the directives of this sacred Synod.

6. From: *Decree on the Ministry and Life of Priests (Presbyterorum ordinis,* Dec. 7, 1965)

N.9. Mindful of this Council's directives on ecumenism, priests should not forget those fellow Christians who do not enjoy full ecclesiastical communion with us.

7. From: *Decree on the Apostolate of Lay People (Apostolicam actuositatem,* Nov. 18, 1965)

N.27. The common patrimony of the Gospel and the common duty of Christian witness resulting from it recommend and frequently require the cooperation of Catholics with other Christians, a cooperation exercised on the part of individuals and Communities within the Church, either in activities or in associations, and on the national or international levels.

Likewise, common human values not seldom call for cooperation between Christians who pursue apostolic aims and those who do not profess Christ's name but acknowledge these values. Through this dynamic yet prudent cooperation, which is of great importance in temporal activities, the laity bears witness to Christ the Savior of the world, and to the unity of the human family.

8. From: *Declaration on Christian Education (Gravissimum educationis,* Oct. 28, 1965)

a.N.1. Children and young people should be trained to take their part in social life, so that by proper instruction in necessary and useful skills they can become actively involved in various community organizations, be ready for dialogue with others, and be willing to act energetically on behalf of the common good.

b.N.11. The Church anticipates great benefits from the activities of the faculties of the sacred sciences.... To these faculties belongs the responsibility of insuring that an ever-deepening understanding of sacred revelation be developed, that the inheritance of Christian wisdom handed down by former generations be more fully appreciated, that dialogue with our separated brethren and with non-Christians be fostered, 'and that questions arising from the development of doctrine be duly solved.

9. From: *Decree on the Church's Missionary Activity* (*Ad gentes,* **Dec. 7, 1965)**

a.N.6. Missionary activity among the nations differs from the pastoral care of the faithful, and likewise from efforts aimed at the restoration of unity among Christians. Yet these two latter activities are very closely connected with the missionary endeavor of the Church because the division among Christians damages the most holy cause of preaching the Gospel to every creature and blocks, for many, their access to the faith. Hence, by the same mandate that demands mission, all the baptized are called to be gathered into one flock that they might be able to bear unanimous witness before the nations to Christ their Lord. And if they cannot yet fully bear witness to the one faith, they should at least be animated by mutual esteem and love.

b.N.12. Furthermore, let the faithful take part in the efforts of those peoples who are waging war on famine, ignorance and disease and thereby struggling to better their way of life and to secure peace in the world. In this activity, the faithful should be eager to offer their prudent aid to projects sponsored by private, public, governmental or international agencies or by various Christian communities and even by non-Christian religions.

c.N.15. The ecumenical should be nurtured in the neophytes. They should appreciate that their brethren who believe in Christ are disciples of Christ, reborn in baptism, and sharers in the many blessings of the People of God.

Insofar as religious conditions permit, ecumenical activity should be fostered in such a way that without any appearance of indifference or confusion and without unhealthy rivalry, Catholics might fraternally cooperate with their separated brethren, by a common—insofar as that is possible—profession before the nations of faith in God and in Jesus Christ, and by a common effort in social, cultural, technical and religious matters, in accordance with the *Decree on Ecumenism.* Let them cooperate together, especially, for the sake of Christ, their common Lord. Let His Name be the bond that unites them! This type of cooperation should be undertaken not only between private persons, but also, subject to the judgement of the local Ordinary, between Churches or ecclesial Communities and their undertakings.

d.N.16. These general requirements for priestly training, including the pastoral and practical prerequisites prescribed by the Council, should be harmonized with an attempt on the students' part to make contact with the particular way of thinking and acting characteristic of their own people. . . . In their philosophical and theological studies, let them consider the points of contact between the traditions and religion of their homeland and the Christian religion . . . The students should learn the history, aim and method of the Church's missionary activity, as well as the peculiar social, economic and cultural conditions of their own people. Let them be educated in the ecumenical spirit, and properly prepared for fraternal dialogue with non-Christians.

e.N.36. So all the children of the Church should have a lively consciousness of their own responsibility for the world, they should foster within themselves a truly Catholic spirit, they should spend their energies in the work of evangelization. Yet, let all realize that the primary and most important contribution one can make to the spread of the faith is to lead a profound Christian life. Their fervor in the service of God and their love for others will cause a new spiritual breeze throughout the whole Church. Then she will appear as a sign raised up among the nations (cf. Is. 11:12), "the light of the world" (Mt. 5:14) and "the salt of the earth" (Mt. 5:13). This witness of their life will achieve its effect more easily if it is borne in unison with other Christian bodies, according to the norms of the *Decree on Ecumenism*, N. 12.

f.N.41. In a fraternal spirit, lay people should collaborate with other Christians, with non-Christians, and especially with members of international organizations, having always before their eyes the awareness that "the building up of the earthly city should have its foundation in the Lord and should be directed towards Him (*Lumen gentium*, N. 46).

g.N.29. In coordination with the Secretariat for Promoting Christian Unity, the Congregation of the Propagation of the Faith will seek ways and means for attaining and organizing fraternal cooperation and harmonious relations with the missionary undertakings of other Christian communities, so that as far as possible the scandal of division might be removed.

10. **From:** *Constitution on the Church in the Modern World* (*Gaudium et spes*, Dec. 7, 1965)

a.N.40. Through each of its members and its community as a whole, the Church believes it can contribute greatly toward making the family of man and its history more human.

Furthermore, the Catholic Church gladly values what other Christian Churches or ecclesial Communities have contributed or are doing cooperatively to achieve this same goal. At the same time, the Church is firmly convinced that there is considerable and varied help that it can receive from the world on preparing the ground for the Gospel. This help it gains from the talents and activity of individuals and from human society as a whole.

b.N.90. For Christians one undoubtedly excellent form of international activity consists in the cooperative efforts which, as individuals and in groups, they make to organizations established or on the way to being set up to foster cooperation between nations. . . . This Council desires that by way of fulfilling their role properly in the international community, Catholics will seek to cooperate actively and positively both with their separated brethren, who together with them profess the gospel of love, and with all who thirst for true peace.

c.N.92. Our hearts embrace also those brethren and communities not yet living in full communion with us; yet to them we are united by our profession of the Father, the Son, and the Holy Spirit, and by the bonds of love. We are mindful that the unity of Christians is today awaited and longed for also by many who do not believe in Christ. For the more this unity progresses in truth and love under the powerful impulse of the Holy Spirit, the more this unity will be a harbinger of unity and peace for the whole world. Let us therefore join our forces and modify our efforts in a way suitable and effective today for achieving this lofty goal, and let us take pains to pattern ourselves daily more and more after the spirit of the Gospel, and work together in a spirit of brotherhood to serve the human family. For this family has been called to become in Christ Jesus the family of the sons of God.

11. **From:** *Constitution on Divine Revelation (Dei verbum,* **November 18, 1965)**

N.22. The Christian faithful should have easy access to Sacred Scripture. . . .

Since the word of God should be readily available at all times, the Church, with motherly concern, sees to it that suitable and correct translations are made into different languages, especially from the original texts of the sacred books. If it should happen that, given the opportunity and the approval of Church authority, these translations are produced in a joint effort with the separated brethren, all Christians will be able to use them.

Chapter Two
DIRECTORY CONCERNING ECUMENICAL MATTERS:

Part One

Introduction

In response to many requests from the Council fathers for more detailed guidelines for ecumenical action than those contained in the Decree on Ecumenism, the SPCU began in March 1965 the drafting of such directives. The procedure was to issue a series of guidelines on specific topics rather than to publish a comprehensive directory.

Shortly after the Council, Paul VI confirmed the SPCU as a permanent organ of the Holy See [*Finis concilio,* Jan. 3, 1966: *AAS* 58 (1966), p. 40]. The SPCU retained also its working structure of bishop-members and consultors.

The SPCU decided that four topics were pressing: 1) the setting up of ecumenical commissions, both diocesan and national; 2) the validity of baptism conferred by ministers of other churches and ecclesial communities; 3) the fostering of "spiritual ecumenism" within the Catholic Church; 4) and related to this, "the sharing of spiritual activity and resources" *(communicatio in spiritualibus);* among them, liturgical worship *(communicatio in sacris).*

The drafts were offered also to the episcopal conferences for comment. In early 1967 the SPCU submitted its final version to Paul VI, who approved the final text for publication. It was so promulgated as Part One of the *Directory* on May 14, 1967, over the signatures of the SPCU's President and Secretary. The only official text is the Latin version, *Ad totam Ecclesiam:* [*AAS* 59(1967), pp. 574–592]. English: SPCU *IS,* 2

(1967), pp. 5–12. The translations, even those of the SPCU, are only provided as a service to those who consult them.

INTRODUCTION

1. "The concern for restoring unity involves the whole Church, faithful and clergy alike. It extends to everyone, according to the talent of each. . . ."[1] The Ecumenical Directory is being published to encourage and guide this concern for unity, so that what was promulgated in this field by the decrees of the Second Vatican Council may be better put into practice throughout the Catholic Church. This must be done in a manner faithful to the mind of the Church. "Ecumenical activity cannot be other than fully and sincerely Catholic, that is loyal to the truth we have received from the Apostles and the Fathers, and in harmony with the faith which the Catholic Church has always professed, and at the same time tending toward that fullness in which our Lord wants His Body to grow in the course of time."[2]

2. The Decree on Ecumenism insists in a number of places that it is the business of the Apostolic See and the bishops, with due regard for the rights of Patriarchs and their synods, to decide ecumenical policy after taking all circumstances into account.[3] Proper care must be taken in these matters so that the ecumenical movement itself is not impeded and the faithful do not suffer harm due to the danger of false irenicism or indifferentism. This is a pastoral care, which will be the more effective as the faithful become more solidly and fully instructed in the teaching and authentic tradition both of the Catholic Church and of the churches and communities separated from her. Against the dangers and harm that may arise, this accurate knowledge of teachings and traditions will be a better safeguard than the kind of ignorance which is often reinforced by false fear: fear of those adjustments which, in accordance with the spirit and decisions of the Second Vatican Council, are necessary to any genuine renewal of the Church.

Ecumenical movement begins with the renewal by which the Church expresses more fully and perfectly the truth and holiness which comes from Christ Our Lord. Everyone of the faithful, as a member of the Church, should share in this renewal in truth and charity so as to grow in faith, hope and charity and bear witness in the Church of God and our Saviour Jesus Christ by his own Christian life.

Since this movement has been set on foot by the Holy Spirit, what follows here is put forward with the intention and in a manner to be of service to the bishops in putting into effect the Decree on Ecumenism, "without obstructing the ways of divine Providence, and without prejudging the future inspirations of the Holy Spirit."[4]

I.

THE SETTING UP OF
ECUMENICAL COMMISSIONS

A. The Diocesan Commission

3. It seems very suitable to set up a council, commission or secretariat, either for several dioceses grouped together or, where circumstances call for it, in each diocese, charged to promote ecumenical activity by the episcopal conference or of the local Ordinary. In those dioceses which cannot have their own commission there should at least be one person delegated by the bishop for these duties.

4. This commission should cooperate with such ecumenical institutions or enterprises as already exist or may be launched, making use of their help where occasion offers. It should also be prompt to help other diocesan work and individual initiative, by exchanging information and ideas with those concerned, to mutual advantage. This should all be done in harmony with the principles and general norms already existing in this matter.

5. To make clearer and foster better the concern for unity which belongs to the Church as a whole, where possible the commission should include among its members not only diocesan clergy but also Religious of both sexes and suitable laymen and women.

6. Besides the other functions assigned to it, the commission should:

a. Put into practice, according to local situations, the decisions of Vatican II on ecumenical affairs;

b. Foster spiritual ecumenism according to the principles laid down in the Decree on Ecumenism (see especially n. 8) about public and private prayer for the unity of Christians;

c. Promote friendliness, cooperation and charity between Catholics and their brothers who are not in their communion;

d. Initiate and guide dialogue with them, bearing in mind the adaptation to be made to the types of participants according to nn. 9 and 11 of the Decree on Ecumenism;

e. Promote in common with our separated brethren joint witness to the Christian faith as well as cooperation in such areas as e.g., in education, morality, social and cultural matters, learning and the arts.[5]

f. Appoint experts to undertake discussions and consultations with the other churches and communities in the diocese;

g. Offer help and encouragement for the instruction and education to be given to clergy and laity and for conducting one's life in an ecumenical spirit, with special emphasis being given to preparing seminary students, to preaching, catechetics and other kinds of teaching dealt with in the Decree on Ecumenism, n. 10;

h. Maintain relations with the territorial ecumenical commission, (see below) adapting the latter's advice and recommendations to local diocesan conditions, and, in addition, when circumstances suggest, useful information should be sent to the Secretariat for Promoting Christian Unity in Rome, which can help the latter in carrying on its own work.

B. The Territorial Commission

7. Each national episcopal conference* and also those which, according to circumstances, include more than one nation—should establish in accordance with their own statutes a commission of bishops for ecumenical affairs assisted by experts. This commission should have a mandate from the episcopal conference of the territory to give guidance in ecumenical affairs and determine concrete ways of acting in accordance with the Decree on Ecumenism and with other ordinances and legitimate customs, taking account of the time, place and persons they are concerned with but also of the good of the universal Church. If possible, this commission should be assisted by a permanent secretariat.

8. The functions of this commission will include all those listed under n. 6 insofar as they enter into the competence of a territorial episcopal conference. In addition let it carry out other tasks, of which some examples are given here:

a. Putting into practice the rules and instructions issued by the Apostolic See in these matters;

b. Giving advice and assistance to the bishops who are setting up an ecumenical commission in their own dioceses;

c. Giving spiritual and material help where possible to both existing ecumenical institutions and to ecumenical enterprises to be promoted either in the field of instruction and research or in that of pastoral care and the promotion of Christian life according to the principles set out in the Decree on Ecumenism, nn. 9 to 11;

d. Establishing dialogue and consultation with the leaders and with ecumenical councils of the other churches and communities which exist on a national or territorial (as distinct from diocesan) scale;

e. Appointing of those experts who, by a public mandate of the Church are designated for the conversations and consultations with experts of the communities referred to under (d) above;

f. Setting up, if need be, a special subcommission for ecumenical relations with the Easterns;

g. Maintaining relations between the territorial hierarchy and the Holy See.

---

* References in this directory to "episcopal conference" also apply, with due consideration for the requirements of law, to the patriarchal synods and synods of major archbishops in the Catholic Eastern Churches.

II.
THE VALIDITY OF BAPTISM
CONFERRED BY MINISTERS OF CHURCHES AND
ECCLESIAL COMMUNITIES SEPARATED FROM US

9. The Church's practice in this matter is governed by two principles: that Baptism is necessary for salvation, and that it can be conferred only once.

10. The ecumenical importance of Baptism is clear from documents of the Second Vatican Council: "He Himself (Jesus Christ) in explicit terms affirmed the necessity of faith and Baptism,[6] and thereby affirmed also the necessity of the Church, for through Baptism as through a door men enter the Church."[7]

"The Church recognizes that in many ways she is linked with those who, being baptized, are honored with the name of Christian, though they do not profess the faith in its entirety or do not preserve unity of communion with the successor of Peter."[8]

"For men who believe in Christ and have been properly baptized are brought into a certain, though imperfect, communion with the Catholic Church . . . all who have been justified by faith in Baptism are incorporated into Christ; they therefore have a right to be called Christians, and with good reason are accepted as brothers by the children of the Catholic Church."[9]

"On the other hand, Catholics must gladly acknowledge and esteem the truly Christian endowments from our common heritage which are to be found among our separated brethren."[10]

11. Baptism is, then, the sacramental bond of unity, indeed the foundation of communion among all Christians. Hence its dignity and the manner of administering it are matters of great importance to all Christ's disciples. Yet a just evaluation of the sacrament and the mutual recognition of each other's Baptisms by different communities is sometimes hindered because of a reasonable doubt about the Baptism conferred in some particular case. To avoid difficulties which may arise when some Christian separated from us, led by the grace of the Holy Spirit and by his conscience, seeks full communion with the Catholic Church, the following guiding principles are put forward:

12. There can be no doubt cast upon the validity of Baptism as conferred among separated Eastern Christians.* It is enough therefore to establish the fact that Baptism was administered. Since in the Eastern Churches the sacrament of Confirmation (Chrism) is always lawfully administered by the priest at the same time as Baptism, it often happens

---

* With regard to all Christians, consideration should be given to the danger of invalidity when Baptism is administered by sprinkling, especially of several people at once.

that no mention is made of the confirmation in the canonical testimony of Baptism. This does not give grounds for doubting that the sacrament was conferred.

13. In respect of other Christians a doubt can sometimes arise:

a. Concerning matter and form. Baptism by immersion, pouring or sprinkling, together with the Trinitarian formula is of itself valid.[11] Therefore if the rituals and liturgical books or established customs of a church or community prescribe one of these ways of baptizing, doubt can only arise if it happens that the minister does not observe the regulations of his own community or church. What is necessary and sufficient, therefore, is evidence that the minister of Baptism was faithful to the norms of his own community or church.

For this purpose generally one should obtain a written baptismal certificate with the name of the minister. In many cases the other community may be asked to cooperate in establishing whether or not, in general or in a particular case, a minister is to be considered as having baptized according to the approved ritual.

b. Concerning faith and intention. Because some consider that insufficiency of faith or intention in the minister can create a doubt about Baptism, these points should be noted:

——The minister's insufficient faith never of itself makes Baptism invalid.

——Sufficient intention in a baptizing minister is to be presumed unless there is serious ground for doubting that he intends to do what Christians do.[12]

c. Concerning the application of the matter. Where doubt arises about the application of the matter, both reverence for the sacrament and respect for the ecclesial nature of the other communities demand that a serious investigation of the community's practice and of the circumstances of the particular Baptism be made before any judgment is passed on the validity of a Baptism by reason of its manner of administration.[13]

14. Indiscriminate conditional Baptism of all who desire full communion with the Catholic Church cannot be approved. The sacrament of Baptism cannot be repeated[14] and therefore to baptize again conditionally is not allowed unless there is prudent doubt of the fact, or of the validity, of a Baptism already administered.[15]

15. If after serious investigation as to whether the Baptism was properly administered, a reasonable doubt persists, and it is necessary to baptize conditionally, the minister should maintain proper regard for the doctrine that Baptism is unique by a) suitably explaining both why he is in this case baptizing conditionally and what is the significance of the rite of conditional baptism; b) carrying out the rite according to the private form.[16]

16. The whole question of the theology and practice of Baptism should be brought up in dialogue between the Catholic Church and the other separated churches or communities. It is recommended that ecumenical commissions should hold such discussions with churches or councils of churches in various regions and, where convenient, come to a common agreement in this matter.

17. Out of reverence for the sacrament of initiation which the Lord instituted for the new covenant, and in order to clarify what is necessary for its proper administration, it is most desirable that dialogue with our separated brethren be not restricted to the sole question of what elements are absolutely necessary for valid Baptism. Attention should also be given to the fullness of the sacramental sign and of the reality signified (or *"res sacramenti"*), as these emerge from the New Testament; this will make it easier for churches to reach an agreement on mutual recognition of Baptism.

18. Placing a proper value on the Baptism conferred by ministers of the churches and ecclesial communities separated from us has ecumenical importance; Baptism is thereby really revealed as the "sacramental bond of unity binding all who are regenerated by it."[17]* Therefore it is to be hoped that all Christians will grow continually more reverent and faithful in their regard for what the Lord instituted concerning its celebration.

19. The Decree on Ecumenism makes clear that the brethren born and baptized outside the visible communion of the Catholic Church should be carefully distinguished from those who, though baptized in the Catholic Church, have knowingly and publicly abjured her faith. According to the decree (n. 3) "one cannot charge with the sin of separation those who at present are born into these communities and in them are brought up in the faith of Christ." Hence, in the absence of such blame, if they freely wish to embrace the Catholic faith, they have no need to be absolved from excommunication, but after making profession of their faith according to the regulations set down by the Ordinary of the place they should be admitted to the full communion of the Catholic Church. What canon 2314 prescribes is only applicable to those who, after culpably giving up the Catholic faith or communion, repent and ask to be reconciled with mother Church.

20. What has just been said of absolution from censures obviously applies for the same reason to the abjuring of heresy.

---

* Cf. also the Report of the Mixed Commission between the Roman Catholic Church and the World Council of Churches (*Oss. Rom.* Feb. 20, 1966, p. 7): The Report of the Fourth International Conference on "Faith and Order," Montreal, 1963, nn. 111, 113, and 154.

III.

21. "This change of heart and holiness of life, along with public and private prayer for the unity of Christians, should be regarded as the soul of the whole ecumenical movement, and merits the name, 'spiritual ecumenism.' "[18]

In these few words the decree defines spiritual ecumenism and stresses its importance in order that Christians may, both in prayer and in the celebration of the Eucharist and indeed in their entire daily life, carefully keep in view the aim of unity. Every Christian, even though he does not live among separated brethren, always and everywhere has his part in this ecumenical movement, through restoring the whole Christian life according to the spirit of the Gospel, as has been taught by the Second Vatican Council—leaving out nothing of the common Christian heritage.[19]

22. It is fitting that prayers for unity be offered regularly at fixed times, e.g.:

a. The week from January 18–25, called the Week of Prayer for Christian Unity, in which often many churches and communities join in praying to God for unity;

b. The days from the Ascension to Pentecost, which commemorate the community at Jerusalem waiting and praying for the coming of the Holy Spirit to confirm them in unity and universal mission.

Additional examples are:

a. The days about the Epiphany, when we commemorate the manifestation of Christ in the world and the link connecting the Church's function with unity;

b. Maundy Thursday, when we commemorate the institution of the Eucharist, the sacrament of unity, and Christ our Saviour's prayer in the supper room for the Church and for her unity;

c. Good Friday, or the feast of the Exaltation of the Holy Cross, when we commemorate the mystery of the Holy Cross—by which the scattered sons of God are reunited;

d. Easter, when all Christians share with one another the joy of Our Lord's Resurrection;

e. On the occasion of meetings or other important events of ecumenical origin or specially likely to serve ecumenical purposes.

23. "It is a recognized custom for Catholics to meet for frequent recourse to prayer for the unity of the Church with which the Saviour Himself on the eve of His death so fervently appealed to His Father 'That they may all be one.' "[20] Therefore, let all pray for unity in a way consonant with Christ's prayer at the Last Supper: that all Christians may achieve "that fullness of unity which Jesus Christ wishes."[21]

24. Pastors should see to it that, as circumstances of places and persons suggest, gatherings of Catholic faithful are arranged to pray for unity; and since the Holy Eucharist is that marvelous sacrament "by which the unity of the Church is signified and brought about,"[22] it is very valuable to remind the faithful of its importance; public prayers for Christian unity should be encouraged at Mass (e.g., during the Prayer of the Faithful or in the litanies called *Ecteniae*) as well as the celebration of votive Masses for Christian unity. Further those rites which have special liturgical prayers of petition, like the *"Litia"* and *"Moleben"* and similar supplications can properly use them to pray for unity.

IV.

SHARING OF SPIRITUAL ACTIVITY
AND RESOURCES WTH OUR SEPARATED BRETHREN

A. Introduction

25. Fraternal charity in the relations of daily life is not enough to foster the restoration of unity among all Christians. It is right and proper that there should also be allowed a certain *"communicatio in spiritualibus"*—i.e., that Christians should be able to share that spiritual heritage they have in common, in a manner and to a degree permissible and appropriate in their present divided state. From those elements and endowments which together go to build up and give life to the Church herself, some, even very many, can exist outside the visible boundaries of the Catholic Church.[23] These elements "which come from Christ and lead to Him rightly belong to the one Church of Christ";[24] they can contribute appropriately to our petitioning for the grace of unity; they can manifest and strengthen the bonds which still bind Catholics to their separated brethren.

26. But these spiritual endowments are found in different ways in the several Christian communities, and sharing in spiritual activity and resources cannot be independent of this diversity; its treatment must vary according to the conditions of the people, churches and communities involved. For present conditions the following guiding principles are offered:

27. There should be regard for a certain give-and-take ("reciprocity") if sharing in spiritual activity and resources, even within defined limits, is to contribute, in a spirit of mutual good will and charity, to the growth of harmony among Christians. Dialogues and consultations on the subject between Catholic local or territorial authorities and those of other communions are strongly recommended.

28. In some places and with some communities, sects and persons, the ecumenical movement and the wish for peace with the Catholic

Church have not yet grown strong,[25] and so this reciprocity and mutual understanding are more difficult; the local Ordinary or, if need be, the episcopal conference may indicate suitable measures for preventing the dangers of indifferentism and proselytism* among their faithful in these circumstances. It is to be hoped, however, that through the grace of the Holy Spirit and the prudent pastoral care of the bishops, ecumenical feeling and mutual regard will so increase both among Catholics and among their separated brethren that the need for these special measures will gradually vanish.

29. The term, sharing of spiritual activity and resources *(communicatio in spiritualibus)* is used to cover all prayer offered in common, common use of sacred places and objects, as well as all sharing in liturgical worship *(communicatio in sacris)* in the strict sense.

30. There is *"communicatio in sacris"* when anyone takes part in the liturgical worship or in the sacraments of another church or ecclesial community.

31. By "liturgical worship" is meant worship carried out according to the books, prescriptions or customs of a church or community, celebrated by a minister or delegate of such church or community, in his capacity as minister of that community.

B. Prayer in Common

32. "In certain special circumstances, such as prayer services 'for unity' and during ecumenical gatherings, it is allowable, indeed desirable that Catholics should join in prayer with their separated brethren. Such prayers in common are certainly a very effective means of petitioning for the grace of unity, and they are a genuine expression of the ties which still bind Catholics to their separated brethren."[26] The decree is dealing with prayers in which members and even ministers of different communities take an "active" part. Where Catholics are concerned, this kind of participation is committed to the guidance and encouragement of local Ordinaries. The following points should be noted.

33. It is to be hoped that Catholics and their other brethren will join in prayer for any common concern in which they can and should cooperate—e.g., peace, social justice, mutual charity among men, the dignity of the family and so on. The same may be said of occasions when according to circumstances a nation or community wishes to make a common act of thanksgiving or petition to God, as on a national feast day, at a time of public disaster or mourning, on a day set aside for remembrance of those

---

* The word "proselytism" is here used to mean a manner of behaving, contrary to the spirit of the Gospel, which makes use of dishonest methods to attract men to a community—e.g., by exploiting their ignorance or poverty (cf. *Declaration on Religious Liberty,* n. 4).

who have died for their country. This kind of prayer is also recommended so far as is possible at times when Christians hold meetings for study or common action.

34. However, common prayer should particularly be concerned with the restoration of Christian unity. It can center on, e.g., the mystery of the Church and her unity, Baptism as a sacramental bond of unity however incomplete, the renewal of personal and social life as a necessary way to achieving unity and the other themes set out under n. 22.

35. The Form of the Service.

a. Representatives of the churches or communities concerned should agree and cooperate in arranging such prayer—in deciding who should take part, what themes, hymns, Scripture readings, prayers and the like should be used.

b. In such a service there is room for any reading, prayer and hymn which manifests the faith or spiritual life shared by all Christians. There is a place for an exhortation, address or Biblical meditation drawing on the common Christian inheritance which may lead to mutual good will and promote unity among Christians.

c. It is desirable that the structure of services of this kind, whether confined to Catholics, or held in common with our separated brethren, should conform to the pattern of community prayer recommended by the liturgical revival.[27]

d. When services are arranged to take place in an Eastern church, it should be borne in mind that an official liturgical form is considered among Orientals as particularly well adapted to prayer of petition; particular consideration should therefore be given to the liturgical order of this Church.

36. The Place.

a. A place should be chosen which is acceptable to all those taking part. Care should be taken that everything is properly prepared and conducive to devotion.

b. Although a church building is the place in which a community is normally accustomed to celebrating its own liturgy, there is nothing which in itself prevents holding the common services mentioned in nn. 32–35, in the church of one or other of the communities concerned if there is need for this and the local Ordinary approves. In fact the situation may make this the suitable thing.

c. It should be remembered when arranging prayer services with the Eastern Orthodox brethren, that all Eastern Christians regard the church as far and away the most suitable place for public prayer.

37. Dress.

There is nothing against the use of choir dress, where circumstances may indicate this and there is common agreement among the participants.

C. Sharing in Liturgical Worship

38. "Yet sharing in liturgical worship *(communicatio in sacris)* is not to be considered as a means to be used indiscriminately for the restoration of unity among Christians. There are two main principles upon which the practice of such common worship depends: First, that of the unity of the Church which ought to be expressed; and second, that of the sharing in means of grace. The expression of unity very generally forbids common worship. Grace to be obtained sometimes commends it."[28]

1. Sharing in Liturgical Worship with our Separated Eastern Brothers

39. "Although these (Eastern) Churches are separated from us, yet they possess true sacraments, above all—by apostolic succession—the priesthood and the Eucharist, whereby they are still joined to us in closest intimacy. Therefore some sharing in liturgical worship *(communicatio in sacris)*, given suitable circumstances and the approval of church authority, is not merely possible but is encouraged.[29]

40. Between the Catholic Church and the Eastern Churches separated from us there is still a very close communion in matters of faith;[30] moreover, "through the celebration of the Eucharist of the Lord in each of these Churches, the Church of God is built up and grows in stature" and "although separated from us, yet these Churches possess true sacraments, above all—by apostolic succession—the priesthood and the Eucharist. . . ."[31]

This offers ecclesiological and sacramental grounds for allowing and even encouraging some sharing in liturgical worship—even Eucharistic—with these churches "given suitable circumstances and the approval of church authority."[32]

Pastors should carefully instruct the faithful so that they will be clearly aware of the proper reasons for this kind of sharing in liturgical worship.

41. The principles governing this sharing set out in the Decree on Eastern Churches[33] should be observed with the prudence that the decree recommends; the norms which apply to Oriental Catholics apply equally to the faithful of any rite, including the Latin.

42. It is particularly opportune that the Catholic authority, whether the local one, the synod or the episcopal conference, does not extend permission for sharing in the reception or administration of the sacraments of Penance, Holy Eucharist or Anointing of the Sick except after satisfactory consultations with the competent authorities (at least local ones) of the separated Oriental Church.

43. In granting permission for sharing in the sacraments it is fitting that the greatest possible attention by given to "reciprocity."

44. Besides cases of necessity, there would be reasonable ground for encouraging sacramental sharing if special circumstances make it material-

ly or morally impossible over a long period for one of the faithful to receive the sacraments in his own Church, so that in effect he would be deprived without legitimate reason of the spiritual fruit of the sacraments.

45. Since practice differs between Catholics and other Eastern Christians in the matter of frequent Communion, confession before Communion and the Eucharistic fast, care must be taken to avoid scandal and suspicion among the Orthodox, created by Catholics not following the Orthodox usage. A Catholic who legitimately communicates with the Orthodox in the cases envisaged here must observe the Orthodox discipline as much as he can.

46. Those Eastern Christians who, in the absence of sufficient confessors of their own church, spontaneously desire to do so may go to a Catholic confessor. In similar circumstances a Catholic may approach a confessor of an Eastern Church which is separated from the Apostolic Roman See. Reciprocity should be maintained here too. Both sides should of course take care to arouse no suspicion of proselytizing.[34]

47. A Catholic who occasionally, for reasons set out below[35] attends the Holy Liturgy (Mass) on a Sunday or holy day of obligation in an Orthodox Church is not then bound to assist at Mass in a Catholic Church. It is likewise a good thing if on such days Catholics, who for just reasons cannot go to Mass in their own Church, attend the Holy Liturgy of their separated Oriental brethren, if this is possible.

48. Because of the close communion between the Catholic Church and the separated Eastern Churches, as described above (n. 40), it is permissible for a member of one of the latter to act as godparent, together with a Catholic godparent, at the baptism of a Catholic infant or adult so long as there is provision for the Catholic education of the person being baptized, and it is clear that the godparent is a suitable one. A Catholic is not forbidden to stand as godparent in an Orthodox church, if he is so invited. In this case, the duty of providing for the Christian education of the baptized person binds in the first place the godparent who belongs to the Church in which the child is baptized.

49. Brethren of other churches may act as bridesmaid or best man at a wedding in a Catholic church. A Catholic too can be best man or bridesmaid at a marriage properly celebrated among separated brethren.

50. Catholics may be allowed to attend Orthodox liturgical services if they have reasonable grounds, e.g., arising out of a public office or function, blood relationships, friendships, desire to be better informed, etc. In such cases there is nothing against their taking part in the common responses, hymns, and actions of the Church in which they are guests. Receiving Holy Communion however, will be governed by what is laid down above, nn. 42 and 44. Because of the close communion referred to earlier (n. 40) local Ordinaries can give permission for a Catholic to read lessons at a liturgical service, if he is invited. These same principles govern

the manner in which an Orthodox may assist at services in Catholic churches.

51. Regarding participation in ceremonies which do not call for sacramental sharing the following should be observed:

a. In ceremonies carried out by Catholics, an Oriental clergyman who is representing his Church should have the place and the liturgical honors which Catholics of equal rank and dignity have.

b. A Catholic clergyman present in an official capacity at an Orthodox service can, if it is acceptable to his hosts, wear choir dress or the insignia of his ecclesiastical rank.

c. There should be meticulous regard for the outlook of the clergy and faithful of the Eastern Churches, as well as for their customs which may vary according to time, place, persons and circumstances.

52. Because sharing in sacred functions, objects and places with all the separated Eastern brethren is allowed for a reasonable cause,[36] it is recommended that with the approval of the local Ordinary separated Eastern priests and communities be allowed the use of Catholic churches, buildings and cemeteries and other things necessary for their religious rites, if they ask for this, and have no place in which they can celebrate sacred functions properly and with dignity.

53. The authorities of Catholic schools and institutions should take care to offer Orthodox clergy every facility for giving spiritual and sacramental ministration to their own faithful who attend such schools and institutions. As far as circumstances allow, and with the local Ordinary's permission, these facilities can be offered on the Catholic premises, including the Church.

54. In hospitals and similar institutions conducted by Catholics, the authorities should promptly advise the Orthodox priest of the presence of his faithful, and give him facilities to visit the sick and administer the sacraments to them in dignified and reverent conditions.

2. Sharing in Liturgical Worship with Other Separated Brethren

55. Celebration of the sacraments is an action of the celebrating community, carried out within the community, signifying the oneness in faith, worship and life of the community. Where this unity of sacramental faith is deficient, the participation of the separated brethren with Catholics, especially in the sacraments of the Eucharist, Penance and Anointing of the Sick, is forbidden. Nevertheless, since the sacraments are both signs of unity and sources of grace[37] the Church can for adequate reasons allow access to those sacraments to a separated brother. This may be permitted in danger of death or in urgent need (during persecution, in prisons) if the separated brother has no access to a minister of his own communion, and spontaneously asks a Catholic priest for the sacraments—so long as he declares a faith in these sacraments in harmony with that of the Church,

and is rightly disposed. In other cases the judge of this urgent necessity must be the diocesan bishop or the episcopal conference. A Catholic in similar circumstances may not ask for these sacraments except from a minister who has been validly ordained.

56. A separated brother is not to act as a Scripture reader or to preach during the celebration of the Eucharist. The same is to be said of a Catholic at the celebration of the Lord's Supper or at the principal liturgical service of the Word held by the Christians who are separated from us. At other services, even liturgical ones, it is allowable to exercise some functions, with the previous permission of the local Ordinary and the consent of the authorities of the community concerned.

57. With the exception already dealt with above (n. 48) it is not permissible for a member of a separated community to act as godparent in the liturgical and canonical sense at Baptism or Confirmation. The reason is that a godparent is not merely undertaking his responsibility for the Christian education of the person baptized or confirmed as a relation or friend—he is also, as a representative of a community of faith, standing as sponsor for the faith of the candidate. Equally a Catholic cannot fulfill this function for a member of a separated community. However, because of ties of blood or friendship, a Christian of another communion, since he has faith in Christ, can be admitted with a Catholic godparent as a Christian witness of the baptism. In comparable circumstances a Catholic can do the same for a member of a separated community. In these cases the responsibility for the Christian education of the candidate belongs of itself to the godparent who is a member of the Church in which the candidate is baptized. Pastors should carefully explain to the faithful the evangelical and ecumenical reasons for this regulation, so that all misunderstanding of it may be prevented.

58. The separated brethren may act as "official" witnesses (bridesmaid or best man) at a Catholic marriage, and Catholics at a marriage which is properly celebrated between our separated brethren.

59. Catholics may be allowed to attend occasionally the liturgical services of other brethren if they have reasonable ground, e.g., arising out of a public office or function, blood relationship or friendship, desire to be better informed, an ecumenical gathering, etc. In these cases, with due regard to what has been said above—there is nothing against Catholics taking some part in the common responses, hymns and actions of the community of which they are guests—so long as they are not at variance with Catholic faith. The same principles govern the manner in which our separated brethren may assist at services in Catholic churches. This participation, from which reception of the Eucharist is always excluded, should lead the participants to esteem the spiritual riches we have in common and at the same time make them more aware of the gravity of our separations.

60. When taking part in services which do not call for sacramental sharing, ministers of other communions may, by mutual consent, take a place suitable to their dignity. So too Catholic ministers who are present at ceremonies celebrated by other communions, may, with due regard for local customs, wear choir dress.

61. If the separated brethren have no place in which to carry out their religious rites properly and with dignity, the local Ordinary may allow them the use of a Catholic building, cemetery or church.

62. The authorities of Catholic schools and institutions should take care to offer to ministers of other communions every facility for giving spiritual and sacramental ministration to their own communicants who attend Catholic institutions. These ministrations may be given in Catholic buildings, in accordance with the above, n. 61.

63. In hospitals and similar institutions conducted by Catholics, the authorities in charge should promptly advise ministers of other communions of the presence of their communicants and afford them every facility for visiting the sick and giving them spiritual and sacramental ministrations.

In an audience granted to the Secretariat for Promoting Christian Unity, April 28, 1967, the Sovereign Pontiff, Paul VI, approved this directory, confirmed it by his authority and ordered that it be published. Anything to the contrary notwithstanding.

Notes

1. *Decree on Ecumenism,* n.5.
2. *Ibid.,* n.24.
3. Cf. n.,4, n.8, n.9.
4. *On Ecumenism,* n.24.
5. *Ibid,* n.12. Cf. *Decree on the Church's Missionary Activity,* n.12.
6. Cf. Mark 16:16; John 3:5.
7. *Constitution on the Church,* n.14.
8. *Ibid.,* n.15.
9. *On Ecumenism,* n.3.
10. *Ibid.,* n.4.
11. Code of Canon Law (CIC), c.758.
12. Cf. Response of the Holy Office, Jan. 30, 1833: "It is sufficient to do what Christians do"; Congregation of the Council, Decrees approved by Pius V, June 19, 1570, cited by the Provincial Council of Evreux, France, 1576.
13. Cf. CIC, c.737.
14. Cf. CIC, c. 732,1.
15. Cf. Council of Trent, S.VII, can.4, CIC, c.737.1.
16. Cf. CIC, c.737,2.
17. *On Ecumenism,* n.22; *On the Church,* n.15.
18. *On Ecumenism,* n.8.
19. *Ibid.,* n.6; *On Church's Missionary Activity,* n.36.
20. *On Ecumenism,* n.8.

21. *Ibid.,* n.4.
22. *Ibid.,* n.2.
23. *Ibid.,* n.3.
24. *Ibid.*
25. *Ibid.,* n.19.
26. *Ibid.,* n.8.
27. *Constitution on the Sacred Liturgy,* nn.30,34,35.
28. *On Ecumenism,* n.8.
29. *Ibid.,* n.15. Cf. *Decree on the Eastern Catholic Churches,* nn.24–29.
30. *On Ecumenism,* n.44.
31. *Ibid.,* n.15.
32. *Ibid.*
33. Cf. nn. 26–29.
34. Cf. Note on n.28.
35. Cf. n.50.
36. *On Eastern Catholic Churches,* n.28.
37. *On Ecumenism,* n.8.

Chapter Three
DIRECTORY CONCERNING ECUMENICAL MATTERS:

Part Two:
Ecumenism in Higher Education

Introduction

Even before Part I of the Ecumenical Directory had been promulgated, the SPCU members and consultors were drafting Part II. It would deal with a single topic: ecumenical principles and practice in "higher education", that is, both clerical and lay studies at the post-secondary level, corresponding in one way or another to the university and major seminary levels.

Bishops and episcopal conferences also contributed their suggestions, and various Vatican curial offices collaborated, especially the Congregation for Catholic Education. The SPCU's plenary session of November 1968 approved the text in substance, just before the death of its first president, Augustin Cardinal Bea. After further revision by a joint commission (the SPCU, the Congregations of the Doctrine of the Faith, and for Catholic Education), Paul VI "approved this Directory, confirmed it by his authority, and ordered that it be published" (April 16, 1969).

The text was promulgated on May 15, 1969. In his official presentation to the press, the SPCU president, John Cardinal Willebrands, said: "The point of departure was a firm ecumenical purpose, that is, the will to put into practice in the field of higher education the teaching of Vatican II on ecumenism. The problem is to harmonize over the whole field strict principles of Catholic faith and of the Catholic conception of ecumenism as well as of good sense, at the same time taking account of a great variety of situations". *Spiritus Domini: AAS* 62(1970), pp. 705–724. English: SPCU *IS,* 10 (1970), pp. 3–10.

INTRODUCTION

The Spirit of the Lord is at work in the present-day ecumenical movement in order that, when the obstacles hindering perfect ecclesiastical communion have been surmounted,[1] the unity of all Christians may at last be restored and shine forth,[2] for all peoples are called to be a single new people, confessing one Jesus, Saviour and Lord, professing one faith, celebrating one eucharistic mystery:[3] "that the world may believe that Thou has sent me," as the Lord said (Jn. 17:21).

All Christians should be of an ecumenical mind, but especially those entrusted with particular duties and responsibilities in the world and in society; hence the principles of ecumenism sanctioned by the Second Vatican Council should be appropriately introduced in all institutions of advanced learning.[4] In fact many have asked for some principles and lines of action which would help everybody to cooperate for the common good of the Catholic Church and the other Churches and ecclesial communities.

Bishops have a special responsibility for promoting the ecumenical movement and it is for them to lay down the required guiding principles. But because of the great variety of institutions of advanced learning it is far from easy to prescribe such guiding principles; there are differences between various nations and regions, differences deriving from varying individual maturity and experience; differences also resulting from the varying state of relationships whether in the ecclesiological sphere or in that of cooperation between the Catholic Church and other Churches or ecclesial communities. It belongs therefore to bishops and episcopal conferences both to translate general principles into practice[5] and to adjust undertakings already on foot to existing conditions as these affect man and matters—and even, as occasion offers, to start new undertakings. It is strongly suggested that episcopal authorities should associate with themselves in this task an appropriate number of religious superiors, men and women, as well as rectors and administrators, specialists in religious education and practicing teachers—and should bring representatives of the students into consultation when necessary.

Since moreover all ecumenical work is conditioned by the abnormal situation that the Churches and ecclesial communities involved in it are divided and at the same time their efforts are directed to restoring unity, the principles set out below will sometimes, because of changed circumstances, be newly applied in practice by competent authority, and the lines of policy will be adapted so as always to go on serving the purpose for which they were put out.

I.
GENERAL PRINCIPLES AND
AIDS TO ECUMENICAL EDUCATION

1. Though some undertakings for fostering ecumenical education mainly concern theological faculties and colleges—which will be treated further on—there are some forms of ecumenical action which are applicable to all higher education. Students and teachers who take part in this kind of undertaking are reminded that they must willingly and generously equip themselves with that solid religious training, maturity of mind and real skill which the nature of the project demands.

2. The purpose of ecumenical programs. The purpose of programs of this type is to increase among students a deeper knowledge of the faith, the spirituality and the entire life and doctrine of the Catholic Church, so that they may wisely and fruitfully take part in ecumenical dialogue, each according to his capabilities,[6] to direct their attention both to that inward renewal of the Catholic Church itself which will help so much to promote unity among Christians, and to those things in their own lives, or in the life of the Church which hinder or slow down progress towards unity;[7] a further purpose is that teachers and students should learn more about other Churches and communities, and so understand better and assess more correctly what unites Christians and what divides them;[8] finally, since these efforts are not to be mere intellectual exercises, the aim is that those taking part in them should better realize the obligation of fostering unity between Christians and so be led to apply themselves more effectively to achieving it. They will also be led to do what is in their power to give joint Christian witness to the contemporary world.

3. Aids to achieving this purpose.

a. Since various academic subjects may have a connection with ecumenism, the following points, which may serve as examples, should be borne in mind:

Where courses or lectures on religion are given in various forms to students, whether as part of the syllabus or occasionally, those who give them should take note of what is said below about the ecumenical aspects of theological teaching.[9]

Courses in philosophy, while providing a solid and coherent understanding of man, of the world and of God based on a philosophical heritage of lasting value, should also take account of contemporary philosophical investigations, and pupils should properly be made aware of the principles which govern these.[10] This because they ought to know and assess properly the philosophical principles which often underlie existing theological and exegetical views among the various Churches and Christian communities.

The style and ways of teaching history should be reviewed so that in dealing with Christian society due consideration is given to the different Christian communities and their whole way of life understood. The events and personalities involved in the various religious divisions should be dealt with fairly and the many attempts to restore unity and bring about renewal in the Church should not be overlooked.

In the other subjects, attention can be paid to those spiritual elements which are part of the common Christian inheritance and are to be found among various Christian communities, e.g., in the field of literature, the arts, music.

b. As far as possible, properly instructed Catholics, so long as they firmly maintain their Catholic heritage, should be encouraged to support undertakings in the field of religious studies proposed by non-confessional universities.

c. Among the various types of activities usually associated with academic institutions, some are more specially suited to promoting the ecumenical movement. These are some examples:

Conferences or study-days dealing with specifically ecumenical themes.

Meetings or associations for study, for joint work or for social welfare work which may provide occasion for ecumenical discussion, or for examining Christian principles of this social action and aids to putting those principles into practice. Those meetings and associations, whether confined to Catholics or including other Christians, should do all they can to cooperate with existing student societies. In halls of residence attached to academic establishments circumstances may suggest exchanges between Catholics, faithfully witnessing to their own belief, and other Christian students, by means of which both, with suitable guidance, may live their lives together in a deeper ecumenical spirit.

In university journals and reviews, space may be assigned for ecumenical news and at least occasionally for more serious articles on ecumenical subjects.

d. Among activities to which special attention should be paid, we should include prayer for unity not only during the Week of Prayer for Christian Unity but at other appropriate times during the year.[11] Subject to local and personal circumstances, and to the rules laid down about liturgical worship in common, joint retreats may well be organized for one or more days under a reliable retreat master.[12]

e. There is a wider field for joint witness in social and welfare work. Students should be prepared for this kind of cooperation and exhorted to take part in it. This will have greater and more precise effect if students not only of theology but of other faculties (e.g., law, sociology, political economy) join forces to promote and carry out the work.

f. Priests engaged in some ministry in these various institutions (chaplains, teachers, student advisors) have a special duty in the matter of ecumenical relations. This duty demands of them both a deeper knowledge of the Church's doctrine and a particular qualification and experience in academic subjects, as well as steady prudence and moderation, if they are to be useful guides to students who want to combine full and genuine loyalty to their own Christian community with a positive and open bearing towards their fellow-students.

II.
THE ECUMENICAL DIMENSION
OF RELIGIOUS AND THEOLOGICAL EDUCATION

1. Spiritual Formation.

Since the Holy Spirit must be regarded as at work in the ecumenical movement, the first thing to be attended to in ecumenical education is conversion of heart—spiritual life and its renewal, for "from newness of mind, from self-denial and from the freest outpouring of charity, desires for unity proceed and mature."[13] This renewal should be rooted in the life of the Church itself, in its liturgy and sacraments; it should be directed to prayer for the unity of all Christians and to the fulfilling of the Church's function in the world. The spiritual life of Catholics must be genuine: centered on Christ the Saviour and looking to the glory of God the Father it will assign to the whole range of religious acts and exercises their due and proper importance.

To give adequate emphasis to the Catholic and apostolic character of the Church,[14] the ecumenical spiritual life of Catholics should also be nourished from the treasures of the many traditions, past and present, which are alive in other Churches and ecclesial communities; such are the treasures found in the liturgy, monasticism and mystical tradition of the Christian East; in Anglican worship and piety; in the evangelical prayer and spirituality of Protestants.

But this linking with other spiritual traditions, if it is not to remain in the realm of theory, should be perfected by practical acquaintance with them where circumstances favor this. Hence some prayer in common and sharing in public worship are to be promoted, in harmony with the rules laid down by competent authority.[15]

2. Doctrinal Education.

Ecumenism should bear on all theological discipline as one of its necessary determining factors,[16] making for the richer manifestation of the fullness of Christ. Nevertheless ecumenism as a separate question may either provide the material of a special course of lectures, if opportunity offers, or at least be the theme of some lectures given in the chief dogma courses.

3. The Ecumenical Aspect in All Theological Teaching.

Ecumenism should embrace these aspects:

a. those elements of the Christian heritage both of truth and of holiness which are found in common in all Churches and Christian communities,[17] though they are sometimes given different theological expression;[18]

b. the spiritual treasury and wealth of doctrine which each Christian community has as its own, and which can lead all Christians to a deeper understanding of the nature of the Church;[19]

c. whatever in matters of faith causes dissension and division, yet can stimulate a profounder examination of the word of God aimed at manifesting what in proclaiming truth are real contradictions and what only seem to be.

4. The Ecumenical Aspect in the Separate Branches of Theology.

In every branch of theology the ecumenical standpoint should make for consideration of the link between the subject and the existing mystery of the unity of the Church. Moreover, when the subject is expounded, pupils should be given a sense of the fullness of Christian tradition in doctrine, spirituality and Church discipline. They will become aware of this when their own tradition is related to the riches of other Christian traditions of East and West, both in their classical forms and in their modern expressions.

This way of paying attention to the patrimonies of other Christian Churches and ecclesial communities is undoubtedly important: in studying Scripture, the common source of the faith of all Christians; in studying apostolic tradition as it is to be found in the Fathers and ecclesiastical writers of the Eastern and Western Church; in liturgical teaching which presents a scholarly comparison of various forms of divine worship and of their doctrinal and spiritual significance; in expounding dogmatic and moral theology with particular regard for questions raised by the ecumenical movement; in Church history, when it carefully traces the unity of the Church itself through the changes brought about by time, and the causes of division among Christians; in teaching canon law, where elements of divine law are to be diligently distinguished from elements of merely ecclesiastical law which can be exposed to change by reason of the passage of time or because of temperament, culture or tradition;[20] finally in pastoral and missionary training and in social studies, in which particularly careful attention is due to the situation in which all Christians find themselves when facing the requirements of the contemporary world. In this way the fullness of divine revelation is expressed better and more completely and the task which Christ entrusted his Church to fulfill in the world is carried out.[21]

5. Conditions of a Genuine Ecumenical Mind in Theology.

Ecumenical action "cannot but be fully and sincerely Catholic— faithful that is to the truth which we have received from the Apostles and Fathers, and in harmony with the faith which the Catholic Church has always confessed."[22] But we should always preserve the sense of an order based on degree, or of an "hierarchy" in the truths of Catholic doctrine which, although they all demand a due assent of faith, do not all occupy the same principal or central place in the mystery revealed in Jesus Christ, since they vary in their relationship to the foundation of the Christian faith.[23]

Students should learn to distinguish between revealed truths, which all require the same assent of faith, and theological doctrines. Hence they should be taught to distinguish between "the deposit of faith itself, or the truths which are contained in our venerable doctrine," and the way in which they are enunciated,[24] between the truth to be enunciated and the various ways of perceiving and more clearly illustrating it,[25] between apostolic tradition and merely ecclesiastical traditions. Already from the time of their philosophical training students should be put in a frame of mind to recognize that different ways of stating things in theology too are legitimate and reasonable, because of the diversity of methods or ways by which theologians understand and express divine revelation. Thus it is that these various theological formulae are often complementary rather than conflicting.[26]

6. Ecumenism as a Special Branch of Study.

Even though all theological training has an ecumenical aspect, courses on ecumenism are not therefore superfluous. The following may be regarded as elements for such courses, leaving room for development as circumstances and time suggest:

a. "Oecumene," "ecumenism"—their historical origins and present meaning.

b. The doctrinal foundations of ecumenism, with special reference to the bonds of communion still holding between Churches and ecclesial communities.

c. The aim and method of ecumenism, the various forms of union and cooperation, the hope of restoring unity, the conditions for unity, full and perfect unity, the practice of ecumenism especially in the sphere of social action.

d. The history of ecumenism, especially of the various attempts made in the course of time to restore unity, and a consideration of their positive and negative features.

e. An account of the "institutional" aspect and present life of the different Christian communions: their doctrinal tendencies, the true causes of divisions, missionary effort, spirituality, forms of divine worship.

f. A number of questions to do with ecumenism: special questions which the ecumenical movement gives rise to about hermeneutics, ministry, divine worship, "intercommunion," tradition, "proselytism" and true evangelization, false irenicism, the laity, the ministry of women in the Church and so on.

g. The spiritual approach to ecumenism, especially the significance of prayer for unity and the various forms of spiritual ecumenism.

h. Existing relations between the Catholic Church and other Churches and ecclesial communities or federations of Churches, as well as the relations which all these have with each other.

i. The importance of the special role which the World Council of Churches has in the ecumenical movement, and the relationships which exist between the Roman Catholic Church and the World Council of Churches.

III.
PARTICULAR GUDELINES
FOR ECUMENICAL EDUCATION

1. Dialogue between Christians in Higher Education.

Careful examination of the general principles governing dialogue between Christians makes it very clear that seminaries, theological faculties and the other institutions of higher education have their own particular role to play in ecumenical dialogue, and that dialogue itself in these institutions is a help towards their fulfilling their function regarding the education of the young.

But dialogue as an element of education demands:

a. sincere and firm fidelity to one's own faith, without which dialogue is reduced to a conversation in which neither side is genuinely engaged;

b. a mind open and ready to base life more deeply on one's own faith because of the fuller knowledge derived from dialogue with others, who are to be reckoned as sharing with us the true name of Christian;

c. investigation of ways and means of concerted effort to establish relations and restore a unity which will not rest on indifference or false irenicism or facile accommodation to the demands of the age, but on a greater fidelity to the Gospel and an authentic profession of the Christian religion which satisfies the demands both of truth and of charity;

d. consultation and cooperation with the pastors of the Church and a due deference for their directions and advice, for dialogue is never a mere exchange between persons and institutions, but of its very nature engages the whole Church;[27]

e. readiness to acknowledge that the members of the various Churches and ecclesial communities are generally best equipped to expound properly the doctrine and life of their own communion;

f. respect for conscience and for the convictions of others in explaining the outlook and doctrine of one's own Church or one's own way of understanding divine revelation;

g. readiness to acknowledge that not everyone is equally equipped for dialogue—there are differences of intellectual training, maturity of mind, spiritual development; hence syllabuses and lectures should be revised so as to correspond to the real needs of the students.

2. Those Who Have Special Ecumenical Tasks.

To fulfill her ecumenical responsibility, the Church must have at her disposal an adequate number of experts in ecumenical matters—clergy and religious, laymen and women. They are needed everywhere—even in regions where Catholics form the greater part of the population.

Among the tasks that may be assigned to them are these: to help bishop and clergy and regional authorities to prepare the faithful to acquire a truly ecumenical mentality; to assist or direct the various diocesan and regional ecumenical commissions; to establish suitable relations with other Christian communities; to give special lectures on ecumenism in seminaries and other educational establishments; to organize ecumenical activity in Catholic schools and institutions; to foster the training of missionaries for their own special kind of ecumenical work.[28]

Besides their solid general theological training, it is desirable that these experts:

a. should have special advanced training in some branch of study—such as theology, exegesis, history, philosophy, religious sociology;

b. should be properly instructed in the principles of the present-day ecumenical movement, in the questions which occupy it, in what it has achieved and has still to achieve. Over and above what they can learn from lectures and research, they should be strongly urged to take every possible part in ecumenical relationships, which they can do by means of meetings, conferences, centers or institutes for ecumenical studies and so on;

c. should be properly instructed in the traditions of those Christians, side by side with whom they live and work. Studies of this sort should as far as possible be done by regular contact with those who know and live such traditions.

3. Those Already Working in a Pastoral Ministry.

In carrying out the established policy of pastoral training for the clergy through clergy councils, special institutes, retreats, days of recollection or pastoral discussion, bishops and religious superiors are earnestly exhorted to make sure that the necessary care is devoted to ecumenism, and also to bear in mind these particular points.[29]

As opportunity offers, special instruction should be provided for priests, religious and laity on the present state of the ecumenical movement, so that they may learn to bring an ecumenical point of view into preaching, into divine worship, into catechism and into Christian life at large. Further, as far as it is possible and prudent, a minister of another Church or community should be invited to explain his own tradition or talk on pastoral problems, which are very often common to all Christian ministers.

Where it seems advisable and the Ordinary agrees, the Catholic clergy should be invited to attend special meetings with ministers of other Churches and communities—for the purpose of getting to know each other better and of solving pastoral problems by a joint Christian effort. This sort of activity often goes best when associations are set up, such as local or regional clergy councils, ministerial associations, etc., or when people join existing associations of the kind.

Theology faculties, seminaries and other seats of learning can make a great contribution to ecumenical effort both by arranging courses of study for clergy doing pastoral work and by urging their own teaching staff to take a ready share in studies and courses organized by others.

4. Concerning Superiors and Teaching Staff in Institutions
for Theological Education.

The general principles set out in Chapter II should shape, guide and give stimulus to the training of all those who are intended to teach theology and related subjects, so that they will be adequately learned and fitted for the office of educating younger priests, students of the sacred sciences, religious and laity.

To help teaching staff to satisfy their ecumenical responsibilities, bishops, whether in their own diocese or together with the bishops of the region or country, religious superiors and those in authority in seminaries, universities and similar institutions should take pains to promote the ecumenical movement and spare no effort to see that their teachers keep in touch with advances in ecumenical thought and action. Moreover, care must be taken to maintain an adequate supply of books, reviews, periodicals and similar publications, Catholic and non-Catholic.

In planning studies, the following points should be given the fullest attention:

a. It seems appropriate to give a special course on ecumenism shortly after theological studies have begun: a broad knowledge of ecumenical matters will help students to a deeper understanding of particular subjects.

b. To intensify devotion to ecumenism and promote familiarity with the whole ecumenical movement, it will be useful from the beginning to take opportunities of providing conferences for pupils. Teachers in class may also usefully assign pupils essays and other exercises on ecumenical themes.

c. Textbooks and other teaching aids should be chosen or written with due care. These works should faithfully set out the opinions of other Christians on matters of theology, history and spirituality, which more-over should not be considered in isolation from life but as embodied in a tradition by which men live.

d. It is most important that students who are being trained for the priesthood or the religious life should learn fully how to conduct themselves in future pastoral dealings with other Christians—e.g., how they may help them in some spiritual need and yet at the same time respect their freedom of conscience and the grace of the Holy Spirit in them.

e. The libraries of seminaries and other institutions of higher education should be kept well supplied with books and periodicals, both those which deal with ecumenism in general and those which give particular treatment of questions of local ecumenical concern are important for the special purpose of the institution.

IV.

INSTITUTIONAL AND PERSONAL COOPERATION
BETWEEN CATHOLICS AND OTHER CHRISTIANS

1. Subject to conditions which vary from place to place, and to the principles already put forward,[30] cooperation between institutions of higher education and relationships on various levels between teachers and students of different Churches and communities can be of the greatest advantage not only to the ecumenical movement at large but to the ecumenical education of teachers and pupils concerned.

2. Such cooperation between Christians in the sphere of higher education can greatly profit the institutions involved; it contributes in fact:

——to fuller knowledge of theology (especially in the matter of useful aids for the science of hermeneutics), and also of other subjects which are treated in institutions of advanced learning;

——to assisting the academic faculty, through the shared use of books and libraries, by providing a greater number of qualified teachers; by cutting down useless or duplicated courses, subject to directions given below;

——to increasing material resources where necessary, e.g., by shared use of buildings, especially libraries and classrooms;

——by multiplying the assistance which the institution can afford to society as a whole: for men will more freely pay attention to the authority and influence of some joint Christian action than to that of single institutions operating in isolation;

——to reinforcing the witness offered to other Christians of the proved worth of the institution—something which men look for from such training over and above the merely academic quality of the teaching.

3. This cooperation and habit of exchanges with their colleagues of other Christian communities continually opens up new paths of scholarly inquiry to teachers, and helps them to fulfill their teaching function better. Furthermore the students can to some degree already be prepared throughout their period of training for future ecumenical work, and with the help of really expert Catholic instructors they can better learn to overcome such intellectual and spiritual difficulties as might perhaps arise from exchanges of this kind.

4. In this cooperation two classes of persons should be distinguished:

a. graduates and those who have completed a general theological training,

b. those who have not yet completed the ordinary curriculum.

5. Episcopal conferences, in drawing up a program of Training for the Priesthood according to the decree *Optatam Totius,* should issue general rules, on lines to be laid down later, about particular cases of cooperation between Catholic seminaries and those of other Christians. But since institutions for training members of religious orders can also take part in this cooperation, major superiors or their delegates should contribute towards drawing up rules in accordance with the decree *Christus Dominus,* n. 35, art. 5 and 6. If particular questions arise about some seminary or institution the Ordinary who has jurisdiction over it must decide, according to the lines laid down by the episcopal conference, which undertakings require his approval and which can be left simply to those in charge of the seminary.

6. Graduates and others who have finished a general theological training. Ecumenical dialogue and action should be advanced by setting up ecumenical institutes and centers in various places and countries and, as circumstances demand, with the approval of lawful authority. These institutes or "centers" as they are called, can be established separately, or as part of some faculty or by cooperation between existing faculties or universities. The structure and aims of these centers can vary. But when they are planned and their programs arranged, it is most desirable to keep in mind the whole ecumenical concern in all its aspects.

7. Of such institutes these types may be distinguished:

a. Centers of ecumenical research in which theological questions on a particular theme are thoroughly thrashed out, and directed towards ecumenical dialogue through inquiry into sources, scholarly exchanges and published writings.

b. Ecumenical theological institutes in which students who have finished their general theological training can be set aside to do specialized work in ecumenical theology by means of special courses and seminars. Such institutes may be either designed for general ecumenical affairs, or they may be devoted to special study in some one subject (e.g., the theology of the Oriental Churches, Protestant theology, Anglican theology, etc.) but this should by no means involve neglecting to keep in view the ecumenical problem as a whole.

c. Associations for the joint study of theological and pastoral questions by ministers of different Churches and communities who meet to discuss the theoretical and practical aspects of their ministry among their own people as well as their common witness to the world.

d. Federations of universities and other institutions to facilitate the shared use of libraries and other resources and to establish closer links between their teachers and students in planning study programs.

8. Interconfessional Institutes. Subject to conditions of time and place, the institutes and centers just referred to may be conducted either by Catholics or by several confessions simultaneously. Joint institutes are particularly useful where churches or ecclesial communities need to examine certain questions together (e.g., mission work, dealings with non-Christian religions, questions about atheism and unbelief, the use of media of social communication, architecture and sacred art and, in the province of theology, explanation of Holy Scripture, salvation history, pastoral theology, etc.) which if they are properly resolved can very much advance Christian unity. The setting up and administration of these institutes should normally be entrusted to those who conduct them, saving the rights of competent ecclesiastical authority.

9. Where it seems advisable, Catholic institutes can, in accordance with n. 5 of the present chapter, become members of associations designed to promote raising the standard of theological education, better training of those intended for the pastoral ministry, better cooperation between religious institutions for advanced learning. Care should however be taken that joining such an association leaves intact the autonomy of the Catholic institute in matters of the program of studies, of the doctrinal content of subjects to be taught, of the spiritual and priestly training of the students insofar as these things are determined by the institutes' own purpose and by rules laid down by legitimate ecclesiastical authority.

10. Those who have not yet finished general theological training. Throughout the whole period of their general theological training, whenever there is question of Catholic students cooperating in their intellectual formation with other Christian students, the principles set out in Chapter III, n. 1, must be especially borne in mind. For these exchanges (arising from joint study, prayer, social action, etc.) will be fruitful insofar as

everybody involved is firmly founded in his own faith and tradition and aware of the purposes of ecumenism and the requirements of ecumenical dialogue.

11. Catholic seminaries, theological schools, houses and training colleges for religious men and women can collaborate with other Christian institutions of a similar kind. This cooperation may take various forms according to local conditions and the character of the institutions concerned, for example, occasional exchange of teachers, mutual recognition of certain courses, various kinds of federation, affiliation to a university. In all this care should be taken that the native character of the Catholic institution is preserved, together with its right to train its own students and expound Catholic doctrine, taking account of what is said below, n. 13.

12. Experts in ecumenism from other communities may be invited to hold conferences in Catholic institutions and even to conduct some courses, so long as the proper character of the institution concerned is respected. Catholic teachers should by all means be ready to do the same for others if they are asked.

13. Catholic students may be allowed to attend lectures at institutions, even seminaries, of other Christians, according to the following guiding principles. These things should be kept in view: a) the usefulness of the course and the solid help it will afford in their training as a whole; b) the public reputation, mastery of his subject and ecumenical mind of the teacher; c) the previous preparation of the pupils; d) their spiritual and psychological maturity, and above all e) the very nature of the branches of study concerned; for the more the doctrinal aspect enters into the subject matter, the more caution should be exercised in allowing pupils to attend. Hence, while ordinary or systematic instruction should be given by Catholic teachers, especially where exegesis, dogmatic and moral theology are concerned, Catholic pupils can attend classes dealing with practical subjects, such as biblical languages, communications media, religious sociology insofar as this new science is based on observation of facts, etc. Subject to the judgment of their superiors, who, as was said earlier, should weigh their scientific and spiritual preparedness, students may also attend lectures of common usefulness even though these have a certain doctrinal aspect—examples are church history and patrology. It is the office of superiors to take decisions in these matters, after consulting with the students, according to the general regulations of the seminary and the directions given by the Ordinary who has jurisdiction over it.[31]

It will do much to make such programs really fruitful in practice if Catholic teachers have a fuller knowledge of the writings, opinions, and ecumenical outlook of those teachers from other Christian communities whose classes pupils are allowed to attend. This will be easier if they meet them often and visit their institutions. Further, it is strongly recommended that seminary superiors periodically hold discussions with their staff and spiritual directors, to review the program of studies, suggest changes, and deal with difficulties that may have arisen. Similar meetings and discussions with colleagues from other Christian seminaries are also recommended.

14. In various parts of the world, the pattern of higher education is very much in a state of transition and many proposals are being put forward for amalgamating the different institutes for the study of religion in public and non-denominational universities. It belongs to episcopal conferences to judge, by appropriate means and with appropriate advice, what part clerical students may take in these schemes. In carefully examining this question, they should pay particular regard to the right and proper intellectual and spiritual education of students for the priesthood as well as of other pupils under the guidance of Catholic authority; also to the active involvement of Catholic teachers in these programs and finally to the complete and assured freedom of the Church's magisterium to determine genuine Catholic doctrines and traditions.

If these joint enterprises are to give useful results, it is to be wished that the governing bodies of universities and faculties shall have as active members Catholics (laymen, clerics, religious) who are really expert in their own field and in ecumenical dialogue.

15. Other Catholic institutions which offer religious instruction, whether to students working for theology degrees or for those from other faculties, should be guided by these same principles but adapted to their own character and to the condition and requirements of their students. What has been said already about the previous religious training and maturity of mind of pupils, and of the special competence and general ability of teachers, is equally applicable to these institutions.

*   *   *

In an audience granted to His Eminence Cardinal John Willebrands, President of the Secretariat for Promoting Christian Unity, April 16, 1970, the Sovereign Pontiff, Paul VI, approved this Directory, confirmed it by his authority and ordered that it be published. Anything to the contrary notwithstanding.

Rome, April 16, 1970

Notes

1. *Decree on Ecumenism (Unitatis Redintegratio),* n.4.
2. *Ibid.,* n.1.
3. *Ibid.,* n.4.
4. The term "institutions of advanced learning" in this document covers all university faculties, academic institutes, diocesan seminaries, institutes or centers

of houses for the training of religious, men and women; it excludes therefore grammar and secondary schools, or (in American usage) high schools.

5. According to the directives laid down in the *Ecumenical Directory,* Part One, nn. 2,6–8.

6. Cf. *On Ecumenism,* nn. 3,5.

7. *Ibid.,* nn. 4,6,7.

8. *Ibid.,* n.3.

9. Cf. II, nn.2–5.

10. *Decree on the Training of Priests (Optatam Totius)* n.15.

11. *Ecumenical Directory,* Part One, nn. 22, 32–34.

12. According to the directives laid down by competent authority, cf. Intr.

13. *On Ecumenism,* n.7.

14. *Ibid.,* n.3.

15. *Ecumenical Directory,* Part One, nn. 25–63. Cf. also "A Declaration of the Secretariat for Promoting Christian Unity on the position of the Catholic Church concerning a common Eucharist between Christians of different Confessions," *Osservatore Romano,* January 12–13, 1970, p.3.

16. *On Ecumenism,* nn. 9–10.

17. *Ibid.,* n.3.

18. *Ibid.,* n. 17.

19. *Ibid.,* n. 4. Cf. Encyclical *Ecclesiam Suam* of Paul VI: AAS 66 (1964), pp. 609ff.

20. *Constitution on the Church (Lumen Gentium),* n. 13. Also, *On Ecumenism,* nn. 4, 16.

21. On Ecumenism, n. 12. Cf. *Decree on the Church's Missionary Activity (Ad Gentes),* nn. 12, 36.

22. *On Ecumenism,* n.24.

23. *Ibid.,* n. 11.

24. Cf. Pope John XXIII's allocution to the Second Vatican Council, October 11, 1962, in *Constitutiones, Decreta, etc.* (Ed. Polyglotta Vaticana), p. 865; also, *On Ecumenism,* n.6; *Constitution on the Church in the Modern World* (Gaudium et Spes), n. 62.

25. *On Ecumenism,* n.17.

26. *Ibid.,* n. 17.

27. *Ibid.,* n. 4.

28. *Ecumenical Directory,* Part One, nn. 3–8.

29. *Decree on the Pastoral Office of Bishops (Christus Dominus),* n. 16; *Decree on the Life and Ministry of Priests* (Presbyterorum Ordinis), n.9.

30. Cf. above, III.1.

31. Cf. above, IV.5.

Chapter Four
REFLECTIONS AND SUGGESTIONS CONCERNING ECUMENICAL DIALOGUE

Introduction

While the SPCU was drafting Part II of the *Directory* ("Ecumenism in Higher Education"), it also was elaborating a document on ecumenical dialogue, that is, between the "Christians of different Churches or Communions." It was then intended to be Part III of the directory. At its plenary session of November 1969 the SPCU approved the text, but with the resolution that it should not be given the same normative authority as Parts I and II, and thus should not be published as an integral part of the directory. Let it be considered, the SPCU later stated in its explanatory note, as "a working document, a qualified and sure guide, which carries weight without, however, being based upon any authority in the juridical sense of the word. . . . Its authority resides uniquely in the fact that it is the result of prolonged reflection made on many levels by those engaged in ecumenical dialogue" [IS, 12 (Dec. 1970), p. 3]. Paul VI approved the SPCU's resolution. On August 15, 1970, the document was promulgated by the SPCU, in English and in French.

The explanatory note mentions that during the drafting stages, the Joint Working Group between the Roman Catholic Church and the World Council of Churches had been responsible for a "working paper" document. The *Reflections and Suggestions* never appeared in Latin; in various languages, the text was sent to episcopal conferences as "an aid at the disposal of ecclesiastical authorities for concrete application of the *Decree on Ecumenism,*" SPCU *IS,* 12 (1970), pp. 5–11.

75

I.

INTRODUCTION

This document concerns only ecumenical dialogue, that is to say, dialogue which is established between the "Christians of different Churches or Communions."[1] The principles on which it rests and the themes which it deals with are in part different from those which characterize the dialogue which the Catholic Church wishes to establish, and in fact does establish, with Judaism, the major religions, with non-believers and with the world. In fact, "We for our part should not wish to exclude anybody from such a dialogue, prompted only by charity and directed towards truth. . . ."[2] These various forms of dialogue cannot be dissociated one from the other; the dialogue which is dealt with here is not unconnected with those forms of dialogue which are the concern of the Secretariats for Non-Christian Religions and for Non-Believers.

In spite of certain contrary appearances, modern man seeks for dialogue as a privileged means of establishing and developing mutual understanding, esteem, respect and love, whether between groups or between individuals. For this reason he is eager to make ever greater use of it at all levels of his life, political, social, economic, educational and religious.

The same is true when individual Christians and Churches or ecclesial Communities concern themselves with ecumenical matters. Dialogue is the indispensable means for their meeting and their witness, at the levels both of thought and action. Thus there have grown up interconfessional groups of the most varied composition and aims, and the need has made itself felt of establishing dialogue structures, as seen in the local and regional ecumenical commissions, the World Council of Churches and the Secretariat for Promoting Christian Unity.

Being aware of these facts, the Second Vatican Council stressed the importance of dialogue between the Catholic Church and the other Churches and ecclesial Communities.[3] The Secretariat for Promoting Christian Unity, taking its inspiration from the concerns, orientations and motives of the Council, proposes to show the nature and aim of this ecumenical dialogue, together with its bases, its conditions, its method, the themes it handles and the forms it takes with a view to favoring and developing it in the present situation.

If concern for the reestablishment of Christian unity involves all the members of the Church, both the faithful and their pastors, each according to his own condition, it belongs to the bishops to be the promoters and guides of ecumenical dialogue.[4] As such, they will also exercise their pastoral vigilance in order to keep the dialogue on the exact lines laid down for it by the Second Vatican Council in the Decree on Ecumenism.

This pastoral vigilance will take into account the double aspect of ecumenical action envisaged by the Council. For if ecumenical action must remain "loyal to the truth we have received from the Apostles and the Fathers, and in harmony with the faith which the Catholic Church has always professed, and at the same time tending towards that fullness with which Our Lord wants His body to be endowed in the course of time,"[5] nevertheless the Council expresses the desire "that the initiatives of the sons of the Catholic Church, joined with those of the separated brethren, go forward without obstructing the ways of divine Providence and without prejudging the future inspiration of the Holy Spirit."[6]

II.
NATURE AND AIM
OF ECUMENICAL DIALOGUE

1. In general terms, dialogue exists between individuals and groups from the moment when each party begins both to listen and reply, to seek to understand and to be understood, to pose questions and to be questioned in turn, to be freely forthcoming himself and receptive to the other party, concerning a given situation, research project or course of action, with the aim of progressing in unison towards a greater community of life, outlook and accomplishment. Each of the parties to the dialogue is ready to clarify further his ideas and his ways of living and acting, if it appears that truth is leading him in this direction. Thus reciprocity and a mutual commitment are essential elements of dialogue.[7]

2. The ecumenical dialogue demands all these elements, which will be made more specific by the aim pursued. This aim has several aspects:

a. Through dialogue, Christians must learn to advance together in their sharing in the reality of the mystery of Christ and of his Church. In this way, they will be able to discern the common elements in their different ways of approaching the revealed mystery and of translating it into their thought, life and witness.

b. Through dialogue, Christians must learn to give common witness to the mission which Jesus Christ confided to His Church, so that all may "before the whole world . . . profess their faith in God, one and three, in the incarnate Son of God, our Redeemer and Lord,"[8] and that thus the world may come to believe.

c. Since the world poses the same question to all the Churches and ecclesial Communities, the latter, listening to the questions together and understanding them through dialogue, and being attentive to the Holy Spirit, will seek together the response that the Lord expects of them in order to serve the world, especially in those places where the Gospel has not been preached.[9]

d. In the sphere of their internal life, a large number of Christian Communions are face to face with the same questions, which however they may each find posed at different levels. Such questions are those concerning the laity, the ministry, liturgy, catechetics, the Christian family, and so on. Does not the Holy Spirit urge Christians to approach jointly these questions also?

Thus it becomes apparent that ecumenical dialogue is not limited to an academic or purely conceptual level, but striving for a more complete communion between the Christian Communities, a common service of the Gospel and closer collaboration on the level of thought and action, it serves to transform modes of thought and behavior and the daily life of those Communities. In this way, it aims at preparing the way for their unity of faith in the bosom of a Church one and visible: thus "little by little, as the obstacles to perfect ecclesial communion are overcome, all Christians will be gathered, in a common celebration of the Eucharist, into that unity of the one and only Church which Christ bestowed on His Church from the beginning. This unity, we believe, dwells in the Catholic Church as something she can never lose, and we hope that it will continue to increase until the end of time."[10]

It is true that dialogue by itself does not suffice to bring about the fullness of unity that Christ wishes; nevertheless, that unity is the ultimate aim of the thoughts and desires of those engaged in dialogue, who are preparing themselves to receive it as the great gift that God alone will bestow, in the way and at the time that He wishes.[11]

III.
BASES OF DIALOGUE

Ecumenical dialogue is rooted in a number of doctrinal and pastoral facts.

1. First, since "the brethren who believe in Christ are Christ's disciples, reborn in Baptism, sharers with the People of God in very many riches,"[12] and since these riches, such as "the written word of God, the life of grace, faith, hope and charity, along with other interior gifts of the Holy Spirit and visible elements,"[13] are accessible to all those who have been baptized, Christians are in a position to communicate to each other the riches that the Holy Spirit develops within them. This community of spiritual goods is the first basis upon which ecumenical dialogue rests.

2. But it is inside their Churches and ecclesial Communities that Christians enjoy these spiritual goods; the Churches and Communities which are separated from the Catholic Church enjoy "a significance and a value in the mystery of salvation. . . . Many of the sacred actions" that they perform are to be recognized as "capable of providing access to the community of salvation."[14] Between them and the Catholic Church therefore there is a certain communion already existing which must be the

starting point for dialogue. This latter will tend towards a more perfect sharing by each Church and ecclesial Community in the very mystery of Christ and His Church,[15] which is the foundation of their communion among themselves.

3. "Our common reference is Revelation as expressed in the witness of the Holy Scriptures. . . . Their witness is centered in Jesus Christ and has meaning through relation to Him."[16] The Holy Spirit in fact is always acting in such a way as to lead the Christian people to live it and to understand it better and so to accomplish its prophetic role. Ecumenical dialogue therefore allows each one to communicate to his brethren the riches of Christ whereby he lives and to accept the riches whereby the others live.

4. Since "every renewal in the Church essentially consists in an increase of fidelity to her own calling, undoubtedly this explains the dynamism of the movement towards unity."[17] In a like manner, all Communions in their effort to renew themselves, are normally led to enter into dialogue, in order to question themselves on "their own faithfulness to Christ's will."[18]

IV.
CONDITIONS FOR DIALOGUE

1. Before it can begin, all dialogue presupposes that an attitude of sympathy and openness between those who will take part has been brought about by more or less spontaneous contacts and exchanges, in the details of ordinary life. It is in such a context of human relationships, which can be very varied, that dialogue of whatever sort usually takes its origin and form.

2. Ecumenical dialogue will be conducted between the participants as between equals.[19] Everything that has been said about the nature, aim and bases of this dialogue, notably concerning reciprocity and mutual commitment, provides a basis for this attitude of equality.

a. In ecumenical dialogue, those who take part recognize honestly that because of existing differences there is an inequality between the different Christian Communions. Hence they reject on the one hand that doctrinal indifferentism which would claim that, before the mystery of Christ and the Church, all positions are equivalent. On the other hand they do not pass any judgement regarding the willingness of one side or the other to be faithful to the Gospel. The Catholic participant, believing as he does that the Lord has confided to the Catholic Church the fullness of the means of salvation and all truth revealed by God, will be ready to give an account of his faith.[20]

b. In ecumenical dialogue, those who take part recognize one another as existing in Christ, since they have been baptized in Him, born again "not from any mortal seed but from the everlasting word of the living and eternal God," (1 Peter 1:23) and able through the Holy Spirit to hear their brethren tell them of the marvellous works of God.

In this dialogue, they recognize together that a certain communion exists between the Christian Communities; nevertheless, they are anxious not to conceal from one another the fact that in the content, development and expression of the faith of the Churches there exist certain differences which must become the object of their dialogue, so that they may attain a more perfect communion.

Each of those taking part will give the others, in a form that they will be really able to grasp and in the most genuine way, witness to the Gospel of Christ as His Church wishes to bear it; he in his turn will listen to the witness expressed by the others.

In brotherly emulation, those taking part become aware that God is calling them to an ever deeper faithfulness to Himself and to the revelation made by Him.

c. On a practical level, equality between the participants in dialogue implies equality of standard in sacred and secular learning and equality in the level of responsibilities held.

3. To be genuine and fruitful, all dialogue requires that those who direct it, if not all those taking part, possess a certain degree of ability. This required competence will vary according to the forms of dialogue and the themes dealt with, but will always presuppose the religious formation demanded by all dialogue which has as its aim the unity of Christians. Yet, competence in the theological field cannot be the only requirement; there is a place for practical skills in all subjects, whether professional, technical, apostolic or spiritual.

Without pretending to say everything that there is to be said on training for ecumenical dialogue, it will be useful here to recall the following considerations.

a. Though it is not required that all Catholic participants should have the same degree of preparation for such dialogue, it is very much to the point that some of them, whether they be clerics or laymen, should have received an adequate training in this field. Among other things, an effective contribution can be made by ecumenical training sessions, programs for reading, correspondence courses, ecumenical centers and chairs of ecumenism in theological faculties. Through these and parallel ways, attention will be given to learning the art of dialogue, to understanding the thought of others and to becoming acquainted with their spiritual life.[21]

Within the framework of this training, it would be a good thing for Catholics taking part in ecumenical meetings to reflect together on the dialogue in which they participate, both beforehand, in order to prepare themselves for it, and also afterwards, to assess its development and results.

b. Given that the Church "has always regarded the Scriptures together with sacred tradition as the supreme rule of faith, and will ever do so . . . , all the preaching of the Church must, like the Christian religion itself, be nourished and ruled by sacred Scripture."[22] Care must therefore be taken to acquire a culture, theology and spirituality of biblical inspiration. It must not be forgotten that "the sacred utterances are precious instruments in the mighty hand of God."[23]

c. The opportunities for encounter between Christians are becoming more numerous as a result of the circumstances of modern life. It is necessary that the faithful and their pastors should fully appreciate their responsibilities in this field and should take pains to be well informed and constantly alert about theological and spiritual matters.

4. With regard to the presentation of doctrine, a few remarks are necessary.

a. On the one hand, dialogue leads to a more exact knowledge of our brethren,[24] to which they will normally be able to open the way for us. On the other hand, the Catholic participant must carefully inform himself of the content of his Church's faith, without either overstating or minimizing it, remembering that ecumenical encounter is not merely an individual work, but also a task of the Church, which takes precedence over all individual opinions.

b. It will be borne in mind that "in Catholic teaching there exists an order or 'hierarchy' of truths, since they vary in their relationship to the foundation of the Christian faith."[25] Neither in the life nor in the teaching of the whole Church is everything presented on the same level. Certainly all revealed truths demand the same acceptance of faith, but according to the greater or lesser proximity that they have to the basis of the revealed mystery, they are variously placed with regard to one another and have varying connections among themselves. For example, the dogma of Mary's Immaculate Conception, which may not be isolated from what the Council of Ephesus declares about Mary, the Mother of God, presupposes, before it can be properly grasped in a true life of faith, the dogma of grace to which it is linked and which in its turn necessarily rests upon the redemptive incarnation of the Word.

c. Approaching together the mystery of Christ, men discover the difficulty of speaking the same Christian language. By language is meant not just vocabulary, but above all mentality, the genius of a culture, philosophical tools, traditions and style of life.

With each one using the language of his own Communion, the same words may signify quite different realities in one Church and in another, while different words may express the same reality. Since it is a question of establishing real and complete communication, of eliminating the risk of misunderstandings and of not travelling unaware along parallel ways, it is absolutely necessary that those taking part in dialogue, even though they be formed by the spirit of the Scriptures and express themselves in a language inspired by the Scriptures, should submit the language they use to a hermeneutic, a critical study.

5. In order to foster in themselves a spirit of true dialogue, and in order to prepare themselves for engaging in dialogue with their Christian brethren, Catholics will take careful note of the legitimate diversity within the Church's unity. Let them take care to promote "mutual esteem, reverence, and harmony, allowing for every legitimate difference, so that we can begin a dialogue among the People of God, pastors or faithful, which may become steadily more fruitful. The things that unite the faithful are stronger than those that divide them. Let there be unity in things essential, liberty in things doubtful, charity in all things."[26]

If Christians are prepared for dialogue within their own Communities, they are equipped to receive the fruits of an interconfessional dialogue. It is important that those who take part in the latter should consider themselves as the voice which must pass on to their own Community the benefits they have received on its behalf during that dialogue.

The Catholic will be careful to check his manner of procedure in the ecumenical dialogue. In particular he will examine how closely he follows the directives and orientations given by the pastors of the Church regarding both the ecumenical task taken as a whole and dialogue in particular. He will normally become acquainted with these directives through the territorial commission for ecumenical questions or the diocesan commission.

Further, since ecumenical dialogue demands a very close fidelity to the life and faith of his Church, he must also be careful to share in the authentic renewals which develop within the Church, considering them "as favorable pledges and signs of ecumenical progress in the future."[27]

His commitment to dialogue can only be lived in a spirit of renunciation, not only of any seeking for personal advantage, but also of confessional triumphalism or the appearance of it. This demands a spiritual climate which disposes the heart and mind to remain, in Christ, attentive to God and to the impulses of His Spirit. The essential qualities here are purity of intention, desire for holiness, an attitude of humility and repentance and above all prayer.

Thanks to this atmosphere, the conviction strengthens "that it will be possible to overcome the disagreements in an atmosphere of active patience, accepting the fact that time will be needed for ideas to mature and to make progress, and retaining at the same time a keen sense of the importance of the dialogue and of its efficacy."[28]

1. *General remarks.* Whether dialogue deals with questions of ecume-

nism or not, its method includes several elements, which appear either in succession or concurrently:

a. Exchange of ideas, whereby each participant explains his point of view on the subject of the meeting. This exchange has the aspect both of information, calling for cqmpetence in the participants and a desire to learn from the others, and of witness, when the facts or ideas set forth evoke in the speakers a religious attitude of faith and piety. It requires on both sides a resolve to be frank in expounding the truth and a resolve to welcome the truth one listens to;

b. The comparing of ideas, whereby the participants try to bring to light the points of divergence, similarity and convergence in the ideas expounded. This demands attentive sympathy for persons and ideas, without which one cannot understand others' positions;

c. Research, by reflecting upon and discussing shared positions; all dialogue, even of the most elementary kind, always has this goal in view;

d. The bringing to light of aspects previously unnoticed; in fact, as dialogue proceeds, the shared positions to which it leads become the starting point for fresh researches and further advances.

2. More specifically, attention is drawn to the following points concerning ecumenical dialogue:

a. Each of the participants, starting from the understanding he has of the revealed mystery, should try to discover, evaluate and take into serious consideration everything in what the other says that seems to him to be of genuine value. The list of such things might be long. Here are a few useful indications for lines of enquiry:

    aa. Truths confessed in common;

    bb. Truths which have been allowed to become obscured in this or that Community as a result of divisions and historical circumstances, and which may be better preserved and sometimes better developed in some other Community;

    cc. True religious insights, valid theological intentions, even in areas of divergence; particular forms of worship, stresses laid on certain aspects of the Christian life, etc.

b. Each partner should seek to expound the doctrine of his own Community in a constructive manner, putting aside the tendency to define by opposition, which generally results in certain positions becoming overstressed or unduly hardened. This is a purifying process; the warping from which our respective theologies suffer can only be corrected at this price.

c. The partners will work together towards a constructive synthesis, in such a way that every legitimate contribution is made use of, in a joint research aimed at the complete assimilation of the revealed datum. This research involves an effort to return to the sources, going back to Christian origins before the appearance of subsequent disagreements. It also calls for an effort at discovery, looking to the future for solutions that will transcend present historical differences.

d. As the ecumenical dialogue proceeds, it opens up new perspectives for those taking part, leads them on to deeper research starting from the points of agreement they have recognized, and helps them to become aware of what adjustments of behavior and thought may seem necessary. "To seek in order to find, to find in order to seek still further": this saying of St. Augustine[29] comes home to them. Thus, thanks to that "brotherly emulation" that dialogue creates, they will be led "to a deeper realization and a clearer expression of the unfathomable riches of Christ."[30]

V.
SUBJECTS FOR DIALOGUE

1. Ecumenical dialogue may cover the content of faith, theological questions, subjects connected with liturgical and spiritual life, history, religious psychology, as well as anything that has to do with the presence, witness and mission of Christians in the world.

2. Subjects will be chosen by the participants taking into account local situations, the degree of specialized knowledge actually available, the qualifications of the participants or their involvement in the world, bearing in mind their confessional allegiance and also real questions that present themselves variously according to country or region and to historical, economic and sociological context. If dialogue is to be really effective at the level of the Christian people, a place must be given not only to the theologian but also to the sociologist, religious psychologist, anthropologist, historian—and above all to the pastor of souls.

3. Since dialogue is not an end in itself, the more experienced groups should be careful not to choose subjects which are too technical. Dialogue must spring from a legitimate desire for shared knowledge of an event or a situation. It is not just an academic discussion. For highly specialized subjects recourse will have to be made to experts who can provide the necessary information. But if the subjects were too technical for a group insufficiently prepared for them, or if specialists were continually called in, there would be a risk of bringing the dialogue to an end, because the participants would no longer be capable of expressing themselves to one another.

4. Attention to real life is fundamental as a guide in the choice of subjects and the way of tackling them. Certain subjects suggested in the Decree on Ecumenism will be the object of special attention, for example: the study of Scripture, the sacramental and liturgical life, notably on

occasions of common prayer or attendance at the liturgical celebrations of the Churches.[31]

Further themes may be found in other documents of the Council or of the World Council of Churches: Revelation, the Church, Mission, the Church in the world, etc.; also in questions raised by modern life, such as the problems of peace, overpopulation, marriage and birth, etc.; further, certain currents of contemporary thought: the philosophy of the "death of God," Marxism, encounter with non-Christian religions, the secularization phenomenon, etc. Whatever they may be, the subjects will be dealt with, in the light of the Gospel, as they affect and make demands upon the present-day life of Christians.

5. In some countries, the questions raised during the crises of the eleventh and sixteenth centuries are today no longer the problem that they once were. Without forgetting historical origins, dialogue about such questions should focus attention on the way they pose themselves here and now. Particularly when dialogue hinges upon a subject relating to faith, it will be a fruitful exercise to begin from the ecclesial witness of those taking part, so as to obtain a clearer picture of how this faith is lived by them today within their Communities.

6. Dialogue, however, like all human effort, has its limits. Certain differences between the Churches rest on data of a historical, psychological and sociological order. They are felt to be still irreducible. Other, deeper ones depend on the way in which one conceives one's own faith and lives it. Dialogue seems powerless here. The participants realize that God is calling them to turn to Him in prayer and that He is teaching them to place their confidence in the power of the Holy Spirit alone.

VI.
FORMS OF DIALOGUE

1. The most frequent form of dialogue is the one which springs up spontaneously when Christians meet one another. It is here that the desire makes itself felt to get to know others better, and that the necessary contacts are made for more organized meetings. It is impossible to regulate such contacts, which are an integral part of the style of modern life. But Christians must be helped to make use of them for acquiring a better knowledge of one another's situation, problems and doctrinal positions.

2. In particular, dialogue is carried on in a spontaneous and unstructured way in many centers of education and study. It is a means of education that allows the participants to get to know and understand better others' opinions and convictions, to see more exactly their way of life and to compare the various options open to men. It is therefore a good

thing to encourage young Catholics to take part in such meetings, at the same time training them and giving them support, so that they may be enriched by contact with others and may bring to such meetings their own witness.

3. Groups of lay people will also meet to face in the light of Christian faith the questions raised by their profession or occupation: problems of law, medicine, politics, business, technology, scientific research, the social sciences, trade union questions, and so on. The initiative for such meetings is the responsibility of the laymen themselves. They will readily call upon experts for questions which are beyond the competence of non-specialist participants.

4. In these various groups, Christians who are deeply aware of present-day problems often make them the subject of conversations, as country, particular time or the professional interests may suggest. Examples of such problems are peace, social justice, hunger, the problems of the underdeveloped countries, the running of cities, the difficulties of young households, etc. If they are attentive to the spirit of the Gospel, the participants are naturally led to joint enquiry, with a view to taking joint action in and for the world; here will be an opportunity for individual Christians and Christian Communions to bear a common witness.

5. As a consequence of these meetings, the legitimate desire to get to know other Christians better in their faith and their ecclesial and liturgical life may lead some people to form more specifically ecumenical groups, or to take part in already existing ones. It is to be desired that these groups should spring from friendly and fraternal personal contacts between Christians of the various Communities. The Catholics will take pains to deepen their faith and to remain in communion of thought and desire with their Church. It will not be forgotten that the Holy Spirit can implant within the faithful charisms through which He means to act for the good of the Church and the world. The organization and conduct of such meetings can of course be entrusted to specially trained laymen, who will, where necessary, call upon theologians.

6. In mixed marriage households, ecumenical dialogue can have its place, with the attendance when desired of the pastors of the Communities concerned. Such dialogue can serve to strengthen the religious life of the family and will in addition be an example of ecumenical clarity.

7. It is natural that the clergy of the different Churches and Communities should wish to meet one another for an exchange of views on the pastoral problems they have to face, so as to get to know the experiences of others, look for the best solutions to problems, take up common attitudes as far as the circumstances and the nature of the problem allow, and, when the occasion offers, decide on a practical course of joint action. Bishops will make a point of taking part in these meetings from time to time and of recommending them to their priests. Such meetings will in fact help to

create an atmosphere favorable to the brotherhood of all Christians. They will also help to replace the rivalries of former times by ties of mutual help and collaboration. In some countries these meetings often take place within recognized organizations, such as Councils of Churches and Ministerial Associations.

8. Ecumenical dialogue can take place between theologians, for example members of ecumenical institutes, universities, faculties of theology and seminaries. It goes without saying that such dialogue requires of the Catholic participants a very serious, specific preparation for the questions on the agenda. Care will be taken to note the necessary differences between the Church's dogma, the great spiritual and liturgical traditions and the legitimate options in the matter of free discussion and research.

9. Dialogues may be two-sided or many-sided. The number and the confessional allegiance of those taking part will be decided according to the subjects studied and to local possibilities. In any event, during the dialogue those taking part must bear in mind the Christian traditions not represented among them. It will often be a good idea to pass on information concerning these meetings to the local ecumenical organizations and, in the case of more international meetings, to the Secretariat for Promoting Christian Unity.

10. In some theological dialogues, the participants are appointed by the hierarchy to attend not in a personal capacity but as delegated representatives of their Church. Such mandates can be given by the local Ordinary, the episcopal conference within its territory or by the Holy See. In these cases the Catholic participants have a special responsibility towards the authority that has sent them.

11. Ecumenical meetings at all levels will take account of the existence of a body of literature which, taken as a whole, amounts to a written form of dialogue between Christians. This written dialogue is particularly fruitful when the publications are interconfessional. Bishops will encourage Catholic publications which, with regard to other confessions, are marked by qualities of understanding and esteem and have a keen sense of truth. These are the qualities that must mark any ecumenical undertaking.

12. Since the participants have a duty to see that the experience gained in these meetings benefits the members of the Church, they will take care to communicate with the pastors of the Church, passing on information regarding their activities to the various commissions for ecumenism (the Secretariat for Promoting Christian Unity, national, regional or diocesan commissions). They will take an active part in initiatives of ecumenical interest, such as societies, libraries, reviews, publications, etc., and do their best to help these towards wider influence and circulation.

From the Vatican, August 15, 1970

Notes

1. *Decree on Ecumenism,* n.4.
2. *Constitution on the Church in the Modern World,* n.92.
3. *On Ecumenism,* nn.4,9,11,18–23; *Church in the Modern World,* n.92; *Decree on the Missionary Activity of the Church,* n.15.
4. *On Ecumenism,* nn.4,5,9; *Missionary Activity,* n.15.
5. *On Ecumenism,* n. 15.
6. *Ibid.*
7. *Dialogue with Non-Believers,* 1,1 : *AAS* 60 (1968), pp. 695–6.
8. *On Ecumenism,* n.12.
9. *Missionary Activity,* nn. 15.4, 29.4.
10. *On Ecumenism,* n.4.
11. *A Working Paper on Ecumenical Dialogue,* prepared by the Joint Working Group between the World Council of Churches and the Roman Catholic Church: SPCU *IS,* 3 (1967), p.34.
12. *Missionary Activity,* n.3.
13. *On Ecumenism,* n.3.
14. *Ibid.*
15. *Ibid.,* n.4.
16. *A Working Paper on Ecumenical Dialogue, op.cit.,* p.34.
17. *On Ecumenism,* n. 6.
18. *Ibid.,* n.4.
19. *Ibid.,* n.9: "par cum pari".
20. *Ibid.,* nn. 3,4,11.
21. *Ibid.,* n.9.
22. *Constitution on Divine Revelation,* n.21.
23. *On Ecumenism,* n.21.
24. *Ibid.,* n.9.
25. *Ibid.,* n.11.
26. *Church in the Modern World,* n.92; cf. *On Ecumenism,* n.4.
27. *On Ecumenism,* n.6.
28. *A Working Paper on Ecumenical Dialogue, op. cit.,* p. 36.
29. *De Trinitate,* XV, II, 2: *PL* 42, 1057: "Et quaeritur ut inveniatur dulcius et invenitur ut quaratur avidius".
30. *On Ecumenism,* n.11.
31. *Ibid.,* chap. 3; *Directory Part One,* nn. 50, 59.

Chapter Five
ECUMENICAL COLLABORATION AT THE REGIONAL, NATIONAL AND LOCAL LEVELS

Introduction

During the Holy Year of 1975, the SPCU published this document (February 22), which responds to the expressed need of many Roman Catholics who work on the local ecumenical commissions which had been established after the Vatican Council, as encouraged by Part One of the 1967 *Directory*.

Already in 1971 the SPCU members and consultors had begun work on a draft. Meanwhile, the Joint Working Group between the World Council of Churches and the Roman Catholic Church had commissioned a study of forms of ecumenical collaboration on regional, national and local levels. The resulting documentation contributed greatly to later revisions of the SPCU draft.

The official introduction to the text is by the SPCU president, John Cardinal Willebrands, and the secretary, Monsignor Charles Moeller. They carefully elucidate the document's purpose and authority:

"It is not a set of directives or prescriptions endowed with authority in the juridical sense of the word. Rather it is a document that gives the kind of information which can help bishops in a certain place decide about the form to be given to the local ecumenical collaboration. But its purpose is to do more than give information. It sets out orientations which do not have the force of law but which have the weight of the experience and insights of the Secretariat.

It should also be clear that an amount of what the document contains does have the force of law when this is taken from

89

sources of the Church's teaching and discipline such as the documents of the Second Vatican Council and the official decisions and directives of the Holy See.

With this status the document is now published. In addition to the approval of the Plenary, the Cardinal President has brought it to the notice of the Holy Father who approved of it being sent to all episcopal conferences as an aid to them in carrying out their ecumenical responsibilities. It is as such an instrument that the document must be understood and this defines both its scope and its limits.

The ecumenical dimension is a prime aspect of the life of the Catholic Church on the universal and on the local level. Catholic principles on ecumenism have been given in the conciliar Decree on Ecumenism. They maintain that ecumenical initiatives must be adapted to local needs, that the local church itself has a real and indispensable contribution to make, while always insisting that every local initiative be taken always in harmony with the bonds of communion in faith and discipline which link the Catholic Church. All of this the present document sets forth clearly.

At the same time it is not all-inclusive, nor does it aim to be so. At their meeting in 1972 the representatives of the Ecumenical Commissions raised many questions about local ecumenism. We believe our document responds to some, chiefly those touching on organised ecumenical work and its national and diocesan structures.

The Second Vatican Council stresses the responsibility of the bishops in this field. "This Sacred Synod . . . commends this work to bishops everywhere in the world for their skilful promotion and prudent guidance". To this end the efforts of pastors and laity must be directed.

The Pope has proposed the theme of spiritual renewal and reconciliation with God and among Christians as one of the principal goals of the Holy Year. We trust that this present document may be a contribution to the realization of this deeply ecumenical perspective."*

1.

THE ECUMENICAL TASK

In November, 1972, addressing representatives of National Ecumenical Commissions, Pope Paul VI described the primary mission of the

* Text: SPCU *IS,* 26 (1975), pp. 8–31.

Church as being to call men to enter into communion with God, through Christ, in the Holy Spirit, and then to help them to live in this communion which saves them and establishes among them a unity as deep and mysterious as the unity of the Father and the Son.[1]

On another occasion, in October 1967, the Holy Father in an allocution to Patriarch Athenagoras, noted that while this unity is to be a sign in the world calling forth faith, present day unbelief too can act like a summons to the churches and ecclesial communities awakening in them an urgent awareness of the need for unity and calling them to act together. "This common witness", said the Holy Father, "one yet varied, decided and persuasive, of a faith humbly self-confident, springing up in love and radiating hope, is without doubt the foremost demand that the Spirit makes of the churches today."[2]

The pre-condition of this ecumenical movement is a renewal in the Church, according to the spirit of the truth and holiness of Jesus Christ, a renewal which must touch every member of the Church and be attested to by the quality of their lives.[3]

As the call of the Holy Spirit to unity through renewal is heard and answered by the Christian communities, the volume of study and joint action grows apace, so that one may speak of the pressure of the ecumenical movement which more and more compels Christians to dialogue, common prayer, practical collaboration and common witness.[4]

The cooperation between churches and ecclesial communities has mission and unity as its aim, not least when it is concerned with social and allied questions. For all Christian communities recognize the proclamation of the Gospel to the world, in deed as well as in word, as their first duty.[5]

The ecumenical movement is a movement of the Spirit wider than any of the particular initiatives through which it is manifested. This ecumenical impulse, which for the Catholic Church is necessarily guided by the principles set forth in the Decree on Ecumenism and the Ecumenical Directory, seeks a great variety of expressions and structural forms and the purpose of this document is to look at some of the more prominent of these. As the Catholic Church in each country becomes more aware of the manifestations of ecumenism in various parts of the world, it has to avoid both isolationism and slavish imitation of other places. Ecumenical initiatives must be adapted to local needs and will therefore differ from region to region, while always remaining in harmony with the bonds of Catholic communion. Further, the quest for a structural local unity is a challenge, but so equally is that for a qualitative unity in the confession of a sound and complete faith. Ecumenical initiatives should be true expressions of the life of the local church, and not simply the work of individuals. They should therefore be carried on under the guidance of the bishop and in close association with the ecumenical commission of the diocese or of the episcopal conference. It is important that ecumenical commissions should consider such local initiatives with discernment and sympathy and where appropriate offer encouragement and support. Ecumenism is an integral part of the renewal of the Church[6] and its promotion should be the constant concern of the local church.

A difficulty is created if ecumenical initiatives are left solely to unofficial groups.[7] Then there is an imbalance in which the full ecumenical responsibility will not be adequately and prudently met. Such difficulties will best be avoided if there is an obvious and sincere commitment to ecumenism by the local church.

2.

THE CATHOLIC UNDERSTANDING
OF LOCAL CHURCH[8]
AND ITS RELATION TO
THE ECUMENICAL MOVEMENT

Ecumenism on the local level is a primary element of the ecumenical situation as a whole. It is not secondary nor merely derivative. It faces specific needs and situations and has its own resources. It has an initiative of its own and its task is a wider one than merely implementing world-wide ecumenical directives on a small scale.[9]

Not only do the local churches direct and assume responsibility for the work of local ecumenism in communion with the Holy See but in the local churches the mysteries of ecclesial communion (baptism, faith in Christ, the proclamation of the Gospel, etc.) are celebrated and thus constantly renewed, and they are the basis of ecumenical collaboration. This collaboration is served by a number of organized bodies some of which will be mentioned later. It must also be borne in mind that at the present time a good number of Christians prefer to work locally in "informal" groups of a more spontaneous nature than in institutional or "formal" groups.

The importance of local ecumenism derives from the significance of local churches in the Catholic Church as set forth in Vatican Council II:

"A diocese is part of the People of God entrusted to a Bishop, to be cared for with the cooperation of his priests, so that in close union with its pastor, and by him gathered together in the Holy Spirit through the Gospel and the Eucharist, it constitutes a particular Church, in which is truly present and operative the One, Holy, Catholic and Apostolic Church of Christ" (*Christus Dominus,* 11).

The same Council taught:

"Individual bishops are the visible, fundamental principle of unity in their particular churches. These churches are moulded to the likeness of the universal Church; in them, and of them, consists the one, sole Catholic

Church. For this reason individual bishops represent their own church; all, together with the Pope, represent the whole Church linked by peace, love and unity" (*Lumen Gentium,* 23).

It further stated:

"This Church of Christ is truly present in all lawful, local congregations of the faithful. These congregations, in attachment to their pastors, themselves have the name of churches in the New Testament. They are, for their own locality, the new people called by God, in the Holy Spirit and in great fullness (cf. *1 Thess.* 1:5). In these churches the faithful are gathered together by the preaching of Christ's gospel; in them, the mystery of the Lord's Supper is celebrated 'so that the whole brotherhood is linked by the flesh and blood of the Lord's body' " (*ibid.,* 26).

Where the people of God, linked in belief and love with their bishop gather to manifest the unity of lived and proclaimed faith, an irreplaceable sacramental expression is given to the living unity of the Catholic Church.[10]

From this Catholic perspective ecumenical responsibilities of the local church emerge clearly. It is through the local church that the Catholic Church is present with many other Christian churches and communities in the same localities and in wider regions such as the territory of an episcopal conference or of an eastern synod. These regions have their distinctive spiritual, ethical, political and cultural characteristics. Within these regions the other Christian churches and ecclesial communities often have the highest level of their churchly authority whereby they make those decisions which direct their life and shape their future. Therefore, the local church or several local churches in the territory of an episcopal conference or a synod can be in a very favorable position to make contact and establish fraternal relations with other Christian churches and communities at these levels.

Through contacts at this point, the other Christian churches and communities may be afforded a fuller understanding of the dynamic of Catholic life as the local church makes it present both in its particularity and in its concrete universality. With the awareness that in a given place it is the vehicle of the presence and action of the Catholic Church, which is fundamentally one, the local church will be ready to take care that its free initiatives do not go beyond its competence and are always undertaken within the limits of the doctrine and the discipline of the whole Catholic Church, particularly as this touches the sacraments. This discipline is a safeguard of the unity of faith. In this way the bonds of fraternal communion with other local churches will be manifested and the role of the Church of Rome serving the unity of all will be evident.

Thus by reason of their Catholic communion the local churches can enrich the ecumenical movement in many localities, and the local church in one region by its activity may generate an impulse that will stimulate further ecumenical developments elsewhere. Through their communion each local church may also gain ecumenical insights which would not spontaneously arise out of its particular or local situations. And in the face of new and serious ecumenical needs, the local church will rightly call upon the resources and experiences of other churches of its communion to help meet these needs and judge the possibilities. Here the work of the Secretariat for Promoting Christian Unity in stimulating an exchange of insights between the local churches may be of special value.

3.
VARIOUS FORMS OF LOCAL ECUMENISM

In addition to the sacramental expression of the unity of the Catholic Church given in the local church, the real but still imperfect communion between Christian churches and ecclesial communities finds expression in a number of forms of ecumenical action and in certain joint organizations. In this section an attempt is made by way of illustration, to describe some of these areas and forms of local ecumenical action.[11] They are not suggested as being normative, for the initiatives described remain always subjected to the pastoral authority of the diocesan bishop or the episcopal conference. The account given here is clearly not exhaustive but provides a context for later sections of this document. It has to be kept in mind that while these fields of action offer many opportunities of ecumenical collaboration, they also entail problems and difficulties which have to be solved in light of Catholic principles of ecumenism.

a. Sharing in Prayer and Worship
At the level of the local churches there are many occasions for seeking the gifts of the Holy Spirit and that "change of heart and holiness of life which, along with public and private prayer for the unity of Christians, would be regarded as the soul of the whole ecumenical movement".[12] Many forms of this "spiritual ecumenism" are emerging today in prayer groups in which members of various confessions assemble.

The Ecumenical Directory expressed the hope that "Catholics and their other brethren will join in prayer for any common concern in which they can and should cooperate—e.g., peace, social justice, mutual charity among men, the dignity of the family and so on. The same may be said of occasions when according to circumstances a nation or community wishes to make a common act of thanksgiving or petition to God, as on a national feast day, at a time of public disaster or mourning, on a day set aside for remembrance of those who have died for their country. This kind of prayer is also recommended as far as possible at times when Christians hold meetings for study or common action".[13]

The Prayer for Unity, as observed either in January or in the week preceding Pentecost, is widespread and continues to be in most places the chief occasion on which Catholics and other Christians pray together. It is promoted by special committees set up for the purpose by ministers' fraternals or associations and very often by councils of churches.

In certain places some of the great festivals of the liturgical year are marked by joint celebrations in order to express the common joy of Christians in the central events of their faith.

On the Catholic side, participation in sacramental worship is regulated by the Decree on Ecumenism (N. 8), the Directory I (42–44, 55), the 1972 Instruction and the Note issued in 1973.[14]

Both participation in common worship and an exact observance of the present canonical limits are a feature of normal Catholic ecumenical activity.

b. Common Bible Work

In 1968, "Guiding Principles for Interconfessional Cooperation"[15] was co-published by the United Bible Societies and the Secretariat for Promoting Christian Unity and there is official Catholic collaboration in 133 Bible translation projects in various places in accordance with these norms.

Many of the 56 national Bible societies that make up the United Bible Societies, working in agreement with a number of episcopal conferences and diocesan bishops, have developed programs of cooperation with Catholics in scripture distribution and promotion of Bible reading (joint national Bible Sunday, Bible Weeks, exhibitions, lectures, distribution training, seminars, etc.). In some cases Catholics have become officers of Bible Societies[16] or episcopal conferences have appointed official representatives to Bible Society Advisory Councils.[17]

Bible Societies are a meeting ground for a very wide group of Christians. Their focus is the translation and distribution of the Scripture and a great variety of Christian bodies can cooperate in this important work. Cooperation in translation, distribution and study of the Scriptures has important repercussions in missionary work, catechetics and religious education at all levels. Interconfessional cooperation in the common translation of the Scriptures has important implications for common understanding of the content of Revelation. The World Catholic Federation for the Biblical Apostolate[18] has come into existence to promote in each episcopal conference an organization that will help to coordinate Catholic cooperation with the Bible Societies and to give priests and people all the help they need for understanding and using the Scriptures.

c. Joint Pastoral Care

Where this exists, it is organized mainly in terms of some specific situation and does not compete with parish-based pastoral work. For instance, in hospitals the chaplains often adopt an ecumenical approach, both for some of their contacts with the patients and for their dealings with the hospital authorities.

In universities, industry, prisons, the armed forces, radio and television, there is increasing evidence that the work of the various churches and ecclesial communities, is coordinated and, even, in a number of places is done jointly to some degree. The rapid social and economic change characteristic of the present age, is extending the fields where such special ministries, either on a city-wide or a geographical basis, are needed (e.g., to youth, drug addicts, etc.). In a few places,[19] a deliberate effort has been made to devise new pastoral approaches on an ecumenical basis in terms of sector ministries, often on a team-basis.[20]

A special area both of responsibility and difficulty concerns mixed marriages. The Motu Proprio *"Matrimonia Mixta"* encourages a joint effort on the part of the pastors of the partners in order to assist them in the best possible way before and during the marriage.

d. Shared Premises

The rule is that Catholic churches are reserved for Catholic worship. As consecrated buildings they have an important liturgical significance. Further they have a pedagogical value for inculcating the meaning and spirit of worship. Therefore sharing them with other Christians or constructing new churches jointly with other Christians can be only by way of exception.

However, the *Ecumenical Directory* (Part I) has stated:

"If the separated brethren have no place in which to carry out their religious rites properly and with dignity, the local Ordinary may allow them the use of a Catholic building, cemetery or church" (N. 61).

"Because sharing in sacred functions, objects and places with all the separated Eastern brethren is allowed for a reasonable cause (cf. *Decree on Eastern Catholic Churches,* N. 28), it is recommended that with the approval of the local Ordinary separated Eastern priests and communities be allowed the use of Catholic churches, buildings and cemeteries and other things necessary for their religious rites, if they ask for this, and have no place in which they can celebrate sacred functions properly and with dignity" (N. 52).

Because of developments in society, because of rapid growth in population and building, and for financial motives, where there is a good ecumenical relationship and understanding between the communities, the sharing of church premises can become a matter of practical interest. It does not seem possible to adduce any one model for this kind of sharing since it is a question of responding to a need or an emergency.[21]

The building of an interconfessional place of worship must be an exception and should answer real needs which cannot otherwise be met. An airport chapel and a chapel at a military camp are examples that meet this condition. An exceptional pastoral situation could also be the reason for such a building as when a government would forbid the multiplication of places of worship or in the case of the extreme poverty of a Christian community, and there the simultaneous use of a church could be allowed.

In a shared church, judicious consideration needs to be given to the question of the reservation of the Blessed Sacrament so that it is done in a way that is consonant with sound sacramental theology, as well as respectful of the sensitivities of those who use the building. In addition to strictly religious considerations, due attention ought to be paid to the practical, financial and administrative problems, as well as to the questions of civil and canon law which are involved.

Clearly, initiatives in the matter of shared premises can be undertaken only under the authority of the bishop of the diocese and on the basis of the norms for the application of those principles fixed by the competent episcopal conference. Before making plans for a shared building the authorities of the respective communities concerned ought first to reach agreement as to how their various disciplines will be observed particularly in regard to the sacraments. Arrangements should be made so that the rules of the Catholic Church concerning "communicatio in sacris" are respected.

It is important that any project for a shared church be accompanied by suitable education of the Catholic people concerned so that its significance may be grasped and any danger of indifferentism is avoided.

c. Collaboration in Education

The Second Part of the *Ecumenical Directory,* devoted to Ecumenism in Higher Education,[22] outlines many of the possibilities. The manner in which they have been realized differs greatly in different places. In this area there can be particular problems and difficulties which call for a high degree of pastoral prudence.[23]

There are now several "clusters" of theological schools and faculties.[24] In some places there is sharing of certain buildings, and especially the use of libraries, some common lectures (within the limits indicated by the Directory) and sometimes two or more confessional faculties have combined to organize a common academic degree course.

In catechetics local needs have led at times to collaboration in the teaching of religion, especially where this has to be done in nondenominational schools. But as long as Christians are not fully at one in faith, catechesis, which is formation for profession of faith, must remain necessarily the proper and inalienable task of the various churches and ecclesial communities.

The list of ecumenical institutes and study centres where there is Catholic involvement, at least by membership on governing boards and among the student bodies, is now quite considerable. Some of these offer courses in ecumenism and study certain topics on an ecumenical basis. Others which depend on a particular confession may concentrate largely on the study of another Christian confession. The experience of an ecumenical community life over a substantial period of time is an important feature of certain ecumenical institutes.

f. Joint Use of Communications Media

A concern for the better quality of religious programmes on radio and television has led to coordination and in some areas to joint planning and use of common facilities. Occasionally, there is an inter-confessional organization with full Catholic participation, with the major part of its radio, publishing and audiovisual work common to the principal churches and ecclesial communities, but giving each the facilities for enunciating its own doctrine and practice.[25] There are a few instances where religious newspapers either Catholic or of other confessions give regular space to other Christian bodies.[26]

g. Cooperation in the Health Field

New concepts of health care are increasingly supplanting earlier attitudes regarding medical work and the place of hospitals. Donor and welfare agencies prefer to supply money for those health programs which manifest a comprehensive approach. Some governments, as they strive to develop national health services, now tend to refuse to deal with a multiplicity of religious groups. So joint secretariats for the coordination of all church-related medical and health programs have come into being, set up with the joint approval of the Catholic episcopal conferences and the national councils of churches.[27] In several places, Catholics participate in the work of the national coordinating agencies recognized by and reporting to the national councils.[28]

In this area of health and medicine there is room for continuing study and discussion between Catholics and other Christians to deepen understanding of the theological significance of Christian involvement in this work and to elucidate common understanding as well as facing up to doctrinal divergences. Particularly where ethical norms are concerned the doctrinal stand of the Catholic Church has to be made clear and the difficulties which this can raise for ecumenical collaboration faced honestly and with loyalty to Catholic teaching.

h. National and International Emergencies

The response to emergency situations has given rise to ecumenical action in raising funds and in administering and distributing them. Although this latter is done in the main by international agencies, normally an attempt is made to work through local organizations, often a council of churches or the agency of a diocese or episcopal conference. Efficiency in the program as well as the witness value of joint charitable concern often dictates that the work be done ecumenically.

i. Relief of Human Need

As the pressures of contemporary life, especially in great cities, become more intense, Christians are aware of their urgent responsibility to minister to the increasing number of people who become casualties of society. In many places therefore Catholics are joining with other churches and ecclesial communities to provide services for people with pressing personal problems whether of the material, moral or psychological order. There are examples of such common organizations of confessions to provide a more effective pastoral and social ministry to distressed individuals.[29]

j. Social Problems

As the Catholic Church engages its full energies in the serious effort for integral human development it works with all men of good will and especially with other Christian churches and ecclesial communities. Hence in particular situations it has been found appropriate to set up joint organizations to study and promote understanding of true human rights, to question those things which frustrate them and to promote initiatives which will secure them.[30] There are also organizations which enable Christians of various confessions to work with people of other faiths for common goals of social justice.[31]

k. Sodepax Groups

Sodepax, the international agency between the Catholic Church and the World Council of Churches for society, development and peace, is promoting several initiatives on a local scale under the direction of local ecumenical agencies.

Since collaboration in the field of development is a major feature of local ecumenical relations, the impetus given by Sodepax on the international levels has led to local groups being set up to promote education in the issues of justice and peace. Some of these also operate under the name of Sodepax while being autonomous and adapted to their own situation.

This has led in some places to the establishment of joint secretariats for education in development, under the aegis of the Catholic Church and a national council of churches.[32]

There are also agencies for development, sponsored by all the Christian confessions of the place, which aim at promoting action for a more just and human society. In some places, this has made clear the desirability of a national or regional council of churches, with Catholic participation, in order that the Christian communities might play a significant role in the development of the region.[33]

Also notable are the considerable numbers of occasional actions in the area of local development which have not given rise to new continuing organizations but have been carried out through existing or ad hoc groups.

l. Bilateral Dialogues

Bilateral dialogues involving the Catholic Church have developed, regionally, nationally, and locally since Vatican II. The structures of the Catholic Church and its theological patterns of encounter have made this kind of relationship fairly easy.[34]

A distinct progress can be noticed in the topics treated by many of the bilateral dialogues. As mutual trust and understanding grows, it becomes possible to discuss doctrinal points hitherto regarded as completely closed. In turn this has an influence on the ecumenical climate of the place. However, problems do arise when the gap in understanding of the ordinary church members and the discussions of the theologians is allowed to grow too great. It is the pastoral task of the church leaders at different levels (episcopal conferences and dioceses) with the aid of the existing organs of consultation (e.g., the national or diocesan ecumenical commission) to ensure that communication takes place in order to overcome the difficulty and to enable the work done by the theologians to be effective and this in a way that accords with the doctrine and discipline of the Church.

Most of the dialogues try to assess the common situation in which all confessions find themselves today, and to clarify existing difficulties in inter-confessional relations as well as outlining new possibilities on the way to unity. Some stick to selected topics, such as ministry, authority, etc., on which they aim at a deeper mutual understanding and possible convergence. Sometimes a specific problem, e.g., mixed marriages, religious education, proselytism, is taken up and a solution sought whether at the level of theological principle or pastoral practice. At times the task is to coordinate relations and to encourage practical cooperation and exchange on different levels.

m. Meetings of Heads of Communions

In certain places the heads of local churches or ecclesial communities meet regularly, sometimes having a permanent "continuation committee". Through their meetings they exchange information about their activities and concerns, share insights and explore areas of possible collaboration and even set on foot appropriate action. It is understood that the heads of communions have to agree on each occasion of collaboration about the extent to which they can commit the members of their particular body. The usefulness of such groups in certain circumstances has been proved beyond dispute.[35]

n. Joint Working Groups

The concept of a joint working group is that it is not itself a decision-making body, but an organ for joint exploration of possible fields of cooperation, study and action, its recommendations being submitted to the parent bodies on each side. Groups have been set up in several countries between the Catholic Church and either a council of churches or a number of churches and ecclesial communities which do not have membership in a council. In intention these groups have been often envisaged as a transitory expression of the relationship. However, their usefulness and the lack of a suitable substitute have led in most cases to their continuance in being. Since they involve a multilateral conversion they can be a handy instrument for coordinating the more local conversations and initiatives and giving them a coherent framework. They have often initiated multilateral theological studies, as well as practical cooperation in the field of social action. Indeed in some instances more theological work seems to have been achieved through these groups than when the Catholic Church has been a member of a council of churches. The implications of baptism, problems connected with mixed marriages, conscience and dissent, authority, development issues and the problem of disarmament are among the topics found on their agendas.

o. Councils of Churches and Christian Councils[36]

These organizations date in some form from the beginning of the 20th century as a means of ensuring cooperation. As they have developed they have come to promote the collaboration of various churches or groups in social projects and now see themselves as servants of the ecumenical movement in its search for a greater measure of unity.

Because of their importance we are going to consider them at greater length in the next chapter.

4.

COUNCILS OF CHURCHES AND CHRISTIAN COUNCILS

A. Description and Clarifications

a. What Councils Are

In various regions of the world, in different countries and even in areas of a particular country, the ecumenical relation between the Christian communities differs and so the structures in which it finds expression also vary. In a number of places this relationship has taken the form of Christian councils and councils of churches. While these councils have their significance from the churches which take part in them, still they are very important instruments of ecumenical collaboration.

The earliest councils in the ecumenical movement were missionary councils composed of mission agencies and were formed to stimulate thinking on missionary problems and to coordinate action for the spread of the Christian message. As service agencies and other church groups took part in them, they were described as Christian councils, and finally as councils of churches when their membership came to be composed of representatives named by the churches.

Among the principal activities of councils are joint service, the collaborative quest for a fuller unity and, to the extent possible, common witness.

Councils are multiple and diverse. Therefore theologically they must be evaluated according to their activity, and according to the self-understanding they advance in their constitutions. That is to say, councils must be considered concretely as they actually exist rather than approached through theories developed concerning them.

b. *Types of Councils*

We may distinguish the following principal types:

—*Local councils of churches,* which involve the different denominations in a small area, e.g., a parish or a deanery. Such councils are not necessarily affiliated to or directed by their national council. Local councils are found in large numbers in the U.S.A. and in Great Britain.

—*State or area councils* are "at various levels below the national and above the strictly local", and their relationship to the larger and smaller councils varies; in England some of the councils of churches in the major conurbations are of this kind; and in some of these a full time secretary acts virtually as "ecumenical officer" of the particular area.

—*National councils of churches* are composed primarily of representatives named by the churches in a country rather than of representatives from councils at a lower level.

—*Regional councils or conferences of churches* include churches from a number of neighbouring countries.

—*The World Council of Churches* is a distinct category. The World Council of Churches does invite selected national councils "to enter into working relationship as associated councils", and it has set up a Committee on National Council Relationships. This does not imply any authority or control over a particular council; in fact, the decision to enter such a relationship rests always with the national council.[37] It has to be borne in mind too that Catholic membership in a local, national or regional council has implications on those levels and is therefore an independent decision, separate and distinct from any decision about relationship to the World Council of Churches.

c. *The Meaning of Conciliarity*

The English word "conciliarity" can convey different meanings. For this reason Catholics need to explain what they mean by it.[38]

The conciliarity which marks the life of the Catholic Church and is sometimes expressed in ecumenical and provincial councils ("conciles"),[39] is based on a full and substantial communion of local churches among themselves and with the Church of Rome which presides over the whole assembly of charity.[40] This communion finds expression in the confession of faith, the celebration of the sacraments, the exercise of the ministry and the reception of previous councils. In this sense a council is a means enabling a local church, a certain group of local churches, or all of the local churches in communion with the bishop of Rome to express the communion of the Catholic Church.

Councils of churches and Christian councils ("conseils") however are fellowships of churches and other Christian bodies which seek to work together, to engage in dialogue and to overcome the divisions and misunderstandings existing among them. Confessing Jesus Christ as Lord and Saviour according to the Scriptures, they engage in joint action, in a quest for unity, and, to the extent that it is possible, in common witness. The fellowship which they embody does not suppose at all the same degree of communion expressed by ecumenical and provincial councils ("conciles").[41]

From this understanding it is clear that councils of churches and Christian councils ("conseils") do not in and of themselves contain in embryo the beginnings of a new Church which will replace the communion now existing within the Catholic Church. They do not claim to be churches nor do they claim authority to commission a ministry of word and sacrament.

d. *Points of Clarification*

i. A distinction has to be made between Christian councils and councils of churches, the former including as voting members bodies and agencies other than churches.

ii. Neither Christian councils nor councils of churches are uniform in history, constitution or operation.

iii. The variety of patterns to be found in councils of churches around the world has grown up naturally; councils are autonomous bodies and no one council of churches is a sub-unit of another, nor has an attempt been made to impose uniformity. At the same time it should be noted that there are close relationships between some councils even though they are structured in different ways.

In general terms these councils at all levels of the churches' life are similar in nature, but their specific functions vary according to the possibilities and needs of each level.

iv. Although the ecumenical movement calls for fellowship and collaboration at all levels, still, given the variety and autonomy of councils of churches, the decision to join a council at one level must be taken on its own merits.

Membership in local councils does not imply that membership in national councils must then be sought, just as local or national membership does not involve membership in the World Council of Churches. The question of membership must be examined separately and afresh at each level.

v. The sole formal authority of councils is that which is accorded them by the constituent members. The degree of commitment to this fellowship of churches, which a council represents, depends entirely upon the churches themselves.

vi. Councils try to make clear that as a general rule they do not have responsibility for church union negotiations, since it is well understood that these are solely the responsibility of the churches directly involved.

vii. Councils do not claim to be the only appropriate organs of churchly cooperation.

B. The Ecumenical Significance of Christian Councils and Councils of Churches

a. The Ecumenical Fact of Councils

The existence of councils of churches constitutes in numerous countries an ecumenical fact which the non-member churches cannot ignore and may well challenge the churches in countries where such councils do not exist.

In some places the trend towards collaboration is hastened when governments refuse to deal with a diversity of agencies in the fields of education, development and welfare and the churches engaged in these areas have to devise joint programs.

b. The Limits of Ad Hoc Bodies for Council-Church Relationships

In the eyes of many councils of churches collaboration with the Catholic Church solely through ad hoc commissions is regarded as insufficient since this kind of collaboration:

i. gives the impression that the ecumenical fact represented by councils is not treated with sufficient seriousness, and

ii. it tends to remain partial and to lack the necessary continuity.

c. The Existing Relation of the Catholic Church to Councils of Churches

The Catholic Church has full membership in national councils of churches in at least 19 countries and in a very large number of state and local councils. There is membership in one regional conference of churches covering a number of countries.[42] In addition, there is considerable Catholic collaboration with councils and certain of their programs at various levels.

Given that "no central guidelines would be found valid for the variety of councils and of particular circumstances",[43] a number of questions and ecclesial considerations may be proposed, to be taken into account in deciding the appropriate relationship with councils.

5.
CONSIDERATIONS CONCERNING COUNCIL MEMBERSHIP[44]

a. Cooperation with Other Churches and Ecclesial Communities

The documents of the Second Vatican Council expound clearly the conviction that the unity which is the gift of Christ already exists in the Catholic Church,[45] although susceptible of completion and perfection,[46] and this qualifies significantly the Catholic participation in the ecumenical movement. However, since the Second Vatican Council's recognition of the *ecclesial* character of other Christian communities,[47] the Church has frequently called upon Catholics to cooperate not only with other Christians *as individuals,* but also with other churches and ecclesial communities *as such.* This cooperation is commended both in matters of social and human concern, and even more in support of Christian testimony in the field of mission.

"Insofar as religious conditions allow, ecumenical activity should be furthered in such a way that without any appearance of indifference or of unwarranted intermingling on the one hand, or of unhealthy rivalry on the other, Catholics can cooperate in a brotherly spirit with their separated brethren, according to the norms of the Decree on Ecumenism. To the extent that their beliefs are common, they can make before the nations a common profession of faith in God and Jesus Christ. They can collaborate in social and in technical projects as well as in cultural and religious ones. This cooperation should be undertaken not only among private persons, but also, according to the judgement of the local Ordinary, among churches or ecclesial communities and their enterprises" (*Ad Gentes,* 15).[48]

The documents published by the Secretariat for Promoting Christian Unity have stressed that the world often poses the same questions to all the confessions and that, in the sphere of their internal life, most Christian communions have to face similar problems.[49]

The nature of the Church, the normal exigencies of the ecumenical situation, and the questions facing all Christian communions in our own day demand that the Catholic Church give positive consideration to the proper expression at every level of her ecumenical relations with other churches and ecclesial communities.

b. Implications of Council Membership

From a theological point of view, membership in a council of churches carries certain implications:

i. the recognition of other member churches as ecclesial communities even though they may not be recognized as being churches in the full theological sense of the word;[50]

ii. recognition of the council of churches as an instrument, among others, both for expressing the unity already existing among the churches and also of advancing towards a greater unity and a more effective Christian witness.

Nevertheless, as the Central Committee of the World Council of Churches said at its Toronto meeting in 1950: ". . . membership does not imply that each church must regard the other member churches as churches in the true and full sense of the word".[51] Therefore the entry of the Catholic Church into a body in which it would find itself on an equal footing with other bodies which also claim to be churches would not diminish its faith about its uniqueness. The Second Vatican Council has clearly stated that the unique Church of Christ "constituted and organized in the world as a society subsists in the Catholic Church which is governed by the successor of Peter and the bishops in communion with that successor, although many elements of sanctification and of truth can be found outside of her visible structure".[52]

c. Councils and Christian Unity

Since councils of churches are not themselves churches, they do not assume the responsibility of acting for churches which are contemplating or have begun to engage in unity conversations. In principle their action is in the practical field. However, because of their facilities and their administrative resources, they are in a position to give important material help and can, upon request of the churches concerned, give a consultative and organisational assistance. While the study of "Faith and Order" questions, which goes on under the auspices of many councils and is authorized by member churches, has a deep importance in stimulating member churches to a deeper understanding of the demands of the unity willed by Christ, and to facing old deadlocks in a new way, nevertheless it is not the task of a council to take the initiative in promoting formal doctrinal conversations between churches. These belong properly to the immediate and bilateral contacts between churches.

d. The Problem of Council Statements

Councils of churches, in some cases more frequently than the member churches themselves, on occasion make public statements on issues of common concern. These are addressed more often to areas of social justice, human development, general welfare, and public or private morality. They are based on theological positions that may or may not be articulated in the statements themselves. Unless explicitly authorized they cannot be considered as official utterances on behalf of the churches, but are offered as a service to the churches. They are often directed also to the wider public or even to specific audiences, such as government authorities. They vary in character from broad statements of position or orientation in general areas to specific stands on concrete questions. In some instances they examine and illuminate a subject, identifying a number of possible approaches rather than adopting a position. This practice of making statements has caused concern in some churches, and calls especially for clarification where the Catholic Church considers the possibility of membership in councils of churches.

i. The Decision-making Process

In attempting to fix criteria to evaluate the deliberative process in a particular council, it will be necessary to give serious consideration to the hesitations and objections of its members. A common declaration which engages the moral responsibility of its members is possible only with the consent of all.

ii. The Authority and Use of Public Statements

Important as is the process by which statements are formulated and issued, equally important is the manner in which they are received—both by the individual members of the churches and by the public at large. Differences in the weight of authority given to official statements within member churches, as well as differences in the normal mode of formulation and issuance of statements, can result in serious difficulties. Efforts have to be made to obviate the confusion that may arise in practice. Such statements should clearly identify the theological principles on which they are based so as to facilitate their acceptance by church members as being in accord with their own Christian commitment. Since councils cannot usurp the position of the churches that comprise their membership, they need to study how best they can determine what matters fall within their own purpose and mandate and to be sure of the approval of member churches before publishing statements.

iii. Regard for Minority Viewpoints

Councils, being composed of separated churches, inevitably face issues on which they cannot reach a perfect consensus. A profound respect for the integrity and individuality of its member churches will lead a council to develop procedures for ensuring that a minority dissent will be adequately expressed for the mutual benefit of the council, its members, and all to whom the council speaks. Provisions have to be made within councils for such expression of minority viewpoints and in this context polarization ought to be avoided.

e. Joint Social Action—Opportunities and Problems

i. In the Apostolic Letter *Octogesima Adveniens,* the Holy Father has written:

"It is up to these Christian communities, with the help of the Holy Spirit, in communion with the bishops who hold responsibility, and in dialogue with other Christian brethren and all men of good will to discern the options and commitments which are called for in order to bring about the social, political and economic changes seen in many cases to be urgently needed" (n. 4).

ii. At a number of points Christian positions permit and encourage collaboration with other spiritual and ideological families. Therefore councils and ecumenical organizations rightly pay serious attention to possible areas of collaboration (e.g., in the field of development, housing, health, and various forms of relief), which concern people of other living faiths as well as Christian churches and ecclesial communities.

iii. Christian social action to which many councils of churches and ecumenical bodies devote a large part of their endeavors also raises questions for theological reflection. In the first place there is the essential role of social action in the proclamation of the Gospel. "Action on behalf of justice and participation in the transformation of the world fully appear to us as a constitutive dimension of the preaching of the Gospel, or, in other words, of the Church's mission for the redemption of the human race and its liberation from every oppressive situation".[53] Further there are questions of morality, especially regarding family life which more and more need to be faced seriously in all their complexity, in particular those which concern population, family life, marriage, contraception, abortion, euthanasia and others. These questions need to be studied with due regard to the moral teachings of the churches concerned and above all taking into account the objective content of Catholic ethics.[54]

6.

PASTORAL AND PRACTICAL REFLECTIONS
FOR LOCAL ECUMENICAL ACTION

a. Full account ought to be given to local needs and problems in organizing ecumenical action; models from other places cannot simply be imitated.

b. Ultimately, it is always the responsibility of the regional or national episcopal conference to decide on the acceptability and the appropriateness of all forms of local ecumenical action. They should do this in cooperation with the appropriate organ of the Holy See, viz. the Secretariat for Promoting Christian Unity.

c. What really matters is not the creation of new structures but the collaboration of Christians in prayer, reflection and action, based on common baptism and on a faith which on many essential points is also common.

d. Sometimes the best form of collaboration may be for one church and ecclesial community to participate fully in the programs already set up by another. At other times parallel coordinated action and the joint use of the results may be more appropriate. In any event, as collaboration becomes closer, a simplification of structures should be sought and unnecessary multiplication of structures avoided.

e. Where joint actions or programs are decided on, they ought to be undertaken fully by both sides and duly authorized by the respective authorities right from the earliest stages of planning.

f. It is necessary that where there are regional, national and local doctrinal bilateral dialogues, episcopal conferences ensure that at the right time there is contact with the Holy See.

g. Among the many forms of ecumenical cooperation councils of churches and Christian councils are not the only form but they are certainly one of the more important. Since regional, national and local councils are widespread in many parts of the world and do play an important role in ecumenical relations, the responsible contacts which the Catholic Church is having with them are welcome.

h. It is normal that councils should want to discuss and reflect upon the doctrinal bases of the practical projects they undertake. But in such cases it is important to clarify the doctrinal principles involved. It should always be clear that when Catholics take part in a council, they can enter into such discussions only in conformity with the teaching of their Church.

i. The first and immediate responsibility for a decision to join a council rests with the highest ecclesiastical authority in the area served by the council. In practical terms this responsibility is not transferable. With regard to national councils the authority would generally be the episcopal conference (where there is only one diocese for the nation, it would be the Ordinary of the diocese). In reaching a decision, there must necessarily be communication with the Secretariat for Promoting Christian Unity.

j. The degree of involvement of different confessions in the same council depends directly on their respective structures especially in those things concerning the nature and exercise of authority. However, it would seem desirable that councils be constituted in such a way that the various members can all accept the full measure of involvement possible for them.

k. Membership in a council is a serious responsibility of the Catholic bishops or their delegates. It is necessary that the Catholic representatives in councils should be personally qualified and, while representing the Church on matters within their competence, they should be clearly aware of the limits beyond which they cannot commit the Church without prior reference to higher authority.

l. It is not enough that the Church simply have delegates in a council or other ecumenical structure; unless they are taken seriously by the Catholic authorities, the Catholic participation will remain purely superficial. For the same reason all participation in ecumenical structures should be accompanied by constant ecumenical education of Catholics concerning the implications of such participation.

7.

OTHER FORMS OF ECUMENISM

A growing number of Christians in certain parts of the world seem to prefer to engage in local action which is ecumenical by means of informal groups of a spontaneous kind. These people are often motivated by renewed appreciation of the word of Christ: " . . . may they be one in us, . . . so that the world may believe it was you who sent me" (*Jn.* 17, 21).

It is the kind of activity which springs up in a common environment or in a common social condition. Or it may arise in response to a common task or need. The result is a large number of highly diverse groups: action groups, prayer groups, community-building groups, reflection and dialogue groups, and evangelizing groups.

A number of groups are made up of Christians who are rediscovering central Christian truths out of their confrontation with a surrounding world which appears de-christianized and de-personalized.

Through their varied experiences they may have new insights of importance for the future growth and direction of the ecumenical movement.[55] It is desirable that there be real communication between the more organized or formal expressions and structures of the ecumenical movement and these groups when they seek to discover new ways of meeting contemporary needs and therefore engage in experimental projects. In connection with the hierarchy of the Church, these informal groups can offer original and inspiring ideas, whereas without such a contact and apart from ecclesiastical direction they run the risk of becoming unfaithful to Catholic principles of ecumenism and even of endangering the faith. If this communication is ignored, there is not only a danger that ecumenism may become detached from the pressing concerns of people in society but these groups themselves may become unbalanced and sectarian. Communication and dialogue are basic to the success of all ecumenical endeavour.

At the same time where there are groups of this kind under Catholic responsibility, it is necessary that they function in full communion with the local bishop if they are to be authentically ecumenical.

Notes

1. Cf. Pope Paul VI, *Allocutio* ad delegatos commissionum "pro oecumenismo" Conferentiarum Episcopalium et Catholicorum Orientalium Patriarchatuum Synodorum partem agentes: *AAS* 64 (1972), p. 761; cf. also *Information Service* 20 (1973), p. 23 (published by the Secretariat for Promoting Christian Unity).

2. Pope Paul VI, *Allocutio* ad Sanctitatem Suam Athenagoram, Patriarcham Oecumenicum, in Vaticana Basilica habita: *AAS* 59 (1967), p. 1051; cf. also *Information Service* 3 (1967), p. 17.

3. Cf. Ecumenical Directory I, *Ad totam Ecclesiam*, Pars Prima, § 2: *AAS* 59 (1967), p. 575; cf. also *Information Service* 2 (1967), p. 5.

4. Here we would make our own the clarification given in the Third Official Report of the Joint Working Group between the World Council of Churches and the Roman Catholic Church, Appendix II, *Common Witness and Proselytism*, in *Information Service* 14 (1971), p. 19: "Modern languages use several biblically derived terms which denote particular aspects of the announcements of the Gospel in word and deed: Witness, Apostolate, Mission, Confession, Evangelism, Kerygma, Message, etc. We have preferred here to adopt 'Witness' because it expresses more comprehensively the realities we are treating".

Worthy of note is section 10 of the *Declaration of the Bishops' Synod* (October 26th, 1974): "In carrying out these things we intend to collaborate more diligently with those of our Christian brothers with whom we are not yet in the union of a perfect communion, basing ourselves on the foundation of Baptism and on the patrimony which we hold in common. Thus we can henceforth render to the world a much broader common witness to Christ, while at the same time working to obtain full union in the Lord. Christ's command impels us to do so; the work of preaching and rendering witness to the Gospel demands it" (*L'Osservatore Romano*, English edition, Nov. 7, 1974, p. 3).

5. Cf. *Common Witness and Proselytism*, A Study Document, in *Information Service* 14 (1971), pp. 18–23.

6. Cf. *Unitatis Redintegratio*, 6.

7. Cf. Section 7 of this document: "Other forms of ecumenism", p. 29.

8. In n. 11 of *Christus Dominus* (cited p. 6), the "particular church" is defined very clearly and is identified with the diocese. The expression "local church" in this document is understood in a broader sense. In the first place it is what is called in the above mentioned text: "the particular church". It is the church also in territories where bishops have formed episcopal conferences or synods (cf. p. 7). Further it exists in all those legitimate gatherings of the faithful under the direction of their pastors in communion with their bishop which we call "the parish" (cf. *Sacrosanctum Concilium*, 42). The expression "local church" is more all-embracing and more easily grasped than "particular church".

9. Cf. J. Ratzinger "*Ecumenism at the Local Level*," in *IS* 20 (1973), p. 4.

10. Cf. Pope Paul VI: *Allocutio* referred to in *Note 1*.

11. In 1973, the Joint Working Group between the Catholic Church and the World Council of Churches commissioned a survey on the problems facing the various churches and ecclesial communities as they carry out their mission and an examination of the consequences for the ecumenical situation. Over twenty countries participated in the survey. The results have been published in the review *One in Christ* XI (1975), N. 1, pp. 30–88. In addition to an extensive reflection on the outcome of the survey, the publication includes appendices describing the situation in several countries.

12. *Unitatis Redintegratio,* 8.

13. *Ecumenical Directory,* 33.

14. *Instructio* de peculiaribus casibus admittendi alios christianos ad communionem eucharisticam in Ecclesia Catholica: *AAS* 64 (1972), pp. 518–525; cf. also *Information Service* 18 (1972), pp. 3–6. *Communicatio* quoad interpretationem Instructionis de peculiaribus casibus admittendi alios Christianos ad communionem eucharisticam in Ecclesia Catholica: *AAS* 65 (1973), pp. 616–619; cf. *Information Service* 23 (1974), pp. 25–26.

15. Cf. *Information Service* 5 (1968), pp. 22–25.

16. This is the case in Nigeria and Zaïre.

17. For example U.S.A. and the Philippines.

18. Silberburgstrasse 121 A, D-7000 Stuttgart 1, West Germany.

19. Examples are to be found in England.

20. Local Guidelines are offered for Catholic participation in these in the booklet *The Sharing of Resources,* published by the Catholic Ecumenical Commission of England and Wales.

21. The experience of shared premises is not yet wide but in a number of places, as in some new towns in England and in "covenanted" parishes in U.S.A. it has led to a situation where certain joint social and pastoral activities are undertaken in common, while the identities of the Catholic Church and the other confessions involved are maintained and their disciplines of worship respected.

22. Cf. Ecumenical Directory II, *Spiritus Domini: AAS* 62 (1970), pp. 705–724; cf. also *Information Service* 10 (1970), pp. 3–10.

23. Cf. *Common Witness and Proselytism,* 22, 25.

24. Mainly in the U.S.A.

25. *Multimedia Zambia* is an example.

26. One such is *Moto,* the Catholic paper of the diocese of Gwelo in Rhodesia. Other examples could be given.

27. Such secretariats exist in India, Tanzania, Malawi and Ghana.

28. For example, Philippines, Uganda and Kenya.

29. One such is the Interconfessional Counselling Service of Porto Alegre, Brazil.

30. There are for instance the Latin American Ecumenical Commission for Human Rights and the Ecumenical Commission for Service in Brazil; cf. also *Message of His Eminence Cardinal Roy* on the Occasion of the Launching of the Second Development Decade, 9 November 1970, Pontifical Commission on Justice and Peace, §§15 and 16.

31. In Indonesia there is the Committee on Community Organization.

32. Such secretariats exist in Australia and New Zealand.

33. There is the Christian Agency for Development in the Caribbean.

34. Cf. a more complete account in: Ehrenström and Gassman, *Confessions in Dialogue,* Geneva, 1975; cf. also the theological review and critique, commissioned by the Catholic Theological Society of America, *The Bilateral Consultations between the Roman Catholic Church in the U.S.A. and other Christian Communions,* July 1972.

35. For instance in Rhodesia, Australia, New Zealand.

36. In the following pages where councils or conferences of churches are dealt with, generally the term "church" is to be understood in a sociological sense and not in a technical theological sense.

37. Cf. the *New Delhi Report* (London 1962), Appendix II, XI, p. 438.

38. The understanding not only of Catholics but of Orthodox, Anglicans and many Protestants finds expression in the description of "conciliarity" given in a paper of the Salamanca Conference (1973) of the WCC Faith and Order Commission.

39. In some languages other than English two distinct words are used to denote the realities for which in English the single word "council" is used. In French for example there are the words "concile" and "conseil"; in Italian "concilio" and "consiglio"; in Spanish "concilio" and "consejo"; in German "Konzil" and "Rat" and in Latin "concilium" and "consilium".

40. Cf. *Lumen Gentium,* 13; *Ad Gentes,* 22; S. Ignatius M., *Ad Rom.,* Praef.

41. In the meeting of the Faith and Order Commission of the WCC held in Accra, 1974, the following comment was made: "The local, national and world councils of churches which perform such a vital role in the modern ecumenical movement do not, obviously, conform to the definition of conciliar fellowship given at Salamanca. They are federal in character and do not enjoy either the full communion or the capacity to make decisions for all their members. They might properly be described as *'pre-conciliar'* bodies".

42. The Caribbean Conference of Churches. At the present time the Catholic Church has full membership in the following 19 national councils of churches: Denmark, Sweden, The Netherlands, Switzerland, Belize (British Honduras), Samoa, Fiji, New Hebrides, Solomon Islands, Papua-New Guinea, Tonga, West Germany, Botswana, St. Vincent (British Antilles), Sudan, Uganda, Finland, Guyana, Trinidad and Tobago.

43. *Minutes: Joint Working Group between the Roman Catholic Church and the World Council of Churches* (meeting held in June, 1971, Bernhäuser Forst, Stuttgart, Germany), December 1971, p. 10 (unpublished).

44. In certain cases where Catholic membership in a national council of churches is under consideration, studies have been undertaken and later published. They are of interest as applying general principles to given situations. Examples are: *The Implications of Roman Catholic Membership of the British Council of Churches* (1972), The British Council of Churches, 10 Eaton Gate, London; *Report on Possible Roman Catholic Membership in the National Council of Churches* (1972), US Catholic Conference, 1312, Massachusetts Avenue, N. W., Washington DC 20005, USA; *Groupe mixte de travail—Comité pour de nouvelles structures oecuméniques,* Office national d'oecuménisme, 1452, rue Drummond, Montréal 107, Canada.

45. Cf. *Unitatis Redintegratio,* 1; *Lumen Gentium,* 8, 13.

46. Cf. *Unitatis Redintegratio,* 6.

47. Cf. *Lumen Gentium,* 15; *Unitatis Redintegratio,* 3 sqq.; etc.

48. Cf. also *Unitatis Redintegratio,* 4, 12; *Apostolicam Actuositatem,* 27.

49. Cf. *Ecumenical Directory,* Part II, §1; *Reflections and Suggestions Concerning Ecumenical Dialogue,* II, 2c and d (a working instrument at the disposal of ecclesiastical authorities for concrete application of the Decree on Ecumenism, published in *Information Service* 12 (1970), pp. 5–11).

50. Cf. *Lumen Gentium,* 15; *Unitatis Redintegratio,* 3; also *Minutes and Report of the Third Meeting of the Central Committee* (Toronto, Canada, July 9–15, 1950). The *Toronto Statement,* while it refers directly to the World Council of Churches, appears to be fully applicable to similar organizations such as a national council of churches.

51. *Ibid.* (Toronto Statement).

52. *Lumen Gentium,* 8.

53. Synod of Bishops, *Justice in the World,* Typis Polyglottis Vaticanis (1971), p. 6; *Documenta Synodi Episcoporum,* De Iustitia in Mundo: *AAS* 63 (1971), p. 924.

54. "And if in moral matters there are many Christians who do not always understand the gospel in the same way as Catholics, and do not admit the same solutions for the more difficult problems of modern society, nevertheless they share our desire to cling to Christ's word as the source of Christian virtue and to obey the apostolic command: 'Whatever you do in word or in work, do all in the name of the Lord Jesus, giving thanks to God the Father through him' (*Col.* 3:17). Hence, the ecumenical dialogue could start with discussions concerning the application of the gospel to moral questions" (*Unitatis Redintegratio,* 23, §3).

55. Cf. *Ecumenical Directory,* Part I, §3.

Chapter Six
SACRAMENTAL SHARING

Introduction

The two principles for sharing in liturgical worship *(communicatio in sacris)* had been stated in the *Decree on Ecumenism* (n.8): "the unity of the Church which ought to be expressed" and "sharing in the means of grace". The *Ecumenical Directory* (Part One, May 1967) detailed the norms for the Decree's application (n.55). Within the next six years the Holy See became aware of differing interpretations and practices. This experience elicited the five following documents.

I
NOTES ON THE APPLICATION
OF THE DIRECTORY*

The Secretariat for Promoting Christian Unity announces:

1. In these last few months, in various parts of the world, Protestant and Anglican Christians have been admitted, here and there, to participate in the Eucharistic Communion during the celebration of Mass although they did not have the permit required by the norms in force and therefore despite the reproval of the competent ecclesiastical authority.

2. It therefore seems necessary to recall herewith the measures adopted by the Second Vatican Council and applied by the Ecumenical Directory (approved by the Holy Father on April 27, 1967: *AAS* 59 (1967), pp. 574–592).

3. "Worship in common is not to be considered as a means to be used indiscriminately for the restoration of unity among Christians. There are

---

* November 18, 1968. Promulgated in Italian, *L'Osservatore Romano;* over the signature of Augustin Cardinal Bea, SPCU President.

two main principles upon which the practice of such common worship depends: first, that of the unity of the Church which ought to be expressed; and second, that of the sharing in means of grace. The expression of unity very generally forbids common worship. Grace to be obtained sometimes commends it. The concrete course to be adopted, when due regard has been given to all the circumstances of time, place and persons, is left to the prudent decision of the local episcopal authority, unless the bishops' conference according to its own statute, or the Holy See, has determined otherwise." (*Decree on Ecumenism,* n. 8)

4. "The celebration of the sacraments is an action of the celebrating community made within the community itself of which the celebration signifies oneness in faith, worship and life. Accordingly, when this unity of faith is lacking regarding the sacraments, participation of the separated brothers with the Catholics, particularly in the sacraments of the Eucharist, Penance and Anointing of the Sick, is forbidden. Nevertheless, since the sacraments are signs of unity as well as fonts of grace (cf. *Decree on Ecumenism,* n. 8), the Church can, for sufficient motives, permit some separated brothers to be admitted to them. This permit can be granted when there is danger of death, or because of urgent necessity (during a persecution, or imprisonment), if the separated brother cannot go to a minister of his own Church and if he asks spontaneously for the sacraments from a Catholic priest, so long as he manifests a faith conforming to the faith of the Church regarding these sacraments, in addition to being well disposed. In other cases of like urgent necessity, the local Ordinary or the episcopal conference will decide.

"The Catholic faithful, in similar circumstances, cannot ask for these sacraments except from a minister who has been validly ordained." (Ecumenical Directory *Ad totam Ecclesiam,* n. 55)

5. These most precise texts determine the conditions required for the admission of an Anglican or a Protestant to receive the Eucharistic Communion in the Catholic Church. The fact that a Christian belonging to one of the confessions mentioned above is spiritually well disposed and spontaneously asks for Communion from a Catholic priest is not sufficient. Two other conditions are necessary: that his faith in the sacraments is in harmony with that of the Church and that he has no access to a minister of his own communion.

The Directory cites, as an example, three cases when, owing to circumstances beyond one's control when these conditions exist: when there is danger of death, or during persecution or imprisonment. In other cases, the local Ordinary or the episcopal conference can give permission, if it is requested, but on condition that it is a matter of cases of urgent necessity similar to those quoted as an example, and under the same conditions.

When one of these conditions is lacking, access to Eucharistic Communion in the Catholic Church is not possible.

II

THE POSITION OF THE CATHOLIC CHURCH
CONCERNING A COMMON EUCHARIST
BETWEEN CHRISTIANS OF DIFFERENT CONFESSIONS*

1. Recently, in various parts of the world, certain initiatives have been taken with regard to common participation in the Eucharist. They have involved on the one hand faithful and clergy of the Catholic Church and, on the other, laity and pastors of other Christian Churches and ecclesial communities. At times there is question of the admission of Catholic faithful to a Protestant or Anglican Eucharistic communion; at other times, participation by Protestants and Anglicans in the Eucharistic communion in a Catholic church; or again, there are common acts of Eucharistic worship jointly celebrated by ministers belonging to Churches and ecclesial communities still separated from one another, and in these the laity of the communities concerned take part.

This subject is of great theological, pastoral and, above all, ecumenical importance and we desire to recall the Church's recently formulated norms concerning it.

2. The Second Vatican Council addressed itself to this subject in the Decree on Ecumenism, *Unitatis Redintegratio.* After having called to mind that common prayers for unity are an efficacious means for asking for the grace of unity and constitute an authentic expression of the bonds by which Catholics remain united with other Christians, the Decree continues:

"Worship in common is not to be considered as a means to be used indiscriminately for the restoration of unity among Christians. There are two main principles upon which the practice of such common worship depends: first, that of the unity of the Church which ought to be expressed; and second, that of the sharing in means of grace. The expression of unity very generally forbids common worship. Grace to be obtained sometimes commends it. The concrete course to be adopted, when due regard has been given to all the circumstances of time, place and persons, is left to the prudent decision of the local episcopal authority, unless the bishops'

---

* January 7, 1970, A *Declaration* from the SPCU. Over the signatures of John Cardinal Willebrands, SPCU President, and of Fr. Jerome Hamer, O.P., Secretary. French Text: *AAS* 62(1970), pp. 184–188. English: SPCU *IS,* 9 (1970), pp. 21–23.

conference according to its own statute, or the Holy See, has determined otherwise." (*Decree on Ecumenism*, n. 8)

3. In applying these general principles, the Council asks us to consider well the "particular situations of the Churches of the East" (*Decree on Ecumenism*, 14) and to draw the appropriate consequences from these facts:

> "Although these Churches are separated from us, they possess true sacraments, above all—by apostolic succession—the priesthood and the Eucharist, whereby they are still joined to us in a very close relationship. Therefore, given suitable circumstances and the approval of Church authority, some worship in common is not merely possible but is recommended". (*Decree on Ecumenism*, 15)

The Decree on the Catholic Eastern Churches, *Orientalium Ecclesiarum*, makes some applications. It permits Eastern Christians not in full communion with the Apostolic See of Rome to be admitted to the sacraments of Penance, of the Eucharist and of the Anointing of the Sick when they find themselves in the specified circumstances. It equally authorizes Catholics to request these same sacraments from Eastern priests whenever necessity or a genuine spiritual benefit calls for it and access to a Catholic priest is physically or morally impossible. It also recommends that the authorities of the Churches involved contact each other about the matter (cf. *Decree on the Catholic Eastern Churches*, 27, 29).

4. The section of the Decree on Ecumenism devoted to "the separated Churches and ecclesial communities in the West" includes Christian confessions of great variety. In it the Council treated the theological problem which underlies Eucharistic sacramental relations with Christian communities where those conditions found in the Churches of the East are lacking:

> "Although the ecclesial Communities separated from us lack the fullness of unity with us which flows from baptism, and although we believe they have not preserved the proper reality of the eucharistic mystery in its fullness, especially because of a deficiency of the sacrament of Orders, nevertheless when they commemorate the Lord's death and resurrection in the Holy Supper, they profess that it signifies life in communion with Christ and await His coming in glory. For these reasons, the doctrine about the Lord's Supper, about the other sacraments, worship and ministry in the Church, should form subjects of dialogue." (*Decree on Ecumenism*, 22)

It should be noted that the doctrinal appreciation of the Eucharist of these communities is bound up with an appeal for dialogue about the Eucharist and the entire sacramental life, and a special mention is made of the ministries of the Church.

It is well known that the Catholic Church attaches a decisive importance to the traditional teaching about the necessity of the ministerial priesthood connected with the apostolic succession, and the conditions in which it exists.

5. The dispositions of the Second Vatican Council were applied through the Ecumenical Directory which was approved by the Holy Father on April 22, 1967 and published in the *Acta Apostolicae Sedis* on July 5 of the same year.

For Eucharistic relations with Eastern Christians not in full communion with the Apostolic See of Rome, the Directory reproduces the dispositions of the Council and determines in a precise way certain useful points especially in what concerns reciprocity and previous agreement between the ecclesiastical authorities of the Churches concerned (*Ecumenical Directory,* 39–47).

6. The Directory went more into detail when treating of those Christian communities with which we do not share the same ecclesiological and sacramental bases that particularly unite us to the Churches of the East. After giving doctrinal justifications of its norms, it formulates these in the following way:

"Celebration of the sacraments is an action of the celebrating community, carried out within the community, signifying the oneness in faith, worship and life of the community. Where this unity of sacramental faith is deficient, the participation of the separated with Catholics, especially in the sacraments of the Eucharist, Penance and Anointing of the Sick, is forbidden. Nevertheless, since the sacraments are both signs of unity and sources of grace (cf. *Decree on Ecumenism,* 8), the Church can for adequate reasons allow access to those sacraments to a separated brother. This may be permitted in danger of death or in urgent need (during persecution, in prisons) if the separated brother has no access to a minister of his own communion, and spontaneously asks a Catholic priest for the sacraments—so long as he declares a faith in these sacraments in harmony with that of the Church, and is rightly disposed. In other cases the judge of this urgent necessity must be the diocesan bishop or the episcopal conference. A Catholic in similar circumstances may not ask for these sacraments except from a minister who has been validly ordained". (*Directory,* 55)

7. In commenting on this passage, one month before his death, Eminence Cardinal Bea, president of the Secretariat for Promoting Christian Unity, endeavored to throw light on its exact meaning:

> "These texts determine precisely the conditions required for admitting an Anglican or a Protestant to Eucharistic communion in the Catholic Church. It is not enough then, that one of these Christians be spiritually well disposed and that he spontaneously requests Communion from a Catholic minister. In the first place two other conditions must be verified: that they hold the faith which the Catholic Church herself professes concerning the Eucharist, and that they are unable to approach a minister of their own confession.
>
> The Directory cites as examples three very special cases, where these conditions can be verified: danger of death, persecution, imprisonment. In other cases, the Ordinary of the place or the episcopal conference will be able to give the permission, if it is asked. The condition must be, however, that urgent necessity similar to that in the cases cited as examples and the same conditions must be verified.
>
> When one of these conditions is lacking, admission to Eucharistic communion in the Catholic Church is not possible". (*Note concerning the application of the Ecumenical Directory, Oss. Romano,* October 6, 1968)

8. With regard to the role which the Directory plays in the pastoral action of the Church, it is useful to recall the words addressed by the Holy Father on November 13, 1968, to the members of the Secretariat for Promoting Christian Unity:

> "We need not tell you that, to promote ecumenism in an efficacious way, one must also guide it, submit it to rules that are quite precise. We regard the Ecumenical Directory not as a collection of advisory principles which one can freely accept or ignore, but as an authentic instruction, an exposition of the discipline to which all those who wish to truly serve ecumenism should submit themselves". (*Osservatore Romano,* November 14, 1968)

9. The Secretariat for Promoting Christian Unity is following this question very closely and itself has taken various initiatives concerning it. Recently, during its plenary assembly (*Congregatio plenaria* of which 40 bishops from all over the world are members), held in Rome from November 18 to 28, 1969, it devoted a great deal of attention to it. At the same time the Secretariat particularly appreciates the work being done all over

the world to deepen the theology of the Church, of ministry and of the Eucharist, both as sacrament and sacrifice, done within the historical context of the division among Christians. It is following with interest and profit the efforts being made to clarify the problem in all its dimensions and to work out a more precise vocabulary. Above all it is pleased with the interconfessional dialogue on this subject which is now taking place on both local and international levels. The Secretariat hopes that these conversations will help to bring about a convergence of positions on the subject. Still, it must be pointed out that, up to the present, these dialogues have not yet produced results which can be adopted on both sides by those who have responsibility in the Churches and ecclesial communities involved.

The Catholic Church, then, is not at present in a position to modify the norms of the *Ecumenical Directory* as given above. The line of conduct traced out there results from the Church reflecting on her own faith and considering the pastoral needs of the faithful. Before considering another way of acting in the matter of a common Eucharist, it will be necessary to establish clearly that any change to be made will remain totally in conformity with the Church's profession of faith and that it will be a service to the spiritual life of her members.

10. At this time when the Week of Prayer for Unity is about to begin, we are taking into account the extent to which the desire for a common Eucharist powerfully stimulates the search for that perfect ecclesial unity among all Christians willed by Christ. This desire can be expressed very appropriately in the celebrations which will take place during this Week of Prayer. As well as the reading of and meditation upon Holy Scripture, these celebrations could in fact include elements which point towards the common Eucharist so much desired: our gratitude for the partial unity already obtained, our regret for the divisions which still remain and our firm resolve to do everything possible to overcome them, and finally our humble petition to the Lord to hasten the day when we will be able to celebrate together the mystery of the Body and the Blood of Christ.

III

CASES WHEN OTHER CHRISTIANS
MAY BE ADMITTED
TO EUCHARISTIC COMMUNION
IN THE CATHOLIC CHURCH*

1. The Question.

We are often asked the question: in what circumstances and on what conditions can members of other Churches and ecclesial communities be admitted to eucharistic communion in the Catholic Church?

The question is not a new one. The Second Vatican Council (in the *Decree on Ecumenism*) and the *Ecumenical Directory* dealt with it.

The pastoral guidance offered here is not intended to change the existing rules but to explain them, bringing out the doctrinal principles on which the rules rest and so making their application easier.

2. The Eucharist and the Mystery of the Church.

There is a close link between the mystery of the Church and the mystery of the Eucharist.

a. The Eucharist really contains what is the very foundation of the being and unity of the Church: the Body of Christ, offered in sacrifice and given to the faithful as the bread of eternal life. The sacrament of the Body and Blood of Christ, given to the Church so as to constitute the Church, of its nature carries with it:

—the ministerial power which Christ gave to his apostles and to their successors, the bishops along with the priests, to make effective sacramentally His own priestly act—that act by which once and forever He offered Himself to the Father in the Holy Spirit, and gave Himself to His faithful that they might be one in Him;

—the unity of the ministry, which is to be exercised in the name of Christ, Head of the Church, and hence in the hierarchical communion of ministers;—the faith of the Church, which is expressed in the eucharistic action itself—the faith by which she responds to Christ's gift in its true meaning.

The sacrament of the Eucharist, understood in its entirety with these three elements, signifies an existing unity brought about by Him, the unity of the visible Church of Christ which cannot be lost.

b. "The celebration of Mass, the action of Christ and of the people of God hierarchically ordered, is the center of the whole Christian life, for the universal Church as for the local Church and for each Christian."

---

* June 1, 1972. An *Instruction* from the SPCU. Over the signatures of John Cardinal Willebrands and Fr. Jerome Hamer, O.P. Latin Text: *AAS* 64 (1972), pp. 518–525. English: SPCU *IS*, 18 (1972), pp. 3–6.

Celebrating the mystery of Christ in the Mass, the Church celebrates her own mystery and manifests concretely her unity.

The faithful assembled at the altar offer the sacrifice through the hands of the priest acting in the name of Christ, and they represent the community of the people of God united in the profession of one faith. Thus they constitute a sign and a kind of delegation of a wider assembly.

The celebration of Mass is of itself a profession of faith in which the whole Church recognizes and expresses itself. If we consider the marvelous meaning of the eucharistic prayers as well as the riches contained in the other parts of the Mass, whether they are fixed or vary with the liturgical cycle; if at the same time we bear in mind that the liturgy of the word and the eucharistic liturgy make up a single act of worship, then we can see here a striking illustration of the principle *lex orandi lex credendi.* Thus the Mass has a catechetical power which the recent liturgical renewal has emphasized. Again, the Church has in the course of history been careful to introduce into liturgical celebration the main themes of the common faith, the chief fruits of the experience of that faith. This she has done either by means of new texts or by creating new feasts.

c. The relation between local celebration of the Eucharist and universal ecclesial communion is stressed also by the special mention in the eucharistic prayers of the pope, the local bishop and the other members of the episcopal college.

What has been said here of the Eucharist as center and summit of the Christian life holds for the whole Church and for each of its members, but particularly for those who take an active part in the celebration of Mass and above all for those who receive the Body of Christ. Communion during Mass is indeed the most perfect way of participating in the Eucharist, for it fulfills the Lord's command, "take and eat."

3. The Eucharist as Spiritual Food.

The effect of the Eucharist is also to nourish spiritually those who receive it as what the faith of the Church says it truly is—the body and blood of the Lord given as the food of eternal life (cf. John VI, 54–58). For the baptized, the Eucharist is spiritual food, a means by which they are brought to live the life of Christ himself, are incorporated more profoundly in Him and share more intensely in the whole economy of his saving mystery. "He who eats my flesh and drinks my blood abides in me and I in him" (John VI, 56).

a. As in the sacrament of full union with Christ and of the perfection of spiritual life, the Eucharist is necessary to every Christian: in our Lord's words, ". . . unless you eat the flesh of the Son of Man and drink his blood, you have no life in you" (John VI, 53). Those who live intensely the life of grace feel a compelling need for this spiritual sustenance, and the Church herself encourages daily communion.

b. Yet though it is a spiritual food whose effect is to unite the Christian man to Jesus Christ, the Eucharist is far from being simply a means of satisfying exclusively personal aspirations, however lofty these may be. The union of the faithful with Christ, the head of the mystical body, brings about the union of the faithful themselves with each other. It is on their sharing of the Eucharistic bread that St. Paul bases the union of all the faithful, "Because there is one loaf" (1 Cor. X, 17). By this sacrament "man is incorporated in Christ and united with His members." By frequent receiving of the Eucharist the faithful are incorporated more and more in the body of Christ and share increasingly in the mystery of the Church.

c. Spiritual need of the Eucharist is not therefore merely a matter of personal spiritual growth: simultaneously, and inseparably, it concerns our entering more deeply into Christ's Church, "which is his body, the fullness of him who fills all in all" (Eph. I, 23).

4. General Principles Governing Admission to Communion.

Where members of the Catholic Church are concerned, there is a perfect parallel between regarding the Eucharist as the celebration of the entire ecclesial community united in one faith and regarding it as sustenance, as a response to the spiritual needs, personal and ecclesial, of each member. It will be the same when, in the Lord's good time, all the followers of Christ are reunited in one and the same Church. But what are we to say today, when Christians are divided? Any baptized person has a spiritual need for the Eucharist. Those who are not in full communion with the Catholic Church have recourse to the ministers of their own communities, as their conscience dictates. But what about those who cannot do this, and who for that or other reasons come and ask for communion from a Catholic priest?

The *Ecumenical Directory* has already shown how we must safeguard simultaneously the integrity of ecclesial communion and the good of souls. Behind the Directorium lie two main governing ideas:

a. The strict relationship between the mystery of the Church and the mystery of the Eucharist can never be altered, whatever pastoral measures we may be led to take in given cases. Of its very nature celebration of the Eucharist signifies the fullness of profession of faith and the fullness of ecclesial communion. This principle must not be obscured and must remain our guide in this field.

b. The principle will not be obscured if admission to Catholic eucharistic communion is confined to particular cases of those Christians who have a faith in the sacrament in conformity with that of the Church, who experience a serious spiritual need for the eucharistic sustenance, who for a prolonged period are unable to have recourse to a minister of their own community and who ask for the sacrament of their own accord; all this provided that they have proper dispositions and lead lives worthy of a Christian. This spiritual need should be understood in the sense defined above (No. 3, b and c): a need for an increase in spiritual life and a need for a deeper involvement in the mystery of the Church and of its unity.

Further, even if those conditions are fulfilled, it will be a pastoral responsibility to see that the admission of these other Christians to communion does not endanger or disturb the faith of Catholics.

5. Differences, in View of These Principles, Between Members of the Oriental Churches and Other Christians.

The *Ecumenical Directory* gives different directions for the admission to holy communion of separated Eastern Christians, and of others. The reason is that the Eastern Churches, though separated from us, have true sacraments, above all, because of the apostolic succession, the priesthood and the eucharist, which unite them to us by close ties, so that the risk of obscuring the relation between eucharistic communion and ecclesial communion is somewhat reduced. Recently the Holy Father recalled that "between our Church and the venerable Orthodox Churches there exists already an almost total communion, though it is not yet perfect: it results from our joint participation in the mystery of Christ and of His Church."

With Christians who belong to communities whose eucharistic faith differs from that of the Church and which do not have the sacrament of Orders, admitting them to the Eucharist entails the risk of obscuring the essential relation between eucharistic communion and ecclesial communion. This is why the Directory treats their case differently from that of the Eastern Christians and envisages admission only in exceptional cases of "urgent necessity." In cases of this kind the person concerned is asked to manifest a faith in the Eucharist in conformity with that of the Church, i.e. in the Eucharist as Christ instituted it and as the Catholic Church hands it on. This is not asked of an Orthodox person because he belongs to a Church whose faith in the Eucharist is conformable to our own.

6. What Authority Decides Particular Cases?— The Meaning of No. 55 of the Directorium Oecumenicum.

No. 55 of the Directory allows fairly wide discretionary power to the episcopal authority in judging whether the necessary conditions are present for these exceptional cases. If cases of the same pattern recur often in a given region, episcopal conferences can give general directions. More often however it falls to the bishop of the diocese to make a decision. He alone will know all the circumstances of particular cases.

Apart from danger of death the Directory mentions two examples, people in prison and those suffering persecution, but it then speaks of "other cases of such urgent necessity." Such cases are not confined to situations of suffering and danger. Christians may find themselves in grave spiritual necessity and with no chance of recourse to their own community. For example, in our time, which is one of large-scale movements of population, it can happen much more often than before that non-Catholic Christians are scattered in Catholic regions. They are often deprived of the help of their own communion and unable to get in touch with it except at great trouble and expense. If the conditions set out in the Directory are verified, they can be admitted to eucharistic communion but it will be for the bishop to consider each cause.

Pope Paul VI, through a letter, dated May 25, 1972, from the Cardinal Secretary of State to the Cardinal President, approved this pastoral Instruction and ordered it to become public law *(jus publicum)*.

IV
CONCERNING CERTAIN INTERPRETATIONS
OF THE "INSTRUCTION, JUNE 1, 1972"*

1. After the publication of the "Instruction Concerning Particular Cases When Other Christians May Be Admitted to Eucharistic Communion in the Catholic Church", on June 1, 1972, various interpretations of it were given, some of which depart from the letter and the spirit of the document. To prevent the spread of such inaccurate interpretations and their consequences, we think it useful to recall to mind a few points.

2. With this Instruction, pastoral in character, the Secretariat for Promoting Christian Unity had no intention of changing the rules laid down by the Vatican Council's *Decree on Ecumenism* and further explained by the *Directorium Oecumenicum*. The intention was to explain that the existing discipline derives from the requirements of the faith and so retains its full vigor.

3. The basic principles of the Instruction are:

a. There is an indissoluble link between the mystery of the Church and the mystery of the Eucharist or between ecclesial and eucharistic communion; the celebration of the Eucharist of itself signifies the fullness of profession of faith and ecclesial communion (cf. *Instruction,* no. 2, a, b, c.).

b. The Eucharist is for the baptized a spiritual food which enables them to live with Christ's own life, to be incorporated more profoundly in him and share more intensely in the whole economy of the Mystery of Christ (cf. *Instruction,* no. 3).

4. Within the full communion of faith, eucharistic communion is the

---

* October 17, 1973. A *Note* from the SPCU. Over the signatures of John Cardinal Willebrands and Monsignor Charles Moeller, the SPCU President and Secretary. Italian Text: *AAS* 65(1973), pp. 616–619. English: SPCU *IS,* 23 (1974), pp. 25–26.

expression of this full communion and therefore of the unity of the faithful; at the same time it is the means of maintaining and reinforcing this unity. But eucharistic communion practiced by those who are not in full ecclesial communion with each other cannot be the expression of that full unity which the Eucharist of its nature signifies and which in this case does not exist; for this reason such communion cannot be regarded as a means to be used to lead to full ecclesial communion.

5. All the same, both the *Directorium Oecumenicum* and the "Instruction", on the strength of what has already been said in the Vatican Council's Decree on Ecumenism, allow the possibility of exceptions insofar as the Eucharist is necessary spiritual nourishment for the Christian life.

6. It is the local Ordinary's responsibility to examine these exceptional cases and make concrete decisions. The Instruction (no. 6) recalls that the *Directorium Oecumenicum* gives the episcopal authority power to decide whether in these rare cases the required conditions are present or not. The episcopal authority's faculty of examining and deciding is governed by criteria laid down in the *Directorium Oecumenicum* (no. 55) and further explained in the *Instruction* (no. 4 b): " . . . admission to Catholic eucharistic communion is confined to particular cases of those Christians who have a faith in the sacrament in conformity with that of the Church, who experience a serious spiritual need for the eucharistic sustenance, who for a prolonged period are unable to have recourse to a minister of their own community and who ask for the sacrament of their own accord; all this provided that they have proper dispositions and lead lives worthy of a Christian".

This criterion is observed if all the required conditions are verified. An objective, pastorally responsible examination does not allow any of the conditions to be ignored.

It must also be noted that the Instruction speaks of particular cases, which are to be examined individually. Hence a general regulation cannot be issued which makes a category out of an exceptional case, nor is it possible to legitimate on the basis of epikeia by turning this latter into a general rule.

Nevertheless, the bishops can in the various situations decide what are the needs that make exceptions applicable, that is to say what constitutes a special case, and they can determine the manner of verifying whether all the required conditions are fulfilled in such a particular case. When particular cases present themselves fairly often in one region, following a recurrent pattern, episcopal conferences can issue some guiding principles for ascertaining that all the conditions are verified in particular cases. Normally however it will be within the competence of the local Ordinary to judge such cases.

7. For other Christians to be admitted to the Eucharist in the Catholic Church the Instruction requires that they manifest a faith in the

sacrament in conformity with that of the Catholic Church. This faith is not limited to a mere affirmation of the "real presence" in the Eucharist, but implies the doctrine of the Eucharist as taught in the Catholic Church.

8. It is to be noted that the *Instruction* (no. 5) calls to mind the fact that the *Directorium Oecumenicum* (no. 34–54) provides for the Orientals not in full communion with the Catholic Church rules different from those regarding other Christians (no. 55–63). For example,

a. since they belong to a community whose eucharistic faith is in conformity with that of the Catholic Church, a personal declaration of faith in the sacrament will not be required of them when they are admitted: in an Orthodox this faith is taken for granted;

b. since the Orthodox Churches have true sacraments and, above all, by virtue of apostolic succession, the priesthood and the Eucharist, concessions for sacramental communion must take account of legitimate reciprocity (no. 43);

c. justifiable reasons for advising sacramental sharing are considerably more extensive.

9. The question of reciprocity arises only with those Churches which have preserved the substance of the Eucharist, the sacrament of Orders and apostolic succession. Hence a Catholic cannot ask for the Eucharist except from a minister who has been validly ordained (*Directorium Oecumenicum,* no. 55).

10. The desire to share the Eucharist fundamentally expresses the desire of the perfect ecclesial unity of all Christians which Christ willed. Interconfessional dialogue on the theology of the Eucharist (as sacrament and sacrifice), on the theology of ministry and of the Church is pursuing its course within the ambit of the ecumenical movement, supported by the promises and prayer of Our Lord; it is stimulated and enlivened by the charity poured into our hearts by the Holy Spirit who has been given to us. We express the hope that the ecumenical movement will lead to a common profession of faith among Christians, and so allow us to celebrate the Eucharist in ecclesial unity, giving fulfillment to the words "Because there is one bread, we who are many are one body" *(1 Co 10, 17).*

This Note has been approved by the Holy Father, who has authorized its publication.

V
CELEBRATION OF THE EUCHARIST
FOR DECEASED NON-CATHOLIC CHRISTIANS*

In some regions Catholic ministers are asked to celebrate Mass in supplication *for the dead* who have been baptized in other churches or ecclesial communities. This occurs especially when the deceased persons have held the Catholic religion in special respect and honor or when they have occupied public office at the service of the whole community.

With regard to private Masses, as is already known, there is no difficulty in celebrating the eucharist for such persons. On the contrary, this may be commended, if there is no prohibition, on several grounds, for example, piety, friendship, gratitude, etc.

With regard to public celebrations the present discipline decrees that Mass is not to be celebrated for those who die outside full communion with the Catholic Church (see canon 1241, compared with canon 1240, §1).

In view of contemporary changes in the religious and social conditions which prompted this discipline, the Congregation has received the question from various regions whether in certain cases even a public Mass may be celebrated for such deceased persons.

The Fathers of the Congregation for the Doctrine of the Faith, at the ordinary congregation of June 9, 1976, weighed all the considerations properly and enacted this decree:

I. The present discipline with regard to the public celebration of Mass in supplication for other Christians is to be retained for the future as the general norm; this is done even out of the necessary consideration for the conscience of such deceased persons who have not fully professed the Catholic faith.

II. Until the promulgation of the new Code, this general norm may be derogated from whenever the following conditions are verified simultaneously:

1. The public celebration of Masses is expressly requested by the family, friends, or subjects of the deceased out of a genuine religious motive.

2. In the judgment of the Ordinary no scandal to the faithful is present.

These two conditions can be verified more easily if it is a question of brethren of the Eastern Churches with which a closer, although not full, communion exists in matters of faith.

III. In these cases a public Mass may be celebrated but on condition

---

* A Decree of The Congregation for the Doctrine of the Faith, over the signatures of Francis Cardinal Seper, Prefect, and Jerome Hamer, O.P., Secretary. June 11, 1976. Text: *AAS* 68(1976), pp. 621–622. English: *Jurist* 37(1977), pp. 168–169.

that the name of the deceased person not be commemorated in the eucharistic prayer, since such a mention presupposes full communion with the Catholic Church.

If other Christians are present together with the Catholic faithful who participate in such Masses, the norms enacted with regard to *communicatio in sacris* are to be very faithfully observed: II Vatican Council, Decree on the Catholic Eastern Churches, *Orientalium Ecclesiarum,* n. 26–29 (*AAS* 57 [1965]:84–85); Decree on Ecumenism, *Unitatis redintegratio,* n. 8 (*AAS* 57 [1965]:98); *Directorium de re oecumenica,* n. 40–42, 55–56 (*AAS* 59 [1967]589, 590–591); Instruction on special cases for the admission of other Christians to eucharistic communion in the Catholic Church, n. 5–6 (*AAS* 64[1972]523–525).

The Supreme Pontiff, Pope Paul VI, at an audience on July 11 with the Cardinal Prefect of the Congregation, ratified the above decisions of the Fathers, derogating to the extent necessary from canons 809 (together with canon 2262, §2, 2°) and 1241, anything to the contrary notwithstanding, approved it, and ordered it to be promulgated.

Chapter Seven
MARRIAGES BETWEEN CATHOLICS AND OTHER CHRISTIANS

Introduction

During the Vatican Council, many bishops called for a revision of the legislation which governed marriages between Catholics and other Christians. Shortly after the Council's last session, the Congregation for the Doctrine of the Faith issued an Instruction on the subject (March 1966); and the Congregation for the Eastern Churches, in February 1967, did the same for marriages between Eastern Catholics and other Eastern Christians. Nevertheless, at the first Synod of Bishops (Sept.–Oct. 1967), mixed marriages was one of the five agenda topics. By a large majority vote, the Synod membership favored the granting of dispensations from canonical form in mixed marriages at the local level and a milder form of the traditional guarantees regarding the religious upbringing of the children. On March 7, 1970 Paul VI promulgated new norms.

I

ON MIXED MARRIAGES

A *Decree* from the Congregation for the Doctrine of the Faith (March 18, 1966)*

The sacrament of matrimony, which our Lord Jesus Christ instituted as a symbol of His union with the Church in order to expand fully its sanctifying efficaciousness and to reproduce in fact for the spouses that great mystery (Eph. 5:32) whereby their intimate communion of life represents the love with which Christ offered Himself for the salvation of

---

* *Matrimonii Sacramentum: AAS* 58(1966), pp. 235–239. Translation in *The Jurist* 26 (1966), pp. 361–366.

131

man, demands more than anything else the full and perfect concord of the spouses themselves, especially regarding religion. "In fact, the union of spirits usually fails or at least is weakened when there is, in regard to the highest and most important matters which men hold sacred, that is, religious truths and feelings, a disparity of conviction and an opposition of wills" (Pius XI, *Casti Connubii*).

For these reasons the Church considers it a most grave duty to safeguard and preserve the gift of faith both for the spouses and for the offspring. Precisely for this reason it tries in every way to see that Catholics be joined in marriage with Catholics only.

The obvious proof of this attentive care of the Church is the ecclesiastical discipline concerning mixed marriages, sanctioned in the norms of the Code of Canon Law, which treats in concrete form of the twofold impediments of mixed religion and disparity of worship. Of these the first prohibits marriages between Catholics and baptized non-Catholics, without prejudice, however, to the validity of the marriage (canons 1060–1064). The second renders null the marriage contracted between a Catholic and a non-baptized person (canons 1070–1071).

Another clear reason for the concern of the Church to preserve the sanctity of Christian matrimony is the form itself, juridically defined in terms of how consent is made manifest. Although in fact in the past there have been diverse norms in this respect, it has always been provided that clandestine marriages were not permitted.

Guided by the same concern, all sacred pastors have the task of instructing the faithful on the religious importance and excellence of this sacrament. They must warn them of the difficulties and dangers inherent in marriage between a Catholic and a non-Catholic Christian and, for even greater reasons, in marriage with a non-Christian. With every opportune means let them study how to insure that young people contract marriage with Catholics.

Nevertheless, one cannot deny that the characteristic conditions of our time have rapidly brought about radical transformations in social and family life, making it more difficult than in the past to observe the canonical discipline regarding mixed marriages.

In truth, as circumstances are now, contracts between Catholics and non-Catholics are much more frequent, the ways of life and the similarity of habits are closer. Thus there is more easily born a friendship between them from which, as experience teaches, more frequent occasions of mixed marriages arise.

Accordingly the pastoral concern of the Church, today more than ever, is that the sanctity of marriage, in conformity with Catholic teaching, and the faith of the Catholic spouse, even in mixed marriages, be safeguarded and that the Catholic education of the children be assured with the greatest possible diligence and efficaciousness.

This pastoral duty is all the more necessary because, as is known, there are current among non-Catholics opinions differing from Catholic teaching concerning both the essence of marriage and its qualities, especially regarding that of its indissolubility, and as a consequence, the matter of divorce and new marriages after civil divorce. Therefore the Church considers it her duty to forearm her faithful so that they may not run dangers regarding the faith and suffer harm both of a spiritual and material nature. Let great care be taken, then, in instructing those who intend to contract marriage on the nature, qualities, and obligations implicit in marriage itself, and on the dangers to be avoided.

Moreover, in this connection that line of conduct cannot be disregarded which Catholics must follow with the brethren who are separated from the Catholic Church, as was laid down in the Second Vatican Ecumenical Council in the *Decree on Ecumenism*. This new discipline suggests that the rigor of the present legislation be mitigated regarding mixed marriages, certainly not as regards divine law, but in regard to certain norms of ecclesiastical law by which the separated brethren often feel offended.

It is easy to understand that this very grave problem has not at all escaped the attention of the Second Vatican Ecumenical Council, which was convened by our predecessor, John XXIII of happy memory, precisely to confront the actual needs of the Christian people. And in fact the council Fathers expressed on this matter various opinions which have been attentively considered, as was proper.

Therefore, after consulting the sacred pastors interested in this matter and after attentively assessing all the circumstances, while retaining the two impediments of mixed religion and disparity of worship (although local ordinaries are granted the faculty of dispensing from them according to the norms contained in the apostolic letter *Pastorale Munus,* n. 19 and 20, when there exist grave causes and so long as the prescriptions of the law are observed), and without prejudice to the legislation special to the Eastern Church, by the authority of His Holiness, Pope Paul VI, the following norms are issued which, should they gain positive approval from practice, will be definitively introduced into the Code of Canon Law which is currently being revised.

I

1. Let it be remembered that it is always necessary to remove from the Catholic spouse any danger to his faith and that provision must be diligently made for the Catholic education of children (cf. canon 1060).*

2. Let the local ordinary or the pastor of the Catholic party take care

---

* "The Church most severely forbids everywhere marriages between two baptized persons of whom one is Catholic, the other a member of a heretical or schismatic sect; if there is danger of perversion for the Catholic spouse, and the offspring, the marriage is forbidden by divine law."

to inculcate in grave terms the obligation to provide for the Catholic baptism and Catholic education of the offspring. For the fulfillment of this obligation a guarantee will be asked for by means of an explicit promise on the part of the Catholic spouse, that is to say by means of the *cautiones.*

3. The non-Catholic party, with due delicacy but in clear terms, must be informed of the Catholic teaching regarding the dignity of matrimony and especially regarding its principal qualities, which are unity and indissolubility. He or she must be informed of the Catholic party's grave obligations to safeguard, preserve, and profess his faith and to have the offspring which will be born baptized and educated in the faith.

And so that this obligation may be guaranteed, the non-Catholic spouse should also be invited to promise openly and sincerely that he will not create any obstacle in the fulfillment of that duty. But if the non-Catholic party thinks he may not formulate this promise without violating his conscience the ordinary must refer the case with all its particulars to the Holy See.

4. Although under usual conditions these promises must be made in writing, it is however within the power of the ordinary—either by means of rules of a general character or in each individual case—to establish that these promises of the Catholic party or of the non-Catholic party or of both be given in writing or not, as well as to determine how mention of the promises is to be inserted into the matrimonial documents.

II

If it is ever the case, as sometimes happens in certain regions, that the Catholic education of the child is rendered impossible, not so much by the deliberate will of the spouses but rather because of the law and customs of peoples, from which the parties cannot separate themselves, the local ordinary after considering everything carefully can dispense from this impediment, provided the Catholic party is disposed, in so far as he knows and is able to do it, to take every possible step that all the offspring to be born are baptized and educated in a Catholic manner and that at the same time this be guaranteed by the good will of the non-Catholic party.

In conceding these mitigations, the Church is also animated by the hope that civil laws contrary to human liberty will be abrogated, such as those which forbid the Catholic education of children or the exercise of the Catholic religion, and accordingly that the force of the natural law be recognized in this matter.

III

In the celebration of mixed marriages, the canonical form must be observed according to the norm of canon 1094.* This is required for the

* "Only those marriages are valid which are contracted before the parish priest or the local Ordinary or a priest delegated by either of them and at least two witnesses. . . ."

very validity of the marriage. If, however, diffculties arise, the Ordinary must refer the case with all its particulars to the Holy See.

IV

In regard to the liturgical form, as an exception to canon 1102, par.2, and canon 1109, par.3, *** local Ordinaries are given the faculty of permitting the celebration of mixed marriages using the sacred rites with the usual blessing and discourse.

V

Any celebration in the presence of a Catholic priest and a non-Catholic minister in the simultaneous exercise of their respective rites must be absolutely avoided. However, it is not prohibited that, the religious ceremony having ended, the non-Catholic minister give some words of good wishes and exhortation, and that prayers be recited in common with non-Catholics. What is referred to above may be done with the consent of the local ordinary and with due precautions to avoid the danger of scandal.

VI

Local ordinaries and pastors should be attentive and vigilant so that families resulting from mixed marriages may lead a holy life in conformity with the promises made, especially as regards the Catholic instruction and education of the offspring.

VII

The excommunication provided by canon 2319, §1, n. 1, for those who celebrate a marriage before a non-Catholic minister is abrogated. The effects of this abrogation are retroactive.

In establishing these new norms, it is the mind and intention of the Church, as has been said above, to provide for the actual needs of the faithful, so as to favor with a warmer sense of charity the reciprocal relations between Catholics and non-Catholics.

With this in mind, let those who have the task of teaching the faithful Catholic doctrine, especially the pastors, expend every effort and constant concern. They will endeavor to do so using all charity with the faithful and always without prejudice to the respect due to others, that is to the non-Catholics, [mindful] of their persuasions held in good faith.

Let the Catholic spouses be concerned to make stronger and to

---

*** "All sacred rites are forbidden; if, however, from this prohibition greater evils were likely to result, the Ordinary might permit some of the usual ecclesiastical ceremonies, always to the exclusion of the Mass." "Marriages between Catholic and non-Catholic parties are to be celebrated outside of the church; if, however, the Ordinary judged prudently that greater evils would follow from the observance of this rule, it is left to his discretion to dispense from it; without the prescription of canon 1102, par.2, ceasing to bind."

develop within themselves the gift of faith, leading always a family life based on Christian virtues. Let them study how to offer also to the non-Catholic party and to the children a shining example.

II
MARRIAGES BETWEEN CATHOLICS
AND BAPTIZED EASTERN NON-CATHOLICS

A *Decree* from the Congregation for the Eastern Church (February 22, 1967).*

The increasing frequency of mixed marriages between Eastern Catholics and non-Catholic Eastern Christians in the eastern Patriarchates and Eparchies as well as in the Latin dioceses themselves, and the necessity of coping with the inconveniences resulting from this, were the reasons why the Second Vatican Council decreed: "When Eastern Catholics marry baptized Eastern Non-Catholics, the canonical form for the celebration of such marriages obliges only for lawfulness; for their validity, the presence of a sacred minister suffices, as long as the other requirements of the law are observed" (*Decree on the Eastern Catholic Churches,* n. 18).

In the exceptional circumstances of today, mixed marriages between the Catholic faithful of the Latin-rite and non-Catholic Eastern faithful are taking place; and diverse canonical discipline has brought about many grave difficulties both in the East and in the West. For this reason, petitions from various regions have been addressed to the Supreme Pontiff, asking him to unify canonical discipline in this matter by permitting also to Catholics of the Latin rite what had been decreed for Catholics of the Eastern rite.

His Holiness Pope Paul VI, after mature reflection and diligent investigation, has resolved to agree to the petitions and desires addressed to him, and as a means of preventing invalid marriages between the faithful of the Latin-rite and the non-Catholic Christian faithful of the Eastern rites, of showing proper regard for the permanence and sanctity of marriages, and of promoting charity between the Catholic faithful and the non-Catholic Eastern faithful, the canonical form for the celebration of these marriages obliges only for lawfulness; for validity the presence of a sacred minister suffices, as long as the other requirements of law are observed.

All care should be taken that, under the guidance of the pastors, such marriages be carefully entered into the prescribed registers as soon as possible; this prescription also holds when Catholic Easterns marry bap-

---

* *Crescens matrimoniorum: AAS* 59(1967), pp. 165–166. Over the signatures of Gustavo Cardinal Testa, Pro-Prefect, and Archbishop Mario Brini, Secretary.

tized non-Catholic Easterns, according to the norm of the conciliar *Decree on the Eastern Catholic Churches,* n. 18.

In conformity with the holiness of marriage itself, non-Catholic ministers are reverently and earnestly requested to cooperate in the task of registering marriages in the books of the Catholic party, whether of the Latin or Eastern rite.

Ordinaries of the place, who grant the dispensation from the impediment of mixed religion, are likewise given the faculty of dispensing from the obligation of observing canonical form for lawfulness if there exist difficulties which, according to their prudent judgment, require this dispensation.

The same Supreme Pontiff has ordered the Sacred Congregation for the Eastern Church, of which he himself is the Prefect, to make known to all this resolution and concession. Wherefore, the same sacred Congregation, after also consulting the Sacred Doctrinal Congregation, at the order of His Holiness, has composed the present Decree to be published in the *Acta Apostolicae Sedis.*

Meanwhile, in order that his new statute may be brought to the attention of those whom it concerns, whether they be Catholics of any rite whatever or Orthodox, the present Decree will go into effect from March 25, 1967, feast of the Annunciation of the Blessed Virgin Mary.

Notwithstanding anything which in any way may be to the contrary.*

III
THE 1967 BISHOPS' SYNOD**

1. Whether the terminology now in use (mixed marriage, impediment of mixed religion, impediment of disparity of cult) should be retained? *Placet* 116; *non placet* 64.

---

* On February 22, 1967, the same day this Decree had been promulgated, Cardinal Augustin Bea, SPCU President, sent a letter to each of the Orthodox Patriarchs, with a copy of the Decree. On April 4, 1967, the Holy Synod of the Patriarchate of Moscow, under the presidency of Patriarch Alexis, acknowledged the letter and resolved: "To express its satisfaction on the removal of serious misunderstandings which frequently take place on the occasion of the performance of mixed marriages between Catholics and Orthodox; to recognize the lawfulness of the sacrament of marriage between Orthodox and Catholics, performed by Roman Catholic priests on those occasions when this marriage is performed with the blessing and approval of the Orthodox Bishop". Cf. *Journal of the Moscow Patriarchate,* 1967, n.5, pp. 4–5. In Russian.

** For the first Bishops' Synod (September 29–October 29, 1967), the SPCU and the Congregation for the Doctrine of the Faith prepared a working document for the almost 200 representatives. After floor discussion, eight propositions were submitted for vote, in order to determine "the mind of the Synod," i.e., a manifestation of opinion that would

2. Whether it is opportune to introduce new terminology such as "inter-confessional marriage," "unequal marriage," or some other? *Placet* 29; *non placet* 110; *placet iuxta modum* 41.

3a. Whether for dispensation from the impediment it is enough for the competent authority to have moral certainty that the Catholic party is exposed to no danger of losing the faith and is ready to do everything in one's power to ensure the Catholic baptism and education of the children? *Placet* 137; *non placet* 6; *placet iuxta modum* 42.

3b. Whether for dispensation from the impediment it is enough for the competent authority to have moral certainty that the non-Catholic party is aware of the obligation in conscience and at least does not exclude the Catholic baptism and education of the children? *Placet* 92; *non placet* 13; *placet iuxta modum* 72 (null 10).

4. Whether the canonical impediment should be done away with? *Placet* 28; *non placet* 128; *placet iuxta modum* 29.

5. Whether the canonical impediment can be eliminated in such a way as to have the following norm: Catholics, who for the validity of their marriage are obliged to the form when they contract among themselves, are held to it only for lawfulness if they marry non-Catholics? *Placet* 33; *non placet* 125; *placet iuxta modum* 28.

6. Whether, in retaining the canonical form for the validity of marriage, Local Ordinaries should be empowered to dispense from it in particular cases, according to their own conscience and prudence, in such a way that the use of this right would no longer be reserved to the Holy See? *Placet* 105; *non placet* 13; *placet iuxta modum* 68.

7. Since a mixed marriage, like any other marriage, can be celebrated at Mass or with a special ceremony outside of Mass, should not pastors of souls, with due regard to the freedom of the contracting parties, be concerned with recommending one or the other of these liturgical forms according to the spiritual background of the parties? *Placet* 153; *non placet* 5; *placet iuxta modum* 27.

8. Whether we should not increase our pastoral care in connection with mixed marriages, not only in previous catechetical instruction of the contracting parties, but likewise through special assistance on the part of pastors for families which have arisen from mixed marriages? *Placet* 171; *non placet* 0; *placet iuxta modum* 16.

---

as such remain unbinding for the Church. A two-thirds majority *(placet)* was required—in this case, 124. However, a *placet iuxta modum* vote counts as a *placet*, since an amendment could only modify a proposal if it went generally in the direction of the proposal; if it went clean contrary to it *(non placet)*, it could be discarded. Text: Official Synod Press Release, October 24, 1967.

IV
DETERMINING NORMS FOR MIXED MARRIAGES

An *Apostolic Letter, Motu Proprio,* from Pope Paul VI (March 31, 1970)*

Mixed marriages, that is to say marriages in which one party is a Catholic and the other a non-Catholic, whether baptized or not, have always been given careful attention by the Church in pursuance of her duty. Today the Church is constrained to give even greater attention to them, owing to the conditions of present times. In the past Catholics were separated from members of other Christian confessions and from non-Christians, by their situation in their community or even by physical boundaries. In more recent times, however, not only has this separation been reduced, but communication between men of different regions and religions has greatly developed, and as a result there has been a great increase in the number of mixed marriages. Also a great influence in this regard has been exercised by the growth and spread of civilization and industry, urbanization and consequent rural depopulation, migrations in great numbers and the increase in numbers of exiles of every kind.

The Church is indeed aware that mixed marriages, precisely because they admit differences of religion and are a consequence of the division among Christians, do not, except in some cases, help in re-establishing unity among Christians. There are many difficulties inherent in a mixed marriage, since a certain division is introduced into the living cell of the Church, as the Christian family is rightly called, and in the family itself the fulfillment of the gospel teachings is more difficult because of diversities in matters of religion, especially with regard to those matters which concern Christian worship and the education of the children.

For these reasons the Church, conscious of her duty, discourages the contracting of mixed marriages, for she is most desirous that Catholics be able in matrimony to attain to perfect union of mind and full communion of life. However, since man has the natural right to marry and beget children, the Church, by her laws, which clearly show her pastoral concern, makes such arrangements that on the one hand the principles of Divine law be scrupulously observed and that on the other the said right to contract marriage be respected.

The Church vigilantly concerns herself with the education of the young and their fitness to undertake their duties with a sense of responsibility and to perform their obligations as members of the Church, and she shows this both in preparing for marriage those who intend to contract a mixed marriage and in caring for those who have already contracted such a marriage. Although in the case of baptized persons of different religious

---

* *Matrimonia mixta: AAS* 62(1970), pp. 257–263.

confessions, there is less risk of religious indifferentism, it can be more easily avoided if both husband and wife have a sound knowledge of the Christian nature of marital partnership, and if they are properly helped by their respective Church authorities. Even difficulties arising in marriage between a Catholic and an unbaptized person can be overcome through pastoral watchfulness and skill.

Neither in doctrine nor in law does the Church place on the same level a marriage between a Catholic and a baptized non-Catholic, and one between a Catholic and an unbaptized person; for, as the Second Vatican Council declared, men who, though they are not Catholics, "believe in Christ and have been properly baptized are brought into a certain, though imperfect, communion with the Catholic Church."[1] Moreover, although Eastern Christians who have been baptized outside the Catholic Church are separated from communion with us, they possess true sacraments, above all the Priesthood and the Eucharist, whereby they are joined to us in a very close relationship.[2] Undoubtedly there exists in a marriage between baptized persons, since such a marriage is a true sacrament, a certain communion of spiritual benefits which is lacking in a marriage entered into by a baptized person and one who is not baptized.

Nevertheless, one cannot ignore the difficulties ·inherent even in mixed marriages between baptized persons. There is often a difference of opinion on the sacramental nature of matrimony, on the special significance of marriage celebrated within the Church, on the interpretation of certain moral principles pertaining to marriage and the family, on the extent to which obedience is due to the Catholic Church, and on the competence that belongs to ecclesiastical authority. From this it is clear that difficult questions of this kind can only be fully resolved when Christian unity is restored.

The faithful must therefore be taught that, although the Church somewhat relaxes ecclesiastical discipline in particular cases, she can never remove the obligation of the Catholic party, which, by divine law, namely by the plan of salvation instituted through Christ, is imposed according to the various situations.

The faithful should therefore be reminded that the Catholic party to a marriage has the duty of preserving his or her own faith; nor is it ever permitted to expose oneself to a proximate danger of losing it.

Furthermore, the Catholic partner in a mixed marriage is obliged, not only to remain steadfast in the faith, but also, as far as possible, to see to it that the children be baptized and brought up in that same faith and receive all those aids to eternal salvation which the Catholic Church provides for her sons and daughters.

The problem of the children's education is a particularly difficult one, in view of the fact that both husband and wife are bound by that responsibility and may by no means ignore it or any of the obligations connected with it. However the Church endeavors to meet this problem, just as she does the others, by her legislation and pastoral care.

With all this in mind, no one will be really surprised to find that even the canonical discipline on mixed marriages cannot be uniform and that it must be adapted to the various cases in what pertains to the juridical form of contracting marriage, its liturgical celebration, and, finally, the pastoral care to be given to the married people, and the children of the marriage, according to the distinct circumstances of the married couple and the differing degrees of their ecclesiastical communion.

It was altogether fitting that so important a question should receive the attention of the Second Vatican Council. This occurred several times as occasion arose. Indeed, in the third session the Council Fathers voted to entrust the question to us in its entirety.

To meet their desire, the Sacred Congregation for the Doctrine of the Faith, on March 18, 1966, promulgated an Instruction on mixed marriages, entitled *Matrimonii Sacramentum,*[3] which provided that, if the norms laid down therein stood the test of experience, they should be introduced in a definite and precise form into the Code of Canon Law which is now being revised.[4]

When certain questions on mixed marriages were raised in the first General Meeting of the Synod of Bishops, held in October 1967[5] and many useful observations had been made upon them by the Fathers, we decided to submit those questions to examination by a special Commission of Cardinals which, after diligent consideration, presented us with its conclusions.

At the outset we state that Eastern Catholics contracting marriage with baptized non-Catholics or with unbaptized persons are not subject to the norms established by this Letter. With regard to the marriage of Catholics of whatsoever rite with Eastern non-Catholic Christians, the Church has recently issued certain norms,[6] which we wish to remain in force.

Accordingly, in order that ecclesiastical discipline on mixed marriages be more perfectly formulated and that, without violating divine law, canonical law should have regard for the differing circumstances of married couples, in accordance with the mind of the Second Vatican Council expressed especially in the Decree *Unitatis Redintegratio* and in the Declaration *Dignitatis Humanae,* and also in careful consideration of the wishes expressed in the Synod of Bishops, we, by our own authority, and after mature deliberation, establish and decree the following norms:

1. A marriage between two baptized persons, of whom one is a Catholic, while the other is a non-Catholic, may not licitly be contracted without the previous dispensation of the local Ordinary, since such a marriage is by its nature an obstacle to the full spiritual communion of the married parties.

2. A marriage between two persons, of whom one has been baptized in the Catholic Church or received into it, while the other is unbaptized, entered into without previous dispensation by the local Ordinary, is invalid.

3. The Church, taking into account the nature and circumstances of times, places and persons, is prepared to dispense from both impediments, provided there is a just cause.

4. To obtain from the local Ordinary dispensation from an impediment, the Catholic party shall declare that he is ready to remove dangers of falling away from the faith. He is also gravely bound to make a sincere promise to do all in his power to have all the children baptized and brought up in the Catholic Church.

5. At an opportune time the non-Catholic party must be informed of these promises which the Catholic party has to make, so that it is clear that he is cognizant of the promise and obligation on the part of the Catholic.

6. Both parties are to be clearly instructed on the ends and essential properties of marriage, not to be excluded by either party.

7. Within its own territorial competence, it is for the Bishops' Conference to determine the way in which these declarations and promises, which are always required, shall be made: whether by word of mouth alone, in writing, or before witnesses; and also to determine what proof of them there should be in the external forum, and how they are to be brought to the knowledge of the non-Catholic party, as well as to lay down whatever other requirements may be opportune.

8. The canonical form is to be used for contracting mixed marriages, and is required for validity, without prejudice, however, to the provisions of the Decree *Crescens Matrimoniorum* published by the Sacred Congregation for the Eastern Churches on 22nd February, 1967.

9. If serious difficulties stand in the way of observing the canonical form, local Ordinaries have the right to dispense from the canonical form in any mixed marriage; but the Bishops' Conference is to determine norms according to which the said dispensation may be granted licitly and uniformly within the region or territory of the Conference, with the provision that there should always be some public form of ceremony.

10. Arrangements must be made that all validly contracted marriages be diligently entered in the books prescribed by canon law. Priests responsible should make sure that non-Catholic ministers also assist in recording in their own books the fact of a marriage with a Catholic.

Episcopal Conferences are to issue regulations determining, for their region or territory, a uniform method by which a marriage that has been publicly contracted after a dispensation from the canonical form was obtained, is registered in the books prescribed by canon law.

11. With regard to the liturgical form of the celebration of a mixed marriage, if it is to be taken from the Roman Ritual, use must be made of the ceremonies in the *Rite of Celebration of Marriage* promulgated by our authority, whether it is a question of a marriage between a Catholic and a baptized non-Catholic (39–54) or of a marriage between a Catholic and an unbaptized person (55–66). If, however, the circumstances justify it, a marriage between a Catholic and a baptized non-Catholic can be celebrated, subject to the local Ordinary's consent, according to the rites for the celebration of marriage within Mass (19–38), while respecting the prescription of general law with regard to Eucharistic Communion.

12. The Episcopal Conferences shall inform the Apostolic See of all decisions which, within their competence, they make concerning mixed marriages.

13. The celebration of marriage before a Catholic priest or deacon and a non-Catholic minister, performing their respective rites together, is forbidden; nor is it permitted to have another religious marriage ceremony before or after the Catholic ceremony, for the purpose of giving or renewing matrimonial consent.

14. Local Ordinaries and parish priests shall see to it that the Catholic husband or wife and the children born of a mixed marriage do not lack spiritual assistance in fulfilling their duties of conscience. They shall encourage the Catholic husband or wife to keep ever in mind the divine gift of the Catholic faith and to bear witness to it with gentleness and reverence, and with a clear conscience.[8] They are to aid the married couple to foster the unity of their conjugal and family life, a unity which, in the case of Christians, is based on their baptism too. To these ends it is to be desired that those pastors should establish relationships of sincere openness and enlightened confidence with ministers of other religious communities.

15. The penalties decreed by canon 2319 of the Code of Canon Law are all abrogated. For those who have already incurred them the effects of those penalties cease, without prejudice to the obligations mentioned in number 4 of these norms.

16. The local Ordinary is able to give a *"sanatio in radice"* of a mixed marriage, when the conditions spoken of in numbers 4 and 5 of these norms have been fulfilled, and provided that the conditions of law are observed.

17. In the case of a particular difficulty or doubt with regard to the application of these norms, recourse is to be made to the Holy See.

We order that what we have decreed in this Letter, given in the form of *"Motu Proprio,"* be regarded as established and ratified, notwithstanding any measure to the contrary, and is to take effect from the first day of October of this year.

APPENDIX

The United States. The Apostolic Letter leaves to Episcopal Conferences the further determination of specific questions. To implement this mandate, the National Conference of Catholic Bishops of the United States, on November 16, 1970, approved the following for U.S. dioceses, effective January 1, 1971:

I. Pastoral Responsibility

1. In every diocese, there shall be appropriate informational programs to explain both the reasons for restrictions upon mixed marriages and the positive spiritual values to be sought in such marriages when permitted. This is particularly important if the non-Catholic is a Christian believer and the unity of married and family life is ultimately based upon the baptism of both wife and husband. If possible, all such programs should be undertaken after consultation with and in conjunction with non-Catholic authorities.

2. In every diocese there shall be appropriate programs for the instruction and orientation of the clergy, as well as of candidates for the ministry, so that they may understand fully the reasons for the successive changes in the discipline of mixed marriage and may willingly undertake their personal responsibilities to each individual couple and family in the exercise of their pastoral ministry.

3. In addition to the customary marriage preparation programs, it is the serious duty of each one in the pastoral ministry, according to his own responsibility, office or assignment, to undertake:

a. the spiritual and catechetical preparation, especially in regard to the "ends and essential properties of marriage (which) are not to be excluded by either party" (cf. *Matrimonia Mixta,* n. 6), on a direct and individual basis, of couples who seek to enter a mixed marriage, and

b. continued concern and assistance to the wife and husband in mixed marriages and to their children, so that married and family life may be supported in unity, respect for conscience, and common spiritual benefit.

4. In the assistance which he gives in preparation for marriage between a Catholic and a non-Catholic, and his continued efforts to help all married couples and families, the priest should endeavor to be in contact and to cooperate with the minister or religious counselor of the non-Catholic.

II. Declaration and Promise

5. The declaration and promise by the Catholic, necessary for dispensation from the impediment to a mixed marriage (either mixed religion or

disparity of worship), shall be made, in the following words or their substantial equivalent:

"I reaffirm my faith in Jesus Christ and, with God's help, intend to continue living that faith in the Catholic Church.

"I promise to do all in my power to share the faith I have received with our children by having them baptized and reared as Catholics."

6. The declaration and promise are made in the presence of a priest or deacon either orally or in writing as the Catholic prefers.

7. The form of the declaration and promise is not altered in the case of the marriage of a Catholic with another baptized Christian, but the priest should draw the attention of the Catholic to the communion of spiritual benefits in such a Christian marriage. The promise and declaration should be made in the light of the "certain, though imperfect, communion" of the non-Catholic with the Catholic Church because of his belief in Christ and baptism. (cf. *Decree on Ecumenism,* n. 3)

8. At an opportune time before marriage, and preferably as part of the usual pre-marital instructions, the non-Catholic must be informed of the promises and of the responsibility of the Catholic. No precise manner or occasion of informing the non-Catholic is prescribed. It may be done by the priest, deacon or the Catholic party. No formal statement of the non-Catholic is required. But the mutual understanding of this question beforehand should prevent possible disharmony that might otherwise arise during married life.

9. The priest who submits the request for dispensation from the impediment to a mixed marriage shall certify that the declaration and promise have been made by the Catholic and that the non-Catholic has been informed of this requirement. This is done in the following or similar words:

"The required promise and declaration have been made by the Catholic in my presence. The non-Catholic has been informed of this requirement so that it is certain that he (she) is aware of the promise and obligation on the part of the Catholic."

The promise of the Catholic must be sincerely made, and is to be presumed to be sincerely made. If, however, the priest has reason to doubt the sincerity of the promise made by the Catholic, he may not recommend the request for the dispensation and should submit the matter to the local Ordinary.

III. Form of Marriage

10. Where there are serious difficulties in observing the Catholic canonical form in a mixed marriage, the local Ordinary of the Catholic party or of the place where the marriage is to occur may dispense the Catholic from the observance of the form for a just pastoral cause. An

exhaustive list is impossible, but the following are the types of reasons: to achieve family harmony or to avoid family alienation, to obtain parental agreement to the marriage, to recognize the significant claims of relationship or special friendship with a non-Catholic minister, to permit the marriage in a church that has particular importance to the non-Catholic. If the Ordinary of the Catholic party grants a dispensation for a marriage which is to take place in another diocese, the Ordinary of that diocese should be informed beforehand.

11. Ordinarily this dispensation from the canonical form is granted in view of the proposed celebration of a religious marriage service. In some exceptional circumstances (e.g., certain Catholic-Jewish marriages) it may be necessary that the dispensation be granted so that a civil ceremony may be performed. In any case, a public form that is civilly recognized for the celebration of marriage is required.

IV. Recording Marriages

12. In a mixed marriage for which there has been granted a dispensation from the canonical form, an ecclesiastical record of the marriage shall be kept in the chancery of the diocese which granted the dispensation from the impediment, and in the marriage records of the parish from which application for the dispensation was made.

13. It is the responsibility of the priest who submits the request for the dispensation to see that, after the public form of marriage ceremony is performed, notices of the marriage are sent in the usual form to:

a. The parish and chancery noted above (12).

b. The place of baptism of the Catholic party.

The recording of other mixed marriages is not changed.

V. Celebration of Marriages between Catholics and Non-Catholics

14. It is not permitted to have two religious marriage services or to have a single service in which both the Catholic marriage ritual and a non-Catholic marriage ritual are celebrated jointly or successively. (cf. n. 13 of *Matrimonia Mixta*)

15. With the permission of the local Ordinary and the consent of the appropriate authority of the other church or community, a non-Catholic minister may be invited to participate in the Catholic marriage service by giving additional prayers, blessings, or words of greeting or exhortation. If the marriage is not part of the Eucharistic celebration, the minister may also be invited to read a lesson and/or to preach. (cf. the *Ecumenical Directory*, Part I, n. 56)

16. In the case where there has been a dispensation from the Catholic canonical form and the priest has been invited to participate in the non-Catholic marriage service, with the permission of the local Ordinary and the consent of the appropriate authority of the other church or commu-

nion, he may do so by giving additional prayers, blessings, or words of greeting and exhortation. If the marriage service is not part of the Lord's Supper or the principal liturgical service of the Word, the priest, if invited, may also read a lesson and/or preach. (cf. *ibid.*)

17. To the extent that Eucharistic sharing is not permitted by the general discipline of the Church (cf. n. 11, *Matrimonia Mixta,* and the exceptions in n. 39 of the *Ecumenical Directory,* Part I, May 14, 1967), this is to be considered when plans are being made to have the mixed marriage at Mass or not.

18. Since the revised Catholic rite of marriage includes a rich variety of scriptural readings and biblically oriented prayers and blessings from which to choose, its use may promote harmony and unity on the occasion of a mixed marriage (cf. *Introduction to the Rite of Marriage,* n. 9), provided the service is carefully planned and celebrated. The general directives that the selection of texts and other preparations should involve "all concerned, including the faithful . . ." (*General Instruction on the Roman Missal,* n. 73; cf. n. 313) are especially applicable to the mixed marriage service, where the concerns of the couple, the non-Catholic minister and other participants should be considered.

VI. Place of Marriage

19. The ordinary place of marriage is in the parish church or other sacred place. For serious reasons, the local Ordinary may permit the celebration of a mixed marriage, when there has been no dispensation from the canonical form and the Catholic marriage service is to be celebrated, outside a Catholic church or chapel, providing there is no scandal involved and proper delegation is granted (for example, where there is no Catholic church in the area, etc.).

20. If there has been a dispensation from canonical form, ordinarily the marriage service is celebrated in the non-Catholic church.

Notes

1. *Decree on Ecumenism,* n. 3.
2. *Ibid.,* nos. 13–18.
3. Cf. *AAS* 58(1966), pp. 235–239.
4. *Ibid.,* p. 237.
5. *Argumenta de quibus disceptabitur in primo generali coetu Synodi Episcoporum,* vol. 2 (Typis Polyglottis Vaticanis, 1967), pp. 27–37.
6. Cf. *Decree on Eastern Catholic Churches,* n. 18; *Crescens matrimoniorum: AAS* 59 (1967), pp. 165–166.
7. *Crescens matrimoniorum, ibid.,* p. 166.
8. Cf. I Peter 3:16.

Chapter Eight
RECEPTION OF ADULT BAPTIZED CHRISTIANS INTO THE CATHOLIC CHURCH (THE RITE)

Introduction

The *Constitution on the Liturgy* (Dec. 4, 1963) decreed that "a new rite be drawn up for those who have already been validly baptized and are converts to the Catholic Church. The rite should signify that they are now admitted into the communion of the Church" (n. 69). The Holy See's Congregation for Divine Worship promulgated the new rite on January 6, 1972. The English translation appeared two years later.*

FOREWORD**

In the interval between the Constitution on the Liturgy and the publication of this ritual, it had become evident that the term "convert" or *neo-conversus* may not be appropriately applied to baptized Christians on the occasion of their entering into full Catholic communion.

The term "convert" properly refers to one who comes from unbelief to Christian belief. Although conversion of life is the continuing imperative of Christian believers, the concept of Christian conversion is applied

---

* *The Rite of Reception of Baptized Christians into Full Communion with the Catholic Church*. Copyright: International Committee on English in the Liturgy. Permission granted. The 1976 publication, from which extracts follow, is under the copyright of the United States Catholic Conference. Permission granted.

** An extract. The Vatican SPCU prepared this foreword.

only in reference to Christian initiation—through baptism, confirmation, and the eucharist—rather than to a subsequent change of Christian communion.

The conciliar *Decree on Ecumenism*, moreover, employs the expression, "imperfect communion," when speaking of Christian communities "separated from full communion with the Catholic Church." "For those who believe in Christ and have been properly baptized are brought into certain, though imperfect, communion with the Catholic Church. Without doubt, the differences that exist in varying degrees between them and the Catholic Church . . . do indeed create many obstacles, sometimes serious ones, to full ecclesiastical communion. . . . All who have been justified by faith in baptism are incorporated into Christ; they therefore have the right to be called Christians, and with good reason are accepted as brothers by the children of the Catholic Church" (n.3).*

Thus the name of the present rite and its contents have been chosen to express, not conversion to Christian faith, but rather admission, reception, and welcome into the fullness of Catholic communion. This is the reason also that the present rite is to be kept entirely distinct from the catechumenate of Christian initiation: "Any confusion between catechumens and candidates for reception into communion should be absolutely avoided" (Introduction, below, no. 5). The rites of the catechumenate and Christian initiation are for unbelievers who come to Christian faith; the present rite is for Christian believers who have been baptized in another church or ecclesial community and who now seek to be received into full communion with the Catholic Church.

Changed Discipline

For the United States, the new rite replaces the discipline in effect since July 20, 1959 (Instruction of the Holy Office; see also decrees of the Plenary Councils of Baltimore: II, no. 242; III, no. 122). This provided, in the case of the reception of already baptized persons, for the abjuration of error by making the profession of faith and for absolution from excommunication; thus admitted to communion, the person could be absolved from his or her sins.

Besides altering the terminology of conversion, the revised rite replaces the discipline described above with one in accord with the directory on ecumenism (May 14, 1967). This includes two substantial changes:

1. The requirement of absolution from excommunication is now suppressed, and no abjuration of heresy is to be made (see nos. 19–20).

2. The previous norm concerning the conditional baptism of the doubtfully baptized has been changed to say that a conditional baptism, "if

* TFS translation.

after serious investigation it seems necessary because of reasonable doubt," is to be celebrated privately (nos. 14–15; see Introduction, below, no. 7).

INTRODUCTION

1. The rite for the reception of one born and baptized in a separated ecclesial community into full communion with the Catholic Church,[1] according to the Latin rite, is arranged so that no greater burden than necessary is demanded for reception into communion and unity[2] (See Acts 15:28).

2. In the case of Eastern Christians who enter into the fullness of Catholic communion, nothing more than a simple profession of Catholic faith is required, even if they are permitted, upon recourse to the Apostolic See, to transfer to the Latin rite.[3]

3. a. The rite should be seen as a celebration of the Church, with its climax in eucharistic communion. For this reason the rite of reception is generally celebrated within Mass.

b. Anything which has the appearance of triumphalism should be carefully avoided, and the manner of celebrating this Mass should be precisely defined. Both the ecumenical implications and the bond between the candidate and the parish community should be considered. Often it will be more appropriate to celebrate the Mass with only a few relatives and friends. If for a serious reason Mass cannot be celebrated, the reception should take place where possible during a liturgy of the word. The person to be received into full communion should be consulted about the form of reception.

4. If the reception is celebrated outside Mass, the connection with eucharistic communion should be made clear. Mass should be celebrated as soon as possible, so that the newly received person may participate fully with his Catholic brethren for the first time.

5. The baptized Christian is to receive both doctrinal and spiritual preparation, according to pastoral requirements in individual cases, for his reception into full communion with the Catholic Church. He should grow in his spiritual adherence to the Church where he will find the fullness of his baptism.

During the period of preparation the candidate may share in worship according to the norms of the *Directory on Ecumenism*.

Any confusion between catechumens and candidates for reception into communion should be absolutely avoided.

6. No abjuration of heresy is required of one born and baptized outside the visible communion of the Catholic Church, but only the profession of faith.[4]

7. The sacrament of baptism may not be repeated, and conditional baptism is not permitted unless there is a reasonable doubt about the fact or validity of the baptism already received. If after serious investigation it seems necessary—because of such reasonable doubt—to confer baptism again conditionally, the minister should explain beforehand the reasons why baptism is conferred conditionally in this instance, and he should administer it in the private form.[5]

The local Ordinary shall determine, in individual cases, what rites are to be included or excluded in conditional baptism.

8. It is the office of the bishop to receive baptized Christians into full communion. But the priest to whom he entrusts the celebration of the rite has the faculty of confirming the candidate during the rite of admission,[6] unless the latter has already been validly confirmed.

9. If the profession of faith and reception take place within Mass, the one to be received—with due regard to the individual case—should confess his sins beforehand. He should first inform the confessor that he is about to be received into full communion. Any confessor who is lawfully approved may receive the confession.

10. At the reception, the candidate should be accompanied if possible by a sponsor, that is, the man or woman who has had the chief part in bringing him to full communion or in preparing him. Two sponsors may be permitted.

11. In the eucharistic celebration or, if the reception takes place outside Mass, in the Mass which follows, communion may be received under both kinds by the one received into communion, by his sponsors, parents, and spouse, if they are Catholics, by lay catechists who have instructed him, and also by all Catholics present, if the numbers or other circumstances suggest this.

12. Episcopal conferences may accommodate the rite of reception to various circumstances, in accord with the *Constitution on the Sacred Liturgy* (no. 63). The local Ordinary, moreover, may adapt the rite, enlarging or shortening it in view of special personal or local circumstances.[7]

13. The names of those received into full communion should be recorded in a special book, with the date and place of baptism also noted.

CHAPTER I
RITE OF RECEPTION WITHIN MASS

14. a. If the reception into full communion takes place on a solemnity or on a Sunday, the Mass of the day should be celebrated. On other days the Mass for the unity of Christians may be used.

b. The reception takes place after the homily. In this the celebrant should express gratitude to God and should speak of baptism as the basis for reception, of confirmation to be received or already received, and of the eucharist to be celebrated for the first time by the newly received Christian with his Catholic brethren.

c. At the end of the homily the celebrant gives a brief invitation for the candidate to come forward with his sponsor and to profess his faith with the community. He may use these or similar words:

N., of your own free will you have asked to be received into full communion with the Catholic Church. You have made your decision after careful thought under the guidance of the Holy Spirit. I now invite you to come forward with your sponsor and profess the Catholic faith in the presence of this community. This is the faith in which, for the first time, you will be one with us at the eucharistic table of the Lord Jesus, the sign of the Church's unity.

15. The one to be received then recites the Nicene Creed with the faithful. The profession of faith is always said in this Mass.

Afterwards, at the celebrant's invitation, the one to be received adds:

I believe and profess all that the holy Catholic Church believes, teaches, and proclaims to be revealed by God.

16. The celebrant then lays his right hand upon the head of the one to be received, unless confirmation follows, and says:

N., the Lord receives you into the Catholic Church.
His loving kindness has led you here
so that, in the unity of the Holy Spirit,
you may have full communion with us
in the faith that you have professed
in the presence of his family.

17. If the one to be admitted has not been confirmed, the celebrant next lays his hands upon the candidate's head and begins the rite of confirmation with the prayer.

All-powerful God, Father of our Lord Jesus Christ,
by water and the Holy Spirit
you freed your son (daughter) from sin
and gave him (her) new life.

Send your Holy Spirit upon him (her)
to be his (her) Helper and Guide.
Give him (her) the spirit of wisdom and understanding,
the spirit of right judgment and courage,
the spirit of knowledge and reverence.
Fill him (her) with the spirit of wonder and awe in your presence.
We ask this through Christ our Lord.

The sponsor places his right hand upon the shoulder of the candidate.
The celebrant dips his right thumb in the chrism and makes the sign
of the cross on the forehead of the one to be confirmed, as he says:

N., be sealed with the Gift of the Holy Spirit.

The newly confirmed responds:

Amen.

The celebrant says:

Peace be with you.

The newly confirmed responds:

And also with you.

18. After the confirmation the celebrant greets the newly received
person, taking his hands as a sign of friendship and acceptance. With the
permission of the Ordinary, another suitable gesture may be substituted
depending on local and other circumstances.

If the one received is not confirmed, this greeting follows the formula
of reception (no. 16).

19. The general intercessions follow the reception (and confirmation).
In the introduction, the celebrant should mention baptism, confirmation,
and the eucharist, and express gratitude to God. The one received into full
communion is mentioned in the first of the intercessions.*

20. After the general intercessions the sponsor and, if only a few
persons are present, all the congregation may greet the newly received
person in a friendly manner. In this case the sign of peace before communion may be omitted. Finally the one received into communion returns to
his place.

21. Then Mass continues. It is fitting that communion be received

* Samples given below.

under both kinds by the one received and by the others mentioned in no. 11.

CHAPTER II
RITE OF RECEPTION OUTSIDE MASS

22. If for a serious reason the reception into full communion takes place outside Mass, a liturgy of the word is to be celebrated.

23. The celebrant vests in an alb (or at least in a surplice) and a stole of festive color. First he greets those present.

24. The celebration begins with (an appropriate song and) a reading from scripture on which the homily is based (see no. 14b).

25. The reception follows, as described above (nos. 14c–19).

26. The general intercessions are concluded with the Lord's Prayer, sung or recited by all present, and the priest's blessing.

27. Then the sponsor and, if only a few are present, all the congregation may greet the newly received person in a friendly way. Then all depart in peace.

28. If in exceptional circumstances the liturgy of the word cannot be celebrated, everything takes place as above, beginning with the introductory words of the celebrant. He should start with a quotation from scripture (for example, in praise of God's mercy which has led the candidate into full communion) and speak of the eucharistic communion which will soon follow.

SAMPLE GENERAL INTERCESSIONS

Brothers and sisters: our brother (sister) was already united to Christ through baptism (and confirmation). Now, with thanksgiving to God, we have received him (her) into full communion with the Catholic Church (and confirmed him [her] with the gifts of the Holy Spirit). Soon he (she) will share with us at the table of the Lord. Rejoice with the member we have just received into the Catholic Church. With him (her), let us seek the grace and mercy of our Savior.

That N. may have the help and guidance of the Holy Spirit to persevere faithfully in the choice he (she) has made, we pray to the Lord.

R: Lord, hear our prayer.

That all Christian believers and the communities to which they belong may come to perfect unity, we pray to the Lord.

R: Lord, hear our prayer.

That the Church (Communion) in which N. was baptized and received his (her) formation as a Christian may always grow in the knowledge of Christ and proclaim him more effectively, we pray to the Lord.

R: Lord, hear our prayer.

That all whom God's grace has touched may be led to the fullness of truth in Christ, we pray to the Lord.

R: Lord, hear our prayer.

That those who do not yet believe in Christ the Lord may enter the way of salvation by the light of the Holy Spirit, we pray to the Lord.

R: Lord, hear our prayer.

That all men may be freed from hunger and war and live in peace and tranquillity, we pray to the Lord.

R: Lord, hear our prayer.

That we who have received the gift of faith may persevere in it to the end of our lives, we pray to the Lord.

R: Lord, hear our prayer.

Prayer

God our Father, hear the prayers we offer. May our loving service be pleasing to you. Grant this through Christ our Lord.

R: Amen.

If the reception is celebrated outside Mass, the transition from the general intercessions to the Lord's Prayer (see no. 26) can be expressed in these or similar words:

Celebrant:

Brothers and sisters, let us join our prayers together and offer them to God as our Lord Jesus Christ taught us to pray.

All:

Our Father ...

If the person received into full communion is accustomed to the final doxology *For the Kingdom*, etc., it should be used in this place.

Notes

1. Cf. *Constitution on the Sacred Liturgy*, n.69; *Decree on Ecumenism*, n.3; SPCU *Ecumenical Directory*, n.19.

2. *Decree on Ecumenism*, n.18.

3. *Decree on the Eastern Catholic Churches*, nos. 25 and 4.

4. SPCU *Directory*, nos. 19–20.

5. *Ibid.*, nos. 14–15.

6. *Rite of Confirmation*, Intr., n.7.

7. SPCU *Directory*, n.19.

Chapter Nine
GUIDING PRINCIPLES FOR INTERCONFESSIONAL COOPERATION IN TRANSLATING THE BIBLE

Introduction

Due largely to the demand of the Vatican Council's *Constitution on Divine Revelation (Dei Verbum)* that there be easy access to Holy Scripture for the christian faithful (cf. n.22), Paul VI, on April 4, 1966, entrusted to the SPCU the task of inquiring of the episcopal conferences about the needs and possibilities of Bible translation and about possible cooperation with other Christians in this field. Cardinal Bea then appointed Walter Abbott, S.J. as the liaison officer with the United Bible Societies (UBS), a council of non-denominational Bible societies that devote themselves to the translation, publication and distribution of biblical texts. A group of UBS and Catholic scholars worked out guidelines for interconfessional cooperation. These were jointly published by the SPCU and the UBS Executive Committee on Pentecost, June 2, 1968. Text: SPCU *IS,* 5 (1968), pp. 22–25.

In April 1969, the SPCU was also responsible for launching the independent World Catholic Federation for the Biblical Apostolate, "which is intended to serve the Bishops in their pastoral responsibilities concerning wider use and knowledge of the Bible" (Paul VI, April 16, 1969. Cf. *Osservatore Romano*, April 17, 1969, p.1).

I.
TECHNICAL FEATURES

A. Textual

1. Common Texts

a. New Testament: For joint translation programs, committees should base the work on critical editions of the Greek text prepared by committees of scholars representing both Protestant and Roman Catholic constituencies. It is proposed that Roman Catholic scholars be represented in the preparation of Bible Society editions of the Greek New Testament including both the edition prepared for translators and the edition designed for more technical purposes. It is planned that this shall be a continuing work.

Though a critical text must form the basis of any adequate translation, it is recognized that conservative tendencies in both Roman Catholic and Protestant constituencies require that certain passages of the New Testament found in the Textus Receptus, but no longer supported by the consensus of modern critical judgment, be included in the text of the translation. In such instances, however, it is necessary that the textual evidence be marked in some way by footnotes or appropriate sigla. The extent of textual adjustment will depend, of course, upon the local situation, and will need to be covered carefully by clear and detailed principles (see section II).

b. Old Testament: The Masoretic text edited by Kittle and published by the Wurtemberg Bible Society, being the most widely used by both Protestant and Roman Catholic scholars, is recommended for use by joint translation committees.

In general, the Masoretic text is to be retained as the basis for translation. Where, however, there are insuperable difficulties in the traditional form of the text, scholars are justified in making use of the evidence provided by the Dead Sea Scrolls and by the ancient versions for other forms of the Hebrew text. New insights provided by related Semitic languages such as Ugaritic should be given due consideration even when they conflict with traditional renderings.

In view of the inadequacies of existing aids on Old Testament textual problems, it is recommended that a joint committee be designated to analyse the textual data and provide required guides for translators including the evaluation of evidence and a summary of scholarly judgment.

2. Canon

Many Bible Societies are in a position to publish editions of the Bible which contain the Apocrypha or the deuterocanonical texts in certain well defined circumstances.

It is recognized that on the one hand an edition of the complete Bible bearing the imprimatur of the Roman Catholic authorities will contain the deuterocanonical texts and that, upon the other hand, while many groups within Protestantism have employed the Apocrypha, a great majority find it impossible to accept an arrangement of the Old Testament which does not clearly distinguish between these texts and the traditional Hebrew canon. It is suggested that these two positions can in practice be reconciled if normally, in editions of the Bible published by the Bible Societies and bearing the imprimatur of the Roman Catholic authorities, the deutero-canonical texts are included as a separate section before the New Testament. In the case of the book of Esther the translation of the Greek text will be printed in the deuterocanonical section while the translation of the Hebrew text will be printed among the books of the Hebrew canon. The deuterocanonical parts of the book of Daniel will be presented as items in the separate section.

B. Exegetical

1. Exegesis

In view of the growing agreement between scholars of both Roman Catholic and Protestant backgrounds a common exegetical basis should be established by the adoption of mutually acceptable commentaries and critical studies recommended by a joint commission.

2. Annotations or Helps For Readers

Both the needs of the reader and the traditional requirements of the Church can be satisfied with the following types of annotations:

a. Alternative readings: those meaningfully significant differences of reading which merit notice, or those readings for which manuscript evidence is both limited and late.

b. Alternative renderings: different interpretations based either on ambiguities in the original language or alternative means of expression in the receptor language.

c. Explanation of proper names: literal renderings of proper names when the message turns on an identification of the so-called etymology, e.g., Isaac, Israel, Jesus (at certain crucial points in the text). (These explanations of proper names are essentially similar to "plays on words" but are here treated as a separate category because of their peculiar nature and widespread occurrence.)

d. Plays on words: the identification of related forms in the original languages, e.g., pneuma meaning both "spirit" and "wind" (John 3).

e. Historical backgrounds: brief identification of historical individuals, places and events which are related to so-called "secular history." Much of this information may be given in the form of maps (with ancient and modern nomenclature) and short explanations provided in a Bible index.

f. Cultural differences: explanations of social, religious, or cultural terms: (i) individuals or groups, e.g., Pharisees, Sadducees, Herodians, etc.; (ii) objects of radically different form and function, e.g., weights and measures (weights, measures and coins must often be explained if a text is to be meaningful); (iii) biblical customs, e.g., "being seated on the right hand" must be explained as implying distinction and honor when in certain societies the "left hand" is the preferred location.

g. Cross references: the listing of other passages (with identification annotations) involving parallel content, similar historical events, quotations, clear cases of allusion, and parallel treatment of subject matter. While reference systems always run the risk of subjectivity and some are outright tendentious, nevertheless it has been possible to prepare reference systems of great usefulness and scholarly objectivity.

h. Section headings: the placing of identificational phrases as titles for significant sections. Readers are increasingly requesting the use of section headings in the text to facilitate location of passages, to indicate where a particular narrative or discourse begins, and to break up the otherwise heavy page of type. Such headings must be set off from the text by location and contrastive type face, should insofar as possible consist of words or phrases from the text, and should be identificational rather than interpretative.

Some committees have considered the possibility of explaining different Roman Catholic and Protestant beliefs by noting that one interpretation is held by Roman Catholics and another by Protestants. Such a procedure does not seem wise, for it tends to accentuate differences; nor is it necessary, for most diversities of interpretation can be covered more objectively by marginal annotations on alternative renderings, if the issue in question is important. Where the matter is not of great consequence, it is better simply to omit reference in the interest of joint undertakings.

Most annotations or helps for readers considered above are located on the specific page in the text where the difficulty arises, but if such a note would occur frequently it is often more satisfactory to summarize the data in tables of weights and measures or glossaries of difficult terms.

Restrictions on the types of annotations in no way preclude Roman Catholic and Protestant constituencies from publishing commentaries as separate volumes to help the reader to understand and appreciate more fully the nature and significance of the Holy Scriptures in the light of their own tradition.

3. Supplementary Features

The addition of certain other features such as index, concordance, maps, illustrations, etc., may be considered for certain types of publications.

Though practically all Bibles are printed with a table of contents listing the books of the Bible, an increasing number are also printed with brief indices which aid the reader in finding specific passages. A concordance from 25,000 to 45,000 lines, for instance, may also be highly useful in encouraging the study of principal Bible themes. Maps have been standard in reference Bibles for many years.

Illustrations pose more complex problems than any other supplementary feature, for there are many different concepts of what is artistic and diverse views as to what is appropriate for the Bible. Furthermore, what is aesthetically pleasing and historically meaningful in one culture may be grossly misunderstood in another. One general tendency, however, is now evident in most illustrations employed in the Scriptures; rather than use merely "decorative pictures" of dubious artistic merit and only passing relevance, publishers are responding to an evident desire on the part of people for pictures which will either provide background information or promote a measure of psychological identification and involvement because of the symbolic and dramatic character of the illustration.

To serve the purpose of joint Roman Catholic and Protestant editions, a preface, if desirable, should be restricted to a commendation of the Holy Scriptures to the reader and should omit appeals to ecclesiastical authority.

It is not normally the practice of the Bible Societies to associate the names of translators or revisers with translations of the Scriptures.

C. Linguistic

1. Orthography

Where Roman Catholic and Protestant constituencies employ different systems of spelling, these must be resolved by the employment of carefully developed scientific principles before any significant steps toward a common translation of the Scriptures can be realized.

Orthographic differences in the mission field are relatively widespread. They have resulted from different language backgrounds and linguistic orientations of early missionaries. Changes in such systems cannot be easily made, but given a significant measure of goodwill and a concern for Christian unity and educational efficiency, it is possible to work out practical solutions. At the same time, it is recognized that the problems of orthography are not merely linguistic but are largely ethnolinguistic. Cultural factors, such as conformity to a prestige language, and the psychological elements of efficiency and rapid reading are often far more important than purely linguistic (or phonemic) considerations.

2. Proper Names

Agreement must be reached on the forms of proper names before any joint text can be adopted or any joint translation undertaken. Factors which complicate such agreement are:

a. the traditional use by Roman Catholics of Latin forms as a basis for transliteration, even including certain inflected forms of Latin words;

b. Protestant use of European languages as a basis for transliteration, most commonly English;

c. the dominance of local, national, or trade languages, e.g. French, Portuguese, Spanish and Swahili, in contrast to systems employed by Roman Catholic and Protestant missionaries;

d. the attachment to particular forms of proper names as symbols of religious difference (forms of names have often been employed as a "badge of distinction");

e. the essentially arbitrary nature of the differences in transliteration, so that no one solution is overwhelmingly superior.

In the case of major languages with relatively long traditions, differences of usage can be resolved by following more closely the Greek and Hebrew forms with two major exceptions: (a) Old Testament persons referred to in the New Testament should have the Old Testament forms of names, and (b) certain widely known forms of names may be so deeply embedded in popular or local usage that they cannot be readily changed.

3. Borrowings

Borrowings of terms (other than proper names) e.g., words for "grace," should be kept at a minimum, since words not already used in the receptor language are empty terms. But if borrowing is regarded as necessary, it should generally be from living languages rather than ancient ones.

Borrowing is of two major types: (a) terms borrowed in the past by normal linguistic processes and often completely absorbed, in which case they are really a part of the vocabulary of the living language, and (b) terms expressly introduced for the first time in Bible translations. These latter types of borrowing are the ones treated here.

Roman Catholics and Protestants have exhibited two rather distinct tendencies in borrowing. For the most part, Roman Catholics have borrowed largely from Latin while Protestants have borrowed from Greek, Hebrew or modern European languages, with theological terms coming from Greek and Hebrew and cultural terms from European languages.

For major languages borrowing should be kept at a strict minimum, for all such languages have a sufficiently large vocabulary or phrasal equivalence to make borrowing relatively unnecessary. For minor languages borrowing should be made from those major living languages from which the languages in question normally appropriate such terms as may be required by expanding technology, commerce, and social intercourse.

4. Style of Language

Any joint Roman Catholic and Protestant translation should aim at a style of language which would be both meaningful and readable in public. It must make sense to those both within and outside the church and be in a language reflecting current usage but sufficiently dignified to be fitting for the importance of the message.

It is wrong to assume that only one legitimate type of translation in major world languages is required. Although it is increasingly less necessary to prepare different translations for diverse geographical dialects many languages include significant socio-economic or ethnic dialects. Such diversity of language and corresponding differences of purpose in translation suggest that more than one style of language may not only be desirable but necessary in many situations.

II.
PROCEDURES

Procedures will differ radically, depending upon the nature of the project (a new translation or revision), upon the level of training and education of the constituency, upon whether the psychological climate is conducive to cooperation, and upon the adherence of one or another constituency to its distinctive traditions. In all tasks at least certain of the following procedural factors figure significantly in the development of a program.

A. Climate for Cooperation

Whether a revision or new translation can be undertaken jointly in a particular area depends largely upon the climate established by the respective constituencies.

The strategic importance of the psychological attitudes of the constituencies involves a basic policy of the Bible Societies, which, though they generally hold the publishing rights for the Scriptures, only do so on behalf of the churches. Therefore, any cooperative undertaking will need for its success as wide an agreement as is possible on the part of the constituencies concerned.

B. Revision vs. New Translation

In general, it is preferable to undertake a new translation rather than attempt a revision of an existing text.

Where Roman Catholics wish to use existing Protestant versions without modification or with such slight changes as to be wholly acceptable to the Protestant constituency, there are usually few if any problems. Similarly, Protestants may wish to use certain Roman Catholic translations on similar bases. However, any serious attempt at revision of existing texts often results in a series of difficulties. It would seem far better where time and circumstances permit, to make a new translation. This makes possible the avoidance of traditional attachments, provides freedom to adopt new forms of language and a more relevant style, demonstrates a real and working ecumenicity, and provides both psychological and scholarly bases for creative decisions.

C. Organizational Structure

For the most adequate development of a translation program, there is need for three groups: 1. a Working Committee, 2. a Review Committee, and 3. a Consultative Group.

1. Working Committee

Consisting of 4 to 6 persons equally divided between Protestant and Roman Catholic constituencies and possessing four essential characteristics:

    a. equal standing,
    b. complementary abilities,
    c. mutual respect, and
    d. capacity to work together.

Moreover, it is essential that these persons have the opportunity to give sufficient time to the work, for their goodwill must be matched by the opportunity afforded to carry out the programme (members of working panels have sometimes been assigned tasks without adequate provision being made for their being able to carry through such projects).

2. Review Committee

Consisting of from 8 to 10 persons specially qualified to make scholarly study of the text, exegesis and style. On such a committee Roman Catholic and Protestant constituencies should be equally represented. The members should make their contribution largely by correspondence, though for certain key issues they may be invited to sit with the Working Committee.

3. Consultative Group

Consisting of 25 to 50 persons, depending upon the language and circumstances, selected not primarily for their technical competence but for their position as church leaders and their being representative of different constituencies: ecclesiastical, political, and geographical. The members provide their assistance entirely through correspondence.

For major languages a double structure is required, one for the New Testament and the other for the Old Testament, and in many circumstances a secretary is essential if the work is to be properly coordinated and decisions adequately recorded.

D. Appointment of Personnel

Working and Review Committees should be selected very carefully after full consultation with all leaders involved, while the members of the Consultative Group may be named by their respective constituencies.

To find the most qualified persons to constitute the Working and Review Committees, it is necessary to use informal decision-making structures. That is to say, an extensive investigation is made by some qualified individuals so as to assess the technical capacities and the probabilities of such persons being able to work together effectively in a committee. After determination, in consultation with church leaders, of the availability of such individuals, they may be formally nominated by their respective churches and appointed by the Bible Societies. Without careful preliminary investigation unsuitable appointments have sometimes been made to the detriment of the whole project.

E. Formulation of Principles

To provide proper guidance to a program, to ensure consistency of the results, and to make possible creative collective efforts, detailed principles must be worked out covering the entire range of technical features, e.g., text to be used, exegetical bases, system of transliteration, level of style, etc.

Adequate formulations of principles provide the best guarantee of success of a translation or revision project. In the first place, adherence to such principles provides the most satisfactory answer to the problems of "authority," for once the principles are agreed upon and accepted by the leaders of the respective constituencies, the translators can proceed with a high measure of assurance that the work will be accepted. In the second place, formulation of such principles makes possible the avoidance of a number of psychological problems, since those concerned may argue for or against the principles rather than for and against each other. Furthermore, principles are a significant aid in the production of greater consistency in the translation, for even in instances where some principle needs to be changed as a result of later experience in the work, all previous materials can be adjusted in keeping with such an alteration of principles, so that the resulting work may be basically uniform.

F. Editorial Supervision

It is essential that someone take the responsibility for "editorial supervision."

Such supervision, however, does not necessarily entail constant "watching" of the work, but rather provides a means by which the translators may have from a competent Bible Society source some guidance as to ways of solving those problems which may have arisen during the course of the work. Moreover, the possibility of such consultation provides a method for eliminating pressures which may build up when there is no such "neutral referee" to which to turn. The mere fact that such consultation is available, either with Bible Society Translations Departments or their Field Representatives, often prevents tensions and the development of strained relations.

G. Types of Editions

If joint translation programs are to lead to meaningful unity in the preparation of editions of the Holy Scriptures, it is important to avoid the production of two different texts (Roman Catholic and Protestant) by two different publishing houses.

If the result of joint effort is merely to produce two different texts to be put out by different publishers, it is almost inevitable that within five to ten years the texts will be further changed and ultimately there will be two different Bibles rather than one joint production. Even when the same text is put out by two different publishers it can become the object of very considerable pressure for minor modifications which within a short time add up to major changes. This does not mean, of course, that there should be only one edition of the Scriptures containing precisely the same supplementary or marginal helps, for a variety of forms of one and the same text can be useful in reaching diverse parts of a constituency. Nevertheless, once an agreement has been made as to a united approach to a translation or revision, it is wise to foresee the need of implementing this unity by continued procedures in publication.

H. Imprint and Imprimatur

An edition prepared jointly by Roman Catholics and Protestants would normally bear the imprint of the Bible Society and the imprimatur of the appropriate Roman Catholic ecclesiastical authority.

The most appropriate form for such an edition published by the Bible Societies would be for the Bible Society imprint to occur on the title page and the imprimatur of the appropriate Roman Catholic authority on the back of the title page, this being the normal procedure for books properly authorized by the Roman Catholic Church.

SUPPORT OF JOHN PAUL II*

I congratulate you all not only on this publishing event but, above all, on what it signifies. For it is a comforting sign of that "hunger and thirst for the word of God" of which the Prophet Amos spoke (*Amos* 8, 11) and which is always a sure guarantee of renewal and strengthening in the faith. Moreover, in this fact there is also a broad approval of the ecumenical effort which has gone into your initiative; for the Word of the Lord is one for all the Churches and these can draw ever nearer to each other to the extent to which they can come together in "hearing and reverence" (*Dei Verbum*, 1) that Word itself.

* On March 20, 1980, the Italian Editorial Committee of the inter-confessional translation of the Bible presented its millionth copy to the Pope. His response: SPCU *IS*, 44 (1980), p. 92.

Chapter Ten
COMMON CALENDAR
AND FIXED EASTER DATE

Introduction

Already in 325, the Council of Nicea was preoccupied that all the local Churches, in both the East and the West, should celebrate Easter on the same day, in order to eliminate the "scandal" of the different dates then in practice. At Nicea it was agreed to celebrate Easter on the Sunday which follows the first full moon after the Vernal Equinox. However, historical events, including the acceptance or rejection of general calendar reforms, again led to different dates. Today, Catholics, Anglicans and Protestants, joined by the Armenian Orthodox and the Syrian Orthodox of India, follow the Nicean formula, calculated according to Gregory XIII's calendar changes (1582). Following the same formula but still maintaining the calculation based on the older Julian calendar are all the Churches of the Byzantine tradition, as well as the Orthodox Coptic, the Ethiopian, and the Syrian Orthodox of Antioch.

In the 20th century, the League of Nations, the United Nations, and church organizations have made various attempts to propose a common fixed date. At the Second Vatican Council, the *Constitution on the Liturgy* (1963) had an appendix which met requests "for the assignment of the feast of Easter to a fixed Sunday and for an unchanging calendar". The Council "would not object if the feast of Easter were assigned to a particular Sunday of the Gregorian calendar, provided that those whom it may concern give their consent, especially the brethren who are not in communion with the Apostolic See". The Council also "does not oppose efforts to introduce a perpetual calendar into civil society".*

---

* *A Declaration on the Revision of the Calendar. AAS* 56 (1964), pp. 133–134. Cf. *Decree on the Eastern Catholic Churches* (1964): "Until all Christians concur, as one hopes, on a fixed day for the celebration of Easter, meanwhile in order to foster unity among the Christians of the same area or country, it is left to the Patriarchs or supreme church authorities of a place to consult all concerned parties and so to reach unanimous agreement on the same Sunday for the feast of Easter" (n. 20).

171

In 1964 Paul VI instructed the SPCU to contact other Churches, especially the Orthodox, and to inquire if mutual consent could be reached. In 1965 the World Council of Churches conducted an inquiry among all its member churches. In 1970 the WCC Faith and Order Department organized a consultation on a Fixed Date for Easter; Catholic, Orthodox, Anglican, and Protestant representatives participated. Further discussions between the WCC and the Holy See led to a coordinated effort. As a result, in his 1975 Easter letters to all the Patriarchs and heads of autocephalous Churches, Paul VI asked if a solution for a common date could be found; later, the SPCU proposed a solution, in the name of the Pope, to the Episcopal Conferences, to the leaders of the Anglican and Orthodox Communions, and to the authorities of the world confessional bodies, e.g., Lutheran World Federation, World Methodist Council. The WCC General Secretary, Dr. Philip Potter, also inquired of the member churches.

The results of this inquiry were evaluated at the WCC General Assembly, held in Nairobi, Kenya, December 1975. There the delegates of the Eastern Orthodox Churches expressed "the unanimous consent of our respective Churches": "no individual Orthodox Church may take any position on this issue without a general Pan-Orthodox decision". Accordingly, the Nairobi Assembly decided that for the present "a specific proposal would not lead to a date uniting all Christians".**

I
LETTER OF PAUL VI TO
ECUMENICAL PATRIARCH DIMITRIOS I*

"I am risen, and I find myself with you." (Opening Antiphon of the Roman Easter Liturgy)

While we celebrate the liturgy of Easter night, "the night that God has illuminated with the splendor of the risen Christ" (Opening Prayer of the Easter Vigil), We think of you, dear brother in Christ, and We desire to share with you the joy which comes to Us from the contemplation of the most grand mystery of our salvation: Christ raised from the dead by the Father's glory, so that we too might live a new life (cf. Rom 6:4).

Our joy, however, is at the same time mingled with sadness, because we are not in a position to celebrate this feast together. Not only have we not arrived at that moment when we could express our faith and common

---

** Cf. *Breaking Barriers: Nairobi 1975*, ed. David M. Paton (Grand Rapids: Wm. Eerdmans, 1976), pp. 193–194.

* March 26, 1975. Letters with similar contents were sent also to all the Patriarchs and other heads of autocephalous Churches. French Text: SPCU Archives. TFS trans.

joy by the common celebration of the Eucharist, "memorial of the death and resurrection of Jesus", but this year five weeks separate us in our celebration "of the day which the Lord has made".

Such a divergence weakens the witness which we Christians ought to give together to the world; it also makes it impossible for us to carry out the intentions of the First Ecumenical Council of Nicea which wished that all Christians be one in the celebration of the great mystery of Christ and of the Church (Cf. Letter of St. Athanasius, written in 359. PG 26.688,BC).

Is it not possible to find a solution to this situation? Ought not our common faith in the Spirit of God who guides His Church lead us to one accord? Already in the past your Church has seriously considered this question. In the Second Vatican Council the Catholic Church has likewise desired to find for the feast of Easter, in accord with the other Churches, a date common to all Christians. The World Council of Churches has made persistent efforts to achieve the same desired end.

The Catholic Church will study with great interest all the proposals which would be made to it, especially those which would come from the Orthodox Churches. It would also desire to meet representatives of the Christian Churches and to discuss with them eventual suggestions in view of concrete steps which could be taken.

The world where we live has perhaps more need than ever to our witness, in the power of the Spirit, of our faith in the resurrection of Jesus Christ, our Lord. His resurrection is moreover the foundation of our entire faith, that faith which many question. Does not St. Paul write that if Christ be not raised, our faith is in vain (I Cor 15:14)? Moved by this conviction and confident in the power of the risen Christ and of His Spirit, We desire that in celebrating the mystery of mysteries with one heart and one voice, we could give glory to God, the Father of Our Lord Jesus Christ, whom He has raised from the dead (Cf. Rom 15:6; Col 2:12).

May the peace and joy of the risen Christ be abundantly granted to Your Holiness, to his clergy and his people!

II

LETTER OF CARDINAL JOHN WILLEBRANDS
TO ORTHODOX LEADERS*

The Church has been convinced from the beginning that it is important that all Christians should celebrate the Lord's resurrection on the

---

* May 18, 1975. Sent to all the Patriarchs and other heads of autocephalous Churches. Letters with similar contents were sent to WCC General Secretary, Dr. Philip Potter, and to leaders of the world confessional bodies. English Text: SPCU Archives.

same date, so as to give a visible witness to their community of faith in this central mystery of the Gospel. The need for this common witness seems stronger than ever today, when speed of communications has, we might almost say, abolished distance. His Holiness Pope Paul VI recently expressed in writing to Your Holiness his wish to collaborate with your Church in finding an agreed solution which would put an end to differences which have caused great inconvenience to the faithful.

The matter has been studied in your Church and in the other Christian Churches as by the World Council of Churches. One may ask if the time has not now come for us to move together towards a decision. The Holy Father has asked me, as President of the Secretariat for Promoting Christian Unity, to explore, in close collaboration with the other Christian Churches and with the World Council of Churches, the practical possibilities of a solution which would not be the imposing of one tradition on another but rather the expression of an agreement to which the Holy Spirit has led us, an agreement according to the mind of the Fathers of the first ecumenical council, whose dearest wish was that all should be united in celebrating the Lord's resurrection.

In 1977 the date of Easter will coincide for all Christians, whatever their method of calculating. That date will be April 10, the Sunday following the second Saturday of April. The declarations made by heads of Churches and the reports of study commissions indicate that this particular Sunday is the most widely acceptable date for Easter.

In the name of Pope Paul VI, I would like to propose that from 1977 onwards Easter be always celebrated on the Sunday following the second Saturday of April.

We should be grateful to Your Holiness if you would let us know what you think of the proposal. We are addressing it simultaneously to all the Christian Churches. Through our contacts with the World Council of Churches we know that it is going to make a comparable proposal to its member Churches asking them to study it and give their views.

If your Church should find itself unable to accept this proposal to fix the celebration of Easter on the Sunday following the second Saturday of April, we would be grateful if Your Holiness would let us know whether your Church would be opposed to the Catholic Church fixing this date in the event of a majority of the other Churches being in favour. We would not wish to take such a decision at the risk of setting up an obstacle to the rapprochement of our Churches, that have been celebrating Easter on the same date for years.

III
LETTER OF CARDINAL WILLEBRANDS
TO CATHOLIC EPISCOPAL CONFERENCES*

The reactions of the Churches and the Communities stemming from the Western traditions of Christianity were almost unanimously favorable to the proposal that from 1977 on Easter should be celebrated on the Sunday following the second Saturday of April. All stressed, however, that such a change should be made only in consultation with the various Churches of the East and with their agreements.

The Orthodox Churches have given serious attention to this proposal. They have publicly stated their desire to see all Christians celebrate Easter together. Because of serious pastoral difficulties existing in certain local Churches, however, they feel that further study and reflection should be made by their Churches before a definite answer can be given. This study is already under way but it is clear that no decision will be possible in the immediate future. Furthermore it seems clear that, if the Churches and Communities of the western tradition were to take their own immediate decision on the proposal, this would not assist us in arriving at the goal of a common celebration by all Christians of the central mystery of their faith.

Under these circumstances, the Holy Father has judged that the situation is not yet ripe enough for the Roman Catholic Church to change its present method of determining the date of Easter or to put into effect this year the proposal that this great feast be celebrated on a fixed Sunday of April.

Circumstances will make it possible for all Christians to celebrate together this year of 1977 the Resurrection of our common Saviour. Although it will not be possible to continue this practice in the immediate years to come, it is our conviction, arising out of the serious reactions to the original proposal made, that the entire Christian world is committed to arriving at a solution to this problem as soon as possible.

* March 5, 1977. Extract: SPCU Archives.

Chapter Eleven
RELATIONS WITH THE ORTHODOX CHURCHES

Introduction

The *Decree on Ecumenism* briefly described the first of "the two types of division which affect the seamless robe of Christ": "The first divisions occurred in the East, either because of the dispute over the dogmatic formulae of the Councils of Ephesus and Chalcedon,* or later by the dissolving of ecclesiastical communion between the Eastern Patriarchates and the Roman See"** (n. 13).

During the preparations for the Second Vatican Council, the SPCU had initiated visits to the heads of these Churches, and most of them delegated official observers to the conciliar sessions. Thus began an increasing "dialogue of charity" by the exchange of visits, letters, and theological conversations between the leaders of the Holy See and of these Eastern Churches.***

---

* Those who did not accept the Council of Ephesus (431) later formed the Church to which the name Nestorian is sometimes given. Those who rejected the Council of Chalcedon (451) have organized Churches more along national lines—the Coptic, Ethiopian, Syrian and Armenian Churches, and the Syrian Church of India. These are sometimes called "pre-Chalcedonian" or "non-Chalcedonian" Churches; more recently, "Oriental Orthodox", to distinguish them from, simply, the "Orthodox" Churches of the Byzantine (both Greek and Slavic) tradition.

** Here the text refers primarily to the Ecumenical Patriarchate of Constantinople, the other Eastern Patriarchates (Alexandria, Antioch and Jerusalem, and the autocephalous Churches of Cyprus and Greece—all of the *Greek* tradition. In the *Slavic* tradition are the Patriarchates of Moscow, Serbia (Belgrade) and Bulgaria (Sophia), as well as the autocephalous Churches of Poland, Czechoslovakia, Finland, and America. The Patriarchate of Rumania (Bucharest) and the Church of Georgia are related to both the Byzantine and the Slavic traditions.

*** In the course of history groups from within the separated Eastern Churches resumed ecclesiastical communion with the See of Rome, while retaining their own hierarchical

I
THE ECUMENICAL PATRIARCHATE

1. The Common Declaration

a. The Common Declaration. Of Pope Paul VI and Patriarch Athenagoras (December 7, 1965) *

1. Full of gratitude to God for the favour which he mercifully granted them in their brotherly meeting in those holy places where the mystery of our salvation was accomplished by the death and resurrection of the Lord Jesus, and where the Church was born by the outpouring of the Holy Spirit, Pope Paul VI and Patriarch Athenagoras I have not lost sight of the intention which they held from then onwards, each for his part, never to omit in the future any of those gestures inspired by charity which might contribute towards the fraternal relationships thus initiated between the Roman Catholic Church and the Orthodox Church of Constantinople. They believe that they are thus responding to the call of divine grace, which today requires that the Roman Catholic Church and the Orthodox Church, as well as all Christians, overcome their differences, so as to be once again 'one' as the Lord Jesus asked of his Father for them.

2. Among the obstacles to be found in the way of the development of these brotherly relationships of trust and esteem, there is the memory of those painful decisions, acts and incidents which led in 1054 to the sentence of excommunication delivered against Patriarch Michael Cerularius and two other persons by the legates of the Roman See led by Cardinal Humbert, legates who were themselves in turn the objects of a similar sentence on the side of the Patriarch and the Synod of Constantinople.

3. One cannot pretend that these events were not what they were in that particularly troubled period of history. But now that today a more

---

organizations and liturgical traditions: *e.g.,* the Armenian, Chaldean, Coptic, Ethiopian, Melchite, Rumanian and Ukrainian Churches. There have also been other groups of Ruthenians, Russians and Greeks. The Maronite Church in Lebanon, which considers that it never broke full communion with Rome, is the only Eastern Catholic Church which does not have a corresponding non-Catholic Communion.

* The consigning to oblivion the mutual excommunications of 1054 and the lifting of the anathemas between Rome and Constantinople took place on the same day. In St. Peter's Basilica, at the last public session of the Second Vatican Council, Monsignor Willebrands, SPCU Secretary, read the joint declaration in French. Then Pope Paul VI exchanged the kiss of peace with Metropolitan Meliton of Heliopolis, the representative of the Patriarch. In the Cathedral of the Phanar at Constantinople, the same text was read in Greek by the Secretary of the Holy Synod of the Patriarchate, in the presence of the Patriarch and of Lawrence Cardinal Shehan (Baltimore) who represented the Pope. *AAS* 58(1966), pp. 20–21. Trans. from *One in Christ,* 2 (1966), pp. 167–169.

calm and equitable judgment has been brought to bear on them, it is important to recognize the excesses with which they were tainted and which later led to consequences which, as far as we can judge, went much further than their authors had intended or expected. Their censures were aimed at the persons concerned and not the Churches; they were not meant to break ecclesiastical communion between the sees of Rome and Constantinople.

4. This is why Pope Paul VI and Patriarch Athenagoras I with his synod, certain that they are expressing the common desire for justice and the unanimous sentiment of charity on the part of their faithful, and remembering the command of the Lord: 'If you are offering your gift at the altar, and there remember that your brother has something against you, leave your gift before the altar and go first to be reconciled to your brother' (Matt. 5:23–24), declare with one accord that:

a. They regret the offensive words, the reproaches without foundation and the reprehensible gestures which on both sides marked or accompanied the sad events of that period;

b. They also regret and wish to erase from the memory and midst of the Church the sentences of excommunication which followed them, and whose memory has acted as an obstacle to a rapprochement in charity down to our own days, and consign them to oblivion;

c. Finally they deplore the troublesome precedents and the later events which, under the influence of various factors, among them lack of understanding and mutual hostility, eventually led to the effective rupture of ecclesiastical communion.

5. This reciprocal act of justice and forgiveness, as Pope Paul VI and Patriarch Athenagoras I with his synod are aware, cannot suffice to put an end to the differences, ancient or more recent, which remain between the Roman Catholic Church and the Orthodox Church and which, by the action of the Holy Spirit, will be overcome thanks to the purification of hearts, regret for historical errors, and an effective determination to arrive at a common understanding and expression of the apostolic faith and its demands.

In accomplishing this act, however, they hope that it will be pleasing to God, who is prompt to pardon us when we forgive one another, and recognized by the whole Christian world. But especially by the Roman Catholic Church and the Orthodox Church together, as the expression of a sincere mutual desire for reconciliation and as an invitation to pursue, in a spirit of mutual trust, esteem and charity, the dialogue which will lead them, with the help of God, to live once again for the greater good of souls and the coming of the Kingdom of God, in the full communion of faith, of brotherly concord and of sacramental life which existed between them throughout the first millennium of the life of the Church.

b. Paul VI's Response to the Declaration*

"Walk in charity in imitation of Christ" (Eph 5:2): These words of exhortation of the Apostle of the Gentiles concern us who are called Christians in the name of our Saviour, and they weigh upon us, particularly in this time which urges us more strongly to broaden the range of charity. Yes, by the grace of God, our souls are enflamed with the desire to make every effort to restore unity among those who have been called to preserve it, since they too have been incorporated into Christ. And we ourselves, who, by intervention of Divine Providence, occupy the Throne of St. Peter, understanding this commandment of the Lord, on several occasions have already indicated our very firm resolution to seize every occasion which may serve and correspond to the accomplishment of this wish of the Redeemer. We turn over in our mind the disastrous events which, after serious dissensions, ended, in the year 1054, with a grave misunderstanding between the Church of Constantinople and that of Rome. It is not without reason that our predecessor, Pope Saint Gregory VII, wrote of this event: "Just as formerly the harmony was beneficial, so was the subsequent cooling of charity injurious on both sides." (*Letter to Michael, Patriarch of Constantinople,* Reg I, 18, ed Caspar, p. 30.) Moreover, it came about that the pontifical legates pronounced a sentence of excommunication against Michael Cerularius, Patriarch of Constantinople, and against two ecclesiastics, and that the patriarch, as well as his synod, had recourse to the same measure. But today the times and moods have changed. We are profoundly happy that our venerable brother, Athenagoras the First, Patriarch of Constantinople, and his synod are of the same disposition as we, that is, that they wish that we be united by charity, [that] "agreeable and healthy bond among souls" (see St. Augustine, *Sermon* 350, 3, *Patrologia Latina* 39, 1534). Also, in the desire to proceed further along the path of fraternal love, which will be able to lead us to perfect unity, and to suppress obstacles and impediments, in the presence of the bishops gathered here in the second Vatican ecumenical council, we proclaim that we regret the words spoken and the deeds carried out and that they cannot be approved. Moreover, we wish to erase from the memory of the Church the sentences of excommunication then given and to retract it from its legacy and we wish that it be covered over and buried by oblivion. We are happy that it has been given to us to accomplish this act of fraternal charity, here in Rome, next to the tomb of the Apostle Peter on the very day when, in Constantinople, which is called the new Rome, the same action is being taken, and at the moment when

---

* December 7, 1965. Immediately after Msgr. Willebrands had read the Common Declaration to the Council Fathers, Augustin Cardinal Bea read the Pope's response, *Ambulate in dilectione. AAS* 58(1966), pp. 40–41. TFS trans. Over the official manuscript are the words, *"Ad futuram rei memoriam".*

the Western Church and that of the East are celebrating in a religious commemoration Saint Ambrose, bishop and doctor of both Churches. May the very merciful God, author of peace, render efficacious this reciprocal good will and may He allow that this public testimony of Christian brotherhood redound to his glory and to the good of souls.

Given from St. Peter's in Rome, and sealed by the Fisherman's ring, on the feast of St. Ambrose, Bishop, Confessor, and Doctor of the Church, December 7, 1965, in the third year of our Pontificate.

*c. Athenagoras's Response to the Declaration**

In the name of the holy, consubstantial, vivifying and indivisible Trinity.

"God is Love (I Jn 4:9): love is the God-given mark of the disciples of Christ, the power which gathers in unity the Church, and the source of its peace, harmony and order, as a perpetual and brilliant manifestation of the indwelling Holy Spirit.

Thus, those to whom God has entrusted the care of the Churches need this "bond of perfection" (Col 3,14) and must give it every attention, care and protection.

And if charity should ever grow cold and the unity in the Lord be ruptured, one must hastily recognize the evil and seek to remedy it.

But through a mysterious disposition of God, a distressing situation befell the Church: the relations between the Churches of Rome and Constantinople have been tested and the charity that binds them has been so strained that anathema has appeared in the very heart of the Church of God: Roman legates, Cardinal Humbert and his companions, while Patriarch Michael Cerularius and his Synod anathematized the writings of those who came from Rome, as well as those who were considered their collaborators. Therefore, the Churches of Rome and of Constantinople, emulating the loving-kindness of God for men should be aware of this matter and should reestablish peace.

But in our time the benevolence of God is manifest to us, showing the way of reconciliation and peace in ways and means that God has disposed in favor of a mutual solicitude blessed and fruitful for the old as well as our New Rome, for the development of their brotherly relations. It has been judged proper and useful to proceed with setting right the deeds of the past and, in whatever degree is possible in each case, to remove those accumulated obstacles which can be eliminated. All of which should be done for the sake of the expansion, the growth, the building up and perfection of charity.

---

* December 7, 1965. Read by the Patriarch to the Holy Synod. At the head of the document: "Athenagoras. By the mercy of God, the Archbishop of Constantinople, the new Rome, and Ecumenical Patriarch". *Tomos Agapis*, n. 129. TFS trans.

Therefore, our humble self, with the venerable and highly respected metropolitans, our brothers and beloved concelebrants in Christ, having deemed the moment propitious in the Lord, and having gathered together and discussed the matter in the Synod, and having taken cognizance of similar dispositions of ancient Rome, we have decided to remove from memory and from the bosom of the Church the aforementioned anathema levied by the Patriarch Michael Cerularius of Constantinople in his Synod.

We therefore proclaim in writing that the anathema handed down in the grand chancellery of our great church in July 1054 of the seventh indiction is, from this moment and for the information of everyone, lifted from the memory and heart of the Church through the mercy of God. Through the intercession of our Lady, Mother of God and ever-virgin Mary, the "Panmakaristos" (all blessed), of the saints and glorious apostles, of Peter, the first cornerstone, and Andrew, the first-called, and of all the saints, grant peace to the Church and protect it forever and ever.

In testimony thereof and as a perpetual sign and attestation, the present patriarchal and synodal act has been drawn up and signed in the sacred register of our holy Church. An authentic, accurate copy has been sent to the holy Church of ancient Rome for due recognition and deposit in its archives.

In the year of salvation, the 7th day of the month of December of the fourth indiction.

Patriarch Athenagoras delivers judgment.

Thomas of Chalcedon, Chrysostom of Neo-Caesarea, Jerome of Rodopolis, Simeon of Irinoupolis, Dorothea of the Isle of Princes, Maximus of Laodicea, Chrysostom of Myra, Cyril of Chaldea, Meliton of Heliopolis and Tyre, Emilian of Milet.

2. Paul VI's Visit to Athenagoras I. (Istanbul, July 25–26, 1967)

a. Address of Paul VI, *Patriarchal Cathedral of St. George.* *

A little more than three years ago, God, in His Infinite goodness, permitted us to meet in that holy land where Christ founded His Church and poured out His blood for her. Both of us had journeyed in pilgrimage toward that spot on which rose the glorious cross of our Saviour and from where, "lifted up from the earth, He draws all things to Himself" (John 12, 32).

Today it is the same love of Christ and His Church which brings us, a pilgrim once again, to this noble land where the successors of the Apostles once assembled in the Holy Spirit to bear witness to the faith of the

---

* July 25. At the end of a liturgical service, in which the Pope and the Patriarch participated. SPCU *IS,* 3 (1967), pp. 10–11.

Church. We recall here the four great ecumenical councils of Nicaea, Constantinople, Ephesus and Chalcedon, which the Fathers had no hesitation in likening to the four Gospels. These were their first meetings, and they came from the entire Christian world of that time. Inspired by the same brotherly love, they provided our faith with a richness and depth of expression which even in our day nourishes the faith and loving contemplation of all Christians.

Can we not see the working of Divine Providence in the fact that this pilgrimage affords us the opportunity of fulfilling the hope of meeting again, which we both expressed in Jerusalem after Your Holiness had told us that, "having sought to meet with one another, together we had found the Lord"?

Is not the secret of our meeting, of the gradual rediscovery of our churches, that unceasing search for Christ and for fidelity to Christ, who unites us in Himself? At the beginning of this year in which we celebrate the 10th centenary of the supreme testimony given to the faith by the Apostles Peter and Paul, we meet once again to exchange the kiss of brotherly love, here where our fathers in the faith assembled to profess with one accord their belief in the Holy Trinity, indivisible and consubstantial.

In the light of our love for Christ and of our brotherly love, we perceive even more clearly the profound identity of our faith, and the points on which we still differ must not prevent us from seeing this profound unity. And here, too, charity must come to our aid, as it helped Hilary and Athanasius to recognize the sameness of the faith underlying the differences of vocabulary at a time when serious disagreements were creating divisions among Christian bishops. Did not pastoral love prompt St. Basil, in his defense of the true faith in the Holy Spirit, to refrain from using certain terms which, accurate though they were, could have given rise to scandal in one part of the Christian people? And did not St. Cyril of Alexandria consent in 433 to abandon his beautiful formulation of theology in the interests of making peace with John of Antioch, once he had satisfied himself that in spite of divergent modes of expression, their faith was identical?

Is this not a field in which the dialogue of charity can be profitably extended, eliminating many obstacles and opening up paths to the full communion of faith in truth? To find ourselves again one in diversity and fidelity can only be the work of the Spirit of Love. While unity of faith is required for full communion, diversity of usages is not an obstacle to it— on the contrary.

Did not Saint Irenaeus, who "bore his name well, since he was a pacifier both in name and by his actions" (Eusebius, *Ecclesiastical History,* 5, 14, 24), say that diversity of usages "confirms the accord of faith" (ibid. 13)? And as the great doctor of the African Church, Augustine, looked upon diversity of usage as one of the reasons for the beauty of the Church of Christ (*Epistle,* 14, 32).

Charity enables us to acquire a better awareness of the very depth of our unity at the same time it makes us suffer more painfully the present impossibility of seeing this unity expand into concelebration, and it spurs us on to do everything possible to hasten the advent of that day of the Lord. Thus we see more clearly that it is incumbent on the heads of the Churches, on their hierarchy, to lead the Churches along the path which leads to the rediscovery of full communion. They must do it by mutual recognition of each other and mutual respect for each other as pastors of that part of the flock of Christ which is entrusted to them, providing for the cohesion and growth of the people of God and avoiding all that could disperse it and throw confusion into its ranks. From now on then, and through such efforts we will be able to render more efficacious testimony to the name of Christ, who wanted us to be one so that the world might believe.

Charity is the vitally necessary environment for the flowering of faith, and communion in faith is the condition for the full manifestation of that charity which is expressed in concelebration.

May the Lord, who for the second time gives us the opportunity for exchanging the kiss of His love, illumine us and guide our steps and our efforts toward that day so much desired. May He grant that we be ever more completely animated by concern for the faithful fulfillment of His will for the Church! May He grant us a vivid sense of that one thing necessary to which all else must be subordinated or sacrificed. It is in this hope that, with "love without pretense" (Romans 12, 9) we greet you with a holy kiss (Romans 16,16).

b. Reply of Athenagoras I, *Cathedral of St. George**

Glory to God the author of every marvel, who has deemed us worthy today, us and the hierarchy, the clergy and the people around us, linked in our prayer with our holy brothers, the chiefs of the local Orthodox churches and the venerated brothers of the other Christian churches, to receive with boundless love and very great honor Your Holiness, dear and venerated, you who have come here to bring the kiss of ancient Rome to its younger sister.

Be welcome, very holy successor of Peter, who have Paul's name and his conduct, as a messenger of charity, union and peace.

Within the bosom of the Church we give you the kiss of the love of Christ.

The Apostles Peter and Andrew, who were brothers, are glad with us,

* Extracts: SPCU *IS,* 3(1967), pp. 11–12.

and in their joy are joined the choir of the holy Fathers of the setting sun
and of the rising sun, of north and of south, who consumed themselves in
the witness of the undivided Church's common faith and in the sanctification of their concelebration in its bosom, as well as with all those generations who have aspired to see this day.

Here are both of us, facing our common and holy responsibility
toward the Church and the world.

Henceforth, whither and how will we continue along our route?

Both the goal and the paths that lead to it are in the hands of God.
But it is not I, it is the Lord who says "may all be one" (John 17, 21).

Obedient to His words and to His will, we are moving toward the
union of all, toward the full communion of charity and of faith, coming to
pass in the concelebration of the common chalice of Christ, in the impatient expectation and the hope of Him who will come to consummate the
times and history in judging the living and the dead.

How will we pursue our road?

According to us, in the disposition of the conscience and of the will of
all Catholics and Orthodox, marked on both parts by manifestations of the
hierarchy, of the clergy and of the faithful, whose voice in these times is a
precious guide and a consolation.

In thus pursuing our road, we humbly believe we are replying to the
exigencies—unavoidable at the present hour—of a history of which God
remains the master.

Called to be servants of the Lord of His Church and of the whole
world, let us collaborate then in the design of God, who leaves the 99
sheep to save the one of them who strayed (Matthew 18, 11) and toward
whom we are held to a common care and a common witness.

However, let us begin with ourselves. Let us make every possible
sacrifice and suppress mutually, with a total abnegation, all that in the past
seemed to contribute to the Church's integrity but which in reality ended
by creating a division difficult to surmount. Let us build the Body of
Christ in reuniting what is divided and in bringing together again what is
scattered (Liturgy of St. Basil).

Let us then apply ourselves, by reciprocal gestures of the Churches,
where it is possible, to reuniting what is divided, in the firm recognition of
the common points of the Faith and of canonical regulations. Let us thus
conduct the theological dialogue according to the principle of the full
community of what is fundamental for the Faith and for the liberty of a
theological, spiritual and creative thought, inspired by the common Fathers, in the diversity of local usage admitted by the Church from its
beginnings.

So doing, we will have in view not only the unity of our two holy
Churches but also a higher service: to offer ourselves together to all other
dear Christian brothers as examples and artisans in the accomplishment of

the whole will of the Lord, which is to reach the union of all so that the world may believe that Christ was sent by God.

But there is more. We have in view all those who believe in a God, Creator of man and of the universe, and, in collaborating with them, we will serve all men without distinction of race, creed or opinion, to promote the good of peace in the world and to establish the kingdom of God on earth.

Full of such sentiments and of such thoughts, we salute Your Holiness' arrival in the East as a new dawn of Rome and of Constantinople, of the Roman Catholic world and the Orthodox world, of all Christianity and of the whole of mankind.

c. Message of Paul VI, *Latin Cathedral of the Holy Spirit**

At the beginning of the Year of Faith being celebrated in honor of the 19th centenary of the martyrdoms of Sts. Peter and Paul, we, Paul, Bishop of Rome and head of the Catholic Church, convinced that it is our duty to undertake all that can serve the universal and holy Church of Christ, once again meet our beloved brother Athenagoras, Orthodox Archbishop of Constantinople and Ecumenical Patriarch, and we are moved by an ardent desire to see the prayer of the Lord realized: "That they may be one, even as we are one, I in them and thou in me. That they may be perfected in unity, and that the world may know that thou hast sent me" (John 17, 22–23).

This desire animates a will resolved to do everything in our power to hasten that day when full communion will be re-established between the Church of the West and that of the East, in view of the recomposition of all Christians in that unity which will permit the Church to bear witness more effectively to the fact that the Father has sent His Son into the world so that in Him all men may become sons of God and may live as brothers in charity and peace.

Convinced that "there is no other name under heaven given to men by which we must be saved" (cf. Acts 4, 12), and no other name which can give them true brotherhood and peace, we are attentive to the message which John, the beloved Disciple, sent from Ephesus to the churches of Asia: "What we have heard we announce to you in order that you also may have fellowship with us and that our fellowship may be with the Father and with His Son Jesus Christ" (1 John 1, 3). What the Apostles have seen, heard and announced to us, God has given us to receive in faith.

Through Baptism "we are one in Jesus Christ" (Galatians 3, 28). The priesthood and the Eucharist unite us even more intimately by virtue of

---

* July 25, at the end of a joint prayer service. A written document, *Anno ineunte,* signed by Pope Paul, and read by SPCU Secretary, Bishop Willebrands. SPCU *IS,* 3 (1967), pp. 12–13.

the apostolic succession (cf. Second Vatican Council's *Decree on Ecumenism*, No. 15).

Such is the profound and mysterious communion which exists between us, participating in the gifts of God to His Church, we are put in communion with the Father by Christ in the Holy Spirit.

Having become sons in the Son in all reality (cf. I John 3, 1–2), we have become also really and mysteriously brothers to each other. This mystery of divine love is realized in every local church, and is this not the reason for the traditional and so beautiful expression, according to which local churches like to call themselves sister churches (cf. *Decree on Ecumenism*, No. 14)?

We lived this life of a sister church for centuries, celebrating together the ecumenical councils which defended the deposit of faith against any alteration. Now after a long period of division and reciprocal incomprehension the Lord grants us that we rediscover ourselves as sister churches despite the obstacles which were then raised between us. In the light of Christ, we see how urgent is the necessity of surmounting these obstacles in order to succeed in bringing to its fullness and perfection that unity— already so rich—which exists between us.

Since we both profess "the fundamental dogmas of the Christian faith on the Trinity, the word of God made flesh of the Virgin Mary" as they "were defined in the ecumenical councils celebrated in the East" (cf. *Decree on Ecumenism*, No. 14) and since we have in common real sacraments and a hierarchical priesthood, it is necessary first of all that in the service of our holy Faith we should work fraternally, seeking together those forms which are suitable and progressive toward development and actualization in the life of our Churches of that communion which already exists, though imperfectly.

It will then be necessary on both sides and through mutual contacts to promote, deepen and adapt the formation of the clergy, and the instruction and the life of the Christian people.

It is a matter of knowing and of respecting each other in the legitimate diversity of liturgical, spiritual, disciplinary and theological traditions (cf. *Decree on Ecumenism*, Nos. 14 and 17) by means of a frank theological dialogue, made possible by the re-establishment of brotherly charity in order to attain accord in the sincere confession of all revealed truths.

In order to restore and preserve communion and unity, care must indeed be taken to "impose no burden beyond what is indispensable" (Acts 15, 28; *Decree on Ecumenism*, No. 18). In hope and charity, sustaining ourselves with continuous supplication, moved by the sole desire for the one thing that is necessary (cf. Luke 10, 32) and resolved to subordinate everything to it, we must continue and intensify our steps forward "in the name of the Lord".

*d. Sermon of Paul VI to Catholics of Istanbul**

Help us, then—all of you, shepherds and flock—help us in the great task we have undertaken and which has been one of the determining reasons for this journey: the recomposition of Christian unity. You feel here its necessity more than others and you also see better than others its progress.

The recent Vatican Council reminded us that this progress is based first of all on the renovation of the Church and on the conversion of the heart. This means that you will contribute to this progress toward unity in the measure in which you enter into the spirit of the council. An effort is demanded from each of us to revise our customary ways of thinking and acting to bring them more into conformity with the Gospel and the demands of a true Christian Brotherhood.

Let us do it generously, trusting that the hour of God will come and that we can hasten its coming by our prayers and our efforts.

We are happy to address this exhortation to you in this city which has a glorious Christian past—the city which had as bishop Saint John Chrysostom, the great Doctor of the East and West, and where the Church once celebrated four of its ecumenical councils and where today the presence of the venerable Patriarch Athenagoras—so zealous, too, for the cause of unity—fills our hearts with hope.

Let us pray together to obtain the grace of a generous response to the appeal of the Church and of the council and the grace of full unity for all those who believe in Christ and profess with their hearts and their lips the one and undivided Trinity, Father, Son and Holy Spirit. Amen.

3. Athenagoras's Visit to Paul VI. (Vatican City, October 26–27, 1967)

a. Address *of Athenagoras I to Paul VI***

Fulfilling the ministry of charity, of unity and of peace, a short while ago we embraced as brothers in Christ, venerated and honored, in our holy Church of the East; today, in this eternal city of the Romans, the abode of the primary leaders of the Apostles, Peter and Paul, and glory of the Christian world, we come to Your Holiness as a brother toward a brother. With these sentiments we return to you the kiss of the charity and of the peace of our Lord Jesus and express to you our profound esteem.

We are particularly happy to do this not just simply toward the venerable Bishop of Rome, bearer of apostolic grace and the successor of a constellation of holy and wise men who made illustrious this See which is the first in honor and order in the living body of the Christian Churches

---

* July 25, Latin Cathedral of the Holy Spirit. Extract: SPCU *IS,* 3 (1967), p. 14.
** October 26, in the presence of the Bishops' Synod, presided over by the Pope. Extracts: SPCU *IS,* 3 (1967), p. 15.

scattered throughout the world, and whose holiness, wisdom and struggles for the common faith in the undivided Church are a permanent conquest and the treasure of the entire Christian world. We are also happy to do this toward a Pope of eminent spiritual worth and Christian inspiration who possesses, in humility, sublime gifts and whose sense of responsibility before the Lord, before the divided Church, before the manifold tragedies of this world leads him each day from actions of charity to acts of edification, to a service befitting God, the Church and mankind.

We stand in this holy place, next to Your Holiness, near the altar, and prepare our heart and spirit for the journey toward a common Eucharist, in the sentiments of the Lord washing the Apostles' feet. In this extraordinarily holy moment, as we do this, we hear the cry of the blood of the Apostles Peter and Paul, the voice of the Church of the catacombs and of the martyrs of the Colosseum inviting us to exhaust all ways and all means to complete the holy work undertaken, that of the perfect recomposition of Christ's divided Church: This is not only to fulfill the Lord's will but also that the world may see the splendor of what is, according to our profession of faith, the Church's first property: unity.

The ecumenical movement, the Second Vatican Council, the pan-Orthodox conferences, the Lambeth conferences and the pan-Christian congresses of the other Christian Churches and confessions, contacts with Your Holiness and between other Christian leaders have laid bare before the eyes of all the weighty wrong of the division of the Church and this in such a way that it is not possible that there should be today a local Church, a responsible pastor or Christian teacher who does not realize the absolute urgency of healing the evil.

On the other hand, the fact that we have all emerged from our isolation and self-sufficiency to search for the solid ground on which the undivided Church was founded, has revealed to us the truth that what unites us is more than what divides us.

These two facts fill our hearts with the certain hope that it will be the entire Catholic Church and the entire Orthodox Church which by common agreement and with a sense of their responsibility, will strike out along the way to their union.

In this common journey, which will be a journey toward truth, a journey toward "what has been believed always, everywhere and by all", we are called upon to continue and intensify the dialogue of charity so as to make it into an event preceding the theological dialogue. As regards the mainly theological dialogue we will direct it on the one side toward interpretation of what is already experienced in common in the Church and on the other side toward research in a spirit of charity and edification, and toward the expression of truth in a spirit of service.

Thus we hope to succeed in appreciating exactly and in distinguishing between those points of the faith which must necessarily be confessed in common and those other elements of the life of the Church which, since they do not touch on faith, can freely constitute, in accordance with the traditions of each of the Churches, the proper aspects of the life of each of them, aspects which are respected by the other.

We cannot, of course, determine how long the journey will take. It is a matter of faith in the final result, of many prayers, of holy patience, of assiduous work, but it is above all a matter of charity. In fact, it is only in charity that we will be able to purify ourselves from all the negative elements we have inherited from the past, that we will be able to remove the obstacles which arise, that we will be able to re-establish fully mutual brotherly trust and that, by creating in mutual respect a new mentality— the mentality of kinship—we will be able to construct in a stable and secure manner the unity of our churches in Christ Jesus, Who is the Head of the Church.

That is why we wanted to dedicate to the Faith, to the renewal and deepening of the Faith, this nineteenth centenary of Peter and Paul's martyrdom, their supreme witness of their faith, love (cf. *Jn.* 15, 13) and hope. How can there be a renewal if it does not result in a strengthening of faith, a more fervent charity, a greater certitude of hope; if it does not revive our faith in this deep mysterious communion effected between us by a like obedience to Christ's Gospel, by the same Sacraments, and especially by the same Baptism and the same priesthood which celebrates the same Eucharist, Christ's one sacrifice, a like episcopacy received from the Apostles to guide God's People to the Lord and preach His word to it (*Unitatis Redintegratio,* 15–17)? There we have so many ways which the Holy Spirit uses to bring us with our whole being towards the fullness of this communion already so rich yet still incomplete, uniting us in the mystery of the Church.

We come now to the other aspect of the action of the Spirit that we mentioned when we began, His action in each member of the Christian Faithful, the fruits of holiness and generosity it produces, another fundamental prerequisite for our drawing closer to one another: change of heart (*UR,* 7) which enables us in our personal life to hear and carry out with ever greater docility the bidding of the Spirit. Without this effort, which must be unceasing, to be faithful to the Holy Spirit Who transforms us into the likeness of the Son (cf. II *Cor.* 3, 11) there can be no true lasting brotherhood. It is only by becoming truly sons in the Son (cf. I *Jn.* 3, 1–2) that we also truly become in a mysterious manner brothers of one another. "We can achieve depth and ease in strengthening mutual brotherhood to the degree that we enjoy profound communion with the Father, the Word and the Spirit" (*UR,* 7). Besides, this effort for holiness provides the setting for the entire common heritage we have recently alluded to, which the Second Vatican Council saw fit to mention at length (UR, 13–18). What help we also have and what bonds of brotherhood in knowing by faith that in this quest to make Christ our own (cf. *Phil.* 3, 12), "we are surrounded by so great a cloud of witnesses" (*Heb.* 12, 1), among whom are, above all, the martyrs of our common faith who are, as you said so graciously when you wrote to announce your visit, the finest ornament of the Church of Rome. All these saints of the East and West are with us here, rejoicing and praying Him Who has begun this wonderful work to bring it to completion. All these saints also, who amid innumerable difficulties, sufferings and temptations remained steadfast as if they saw the invisible, teach us by their example to strain forward to what lies ahead (cf. *Phil.* 3, 13) "looking to Jesus the pioneer and perfecter of our faith" (*Heb.* 12, 2).

All this is certainly brought to our minds and expressed symbolically in the fact that your visit is taking place when the Church of the West is preparing to celebrate the feast of All Saints. We shall look with eyes of faith on this assembly of the people of the elect, gathered around Christ, risen and glorious, seated at the right hand of the Father, and united in a fraternal love that nothing must be allowed to lessen, and inspired alone by the desire to carry out what the Spirit asks of the Church, we shall, in a hope stronger than all obstacles, go forward *in the name of the Lord.*

b. Address *of Paul VI to Athenagoras I* *

You, dearly esteemed Brother, have for a considerable time made no secret of your desire to visit us in our Church of Rome. Now today we see that the Lord has allowed us to have you in our midst, the representative of the traditions of the Churches "of Pontus, Galatia, Cappadocia, Asia and Bithynia" to which "Peter, the apostle of Jesus Christ" (I *Pet.* 1, 1), long ago wrote his letter, a faithful reflection of the life, faith and hope of the early Church. That letter with its instruction and exhortations also carried the greetings of the Church of Rome to those Churches (cf. I *Pet.* 5, 13). It is thus a first testimony to the relations which developed so fruitfully in the following centuries, although we must admit that these have not been without clashes and misunderstanding. Even after the unhappy breach between us had been made, efforts were unceasing, notably in the 13th and 15th centuries, to repair it. Alas, these attempts did not have lasting positive effects. But we may ask if they have ever been freer than they are today of every political element or of any other purpose than the sole desire of realizing Christ's will for His Church. In fact, on both sides we are impelled by the single desire of purifying our souls in obedience to truth to love one another sincerely as brothers, loving one another earnestly from the heart (cf. I *Pet.* 1, 22). This rightness of our intentions and the sincerity of our decision are surely a sign of the Holy Spirit's action, His powerful action of profound renewal that we are

* October 26, in reply to Athenagoras I, St. Peter's Basilica. Extracts: *AAS* 59 (1967), pp. 1048–1053. SPCU *IS,* 3 (1967), pp. 16–18.

experiencing and marvelling at in the Church and in every member of the Christian Faithful.

We are pleased to repeat this and to reflect on it with you during this Year of the Faith at the beginning of which we desired to visit you in your noble country. In visiting Smyrna and Ephesus we heard echoing in our hearts the message addressed by the Spirit through John to the Churches of Asia Minor: "He who has an ear, let him hear what the Spirit says to the Churches" (*Rev.* 2, 7, 11, 17, 29; 3, 6, 13, 22). The Spirit gives us to know Christ (cf. I *Cor.* 12, 3), to guard the truths entrusted to the Church (cf. II *Tim.* 1, 14), to penetrate the mystery of God (cf. I *Cor.* 2, 11) and His truth (cf. *Jn.* 16, 13), for He is life (cf. *Gal.* 5, 25) and inward transformation (cf. *Rom.* 8, 9, 13). And He demands with greater insistence than ever that we be one that the world may believe (cf. *Jn.* 17, 21). This request of the Holy Spirit we see manifested first of all in the movement of renewal that He is bringing about everywhere in the Church. This renewal, the desire to be more attentive and receptive in our faithfulness, is in fact the most fundamental prerequisite for our drawing closer to one another (*Unitatis Redintegratio,* 6). The Second Vatican Council in the Catholic Church is one of its stages. Its decisions are being followed out with prudence and determination on every level of the Church's life. The Synod of Bishops gathered here, is a sign of it; today when problems are on a world scale it guarantees in new forms a better cooperation between local Churches and the Church of Rome which presides in charity (St. Ignatius, *Rom.* title). We have also undertaken the revision of our Canon Law, and without waiting for its completion have already promulgated new directives with a view to removing certain obstacles to development in the daily life of the Church and of the brotherhood we are increasingly finding again between the Orthodox Church and the Catholic Church.

We know that a like effort for renewal is in progress in the Orthodox Church and we are following its development with love and attention. You also are experiencing the need we have mentioned of securing a better cooperation between local Churches. The first Panorthodox Conference at Rhodes, the fruit in great measure of the patient and persevering efforts of Your Holiness, marked an important stage on this path, and it is significant that the program it set itself, although worked out previously and independently, bears in essentials a striking resemblance to that of the Second Vatican Council. Is that not a further sign of the Spirit's action, urging our Churches to active preparation so as to make possible the re-establishment of their full communion with one another?

We should on both sides take courage and follow up this effort developing it as much as we possibly can by contacts and by a cooperation whose forms we should work out together. Far more than by a discussion of the past, it is in a positive collaboration towards giving a response to what the Spirit asks of the Church today that we shall eventually surmount the obstacles still separating us.

If in our efforts for renewal we see a sign of the action of the Spirit urging us on to re-establish full communion with one another and preparing us for it, does not the contemporary world, filled with unbelief in many forms, also give us a peremptory reminder of the need we have for unity with one another? If the unity of Christ's disciples was given as the great sign that was to call forth the faith of the world, is not the unbelief of many of our contemporaries also a way whereby the Spirit speaks to the Churches, causing in them a fresh awareness of the urgency there is to fulfil this precept of Christ, Who died "to gather into one the children of God who are scattered abroad" (*Jn.* 11, 52)? This common witness, one yet varied, decided and persuasive, of a faith humbly self-confident, springing up in love and radiating hope, is without doubt the foremost demand that the Spirit makes of the Churches today.

c. Address *of Athenagoras to Augustine Cardinal Bea**

As we are thus bearers of this precious treasure, we are called in our apostolic ministry to dedicate all our activity towards the end that throughout the world there might shine forth the apostolicity of the Holy Church of Christ in holiness and in unity so that its witness to the world might be more effective, that the proclamation of the Gospel might be made to every creature, and that the grace and the kingdom of God might come upon all men.

For this reason we have come, that, along with the holy Head of the Roman Catholic Church, so dearly loved and deeply esteemed by us, and together with all of you we might give common witness to that common desire which now possesses all of us: to follow along that path in a spirit of love and patience as each of us corrects the errors of the past and everything which has contributed to our division, and makes straight the ways of the Lord.

Our thoughts also go out to that great and holy moment when the Bishops of the East and of the West, in a common celebration of the Eucharist around the same altar, will raise up the chalice of the Lord. Perhaps that hour will be slow in coming. The hour of love, however, is already here; it is this one.

Let us love one another, brothers, that with one accord we may make our profession of faith.

* October 26, at a reception in honor of the Patriarch, given by the Holy See, Vatican City. Extracts: SPCU *IS,* 3 (1967), p. 19.

d. Common Declaration of Paul VI and Athenagoras I*

Pope Paul VI and the Ecumenical Patriarch Athenagoras I give thanks in the Holy Spirit to God, the author and finisher of all good works, for enabling them to meet once again in the holy city of Rome in order to pray together with the Bishops of the Synod of the Roman Catholic Church and with the faithful people of this city, to greet one another with a kiss of peace, and to converse together in a spirit of charity and brotherly frankness.

While recognizing that there is still a long way to go on the road toward the unity of all Christians and that between the Roman Catholic Church and the Orthodox Church there still remain points to clarify and obstacles to surmount before attaining that unity in the profession of faith necessary for re-establishing full communion, they rejoice in the fact that their meeting was able to contribute to their Churches' rediscovering themselves still more as sister Churches.

In the prayers they offered, in their public statements and in their private conversation, the Pope and the Patriarch wished to emphasize their conviction that an essential element in the restoration of full communion between the Roman Catholic Church on the one side and the Orthodox Church on the other, is to be found within the framework of the renewal of the Church and of Christians in fidelity to the traditions of the Fathers and to the inspirations of the Holy Spirit Who remains always with the Church.

They recognize that the true dialogue of charity, which should be at the basis of all relations between themselves and between their Churches, must be rooted in total fidelity to the one Lord Jesus Christ and in mutual respect for each one's traditions. Every element which can strengthen the bonds of charity, of communion, and of common action is a cause for spiritual rejoicing and should be promoted; anything which can harm this charity, communion and common action is to be eliminated with the grace of God and the creative strength of the Holy Spirit.

Pope Paul VI and the Ecumenical Patriarch Athenagoras I are convinced that the dialogue of charity between their Churches must bear fruits of a cooperation which would not be self-seeking, in the field of common action at the pastoral, social and intellectual levels, with mutual respect for each one's fidelity to his own Church. They desire that regular and profound contacts may be maintained between Catholic and Orthodox pastors for the good of their faithful. The Roman Catholic Church and the Ecumenical Patriarchate are ready to study concrete ways of solving pastoral problems, especially those connected with marriages between Catholics and Orthodox. They hope for better cooperation in works of

---

* October 28, at the end of the Patriarch's visit. *AAS* 59 (1967), pp. 1054–1055.

charity, in aid to refugees and those who are suffering and in the promotion of justice and peace in the world.

In order to prepare fruitful contacts between the Roman Catholic Church and the Orthodox Church, the Pope and the Patriarch give their blessing and pastoral support to all efforts for cooperation between Catholic and Orthodox scholars in the fields of historical studies, of studies in the traditions of the Churches, of patristics, of liturgy and of a presentation of the Gospel which corresponds at one and the same time with the authentic message of the Lord and with the needs and hopes of today's world. The spirit which should inspire these efforts is one of loyalty to truth and of mutual understanding, with an effective desire to avoid the bitterness of the past and every kind of spiritual or intellectual domination.

Paul VI and Athenagoras I remind government authorities and all the world's peoples of the thirst for peace and justice which lies in the hearts of all men. In the name of the Lord, they implore them to seek out every means to promote this peace and this justice in all countries of the world.

4. Further Contacts Between the Holy See and the Patriarchate*

a. Paul VI to Athenagoras **

It is a great comfort to us to know how many pastors and faithful have drawn from the events of these recent months fresh inspiration to enter into the dialogue of charity which should lead us to rediscover full communion in the love of Christ and in the service of our neighbour. It is indeed above all the Christian people, led by its pastors, which ardently desires to see the dawn of the day when the Lord will give them the grace to celebrate together the Sacred Eucharist and through which this communion is fully signified and bestowed on us.

Our heart is thus full of hope. God, who has begun this work will complete it (cf. *Phil.* 1, 6). Trusting in Him who has promised to be always with us (cf. *Mt.* 28, 20) and in His Spirit who by virtue of the Gospel creates and continually renews the Church's youth, setting it on the path of perfect union with its Spouse, We express to you, dear brother in Christ, Our firm will to continue and deepen Our efforts in common with you and with all the venerable heads of the Orthodox Churches that in us and through us may be wrought the mysterious designs of God for the world which He made and loves with an eternal love.

---

* Included here are but a few of the papal messages exchanged with Athenagoras I, and after his death (July 7, 1972), with his successor, Dimitrios I. There were also visits between official delegations of the two Churches. Such contacts continued during the pontificates of John Paul I and John Paul II.

** Letter of March 13, 1968. Extract: SPCU *IS,* 5 (1968), p. 9.

b. Athenagoras I to Paul VI*

The work of furthering charity among the brethren and of unity within the Church is a godly one; we, therefore, are co-workers with God.

It is right that, having been granted this gift of co-operating with God and of preparing the way to rapprochement between the Churches and towards union, we should again and with frequency give praise to him who has accomplished such wonders.

c. Athenagoras I to Paul VI**

Actually, even if the Eastern Church and the Western Church are separated, for causes known to the Lord, they are not divided, however, in the substance of communion in the mystery of Jesus, God made man, and of his divine-human Church.

We have broken away from mutual love and we are deprived of the boon of unanimous confession of Christ's faith; we have been deprived of the blessing of going up together towards the one altar for the sacrifice instituted by the Lord shortly before his passion; we have been deprived of the blessing of perfect and unanimous harmonious communion in the same precious eucharistic Body and Blood, even if we have never ceased to acknowledge that the apostolic priesthood and the sacrament of the divine Eucharist of each of us are both valid.

But lo! at the present time there is abundantly manifested the anxious desire of the faithful of both East and West to enjoy unanimously in love the communion of the truth of the faith and of its profession, which is celebrated and fulfilled in the same holy cup; and grace has been shed on us abundantly. Illuminated by this grace, today we see clearly that the holy cause of the visible unity of the Church and of the full communion of the faithful in it is not a work subject to human reasonings and desires, the conceptions of man being insecure, but an experience lived in the life of Christ who is in his Body, the Church.

As, in the course of history, we moved negatively towards division, so, through a new experience of life, we are called positively to walk towards perfect unity in concelebration and in the communion of Christ's precious Blood in the same holy chalice. We agree with Your Holiness that it is necessary to strengthen the community of ecclesiastical life in the East and in the West, promoting a real and sure brotherhood at the level of the clergy and of the people of the Roman Catholic and Orthodox Church.

We are writing to you from the East a few days before the Lord's passion. The table is ready in the Upper Room and Our Lord wishes to eat the paschal supper with us. Shall we say no?

It is true, the obstacles arising from historical inheritance and other

* Letter of May 28, 1968. Extract: SPCU *IS,* 5 (1968), p. 8.
** Letter of March 21, 1971. Extract: SPCU *IS,* 15 (1971), pp. 4–5.

origins still remain and the enemy of the Kingdom of God maintains them. But have we not believed in Him who said that things impossible for men are possible for God and that everything is possible for him who believes?

d. *Paul VI to Metropolitan Meliton* *

Rejoicing at having re-discovered that (the Patriarchate of Constantinople and the Church of Rome) are branches of the same tree, born of the same root, they are now suffering at not having yet been able to consummate, by drinking at the same mystical chalice, that perfect communion which sanctions between the two communities the organic and canonical union characteristic of the one Church of Christ.

And, Metropolitan Meliton, kindly tell that saintly Patriarch and the venerated Brothers and Faithful gathered around him, how this happy celebration, which took place in the Church that the historical and theological tradition of the Western Church calls "omnium urbis et orbis ecclesiarum mater et caput" (Clem. XII) because it is the Cathedral of the Bishop of Rome, the successor of blessed Peter the Apostle, far from flattering our human ambition because of the pastoral office entrusted by Christ to be one who sits on this chair, namely, to act as "the perpetual and visible source and foundation of the unity of the bishops and of the multitude of the faithful" (*Lumen Gentium,* no. 23), has profoundly recalled to our conscience this weighty privilege of ours. Here, more than elsewhere, we feel ourself "a servant of the servants of God". Here we think of ourself as a brother with our brothers in the episcopate and in collegial solidarity with them. Here we think of the resolution of another great predecessor, Gregory the Great, who, while asserting his apostolic function (cf. *Reg.* 13, 50), wished to consider the honor of the whole Church and the efficiency of the individual local Bishops, his own honor (cf. *Reg.* 8, 30: P.L. 77, 933). Here we remember St. Cyprian's conception of the unity of the Church: "una Ecclesia per totum mundum in multa membra divisa" (*Ep* 36, 4), that is, like a composite and articulated body, in which parts and groups can be modelled in particular typical forms, and functions can be distinct, though fraternal and converging. Here, in the heart of unity and at the center of catholicity, we dream of the living beauty of the Bride of Christ, the Church, wrapped in her many-colored

---

* January 25, 1972. The Pope delivered the address in the Lateran, the Cathedral of Rome, during a Prayer Celebration on the occasion of the Week of Prayer for Christian Unity. Besides "the cardinals, bishops, prelates and clergy of the Roman Curia and of the Diocese of Rome with the faithful People of the Roman Church," an Orthodox delegation from the Patriarchate of Constantinople also participated. The leader of the delegation was Metropolitan Meliton of Chalcedon, who on the previous day had presented the Pope with *Tomos Agapis* (trans. *Volume of Charity*), containing all the documents exchanged between the Patriarchate and the Holy See, 1958–1970. Extracts: *AAS* 64 (1972), pp. 195–198. English SPCU *IS* 16 (1972), pp. 9–10.

garment (Ps. 44, 15), clothed, we mean, in a legitimate pluralism of traditional expressions. Here we seem to hear the limpid echo of a distant voice of yours: "O you, Peter, the foundation stone of faith!" (cf. Menei, V, 394).

So it remains for us to invoke that divine assistance which strengthens our weakness in practicing the necessary virtues in order that ecumenism can reach its happy conclusion. We will say with St. Paul that we are "sure that he who began a good work in you will bring it to completion at the day of Jesus Christ" (*Phil* 1, 6), convinced that at the completion of the great enterprise of composing the unity of Christians again, one condition will necessarily be requested of all of us, a dilatation of charity: "Dilatentur spatia caritatis", may the frontiers of love be expanded, we will say, to use an expression of St. Augustine that is dear to us (*Serm* 69; P.L. 38, 440–441). A dilatation of charity: which will make it possible for us all to find ourselves once more brothers in the same Church, members of the same body of Christ. Then we will add to the "Tomos Agapis" a new, last and splendid page: the page of unity.

e. Paul VI to the Holy Synod of Constantinople*

We have heard with great emotion of the death of our brother and dear friend in Christ, His Holiness Patriarch Athenagoras. We send you our most sorrowful condolence on the loss which has struck the entire Orthodox Church, and we pray the Lord to receive into His heavenly Kingdom him who was the great protagonist of reconciliation between all Christians and between our two churches in particular.

We recall the encounters we had with the Venerable deceased Patriarch at Jerusalem, Istanbul and Rome; and we render thanks to the Lord in the hope that the work begun by Athenagoras I will be continued, for the greater glory of God and the good of His Church.

We unite ourselves with you in prayer on this day of sorrow and we recommend your Church to the favour of the Lord.

f. Paul VI to those in St. Peter's Square**

... (On) the death of the venerated Greek Orthodox Patriarch of Constantinople, Athenagoras. The whole world spoke about it with the reverence and admiration due to superior men who personify an idea which invests the destinies of history and tends to interpret the thoughts of God. Athenagoras, even in his exterior, majestic and hieratic appearance, revealed his inner dignity, and his grave and simple conversation had accents of simple evangelical goodness. He commanded reverence and

---

* July 7, 1972. A telegram. SPCU *IS,* 19 (1973), p. 4
** July 9, 1973, before the Pope recited the noon "Angelus". Extracts: SPCU *IS,* 19 (1973), p. 4.

sympathy. And we also are among those who greatly admired and loved him; and for us he had a friendship and trust that always moved us, the memory of which now increases our sorrow, and our hope is that we may still have him as a brother close to us in the Communion of the Saints.

You know why we recommend this great man to you, a man of a venerated Church but one which is still not joined to our Catholic Church: it is because he was a constant advocate and apostle of the reunification of the Greek Orthodox Church with the Church of Rome and also with the other Churches and Christian communities which are not yet reintegrated in the one communion of the Mystical Body of Christ.

Three times we had the good fortune of meeting him personally, and a hundred times have we exchanged letters, always mutually promising to make every effort to re-establish perfect unity in faith and in the love of Christ among us, and he always synthesized his feelings in one supreme hope: that of being able to drink from the same chalice with us, that is, to celebrate the eucharistic sacrifice together, the synthesis and the crown of our common ecclesial identification with Christ. And this we too have so much desired.

Now this unfulfilled desire must remain his heritage and our task. In our devoted remembrance of Patriarch Athenagoras, let us pray that through the intercession of the Blessed Virgin Mary, the Mother of Christ and of His Church, this hope may be fulfilled.

g. Paul VI to Dimitrios I*

Our envoy will also bring you, venerable Brother, the expression of our firm hope that the Lord will grant us the light and strength necessary for reaching the end of the road leading to the full communion of our Churches. We have begun to walk along this road with your predecessor Athenagoras I, whom we had the joy of meeting several times and whom we esteemed and loved so deeply. We avail ourself of the occasion to assure you that not only do we pray continually for this intention but that, in order to accomplish this work, we are ready to collaborate in all the initiatives at present judged possible, in the spheres of both study and action.

h. Dimitrios I to Paul VI**

By means of this our fraternal letter to Your Holiness, which is our reply, we state that it is also our holy desire that the road once embarked upon, through the will and good pleasure of God, in these recent years,

---

* November 20, 1973. A letter delivered by John Cardinal Willebrands, SPCU President, as papal envoy to the Holy Synod, celebrating the feast of St. Andrew, patron of the Church of Constantinople. Extract: SPCU *IS,* 23 (1974), p. 14.
** Letter of December 6, 1973. Extract: SPCU *IS,* 23 (1974), p. 15.

towards unity should not be limited to the mere rediscovery of communion of brotherly love, but should consist in a widening of encounters and collaboration and should be extended—having in common thoughts, dispositions and action—to the entire field of the Churches of East and West, in holiness, fidelity and veneration towards the truth transmitted by the Apostles and towards the consciousness of the structure of the Church, until we attain to full and perfect unity, unity in faith and in the truth of our common Saviour and Lord Jesus Christ, in the common profession of faith, to his glory and to that of the Church, which is One, Holy, Catholic and Apostolic.

i. Dimitrios I to Paul VI*

Actuated by love of God, serving Him and Him only, following the path of his Love, our eyes fixed to the end on the ultimate, perfect aim, that is, unity in love, confession of the one Faith in our Lord Jesus Christ, and, by this confession, the attainment of communion in the Holy Eucharist, here we are, by divine Providence, ten years after the cancelling of the millenary anathema which had troubled the holy life of our Churches, by a condemnation of which God alone is the judge.

With a deep love of the Holy Church, we present to the Love of the Divine Word the blessed event itself—with all its historic significance— and also the celebration of its tenth anniversary.

Living, through his mercy, the mystery of the Lord's Body in the East as a Bishop—the least of Bishops—and watching as is fitting over the Holy Church and the world within her, we have acquired the conviction that, in the Church, the time for words is past. In the world, words, which still circulate, lead it astray; but we, although in the world, are not of the world.

Contemplating, from the East, the Church and the world in this way, we think that the world is now being judged.

Where, then, is the Church, O Holy Brother? At the very center of this judgment, or outside it? It is not to Your loved and respected Holiness that we are posing this question, but to ourselves and, through us, to the whole militant Church of Christ on earth.

Evaluating, therefore, from here what concerns the Church, we venture to say to Your Holiness that up to now we have not run in vain, bearing aloft the testimony of the Lord's Cross in this sacred land of the East, and that the hour of the Word, which transcends our words, the hour of God's Word, has already struck.

---

* Message of December 14, 1975. On this Sunday, the Pope presided at a celebration in the Sistine Chapel to commemorate the tenth anniversary of "the lifting of the anathemas" (Dec. 7, 1965). A similar ceremony took place in the Church of St. George in the Phanar, presided over by Dimitrios I. This message was read at the Sistine Chapel ceremony. Extracts: SPCU *IS,* 31 (1976), p. 2.

It is in the Word of God that our Holy Church of Christ in Constantinople embraced the Bishop of Rome and the Holy Church of Rome, in an act which is like a perfume of praise rising towards God from the pentarchy of the One, Holy, Catholic and Apostolic Church, in which the Bishop of Rome is designated to preside in love and honor; it embraces him, rendering him all the honor that is due to him through this designation.

j. Paul VI's Response to Dimitrios I*

Yes, we can still see vividly before our eyes the magnificent spectacle of the celebration in St. Peter's Basilica, ten years ago, parallel to what was happening in the church of St. George of the Phanar, when we carried out the solemn and sacred ecclesial act of lifting the ancient anathemas, an act with which we wished to remove the memory of these events for ever from the memory and the heart of the Church.

The enthusiasm and piety with which this action was received by the praying congregation in St. Peter's Basilica showed us clearly that this event was really desired by the Lord. In fact the Council Fathers, who were finishing their conciliar work with God's blessing, were present on that occasion, as were the religious families and an immense multitude of laymen from various parts of the world.

The conscience of the faithful of the Church saw in this act a sign of atonement for regrettable acts on both sides and the manifestation of a determination to construct together, in obedience to the Lord, a new era of brotherhood, which should lead the Catholic Church and the Orthodox Church, "with the help of God, to live once more, for the greater good of souls and the coming of the kingdom of God, in the full communion of faith, brotherly concord and sacramental life which existed between them in the course of the first millennium of the Church's life" (Joint Declaration of 7 December, 1965: *AAS* 58, 1966, p. 21).

Ten years after this event, we renew to the Lord our fervent and humble gratitude, now enriched with new and even more important reasons. This act has, in fact, set free so many hearts which, up till then, had been prisoners of their bitterness, locked in reciprocal distrust. Mutual charity has found its intensity again and has become active once more. All of us, at the same moment, heard the voice of the Lord, asking each of us: "Where is your brother?" (*Gen* 4, 9). Then we began to look for one another and we met as brothers on two other occasions with the venerated Patriarch Athenagoras of holy memory, whom we esteemed and loved so much, and on various other occasions with so many worthy pastors of the Eastern and Western Churches. These new dispositions of spirit have

---

* Discourse of December 14, 1975, in the Sistine Chapel, after the above message of Dimitrios I had been read. Extracts: SPCU *IS,* 31 (1976), pp. 3–4.

spread more and more through the action of the Holy Spirit within the Christian people.

In this way, a deep purification of memory clears an ever wider path for itself. It was in this perspective that the Second Vatican Council had clearly declared: "It is from newness of attitudes, from self-denial and unstinted love, that yearnings for unity take their rise and grow toward maturity" (Decree *Unitatis Redintegratio,* n. 7).

The Holy Spirit has enlightened our intelligences and has brought us to see with increased lucidity that the Catholic Church and the Orthodox Church are united by such a deep communion that very little is lacking to reach the fullness authorizing a common celebration of the Lord's Eucharist "by which the unity of the Church is both signified and brought about" (ibid., n. 2). In this way more stress is laid on the fact that we have in common the same sacraments, efficacious signs of our communion with God, and particularly the same priesthood, which celebrates the same Eucharist of the Lord, as well as the same episcopate received in the same apostolic succession to guide the people of God; and also that "for centuries, celebrating together the ecumenical councils that have defended the deposit of the faith against all alteration", we have lived "this life of sister-Churches" (Brief *Anno Ineunte: AAS* 59, 1967, p. 853).

It is charity that has enabled us to become aware of the depth of our unity. In the course of recent years, we have also seen the development of a sense of joint responsibility as regards the preaching of the Gospel to every creature, which is seriously harmed by the persisting division among Christians (Decree *UR,* n. 1).

Today the relations between our Churches are entering a new stage with the creation of new instruments of dialogue, which, based on the great acquisitions of the last ten years, are called to increase the communion between our two Churches until it reaches fullness.

Beloved Brothers, we bring you the good news that the Orthodox Churches, on the initiative of the Ecumenical Patriarchate, have decided to set up a pan-Orthodox commission to prepare the theological dialogue with the Catholic Church, and also that this same Patriarchate of Constantinople has set up its own special commission to converse with the Church of Rome. We deeply appreciate this initiative and we declare to you that we are quite ready to do the same on our side in order that we may approach full communion by progressing together along the "way that is better than any other" (1 *Cor* 12, 31), the way of mutual charity.

We hope that these new instruments will be bearers of Christian brotherhood and ecclesial communion, and inspired by a sincere love for the whole truth. There comes to our mind what we wrote to our beloved Brother Athenagoras, of venerable memory: "It is necessary in the first place, in the service of our holy faith, to work fraternally to find together suitable and gradual forms to develop and actualize in the life of our

Churches the communion which, though imperfect, exists already" (Cf. Brief *Anno Inuente: AAS* 59, 1967, p. 854).

In this way, our hearts being "rooted in love, founded on love" (*Eph* 3, 17), professing "the basic dogmas of the Christian faith" such as they "were defined in Ecumenical Councils held in the East" (Cf. Decree *UR*, n. 14), living of the life of the sacraments which we have in common and in the spirit of the communion of faith and charity that springs from these divine gifts and is strengthened in them, armed with power, by his Spirit, in order that the inner man may be strengthened (cf. *Eph* 3, 16), may we be able to progress together in identifying the divergences and difficulties that still separate our Churches, and finally overcome them by a reflection of faith and docility to the impulses of the Spirit.

In this way, in respect of a legitimate liturgical, spiritual, disciplinary and theological diversity (cf. Decree *UR*, nn. 14–17), may God grant us to construct, in a stable, certain way, full unity between our Churches!

This dialogue, long before arriving at its final purpose, must aim at influencing the life of our Churches, reviving common faith, increasing mutual charity, drawing closer the bonds of communion, bearing joint witness that Jesus Christ is the Lord and that "this alone of all the names under heaven has been appointed to men as the one by which we must needs be saved" (*Acts* 4, 12).

It is the divine Spirit Himself who asks us to carry out this task. And does not the unbelief that seems to be spreading in the world and to tempt even the faithful of our Churches, does it not call too for a better testimony of faith and unity on our side? Should not this situation drive us to do our utmost to reach, as soon as possible, this unity that Christ asked of his Father for those who believe in Him so that the world may believe (cf. *Jn* 17, 21)?

We are thus called to communicate to others the hope that is in us and to answer for it (cf. *1 Pet* 3, 1).

*k. Paul VI's Last Message Sent to Dimitrios I**

The presence at Rome of the delegation presided over by His Eminence the Metropolitan of Chalcedon, Meliton, and sent by Your beloved Holiness to take part in the liturgical celebration of the feast of the Apostles Peter and Paul, has increased our joy on this blessed day.

We are very grateful to Your Holiness for sending this delegation, and particularly for the fraternal message of communion and of charity which you willed to entrust to it for us. We are glad also to see that the contacts between our Churches are increasing and deepening in the common prayer and liturgy that are at the very heart of the Church's life.

The participation of a delegation from the Roman Catholic Church at

---

* July 15, 1978, three weeks before the Pope's death. Text: SPCU *IS*, 38 (1978), p. 2.

the celebrations for the feast of Saint Andrew in your patriarchal See, and that of a delegation from your Church at the celebrations for the feast of Saints Peter and Paul, concretise and reinforce the spiritual links uniting Catholic and Orthodox. These celebrations permit us to renew before the Lord our common involvement in the search for full unity. For the People of God, and in front of the world, they provide a witness to charity and they constitute the pledge of the hope that animates us to celebrate one day together the one Eucharist of the Lord.

In this spirit of fraternity and in this will of agreement to do all that is possible to obey the Lord's commandment, we express to you, beloved Brother, our affection in the Lord.

l. Dimitrios I's Declaration upon Paul VI's Death*

The Ecumenical Patriarchate and We ourselves have felt deep distress at the news of the death of Pope Paul VI. We share with all our hearts in the grief of the holy Roman Catholic Church and of the Roman Catholic world in general.

Pope Paul VI was one of the great popes of our time. He can be described unhesitatingly as the pope of renewal within the Roman Catholic Church, of reconciliation between Christians, of understanding and cooperation between all religions; as defending and working for human dignity with particular affection and concern for the abandoned and outcast; as the herald of the rights of man and of the suppression of racial discrimination; as the defender of religious freedom and the champion of world peace.

Pope Paul VI indeed lived up to his historic responsibilities at a crucial time of change within the Roman Catholic Church and within the Christian world, and in the midst of universal confusion. He combined apostolic courage with the wisdom and patience of the Fathers, taking as his constant rule the recommendation of the apostle Paul: '. . . and the greatest of these is charity' (*1 Cor* XIII, 13).

As ecumenical Patriarch and speaking for the ecumenical patriarchate at this moment of his departure from this world, we judge it our duty to recall and to emphasize five historic stages in the relations of the Ecumenical Patriarchate and the Vatican, and more generally in the reconciliation of the Orthodox and Roman Catholic Churches:

1. The meeting at Jerusalem between Pope Paul VI and our predecessor of everlasting memory, Patriarch Athenagoras I, in 1964.

2. The lifting of the anathemas between the Churches of Rome and Constantinople in 1965.

3. Pope Paul VI's visit to the ecumenical Patriarchate in 1967.

* August 7, 1978. Text: SPCU *IS* 38 (1978), p. 13.

4. The return visit of our predecessor Patriarch Athenagoras I in 1967 and his warm welcome at the Vatican.

5. Pope Paul VI's personal support for the great cause of dialogue between the Orthodox and Roman Catholic Churches and the movement from a dialogue of charity to the stage of theological dialogue.

We know that Pope Paul VI's swan song was his joy at Orthodoxy and Roman Catholicism entering into theological dialogue.

The Christian Church, all religions, the world and all mankind feel and should feel the loss of this pope's personality. We shall miss him, the evangelist in our time of charity, reconciliation and peace.

Nevertheless this evangelist leaves a holy legacy, great but also heavy upon us. As ecumenical Patriarch, we believe we too have a responsibility towards that legacy, and that an equal responsibility rests upon the Roman Catholic Church and upon him whom it will choose as successor to Paul VI.

Following the death of Paul VI we are all called to take up once again our responsibilities towards the reconciliation and unity of Christians and the building of universal peace.

*m. Dimitrios I's Declaration on John Paul I's Election**

In the present state of relations between Old and New Rome, and more generally between the Orthodox and Roman Catholic Churches, the election of a new Pope is no longer an internal matter for the Roman Catholic Church, but takes on an ecumenical dimension. After Popes John XXIII and Paul VI, the Pope of Rome now holds a new historic position, and a responsibility in the most sacred cause of Christ's Church.

In the same spirit of greeting the election of our brother the new Bishop of Rome, we voice to him not only our joy for the succession to the See of Rome, but also our hope for the continuation of the Christian ecumenical spirit of his two predecessors. We pray that our common Lord, Head of the Church, will strengthen the new Pope in the carrying out of his historical responsibilities towards the Holy Roman Catholic Church, towards Christianity and towards mankind.

5. John Paul II's Visit to Dimitrios I (Istanbul, November 29–30, 1979)

*a. Address of John Paul II to Dimitrios I***

The fundamental dogmas of Christian faith, of the Trinity and of the incarnate Word of God, born of the Virgin Mary, were defined by the Ecumenical Councils which were held in this city or in neighboring cities

---

* August 28, 1978. Extract: SPCU *IS,* 38 (1978), pp. 29–30.
** November 29, St. George's Cathedral of the Patriarchate. Extract: *L'Osservatore Romano* (Eng), Dec. 3.

(cf. Decree *Unitatis Redintegratio,* n. 14). The very formulation of our profession of faith, the *credo,* took place in these first Councils celebrated together by the East and the West. Nicaea, Constantinople, Ephesus, Chalcedon, are names known to all Christians. They are particularly familiar to those who pray, who study and who work in different ways for full unity between our sister-Churches.

Not only have we had in common these decisive Councils, pauses, as it were, in the life of the Church, but for a millennium these two sister-Churches have grown together and developed their great vital traditions.

The visit I am paying today is intended to signify a meeting in the common apostolic faith, to walk together towards this full unity which sad historical circumstances have wounded, especially in the course of the second millennium. How could I fail to express our firm hope in God in order that a new era may dawn?

b. *Welcoming Address of Dimitrios I to John Paul II**

Your coming here, full of Christian charity and simplicity, means far more than a mere meeting between two local bishops; we consider it a meeting of the Western and Eastern Churches.

For this reason the joy we feel on the occasion of this exceptional and historic visit of Your Holiness, is not limited either to this church or to this day, for our meeting is set in the universality and eternity of the divine redemption of mankind.

The meeting takes place locally but it is connected geographically according to the ecclesiastical formulation with the whole West and East—and according to the modern geographical formulation of ecumenism—it is connected also with the North and the South.

The meeting takes place today, but it is connected with the distant past, the past of the common Apostles, the common Fathers, the common Martyrs and Confessors, the Ecumenical Councils, concelebration on the same altar and communion in the same chalice. It is connected also with the recent past, the past of our two great predecessors, Pope Paul VI and Patriarch Athenagoras I. Moreover, this meeting today is intended for God's future—a future which will again live unity, again common confession, again full communion in the divine Eucharist.

We believe that at this moment the Lord is present among us here, and that the Paraclete is upon us—that the two brothers Peter and Andrew are rejoicing with us—that the spirits of the common Fathers and Martyrs are hovering over us, to inspire us. But at the same time we feel arriving right in front of us, right in front of our responsibility, the anxious expectation of the divided Christians, the anguish of the man without recognized human rights, without freedom, without justice, without bread,

---

* November 29, St. George's Cathedral. Extracts: *O.R.* (Eng), Dec. 3.

without medical care, without education, without security and without peace.

c. Homily of John Paul II in Holy Spirit Church*

Today, then, we are celebrating an apostle, the first of the apostles to be called, and this feast reminds us of this fundamental requirement of our vocation, of the vocation of the Church.

This apostle, the patron saint of the illustrious Church of Constantinople, is Peter's brother. Certainly, all the apostles are bound to one another by the new brotherhood that unites all those whose hearts are renewed by the Spirit of the Son (cf. Rom 8:15) and to whom the ministry of reconciliation is entrusted (cf. 2 Cor 5:18), but that does not suppress, far from it, the special bonds created by birth and upbringing in the same family. Andrew is Peter's brother. Andrew and Peter were brothers and, within the apostolic college, a greater intimacy must have bound them, a closer collaboration must have united them in the apostolic task.

Here again today's celebration reminds us that special bonds of brotherhood and intimacy exist between the Church of Rome and the Church of Constantinople, that a closer collaboration is natural between these two Churches.

Peter, Andrew's brother, is the leader of the apostles. Thanks to the inspiration of the Father, he fully recognized, in Jesus Christ, the Son of the living God (cf. Mt 16:16); owing to this faith, he received the name of Peter, in order that the Church may rest on this Rock (cf. Mt 16:18). He had the task of ensuring the harmony of apostolic preaching. A brother among brothers, he received the mission of strengthening them in the faith (cf. Lk 22:32); he is the first to have the responsibility of watching over the union of all, of ensuring the symphony of the holy Churches of God in faithfulness to "the faith which was once for all delivered to the saints" (Jude 3).

It is in this spirit, animated by these sentiments, that Peter's successor has wished on this day to visit the Church whose patron saint is Andrew, to visit its venerated pastor, all its hierarchy and all its faithful. He has wished to come and take part in its prayer. This visit to the first see of the Orthodox Church shows clearly the will of the whole Catholic Church to go forward in the march towards the unity of all, and also its conviction that the re-establishment of full communion with the Orthodox Church is a fundamental stage of the decisive progress of the whole ecumenical movement. Our division may not, perhaps, have been without an influence on the other divisions that followed it.

---

* November 29, during a concelebration of the Eucharist. Present at the Liturgy were Dimitrios I, the Armenian Patriarch Kalustian, and members of the Patriarchate's Holy Synod. Extracts: *O.R.* (Eng), Dec. 10.

For nearly a whole millennium, the two sister-Churches grew side by side, as two great vital and complementary traditions of the same Church of Christ, keeping not only peaceful and fruitful relations, but also concern for the indispensable communion in faith, prayer and charity, which they did not at any cost want to question, despite their different sensitivity. The second millennium, on the contrary, was darkened, apart from some fleeting bright intervals, by the distance which the two Churches took in regard to each other, with all the fatal consequences thereof. The wound is not yet healed. But the Lord can cure it and he bids us do our best to help the process. Here we are now at the end of the second millennium: is it not time to hasten towards perfect brotherly reconciliation, so that the dawn of the third millennium may find us standing side by side, in full communion, to bear witness together to salvation before the world, the evangelization of which is waiting for this sign of unity?

On the practical plane, today's visit also shows the importance that the Catholic Church attaches to the theological dialogue which is about to begin with the Orthodox Church. With realism and wisdom, in conformity with the wish of the Apostolic See of Rome and also with the desire of the pan-Orthodox Conferences, it had been decided to reestablish relations and contacts between the Catholic Church and the Orthodox Churches which would make it possible to recognize each other and create the atmosphere necessary for a fruitful theological dialogue. It was necessary to create again the context before trying to rewrite the texts together.

This period has rightly been called the dialogue of charity. This dialogue has made it possible to become aware again of the deep communion that already unites us, and enables us to consider each other and treat each other as sister-Churches. A great deal has already been done, but this effort must be continued. It is necessary to draw the consequences of this mutual theological rediscovery, wherever Catholics and Orthodox live together. Habits of isolation must be overcome in order to collaborate in all fields of pastoral action in which this collaboration is made possible by the almost complete communion that already exists between us.

We must not be afraid to reconsider, on both sides, and in consultation with one another, canonical rules established when awareness of our communion—now close even if it is still incomplete—was still dimmed, rules which, perhaps, no longer correspond to the results of the dialogue of charity and to the possibilities they have opened. It is important in order that the faithful on both sides realize the progress that has been made, and it would be desirable that those who are put in charge of the dialogue should be concerned to draw the consequences, for the life of the faithful, of future progress.

This theological dialogue which is about to begin now will have the task of overcoming the misunderstandings and disagreements which still exist between us, if not at the level of faith, at least at the level of theological formulation. It should take place not only in the atmosphere of the dialogue of charity, which must be developed and intensified, but also in an atmosphere of worship and availability.

It is only in worship, with a keen sense of the transcendence of the inexpressible mystery "which surpasses knowledge" (Eph 3:19), that we will be able to size up our divergences and "to lay . . . no greater burden than these necessary things" (Acts 15:28) to re-establish communion (cf. Decree *Unitatis Redintegratio,* n. 18). It seems to me, in fact, that the question we must ask ourselves is not so much whether we still have the right to remain separated. We must ask ourselves this question in the very name of our faithfulness to Christ's will for his Church, for which constant prayer must make us both more and more available in the course of the theological dialogue.

If the Church is called to gather men in praise of God, St Irenaeus, the great Doctor of the East and of the West, reminds us that "the glory of God is living man" (*Adv. Haer.* IV, 20, 7). Everything, in the Church, is ordained to allowing man to live really in this full freedom which comes from his communion with the Father through the Son in the Spirit. St Irenaeus, in fact, goes on at once: "and man's life is the vision of God", the vision of the Father manifested in the Word.

d. Discourse *of John Paul II on Feast of St. Andrew* *

Let us now extend our meditation to the mystery of the Church. St Andrew, the first one called, the Patron Saint of the Church of Constantinople, is the brother of St Peter, the leader of the apostles, the Founder with St Paul of the Church of Rome and its first Bishop. On the one hand, this fact recalls to us a drama of Christianity, the division between the East and the West, but it also recalls the deep reality of the communion that exists, in spite of all divergences, between the two Churches.

How we must thank the Lord for having brought forth, in the course of the last few decades, enlightened pioneers and indefatigable architects of unity, such as Patriarch Athenagoras, of venerated memory, and my great predecessors, Pope John XXIII—whose memory this city and this Church treasure—and Pope Paul VI who came to meet you before me! Their action was fruitful for the life of the Church and for the pursuit of full unity between our Churches, which rest on the one cornerstone, Christ, and are built on the foundation of the apostles.

The more and more intense contacts in the last few years have caused us to discover again the brotherhood between our two Churches and the reality of a communion between them, even if it is not perfect. The Spirit

* November 30, at end of the Liturgy concelebrated by Dimitrios I and the Holy Synod in the Orthodox Church of St. George. Extracts: *O.R.* (Eng), Dec. 10.

of God has also shown us more and more clearly the necessity of realizing full unity in order to bear a more effective witness for our time.

We are on the eve of the opening of the theological dialogue between the Catholic Church and the Orthodox Church as a whole. This is another important phase in the process towards unity. Starting from what we have in common, this dialogue will be called upon to identify, tackle and solve all the difficulties that still forbid us full unity. Tomorrow, I will take part in the celebration of the feast of St Andrew in the church of the Ecumenical Patriarchate. We will not be able to concelebrate. That is the most painful sign of the misfortune that befell the one Church of Christ with division. But, God be thanked, for some years we have now been celebrating together the feast of the patron saints of our Churches, as a token and actual desire for full concelebration. In Rome, we celebrate the feast of SS Peter and Paul in the presence of an Orthodox delegation, and at the Ecumenical Patriarchate the feast of St Andrew is celebrated with a Catholic delegation present.

Communion in prayer will lead us to full communion in the Eucharist. I venture to hope that this day is near. Personally, I would like it to be very near. Have we not already in common the same eucharistic faith and the true sacraments, by virtue of the apostolic succession? Let us hope that complete communion in faith, especially in the ecclesiological field, will soon permit this full "communicatio in sacris". My venerated predecessor, Pope Paul VI, had already desired to see this day, just like Patriarch Athenagoras I. Speaking of the latter immediately after his death, he expressed himself as follows: "He always summed up his sentiments in one supreme hope: to be able to 'drink from the same chalice' with us, that is, to celebrate together the eucharistic sacrifice, the synthesis and the crowning of common ecclesial identification with Christ. We, too, had longed for this so much! Now this unfulfilled desire must remain our heritage and our commitment" (Angelus of 9 July 1972). For my part, taking up this legacy, I ardently share this desire, which time and progress in union can only deepen.

And now, dear brothers and sisters, I ask you to pray fervently, in the course of this eucharistic sacrifice, for the full communion of our Churches. Progress in unity will be based on our efforts, on our theological work, on our repeated steps, and especially on our mutual charity; but it is at the same time a grace of the Lord ... Let us beseech him to remove the obstacles that have so far delayed the course towards full unity. Let us beseech him to give all those who are collaborating in the rapprochement his Holy Spirit, who will lead them towards full truth, expand their charity, and make them impatient for unity. Beseech him that we ourselves, pastors of the sister Churches, may be the best instruments of his plan, we whom Providence has chosen, at this hour of history, to govern these Churches, that is, to serve them as the Lord wishes, and thus serve the one Church, which is his Body.

In the course of the second millennium, our Churches had become petrified, as it were, in their separation. Now the third millennium of Christianity is drawing near. May the dawn of this new millennium rise on a Church that has found again her full unity, in order to bear witness better, in the midst of the exacerbated tensions of this world, to God's transcendent love, manifested in his Son Jesus Christ.

God alone knows the times and the moments. As for us, let us watch and pray, in hope, with the Virgin Mary, the Mother of God who keeps watch constantly over her Son's Church, as she kept watch over the apostles. Amen.

*e. Address of Dimitrios I on Feast of St. Andrew**

Christians of other Churches and confessions may have been wondering if this dialogue between the Roman Catholic Church and the Orthodox Church, the beginning of which we bless today, is our final purpose. We could both answer this question in the negative, and we could add at once that our further and principal aim is not just the unity of the two Churches, but the unity of all Christians in the one Lord and in participation in the same chalice.

To those non-Christians who might be wondering what significance Christian unity would have for them, if it would constitute a coalition and front of Christians against non-Christians, we could answer that the Christian unity pursued is not turned against anyone, but that it rather constitutes a positive service for all men, regardless of their sex, race, religion and social class—in accordance with the fundamental Christian principle that "there is neither Jew nor Greek, there is neither slave nor free, there is neither male nor female" (Gal 3:28).

Certainly, various obstacles rear up before us. In the first place we have the serious theological problems which concern essential chapters of Christian faith, for the solution of which we are starting the theological dialogue. But at the same time there are obstacles coming from mistrust, irresponsibility, fear—like that of the disciples in the garden of Gethsemane—non-theological factors concerning Christian differences, intolerance and fanaticism which set Christians and religions against one another—in a word, all the obstacles that come from the arms of Lucifer. It is from Lucifer, moreover, that there come all heresies and divisions and all opposition between man and God and between men themselves.

We live and work for the accomplishment of God's will and for the

---

* November 30, St. George Church, following discourse of John Paul II. Extracts: *O.R.* (Eng), Dec. 10.

preaching of love, unity and peace at a critical hour of the history of mankind. At an hour when the person and spirit of evil, Lucifer, is tempting humanity beyond its strength.

Really, Your Holiness, we find ourselves before an exaltation of temptation and of the activity of the Evil One in the world, in all fields, religious, social, cultural and political, to such an extent that we see before us a phenomenon, a sign of the times. To such an extent that we see in front of us a sole victim, man, the image of God. We are up against a phenomenon, a sign of the times, which can be described as a return to an age of religious fanaticism, wars of religion, and the self-destruction of men and their faith, and always in the name of God.

Before this image of mankind, an image that appears before us in its stark and tragic reality, when we are threatened with a diabolic anarchy, Your Holiness comes in our midst so that we may preach peace and goodness together in all directions.

f. Common Declaration*

We, Pope John Paul II, and the Ecumenical Patriarch Dimitrios I, give thanks to God who has granted us the possibility of meeting to celebrate together the feast of the apostle Andrew, the one first called and the brother of the apostle Peter. "Blessed be the God and Father of our Lord Jesus Christ, who has blessed us in Christ with every spiritual blessing in the heavenly places" (Eph 1:3).

Seeking only the glory of God through the accomplishment of his will, we affirm again our resolute determination to do everything possible to hasten the day when full communion will be re-established between the Catholic Church and the Orthodox Church and when we will at last be able to concelebrate the divine Eucharist.

We are grateful to our predecessors, Pope Paul VI and Patriarch Athenagoras I, for everything they did to reconcile our Churches and cause them to progress in unity.

The progress made in the preparatory stage permits us to announce that the theological dialogue is about to begin and to make public the list of the members of the mixed Catholic-Orthodox commission that will be responsible for it.

---

* November 30, Feast of St. Andrew. Signed by Pope and Patriarch in the Phanar of the Patriarchate. The constitution of the Mixed Catholic-Orthodox Commission for Theological Dialogue was also announced. The 31 Roman Catholic members are presided over by Cardinal John Willebrands, Archbishop of Utrecht and SPCU President. The Orthodox members represent the Ecumenical Patriarchate; the Patriarchates of Alexandria, of Antioch, of Jerusalem, of Moscow, of Serbia, of Rumania, and of Bulgaria; the Church of Cyprus, of Greece, of Georgia, and of Finland. Text: *O.R.* (Eng), Dec. 10.

This theological dialogue aims not only at progressing towards the re-establishment of full communion between the Catholic and Orthodox sister-Churches, but also at contributing to the multiple dialogues that are developing in the Christian world in search of its unity.

The dialogue of charity (cf. Jn 13:34; Eph 4:1–7), rooted in complete faithfulness to the one Lord Jesus Christ and to his will over his Church (cf. Jn 17:21), has opened up the way to better understanding of our mutual theological positions and, thereby, to new approaches to the theological work and to a new attitude with regard to the common past of our Churches. This purification of the collective memory of our Churches is an important fruit of the dialogue of charity and an indispensable condition of future progress. This dialogue of charity must continue and be intensified in the complex situation which we have inherited from the past, and which constitutes the reality in which our effort must take place today.

We want the progress in unity to open up new possibilities of dialogue and collaboration with believers of other religions, and with all men of goodwill, in order that love and brotherhood may prevail over hatred and opposition among men. We hope to contribute in this way to the coming of true peace in the world. We implore this gift of him who was, who is, and who will be, Christ our one Savior and our real peace.

g. Address of John Paul II to the Catholic Community in Ankara*

Today, for you Christians who reside in Turkey, your destiny is to live in the framework of a modern State—which makes provision for the free expression of their faith by all without identifying itself with any—and with persons who, in their vast majority, though not sharing the Christian faith, declare that they are "obedient to God", "submissive to God", and even "servants of God", according to their own words, which link us with the words of St Peter just quoted (cf. ibid. 2:16). They have, therefore, like you, the faith of Abraham in the one almighty and merciful God. You know that the Second Vatican Council spoke out openly on this subject, and I myself recalled in my first encyclical *Redemptor Hominis* that "the Council . . . expressed its esteem for the believers of Islam, whose faith also looks to Abraham" (n. 11).

Allow me to recall here before you these words of the Council's Declaration *Nostra Aetate:* "The Church has also a high regard for the Muslims. They worship God ("together with us", we read in another text of the Council, *Lumen Gentium,* n. 16), who is one, living and subsistent,

---

* November 28, during a prayer service in the Chapel of St. Paul at the Italian embassy. Extract: *O.R.* (Eng), Dec. 3.

merciful and almighty, the Creator of heaven and earth, who has also spoken to men. They strive to submit themselves without reserve to the hidden decrees of God, just as Abraham submitted himself to God's plan, to whose faith Muslims eagerly link their own. Although not acknowledging him as God, they worship Jesus as a prophet; his virgin Mother they also honour, and even at times devoutly invoke. Further, they await the day of judgment and the reward of God following the resurrection of the dead. For this reason they highly esteem an upright life and worship, especially by way of prayer, alms-deeds and fasting" (Declaration *Nostra Aetate* n. 3).

My brothers, when I think of this spiritual heritage and the value it has for man and for society, its capacity of offering, particularly to the young, guidance for life, filling the gap left by materialism, and giving a reliable foundation to social and juridical organization, I wonder if it is not urgent, precisely today when Christians and Moslems have entered a new period of history, to recognize and develop the spiritual bonds that unite us, in order to preserve and promote together for the benefit of all men, "peace, liberty, social justice and moral values" as the Council calls upon us to do (Declaration *Nostra Aetate,* ibid.).

Faith in God, professed by the spiritual descendants of Abraham— Christians, Moslems and Jews—when it is lived sincerely, when it penetrates life, is a certain foundation of the dignity, brotherhood and freedom of men and a principle of uprightness for moral conduct and life in society. And there is more: as a result of this faith in God the creator and transcendent, man finds himself at the summit of creation. He was created, the Bible teaches, "in the image and likeness of God" (Gen 1:27); for the Koran the sacred book of the Moslems, although man is made of dust, "God breathed into him his spirit and endowed him with hearing, sight and heart", that is, intelligence (Sura 32:8).

For the Moslem, the universe is destined to be subject to man as the representative of God; the Bible affirms that God ordered man to subdue the earth, but also to "till it and keep it" (Gen 2:15). As God's creature, man has rights which cannot be violated, but he is equally bound by the law of good and evil which is based on the order established by God. Thanks to this law, man will never submit to any idol. The Christian keeps to the solemn commandment: "You shall have no other gods before me" (Ex 30:3). On his side, the Moslem will always say: "God is the greatest".

I would like to take advantage of this meeting and the opportunity offered to me by the words that St Peter wrote to your predecessors to invite you to consider every day the deep roots of faith in God in whom also your Moslem fellow citizens believe, in order to draw from this the principle of a collaboration with a view to the progress of man, emulation in good, the extension of peace and brotherhood in free profession of the faith peculiar to each one.

6. Contacts between John Paul II and the Patriarchate

John Paul II to the Official Orthodox Delegation* (Vatican City, June 28, 1980)

The theological dialogue which has been opened officially in the island of Patmos is an important event, and in the relations between Catholics and Orthodox it is the major event not only of this year, but for centuries.** We are entering a new phase of our relations, for the theological dialogue constitutes an essential aspect of a wider dialogue between our Churches. The Catholic Church and the Orthodox Church as a whole are engaged in this dialogue. In this way we have found the general framework and the efficacious instrument to identify, in their real context, beyond preliminary prejudice and reservations, the difficulties of every kind which still prevent full communion.

The theme chosen for the first phase of the dialogue is the following: "The mystery of the Church and of the Eucharist in the light of the mystery of the Holy Trinity". This theme deserves the deepest consideration, for it takes us to the very heart of Christian identity. The fact of having accepted the proposal made by the two preparatory commissions, Catholic and Orthodox, to start out in the theological dialogue from what we have in common, offers this dialogue the most solid basis and the most promising perspective.

---

* Since 1977 an annual exchange of delegation visits takes place between the Ecumenical Patriarchate and the Holy See on their respective patron feast days (Saints Peter and Paul at Rome, June 29; Saint Andrew the Apostle at the Phanar, Constantinople, November 30). The Pope has urged that such meetings—"the dialogue of charity"—take place wherever Catholics and Orthodox live together, "in order to create gradually the necessary conditions for full unity." Extract: SPCU *IS*, 44(1980), p. 101.

** May 29–June 4, 1980. For the texts of major addresses on both sides, cf. SPCU *IS*, 44(1980), pp. 103–112. The Joint Commission unanimously adopted the agenda for the first phase of the dialogue as drawn up in 1978 by the preparatory working committee: the sacraments of the Church, a theological reflection on sacramental experience. Such dialogue should be freed as much as possible from "the problematic created by the scholastic theology on both sides" and should concentrate on more recent theological efforts which rely on "the tradition of the ancient Church," the Church as the realized expression of "the Sacrament of Christ" and the Eucharist as "the sacrament par excellence of the Church." Other questions are directly related; for example, the relation of the sacraments to "the structure and government of the Church (or the canonical unity of the Church") and the Eucharist as an expression of the local church gathered around one bishop and the communion of all the local churches. The long preparatory document has been published only in the Greek journal, *Orthodoxos Typos* (Athens), Dec. 19, 1980. John Paul II wrote Dimitrios I on Nov. 24, 1980: "The old differences that had led the Eastern and Western Churches to cease celebrating the Eucharist together are going to be tackled in a new and constructive way. Both the subject chosen for the first phase of the dialogue and its general perspectives bear witness to this." SPCU *IS*, 45(1981), p. 23.

II
THE RUSSIAN ORTHODOX PATRIARCHATE

1. Pope Paul VI to Patriarch Alexis*

The restoration of the patriarchate is an event which is full of meaning in the religious life of the Russian Orthodox Church. This return to the ancient traditions of your Church, which had been prepared for by many years of study and of work by the clergy and laity, represents an important step in the task of spiritual renewal of the Russian Orthodox Church. We hope that this reaffirmation of your ancient tradition will serve to deepen the religious spirit of your people and that it will be a source of renewed strength for those Christians who seek to bear witness to Christ in a world that has so much need of Him.

We are most happy also that God has granted that relations between our Churches should increasingly improve, particularly in recent years. If, in the past as in recent years, there have been difficulties and misunderstandings and especially some most regrettable happenings which have come between the Catholic and the Russian Orthodox Churches, we can see in the contacts that have been made in the recent past a token of a new development of brotherly love, of mutual understanding and of common effort to dispel the differences which still exist between the See of Rome and the Patriarchate of Moscow.

With this hope and again expressing our wish to do all in our power to reunite all Christ's disciples, as our Saviour so desires, in one single spirit and with one heart, in praising the Lord and as his faithful servants in the world of today, we recommend our delegates to Your Holiness and trust that he who is the source and the end of every good work will bless Your Holiness, your clergy and faithful and will lavish on you his joy, his strength and consolation.

2. Letters of Paul VI Concerning 1968 Czechoslovakia

Introduction

On April 28, 1950, the Catholic Byzantine rite Diocese of Prešov in Czechoslovakia was forcibly suppressed, and its more than 300,000 faithful were officially declared members of the Orthodox Church related to the Moscow Patriarchate. Then, in 1951 the Orthodox Church in Czechoslovakia had formed an autocephalous metropolis with four dioceses. In

---

* Letter of May 23, 1968, the Feast of the Ascension. On the occasion of the 50th anniversary "of that day on which the Synod of the whole Orthodox Church of Russia reestablished the patriarchal See of Moscow." A papal delegation, headed by Archbishop George Dwyer (Birmingham, England), was present at the Moscow celebrations. Extract: SPCU *IS,* 5 (1968), p. 9.

early 1968, in the new political climate brought about by President Svoba-
da's and Prime Minister Dubcek's government, the Eastern Catholics had
the opportunity to renew communion with the See of Rome. A majority of
the parishes opted for this restoration, and these decisions are still respected. But during the 1968 process, disputes broke out between Catholics and
Orthodox over controversial congregational choices, property rights, etc.
The disputes occasioned an exchange of letters with Paul VI from the
Patriarch of Moscow and the Metropolitan of Prague. Only the papal
letters are available.

a. To Patriarch Pimen *

We share your pain in knowing that the reaffirmation by certain
Catholics of the communion which they have preserved with this See of
Rome—despite the difficulties Your Holiness well knows—have been
accompanied by acts of violence and of coercion on one part and the other.
These acts are opposed to the spirit of understanding and fraternal charity
which ought to spring from our common profession of faith in our great
God and Savior, Jesus Christ.

We ought to recall that the Roman Catholic Church, as the Orthodox
Church, is based on the ancient canons of the Church, which hold firmly
that there is no council and thus no decision can be considered as conciliar
and valid without the participation and acceptance of the bishops, established by the Holy Spirit as successors of the Apostles and pastors of the
Lord's flock. That fundamental character of conciliarity was lacking in
1950, and in the preceding years, when certain groups have broken
relations of full common existing between the Holy See and certain local
Churches. In this context, one better understands how an important
number of faithful has maintained in their heart a spirit of that union and
manifest it when circumstances so permit.

We can nevertheless assure Your Holiness that Our profound desire
and Our firm will are that the solution of these problems ought to be
sought and found in an atmosphere of real collaboration, assuring both
sides complete respect for the freedom of each believer, manifesting christian charity which ought to reign between brothers, and rejecting completely all violence, all coercion of any form of indiscreet proselytism. We
will do whatever is possible, although present circumstances do not favor
us, to realize that desire in the concrete situation of Czechoslovakia.

In the past, the relations between our Churches sometimes suffered
because of factors foreign to the Gospel which we preach. If Our apostolic
charge does not permit us to refuse persons or groups of persons the
possibility of entering into full communion with the Roman Catholic

* October 21, 1968. The Patriarch's letter is dated August 14. French Extract: SPCU
Archives. TFS trans.

Church, be assured that We will never permit that for reasons relating strictly to personal conviction and freedom of conscience, to the exclusion of every motivation which could restore sentiments foreign to this conviction.

In the common declaration which God permitted Us to publish with His Holiness Patriarch Athenagoras in October 1967, one reads: "They (Pope Paul VI and Ecumenical Patriarch Athenagoras) recognize that the true dialogue of charity, which should be at the basis of all relations between themselves and between their Churches, must be rooted in total fidelity to the One Lord Jesus Christ and in mutual respect for each one's traditions. Every element which can strengthen the bonds of charity, of communion, and of common action is a cause for spiritual rejoicing and should be promoted; anything which can harm this charity, communion and common action is to be eliminated with the grace of God and the creative strength of the Holy Spirit" (*AAS*, 1967, p. 1054). These affirmations remain always valid for Us, and from the depths of Our heart, We wish to express them again to Your Holiness.

With these sentiments, We propose to Your Holiness that, through mutually suitable means, exchanges of views will take place between the Church of Rome and the Russian Orthodox Church in order to discuss what Your Holiness presents as an obstacle on the way to reinforcing the fraternity and love between the Roman Catholic Church and the Orthodox Churches. We have instructed our Secretariat for Promoting Christian Unity to be ready to receive eventual proposals from Your Holiness. We can assure Your Holiness that the Holy See does not cease, in the case which occupies us, to give directives which conform to an action of charity and mutual respect, on the occasion, in particular, of the controlled return of ecclesiastical properties.

b. To Dorotheos, Metropolitan of Prague and All Czechoslovakia*

With Your Beatitude we strongly deplore that the relations between the Catholic Church and the Orthodox Church in Czechoslovakia have been infected on both sides by the excess and violence which have accompanied the recent development of the religious situation in your country. Such acts are directly opposed to the spirit of understanding and brotherly love which ought to spring from our common profession of faith in our Savior Jesus Christ. Many times we have insistently given directives that everything be done to avoid such acts, and thus we are deeply satisfied to know of the common declaration which has been read on Sunday, November 17, in all the Catholic and Orthodox churches of Slovakia. We are

---

* December 3, 1968. The Metropolitan's letter is dated September 9. French Extract: SPCU Archives. TFS trans.

convinced that with such dispositions of mutual, fraternal generosity, the remaining difficulties could be regulated.

In the past the relations between the Catholic Church and the Orthodox Church in Czechoslovakia have been troubled for motives foreign to the Gospel we preach. Such as are the shadows of this sad history, we recall that the Catholic Church, as does the Orthodox Church, basing themselves on the canonical rules of the ancient Church, firmly holds that there can be no authentically canonical and valid decisions without the participation and acceptance of the bishops whom the Holy Spirit establishes as successors of the apostles and pastors of the Lord's flock. That fundamental character of conciliarity was lacking at the assembly which took place at Prešov, April 28, 1950. In this context one understands why an important number of faithful has maintained in their heart a spirit of that union and manifest it when circumstances so permit.

We can nevertheless assure Your Beatitude that our profound desire and our firm will are that the solution of these problems ought to be sought and found in an atmosphere of real collaboration which assures complete respect for the freedom of each believer, manifests the christian charity which ought to reign among brothers, and totally rejects all violence, all coercion or any other form of pressure which tends to determine the adhesion of the faithful to one or the other community.

If our apostolic charge does not permit us to refuse to persons or to communities the possibility of entering into full communion with the Church of Rome, be assured that we will never permit that except for strictly relevant reasons of personal conviction and of the free choice of consciences, with the exclusion of any motivation which is not religious, and with an active preoccupation to avoid whatever would wrong the Orthodox Church.

3. Paul VI to Russian Orthodox Delegation*

We cordially welcome you after the completion of the fourth encounter in a series of providential meetings between the Catholic Church and the Russian Orthodox Church. We know that you have dedicated yourselves with diligence and fidelity to the examination of the theme: "The Christian Proclamation of Salvation in a World of Transformation". We realize what an important and complex subject you have treated, in a spirit of sincere effort to be better equipped to bring the liberating and uplifting

---

* July 3, 1975, during a private audience with a delegation of the Moscow Patriarchate, headed by Metropolitan Nikodim (Leningrad and Novgorod). The delegation had come from a "theological conversation" between Roman Catholic and Russian Orthodox representatives, in Trent, Italy. This was the fourth of the series which began in Leningrad (1967), and continued in Bari, Italy (1970) and Zagorsk, USSR (1973), then Trent, Italy (1975) and Odessa (1980). Extract: SPCU *IS,* 28 (1975), p. 10.

message of salvation to the men and women of our time. We know that your method has been persevering and that the meetings have not lost sight of the final goal of Christianity and of its supernatural and transcendent aims. At the same time your solicitude has been directed to apostolic effectiveness, in order "that the word of the Lord may speed on and triumph" (*2 Thess* 3, 1).

It is our ardent prayer that these joint efforts may bear lasting fruit. We pray that the divisions of centuries will be overcome in the truth and charity of Christ, and that the Holy Spirit will bring to completion a work that has been begun under his inspiration—a work that is indeed manifested among the signs of the times.

It is the world that is awaiting with anxiety to enjoy in its fullness the liberating and salvific message of the Lord. We must go forward, dear friends and brothers, intent on rendering this service in the name of Jesus to those who await his Coming.

4. Paul VI to Patriarch Pimen*

We have requested our venerable brother Ramon Torrella Cascante, Titular Bishop of Minervino Murge and Vice-President of our Secretariat on Christian Unity, to convey to Your Holiness our fraternal greetings and our assurance that we have given serious attention to your letter of December 22, 1977, in which you inform us of the "Appeal to Religious Leaders and Believers Throughout the World" from the heads and representatives of confessions and religious associations of the Soviet Union concerning the neutron bomb.

Aware of our joint responsibility to defend the sacred gift of life and to advance the cause of peace among nations, we have not failed to study this serious problem in all its moral and human aspects, together with Your Holiness and the other signatories to this appeal.

We shall continue to do everything possible, as we have in the past, to persuade all to immediately study concrete and effective means to protect mankind—beginning with Europe, which risks most—from the fearful losses that could be caused by the accidental use of nuclear weapons in any form, whether already in existence or yet to be developed.

To this end we shall continue to insist that responsible leaders throughout the world immediately initiate and carry through negotiations

---

* Letter of May 22, 1978. On December 14, 1977, a conference of heads and representatives of Churches and religious associations in the Soviet Union was held in Zagorsk to discuss "the threat to peace and security in Europe and the whole world in connection with the plans to produce the neutron bomb". The conference adopted an appeal "addressed to religious leaders and believers throughout the world". Patriarch Pimen sent the appeal with a covering letter to Pope Paul VI, who replied. Text: *Journal of the Moscow Patriarchate* (Eng. ed.), n. 10 (1978), p. 30.

to cease production of weapons of this type—as well as other means of mass annihilation—and totally eliminate existing arsenals.

We hope that the forthcoming UN Special Session on Disarmament will be a good occasion to begin resolute and courageous action in this direction.

As for us Christians and all who believe in God the Father and the Lord of Life, we shall accompany with our prayers the efforts of the statesmen occupied with this just, necessary, and complex question so that they may not lack courage, wisdom, and good will in this matter.

May our preaching and our example with God's help imbue men's hearts with a feeling of brotherhood and resolution for peace!

5. Pimen's Sermon upon Paul VI's Death*

We are gathered today in our cathedral to accompany in prayer along "the way of all the earth" (*Jos* 23, 14) our most loved brother in the Lord, Pope Paul VI, head of the Roman Catholic Church, who died a holy death last Sunday. We weep for the death of this truly exceptional head of the Roman Church. In our telegram to His Eminence the Cardinal Chamberlain, John Villot, we have expressed our profound sharing in the sorrow of the whole Roman Catholic Church and we have emphasized how we valued the dead pope's commitment to establishing fraternal relations between the Roman Catholic and Russian Orthodox Churches. The fifteen years of Paul VI's pontificate were marked by this commitment towards Orthodoxy as a whole and towards each Orthodox local church. In that time he gave many proofs of his personal brotherly feeling towards Orthodoxy. He worked hard so that the Catholic-Orthodox dialogue of charity might open out into theological dialogue and today by God's mercy we are on the threshold of that. Warmly and fraternally he greeted many representatives of the Orthodox local churches visiting the eternal city; both during his pilgrimage to the Holy Land and on visits to a variety of other countries he received the representatives of Orthodoxy. Above all it was during Paul VI's pontificate that the Second Vatican Council was continued and brought to completion, which has revived in the Roman Church many of the norms of the ancient undivided Church.

We are glad to give testimony to the fact that in this period there has been consolidated that fraternal character in Roman Catholic/Russian Orthodox relations which is today such a deep joy to us. We look back with deep gratitude on how much Pope Paul VI did for this; he gave his blessing to the Secretariat for Promoting Christian Unity to set on foot various forms of collaboration with our Church, and this has been given

---

* August 9, 1978, during the Liturgy in memory of Paul VI, Cathedral of the Epiphany, Moscow. Extract: *Journal of the Patriarchate of Moscow* (Eng. ed.), N. 10, 1978, pp. 55–56.

living expression under the direction of Cardinal Willebrands. One of the most important forms of this collaborations is the theological conversations between representatives of the Russian Orthodox and Roman Catholic Churches.

These conversations take place in the territory of each church alternately and we know what a warm interest Pope Paul VI took in them. We too value highly these theological conversations, in which are examined problems and doctrinal questions connected with the task our Churches have of meeting the needs of contemporary man.

We recall with deep satisfaction the sharing by representatives of our two Churches in important visits in the life of each Church during Pope Paul VI's pontificate. The exchange of pilgrim groups which was supported by Pope Paul is an important form of spiritual communion between Churches. For our part we have always received and will always receive lovingly Catholic pilgrim groups which visit the holy places of the Russian Orthodox Church; and we ourselves gladly send pilgrims from our Church to Italy to visit the sacred places of the undivided Church. We are grateful to Paul VI of holy memory for having constantly maintained a personal welcome full of Christian love for representatives of the Russian Orthodox church visiting Rome. Many of our bishops, priests and laity met him and have witnessed to the charm of his personality, his deep spiritual qualities and his piety.

We point with satisfaction to the great development of ecumenical activity in the Roman Catholic Church in these last fifteen years, including relations with the World Council of Churches. We note also, with sympathy the Roman Catholic Church's good relations with non-Christian religions during Pope Paul VI's Pontificate.

And here we touch on one of the deceased pope's most important merits—his zealous services to the consolidation of peace and justice in relations between peoples. Throughout his pontificate Paul VI was concerned with questions on which depends the present and future of humanity—questions of war and peace. The world heard from the pope appeals for peace in Vietnam, in the near East, at all those points on the earth at which blood has been shed and where the death which came into the world through sin (cf. *Rom* V, 12) has reaped its fruits. And we all remember the passionate appeal for a lasting, just and universal peace which Paul VI addressed to the general assembly of the United Nations during a visit to its headquarters in New York. We remember gratefully the contribution his Holiness made to the success of conferences for disarmament and collaboration in Europe. We think no less gratefully of his continual anxiety for the advent of a peace without armaments, a peace in which love will reign among men.

Again recently, during the celebration of the sixtieth anniversary of the re-establishment of the patriarchal see of Moscow, we received from

Pope Paul VI a message, these thoughts from which deserve to be quoted: "In these last fifteen years relations between the Catholic Church and the Orthodox Church have taken on new dimensions, opening up new paths for theological dialogue and practical collaboration with the aim of putting an end to past hostility and replacing it with that mutual consideration and disinterested love which should mark disciples of Christ". It was just this aim that Paul VI pursued, and this we receive from him today as his legacy.

6. Christian Millennium in the Ukraine

Introduction

In preparation for the millennium celebration of christian faith in the Ukraine, John Paul II addressed a long letter to Josyf Cardinal Slipyj, Major Archbishop of Lviv for Ukrainians, who is exiled in Rome. The papal letter prompted unfavorable comments from the Orthodox, especially the Russian, because of a possible misinterpretation of the historical reunited Eastern Churches as a future ecumenical model. In the name of the Pope, Cardinal Willebrands clarifies the present Roman Catholic position.

a. Letter of John Paul II to Josyf Cardinal Slipyj*

That union truly entered upon the whole interwoven history of peoples: Ruthenians and Lithuanians and Poles, who at that time lived in just one kingdom. Although that common history pertains to a time past and gone, nevertheless the religious and ecclesial force of that union at Brest persists till now and bears abundant fruit. And indeed the origin of this fruitfulness was and, without doubt, is the very blood shed by Saint Josaphat, Bishop and Martyr, who, as though he were a seal, imprinted this seal upon the difficult reconciliation of the divided Church between the 16th and 17th century. In addition, that union similarly bore fruit in the lives of many bishops and priests and other undaunted confessors of the faith all the way to these our own times.

Formerly, as was its mode, and at the present time, the Apostolic See always attributes a special importance to this same union which shines forth in the very difference of the Byzantine rites and ecclesial traditions: the slavonic liturgical language, the ecclesiastical music, and in all the

---

* May 19, 1979. The Pope first describes the missionary beginnings in the region of "Rus", when "the Church of the West and of the East were still united"; the division of the two in the 11th century, "which brought great pain and bitterness to Christians then and to our own day"; the Ukrainian Christians' centering around the Patriarchate of Constantinople's authority; and the several attempts for reunion with the See of Rome, which culminated in the Union of Brest-Litovsk, 1596. Latin Extracts: *AAS* 71 (1979), pp. 522–527. TFS trans.

forms of piety which so deeply inhere in the history of your people. For these things reveal its spirit and assuredly establish in a certain manner its own character, as well as a diversity. That, for example, is proven as often as the sons and daughters of the Ukrainian nation, upon relinquishing their own citizenship, stay always, even as emigrants, associated with their own Church which through their own tradition and language and liturgy remains for them, as it were, a spiritual "fatherland" in foreign nations.

The Second Vatican Council again took up the great work of ecumenism. For the Church is indeed eager to promote the unity of Christians, while she, of course, attempts new ways of doing so which are better suited with the mentality of people of our age. In fact, even other Christian communities, among which are found the independent or "autocephalous" Churches of the East, have at this time equally prescribed the same plan for themselves. Many declarations, proclamations, and delegations show that point fully and distinctly; but especially does the common prayer by which we are all associated in order to fulfill the will of our Lord as expressed by His own prayer: "Father, that they may be one" (Jn. 17:11).

Ecumenical enterprises of our day, that is, that propensity toward mutual approach and communion—especially between Churches of the West and of the East—can neither omit nor minimize the importance and advantage of the different efforts of restoring unity to the Church which have been made in the past centuries and which had a successful outcome— even if only partially. Considered as proof of this truth is your Church among other Eastern Catholic Churches which possess their own rite. Without doubt, a genuine ecumenical spirit—according to the more recent meaning of the word—ought to be shown and also proved by a special respect towards your Church, as well as towards the other Catholic Churches of the eastern world which have their own distinct rites. In the future we expect very much from the very motive and testimony of an ecumenical spirit which our Brothers of the Orthodox Churches, Patriarchs and Bishops, are displaying, as also their clergy and all the communities at whose traditions and forms of piety the Catholic Church and the Apostolic See look with the greatest veneration and esteem.

Moreover, the same need [for an ecumenical spirit] arises from the principle of religious freedom which constitutes one of the chief doctrines of "The Universal Declaration of Human Rights" itself (United Nations General Assembly, 1948) and which is found in the constitutions of individual States. On the strength of that principle, which the Apostolic See has repeatedly invoked and proclaimed, it is permitted to every believing person to profess one's own faith and also to be a participant of the community of the Church to which one belongs. However, the observing of this principle of religious freedom demands that the rights of the Church of living and functioning be acknowledged for the vicinity to which the individual inhabitants of any State belong.

With the enthusiastic announcement of such an illustrious remembrance as that of your anniversary and with the fervent exhortation to pray conscientiously, we are turned in mind toward all the Churches and Christian Communities with whom we are not yet enjoying full communion—but with whom Christ alone joins us all together. May our thoughts and minds—obviously following Christ who sent His Apostles "even to the very ends of the earth"—be directed at this moment into the holy region of "Rus" which one thousand years ago accepted the gospel and received baptism!

*b. Letter of Metropolitan Juvenaly to Cardinal John Willebrands**

Our Church has become aware of the contents of the letter from His Holiness Pope John Paul II to His Eminence Josyf Cardinal Slipyj (March 19, 1979) "concerning the preparation for the 1000th year of the Christian Ukraine". We continue to learn also of the reactions to this letter in various Churches and by individual theologians; the comments on the contents are, in general, unfavorable. I meet the same reaction among my brother bishops and other members of the Russian Orthodox Church, who are convinced that a public analysis of the letter's contents is necessary.

I have noticed that the letter appears to contradict the spirit of Second Vatican Council decisions and deviates from the relations which have taken shape since the Council between the Roman Catholic Church and the Local Orthodox Churches. Thus, the *Decree on Ecumenism,* which concerns the relations with the Eastern Churches, affirmed, in part (n. 18): "This sacred Council ... confirms what previous Councils and Roman Pontiffs have proclaimed: in order to restore communion and unity or to preserve them, one must 'impose no burden beyond what is indispensable' (Acts 15:28). It is the Council's urgent desire that every effort should be made from now on toward the realization of this unity in the various organizations and living activities of the Church, especially by prayer and by fraternal dialogue on points of doctrine and the more pressing pastoral problems of our time. ... If this task is carried on wholeheartedly, this sacred Synod hopes that after the removal of the wall dividing the Eastern and Western Church, at last there may be but one dwelling, firmly established on the cornerstone, Christ Jesus, who will make both one".

However, the letter to Cardinal Slipyj contains the statement that "Unia" continues to be an important way towards the restoration of unity, and that "the Union of Brest has preserved up to this day all its ecclesiastical and religious force", and that "the Apostolic See has always given an exceptionally important significance to this union". This passage gives the

* September 4, 1979. Addressed to the President of the SPCU. The Metropolitan of Krutitsy and Kolomna is the President of the Department for External Church Affairs of the Patriarchate of Moscow. Russian Text: SPCU Archives. TFS trans.

impression that a change has taken place in the ecumenical policy of the Holy See towards its mutual relations with the Orthodox Churches and towards the ecumenical concord of the Churches.

We do not speak now of some historical inaccuracies, from our point of view; they also can elicit discussion.

Your Eminence, you know that during these last years through the strenuous efforts and the zealous prayer of the Roman Catholic and the Russian Orthodox Churches, fraternal relations have been established between us. In this, great service has been rendered by the Secretariat for Promoting Christian Unity headed by you and by you personally, dear Bishop. And now I, as President of the Department for External Church Affairs, cannot permit that an official reaction of my Church concerning the above mentioned letter be made public before I have received from you suitable information concerning the true meaning of this move.

This letter is dictated with the fervent wish to avoid a useless polemic and misunderstanding of interchurch relations. And I would be very happy to receive from you a timely answer.

c. Response of Cardinal Willebrands to Metropolitan Juvenaly *
Your Eminence, dear Brother in Christ,

I have read with greatest attention your letter of September 4, 1979, concerning a letter which His Holiness, Pope John Paul II, sent to His Eminence, Cardinal Josef Slipyj. The frankness and sincerity with which you expressed your own thought and that of other members of your Church is for me an encouraging sign of the brotherly confidence and mutual respect which have developed during these past years not only between us but also between our Churches.

I brought your letter to the Holy Father's attention. I was able to discuss personally with him its contents and meaning. He has examined what I wish to express below, and in his name I write you.

The letter to Cardinal Slipyj had a very precise purpose. The Holy Father did not intend to express in it his thought on the relations between the Church of Rome and the Orthodox Churches. On this subject, Pope John Paul II has clearly expressed himself from the moment of his election to the See of Rome. He affirms his intention to continue efforts at deepening the relations of prayer, of study, of mutual respect and brotherly love between our Churches, in order to reach that full ecclesial communion which the Lord of the Church desires.

To avoid giving to the Pope's letter a significance the author did not intend, I would like, first of all, to recall the ecumenical intentions of the Roman Catholic Church as they have been expressed in the Vatican Council and by Popes Paul VI and John Paul II.

* September 22, 1979. French Text: SPCU Archives. TFS trans.

In his address to the Christian delegations for the inauguration of his pontificate—and we remember, Your Eminence, that you presided over the delegation from the Patriarchate of Moscow—Pope John Paul II said: "We are eager to tell you of our firm resolve to go forward along the path to unity in the spirit of the Second Vatican Council and in following of our predecessors' example". He added: "Please say to those whom you represent, and to everyone, that the commitment of the Catholic Church to the ecumenical movement, such as it was solemnly expressed in the Second Vatican Council, is irreversible" (*Osservatore Romano,* Oct. 23–24, 1978). Here are very clear words; they leave no doubt about the ecumenical commitment of the present Pope. Furthermore, he repeated the same thoughts in his letter to His Holiness, Patriarch Pimen, on December 20, 1978, in the addresses he has given to groups of bishops and faithful of our Church, as well as to members of various Orthodox Churches who have visited him during the eleven months of his pontificate.

The Second Vatican Council clearly testified to the fact that the Catholic Church recognizes in the Orthodox Churches true Churches which, through the priesthood received in the Apostolic succession, celebrate the Eucharist of the Lord and administer His sacraments. The Council respected their own disciplines, their spiritual traditions and the various doctrinal expressions of the same christian faith which have developed among them and are rooted in the most ancient and authentic traditions of the one Church of Christ. If over the centuries and for reasons which were not always strictly religious, canonical and doctrinal differences have developed between our Churches, we always remain nonetheless "sister Churches". This expression neither is ambiguous nor results from emotional rhetoric; it wishes to express the truth of a communion in the mystery of Christ which, despite these differences, continues to unite us and to unite our Churches.

Your Eminence has said, we are trying today to arrive at a full expression of this communion through prayer and through fraternal dialogue on the points of doctrine on which we still disagree, as well as on the most urgent pastoral problems of our times. The union for which we search, then, is not the absorption of one by the other, or the domination of one over the other, but the full communion between Churches which share the same faith and the same sacramental life. This communion is visibly expressed through structures which correspond to most ancient authentic traditions and to Christ's will for His Church.

In the past these principles were not always grasped with the same clarity; sometimes they were understood and applied in too partial a manner, conditioned by the religious and political situation of a given period. This is not the place to attempt judgement on this past or to doubt the good will of our ancestors in the faith. However, under the light of the Holy Spirit, the evolution of theological reflection and the growth in mutual love allow us to discern in a broader and deeper way the ecclesial communion which should reign between our Churches. We are reviewing our common past better to overcome whatever in this past could cause opposition between us and thus to reestablish true peace between our Churches.

In this context one should consider the letter to Cardinal Slipyj. Pope John Paul II addressed himself to a particular Church which bears its own history and traditions, and is presently undergoing a difficult trial. He did not intend to treat either the theology which should inspire our common search for full ecclesial communion or the method for our development of the relations between our Churches, today and for the future.

For the Catholic Ukrainians, both in their country and elsewhere, the Union of Brest has always had special significance. Through political changes and pressures over many centuries, these Catholics consider themselves bound to the See of Rome by a communion which they wish to express visibly in ecclesiastical structures. The Pope wished to extricate this communion from political and national elements in order to stress the permanent religious and ecclesial value it maintains for those Catholics who still find in their particular Church today a fruitful expression of their religious life, and in order to encourage them to remain faithful to this spiritual heritage. There was no intention whatever of presenting the Union of Brest as the model for our relations with the Orthodox Churches today or as one for the contemplated future union.

Sometimes one meets in certain Orthodox circles a tendency to judge the experience of the united Catholic Churches in a totally negative manner. Some would even have wished that their suppression be the preliminary condition to the dialogue with the Church of Rome. In a letter to His Holiness, Patriarch Alexis on October 21, 1968, Pope Paul VI wrote: " . . . our apostolic charge does not permit us to refuse persons or groups of persons the possibility of entering into full communion with the Roman Catholic Church". He immediately added: "Be assured that we will never permit this except for reasons which flow from personal and free conviction of conscience, and excludes every motivation which could arise from sentiments foreign to this conviction".

In accord with this same spirit Pope John Paul II asks that one correctly appreciate the deeds of past centuries which intended reestablishing the unity of the Churches. Out of these efforts, carried out in circumstances different from ours and inspired by a theology which is no longer that of today, were born the united Catholic Churches. Their existence has allowed some Christians to express their communion with the Church of Rome, in accordance with the demands of their conscience. Inside the Catholic Church they have brought to mind concretely the fact that the Latin tradition was not the only truly authentic christian tradition. In this sense their existence has been and remains beneficial. On the other hand, one must recognize that, unhappily, their foundation also has caused a rupture of communion with the Orthodox Churches and created new tensions between Catholics and Orthodox.

This complex inherited situation is part of the reality within which our ecumenical task should develop today, a constant effort at renewal and of deepened faithfulness. We must profit from the lessons of the past and be docile to what the Holy Spirit is today saying to the Churches to guide them into unity. More than ever in our history, our effort must be separated from every political element, from every aim which deviates from the sole desire to realize Christ's will for His Church. This is Pope John Paul II's thought. He does not think of taking inspiration from a model of the past, but he calls for fidelity and docility to Him who makes everything new.

Your Eminence and very dear Brother, through this letter I assure you that in writing to Cardinal Slipyj, the Pope desired to address himself to a Church and to the faithful who, throughout the changing periods of history up to our own days, have suffered for their fidelity to the See of Rome. They are preparing to celebrate a millennium which is particularly important in their history and in yours. In effect, even if he does not say so in his letter, without hesitation the Pope recognizes in your Russian Orthodox Church an heir to the glorious tradition of Saint Vladimir and of the ancient Church of Kiev which is at the foundation of the faith and perseverance of your christian people.

Inspired by a love without pretense, we desire to continue our efforts towards deepening the brotherly relations between our Churches, so that peace may come about among all, including our Catholic Ukrainian brothers, and that thus we may arrive at that full ecclesial communion for which we are laboring, not according to the models of the past but by seeking to follow the ways the Holy Spirit points out to the Church today as He guides her into all truth and into the peace' which surpasses every sentiment.

You know how much I take to heart this work which was undertaken in cooperation with my Orthodox brothers, and how this task is at the center of my life. I am sure that the Lord who has begun this work among us will bring it to fulfillment.

III

RELATIONS WITH THE ARMENIAN ORTHODOX CHURCH

Visit of Catholicos Vasken I to Paul VI* (Vatican City, May 8–12, 1968)

1. Address of Vasken I to Paul VI**

Your Holiness,

We come to you from a distant world, from the country of biblical Ararat, from Armenia and from the holy city of Etchmiadzin, the cradle and centre of the Christian faith of the Armenians throughout the centuries.

We come to you also from very remote times, stretching back through so many centuries of Christian testimony, to the age of Christ. The Armenian people and its Church preserve these testimonies tenaciously, beginning from those of the times of the apostles St. Thaddaeus and St. Bartholomew, and of St. Gregory the Illuminator, to whose spiritual heritage the Armenian apostolic Church is anchored.

From the second half of the 5th century, the Armenian Church, while remaining firm and faithful to the dogmas and fundamental truths of Oriental Orthodoxy, lived and developed, according to the logic of evolution and historical events, in a direction that was her own, in the ambit of her national life, defending in the course of the centuries the frontiers of Christianity and of civilization in the East, often at the cost of the martyrdom of her body.

The two historical sees of the Armenian Church of Jerusalem and of Turkey, the first founded on the testimony of the apostle St. James, the son of Zebedee and of St. James, the Lord's brother, the second organized in the fifteenth century as the see of the Armenian catholicate of Cilicia, also founded in the fifteenth century, constitute, with the Holy See of Etchmiadzin as their head, one indivisible hierarchical body, with the same apostolate in the life of the Armenian people.

And today with the help of God, the Armenian Church with its hierarchical sees and its dioceses both in Soviet Armenia and abroad, is experiencing a period of spiritual and material progress.

And we come to you with the warm wish that in the world of today a new way illuminated by the light of the Gospel may be opened victoriously, the way in favour of which Your Holiness is striving with such

---

* His Holiness Vasken I is the Supreme Catholicus of all the Armenians, whose see is at Holy Etchmiadzin in Soviet Armenia. On his official visit he was accompanied by Yegishe Derderian, Patriarch of the Armenians of Jerusalem, and Chenork Kaloustian, Patriarch of the Armenians of Turkey.

** May 9, in the Sistine chapel, after a joint prayer service of chants and readings from the Armenian and Roman liturgies. Extracts: SPCU *IS,* 11 (1970), pp. 4–5.

overflowing love and such bold wisdom, thus continuing the work undertaken by the luminous vision of blessed Pope John XXIII.

And perhaps we will not be mistaken if we consider as being of primary importance in this work the imperatives of the implementation of the unity of the Churches and the strengthening of peace in the world.

The Armenian Church is happy to take part in the ecumenical movement and, in agreement with her sister Churches, to progress towards unity in love of Christ, relying on her centuries-old spiritual heritage and on her hierarchical organization.

Humanity needs, more than ever perhaps today, a spiritual equilibrium and a moral discipline, to which we think the Churches with their united forces can contribute greatly, spreading over the contemporary world the light of the Gospel, directed not against science, not against this or that social doctrine, this or that political system, but with an ever growing charity, towards all men, and through a deep faith and optimism, towards man and towards his genius for good.

Although we regretfully observe in life today manifestations of disorderly and unhealthy tendencies, of social injustices, of hatred between nations, sometimes causing wars of bloodshed that deeply distress our conscience, we believe nevertheless that all these phenomena represent, perhaps, defects of growth in the new development of human life moving towards the birth and formation of a new spiritual and moral equilibrium and a new awareness of the universal brotherhood of the peoples.

We have come to your Holy See in Rome to pray with Your Holiness, in order that Love and loyalty may meet, Justice and Peace embrace (*Psalm* 84, 11) on earth, so that our feeling that we must put out the fire of war may become stronger and that we, heads of the Churches, may constantly operate for the one precise purpose of indicating to all nations and all states the ways of unity, brotherhood, and peaceful coexistence. It is no longer possible for men and ourselves, servants of Christ's Church, to be resigned to the idea of war. Every war is a crime.

Our Church and our people have the tragic experience of past wars, especially the First World War of 1915, when the whole of western Armenia was exterminated with the martyrdom of nearly two million Armenian Christians, an event which represented the first genocide of our century.

Let us pray always that such tragedies will never be repeated in any part of the world, to the detriment of any people.

The Church of Christ must be on the lookout, firmly attached to her apostolate, in a spirit of peace, following the example of Our Lord who, during the storm, at the moment of shipwreck, said to his despairing disciples: "Why are you afraid? Men of little faith!"

We must believe that the "winds and seas" of our times will also be subjected to the imperative of peace.

We think it is necessary that all our Churches and all of us should humbly and loyally rally round the divine Master, obeying him, in order to be able, with our prayers and common efforts, to subdue "the winds and the seas", so that all storms will cease and the great Peace will reign.

The day when all men on earth have reached the peaks of reason, with the firm conviction that all men, all nations, are brothers without any distinction, as God's one people, that day the greatest miracle in history will have taken place.

2. Response of Paul VI to Vasken I*

This morning at this historical meeting We cannot but call to mind the special regard of our predecessors the Sovereign Pontiffs for the noble Armenian nation and especially the affection shown so openly by Benedict XV. We also like to recall the decision taken by Gregory XIII and put into effect by Leo XIII of setting up in Rome the Armenian College which is so dear to Us. You know also how pleased We are to count our venerable brother, Cardinal Gregory Peter Agagianian, originally from Armenia, among our close collaborators. He presides over one of the most important offices of the Holy See, the Congregation for the Evangelization of Peoples. Nor can we forget all the Armenian Catholics in different parts of the world and their undying fidelity.

In former times contacts were frequent, notably from the twelfth to the fourteenth centuries, when full communion had been re-established between Rome and the Armenian Church. Close ties continued to exist also in the sixteenth and seventeenth centuries between the Sees of Rome and Etchmiadzin, as together they acknowledged the mystery of the Word of God, become one of us to save us and to make it possible for us to become, in Him, sons of God, members and brothers one of another. It was, for example, after receiving the envoys of the Catholicos Michael, that Pope Paul VI gave his approval to the establishment of an Armenian printing press at Rome. Besides these contacts, opportunity to express deep agreement in the faith was frequently given by exchange of letters and envoys.

If we have come to divergent expressions of the central mystery of our faith, because of unfortunate circumstances, cultural differences and the difficulty of translating terms worked out with much effort and given precise statement only gradually, then research into these doctrinal difficulties must be undertaken again in order to understand what has brought them about and to be able to overcome them in a brotherly way.

Pius XII, in his encyclical *Sempiternus Rex* in 1951, chose to quote one of your great theologians, who was also a fine poet, the Catholicos Nerses IV. In the twelfth century this Catholicos had written to Emperor

* May 9, Sistine chapel. Extracts: SPCU *IS,* 11 (1970), pp. 5–6.

Manuel Comnenius: "In no way do we introduce confusion, change or alteration into the union of Christ, as do the heretics. We affirm one single nature to signify the hypostasis that you also acknowledge in Christ; this we admit to be legitimate and it has entirely the same meaning as our formula 'one single nature' ... We do not refuse to say 'two natures' as long as this is not by way of division as Nestorius holds, but rather to indicate the absence of confusion, against Eutyches and Apollinaris" (*AAS* 43 [1951] pp. 636–637). Has not the time come to clear up once and for all such misunderstandings inherited from the past, and this in a dialogue such as your Church, along with the other Churches meeting at Addis Ababa in 1965, has outlined in principle? The way that leads to agreement on these questions has already been cleared by the theologians in thorough studies and in profitable meetings. We are ready to commit ourselves to this course and to react positively to this decision. More than that, We desire it, just as We ardently desire to leave nothing undone that could hasten the day when we may seal in a concelebration the full unity once again recovered by our Churches. The frequent contacts we mentioned a minute ago diminished to the point of disappearance, to be replaced, unfortunately, by clashes that were sometimes violent. That period is over and our One Lord Jesus Christ is leading us towards one another by continually inciting us to greater vigilance and to renewed fidelity. Is it not significant that we resumed our relations on the occasion of the Second Vatican Council, which gave such intense expression in the Catholic Church to this effort of renewal, and at which Council Your Holiness was good enough to be represented by delegated observers?

3. The Common Declaration*

Paul VI, Bishop of Rome, Pope of the Catholic Church, and Vasken I, Supreme Catholicos-Patriarch of all Armenians, thank the Lord for having permitted them to pray together, to meet each other and exchange the holy kiss of peace, especially during this period of preparation for the great feast celebrating the Descent of the Holy Spirit upon the Apostles.

Conscious of their duties as pastors, they invite all Christians, especially those of the Catholic Church and the apostolic Armenian Church, to respond with greater fidelity to the call of the Holy Spirit stimulating them to a more profound unity which will accomplish the will of our common Saviour, and will render fruitful the service of the world by Christians.

This unity cannot be realized unless everyone, pastors and faithful, really strive to know each other. To this end, they urge theologians to apply themselves to a common study directed towards a more profound knowledge of the mystery of Our Lord Jesus Christ and revelation made in

* May 12, 1970. Vatican City. French Text: *AAS* 62 (1970), pp. 416–417. English SPCU *IS*, 11 (1970), p. 10.

Him. Faithful to the tradition handed down by the Apostles and the Fathers, and at the same time, aware of the demands of a world seeking God in the new developments of our age, they will be able to open up new avenues which will overcome the differences that still exist and bring their Churches to a more perfect unity in the profession of their faith in the face of the world. On their part, the Pope and the Catholicos will strive to do all they possibly can to support these efforts and give them their pastoral blessing.

However, the efforts run the risk of remaining sterile unless they are rooted in the whole life of the entire Church. This is why we hope that a closer collaboration will develop in all possible domains of the Christian life. Prayer in common, mutual spiritual aid, joint efforts to find really Christian solutions to the problems of the world today, will be precious means in the service of this search for a full unity so greatly desired.

This search accomplished together, this collaboration must be based on the mutual recognition of the common Christian faith and the sacramental life, on the mutual respect of persons and their Churches. If the unselfish efforts they wish to foster wholeheartedly are inspired with this spirit and implemented in this manner, then we are confident that the Spirit of truth and love will give to the members of the Catholic Church and the apostolic Armenian Church this truly Christian fraternity which is the fruit of His action in them.

In the name of this fraternity, Pope Paul VI and the Catholicos Vasken I raise their voices in solemn appeal to all those who exert influence on the life of nations and peoples so that they may strive to seek and to find all possible means to end wars, hatred, moral and physical violence, any oppression whatsoever of man by man. May the One who is our peace grant that this appeal be heard.

IV
RELATIONS WITH THE SYRIAN ORTHODOX CHURCH

1. Visit of Mar Ignatius Jacob III to Paul VI (Vatican City, October 25–27, 1971)

a. Address of Paul VI to the Patriarch*

In your person we salute a Church which sees in the faith and devotion of the apostolic community of Antioch the roots and foundation of its own Christian witness. We are particularly happy to welcome an

---

* His Holiness, the Syrian Orthodox Patriarch of Antioch and All the East. At the end of a common prayer service in the Matilda chapel, October 25. Extracts: SPCU *IS,* 16 (1972), pp. 3–4.

exalted visitor from Damascus, where, in receiving the holy waters of baptism, the Apostle of the Nations, whose name we bear, began that life of total commitment to the Lord Jesus Christ which was to lead him to this city of Rome and the supreme sacrifice of his life out of love for that Lord . . .

The history of the relations between our Churches shows many lights and shadows. We recognize that difficulties which have been created over centuries are not always easily overcome. Each of us is motivated by a sincere desire to be faithful to our Fathers in the faith and to the tradition they have handed down to us. Yet this very desire to be faithful to them impels us to search with ever greater zeal for the realization of full communion with each other.

We share a common sacramental life and a common Apostolic tradition, particularly as affirmed in what is popularly called the Nicene Creed. The dogmatic definitions of the first three Ecumenical Councils form part of our common heritage. Thus we confess together the mystery of the Word of God, become one of us to save us and to permit us to become in Him sons of God and brothers of each other.

It is in total submission to this Lord and Saviour, God the Son Incarnate, that we will be able to find the way towards that reconciliation which will bring us to perfect communion. The Syrian Orthodox Church in union with her sister Oriental Orthodox Churches, meeting in Addis Ababa in 1965, has already determined to press forward for a dialogue which will help overcome the misunderstandings of the past. Already theologians are working with renewed effort to throw new light on the mystery of the one Lord Jesus Christ. If they recognize that there are still differences in the theological interpretation of this mystery of Christ because of different ecclesiastical and theological traditions, they are convinced, however, that these various formulations can be understood along the lines of the faith of the early councils, which is the faith we also profess (cf. Pope Pius XII, in Encyclical *Sempiternus Rex, AAS,* 1951, pp. 636–637).

We, as pastors, can encourage the common efforts being made for a deeper and more comprehensive understanding of this mystery which, far from raising doubts about our two different ecclesiastical traditions, can reinforce them and show the basic harmony which exists between them.

The task is the more urgent because of the demands which are being made upon the Churches today. In a world which is struggling to give birth to new ideas, to new developments which can enable all men to share in the gifts of God's creation, to new relationships between men and nations which will ensure peace with justice, we are called to proclaim the "one Lord, one faith, one baptism and one God who is Father of all, over all, through all and within all" (*Eph* 4:5–6).

If we can carry on this task in fraternal communion we will contribute in an even more perfect way to that service of the world which is an essential part of the mission of the Church. We will be fulfilling our vocation to see the mystery of the compassion of God translated into Christian compassion between men and for men.

In the visit of Your Holiness we see a new testimony to our common desire to carry out this mission and fulfil this vocation.

b. *Address of the Patriarch to Paul VI**

After 1520 years of break, mutual anathemas and the like, the heads of these two most ancient Churches in Christendom meet each other as brothers in an atmosphere of love and fraternity. Time is a healer of all wounds. It was at Chalcedon in 451 that the break took place. But now both Churches recognize that what took place there was, unfortunately, a stab to the heart of Christendom.

Thank God, those days of unhappy relations are now a thing of the past; and today there is real love and cooperation between our two Apostolic Sees, and Christian communion in general.

In the 20th century there has never been a movement more fruitful than the ecumenical movement, and we recognize with appreciation the constructive role Your Holiness' illustrious predecessor and your good self have played in this field. We on our part look forward to the day when we will have even a greater visible unity and that too without sacrificing our individuality and the cultural contribution each of our Churches can make towards the speedy spreading of the Kingdom of God on earth.

c. *Address of Paul VI to the Patriarch***

Throughout the centuries, in times of glory and in times of great suffering, your Church has given witness to Our Lord Jesus Christ, the only-begotten Son of God made man for our salvation. Preachers, scholars and pastors have all contributed to deepening the understanding of the Incarnation of the Son of God and to making the significance of God's condescension towards man a living reality for your people. Many of them bore witness to their faith by the supreme sacrifice of their lives.

We are happy that Your Holiness has personally been able to visit the Church of Rome which, under God's grace, has also struggled to fulfil its mission through the devoted actions of its own teachers, pastors and witnesses to her faith.

These Fathers in the faith and these saints and martyrs call out to us to apply ourselves with renewed dedication to that mission, under the inspiration of the Holy Spirit, who is ever ready to offer us new light and

---

* October 25, Matilda chapel. Extract: SPCU *IS*, 16 (1972), p. 4.
** October 27, in the Synod Hall, in the presence of the Synod Bishops, then in session. Extracts: SPCU *IS*, 16 (1972), p. 4.

strength. We ourself and our brothers in the episcopate, with humility but also with great confidence, are determined to listen to these promptings of the Spirit and to strive to carry them out to the best of our ability. That is the underlying principle of the work of this Synod of Bishops which is gathered here and which extends today its heartfelt greeting to Your Holiness.

All of us are encouraged by the fact that your own Church, in union with your sister Oriental Orthodox Churches, is also actively engaged in searching for new ways to carry on her mission in a spirit of unity and docility to what the Spirit is saying to the Churches. Your visit to us makes us even more confident that our Churches will find means for greater cooperation in our common task and, at the same time, will open up the road to that full communion so ardently desired by all of us.

As we pray that the Lord of the Church may lead us to full reconciliation, we are mindful also of the particular needs of the Middle East where so many of your faithful are to be found. May this meeting with Your Holiness be a new stimulus to all Christians, especially to those of that area, to work for reconciliation in Christ among themselves and to search out, with imagination and tenacity, a durable peace with justice for all who dwell in those lands so dear to us.

d. The Common Declaration*

As they conclude their solemn meeting which marks a new step in the relations between the Roman Catholic Church and the Syrian Orthodox Church, His Holiness Pope Paul VI and His Holiness Mar Ignatius Jacob III humbly render thanks to Almighty God, for having made possible this historic opportunity to pray together, to engage in a fraternal exchange of views concerning the needs of the Church of God and to witness to their common desire that all Christians may intensify their service to the world with humility and complete dedication.

The Pope and the Patriarch have recognized the deep spiritual communion, which already exists between their Churches. The celebration of the sacraments of the Lord, the common profession of faith in the Lord Jesus Christ, the Word of God made man for man's salvation, the apostolic traditions which form part of the common heritage of both Churches, the great Fathers and Doctors, including Saint Cyril of Alexandria, who are their common masters in the faith—all these testify to the action of the Holy Spirit who has continued to work in their Churches even when there have been human weakness and failings. The period of mutual recrimination and condemnation has given place to a willingness to meet together in

---

* October 27. Signed by the Pope and Patriarch in the presence of the Synod Bishops. French Text: *AAS* 63 (1971), pp. 814–815. English SPCU *IS,* 16 (1972), p. 5.

sincere efforts to lighten and eventually remove the burden of history which still weighs heavily upon Christians.

Progress has already been made and Pope Paul VI and the Patriarch Mar Ignatius Jacob III are in agreement that there is no difference in the faith they profess concerning the mystery of the Word of God made flesh and become really man, even if over the centuries difficulties have arisen out of the different theological expressions by which this faith was expressed. They therefore encourage the clergy and faithful of their Churches to even greater endeavours at removing the obstacles which still prevent complete communion among them. This should be done with love, with openness to the promptings of the Holy Spirit, and with mutual respect for each other and each other's Church. They particularly exhort the scholars of their Churches, and of all Christian communities, to penetrate more deeply into the mystery of Christ with humility and fidelity to the Apostolic traditions so that the fruits of their reflections may help the Church in her service to the world which the Incarnate Son of God has redeemed.

This world, which God so loved as to send His only begotten Son, is torn by strife, by injustice and by the inhumanity of man towards man. As Christian Pastors, the Pope and the Patriarch raise their common appeal to the leaders of the peoples to increase the efforts towards achieving lasting peace among nations and towards removing the obstacles which prevent so many men from enjoying the fruits of justice and religious freedom. Their appeal is directed to all areas of the world and in particular to that land hallowed by the preaching, the death and the resurrection of our Lord and Saviour Jesus Christ.

2. Visit of Mar Ignatius Jacob III to John Paul II* (Vatican City, May 13–16, 1980)

Our love of that same Risen Lord, our devotion to that apostolic faith and the Christian witness received from our Fathers is what makes our meeting today so full of meaning. Together we repeat the inspired words of Peter: "You are the Christ, the Son of the living God" (*Mt* 16:16). Together we confess the mystery of the Word of God, made man for our salvation, who is the image of the invisible God, the firstborn of every creature (cf. *Col* 1:15), in whom it has pleased the Father to re-establish all things (cf. *Eph* 1:10). This is the Lord we proclaim; this is the Lord we seek to serve, in fidelity and truth; this is the Lord whose Spirit impels us to search with ever greater zeal for the fullness of communion with each other.

* Shortly after his return to Damascus, the Patriarch died (June 25). In his spiritual testament he hoped for a christological formula for the reestablishment of full communion between the Catholic Church and the pre-Chalcedonian Churches. John Paul II addressed the Patriarch during the visit (May 14): Extracts: SPCU *IS*, 44(1980), p. 93.

By baptism we are one in the Lord Jesus Christ. The priesthood and the Eucharist which we share because of the apostolic succession bind us even closer together. The world in which we live and for which Christ gave himself as a ransom for many has need of a united Christian witness in order to be able to hear his word better and respond to his message of love and reconciliation.

Yes, this is a message, or rather an urgent appeal for reconciliation among those who bear his name. For centuries we have been estranged from each other; misunderstanding and mistrust have often marked our relationships. By God's grace we are seeking to overcome that past.

Nine years ago, Your Holiness and my revered predecessor Paul VI met in this very place to give clear testimony to a mutual dedication to this task of Christian reconciliation. At that time you recognized that, even if over the centuries difficulties have arisen because of the different theological expressions which have been used to express our faith in the Word of God made flesh and become really man, the faith we intend to proclaim is the same. In words that were both encouraging and prophetic you said together: "The period of mutual recrimination and condemnation has given place to a willingness to meet together in sincere efforts to lighten and eventually remove the burden of history which still weighs heavily upon Christians" (cf. Common Declaration of 27 October 1971).

These words have not remained simple expressions of good intentions. In the framework of the "Pro Oriente" meetings* between the Catholic and Eastern Orthodox Churches, theologians from both our Churches have searched into and sought to resolve questions which still cause some difference among us and prevent full canonical and Eucharistic Communion. Some of the distinguished bishops present today have taken an active part in these conversations. We are grateful to God and to all these devoted men for the real progress which has been made.

On the level of pastoral care for Christian emigrants there has been fruitful cooperation for disinterested service towards those who, in search of an improvement of the material conditions of their lives, feel the deep need of spiritual support in their new surroundings. I would also like to express my personal appreciation for the delegation Your Holiness sent on the occasion of my election as Bishop of Rome.

Your Holiness, we meet together just after my return from an intensive journey in Africa, a journey filled with many precious experiences. One thing is clear, though. I am more than ever convinced that the world in which we live hungers and thirsts for God, a longing that can be fulfilled only in Christ. As pastors of Churches sharing in apostolic

---

* Cardinal Franz König of Vienna established the Pro Oriente foundation in 1964 for unofficial dialogues with the Orthodox and other Eastern Churches such as the Syrian and the Coptic. Extensive resumés appear in *Wort und Wahrheit.*

traditions, we are called upon in a special way to carry on the apostolic mission of bringing Christ and his gifts of salvation and love to our generation. Our disunity is an obstacle to fulfilling this mission. Our disunity obscures the voice of the Spirit who is striving to speak to mankind through our voices. But our meeting today is sign of our renewed desire to be more attuned to what the Spirit is saying to the Churches. Encouraged by what the Lord has already accomplished in us and through us, we look forward in hope to the future, not minimizing the difficulties but putting our firm trust in him who said "Behold I am making all things new" (*Rev* 21:5).

V
THE COPTIC ORTHODOX CHURCH

1. Visit of Amba Shenouda III to Paul VI* (Vatican City, May 4–10, 1973)

a. Address of Paul VI to Amba Shenouda III**

We meet at a time when Christians are asking themselves about the meaning of the faith they profess and the mission they have to the world. You come to this ancient See of Rome, bearing with you the traditions of the ancient See of Alexandria, of its apostles, its martyrs, its doctors, its holy monks and the vast army of its people, who have given witness to their faith in periods of great darkness. It is our hope that through our discussions and prayer we may make a significant contribution towards understanding each other better, thus making it possible to help Christians find valid answers to the questions they are asking themselves today.

We realize that God is presenting us with a great challenge. We do not expect to overcome immediately the difficulties that fifteen centuries of history have created for us. But we do hope to be able to set out upon a way which will lead to our overcoming these difficulties. For our part, we approach these meetings in a spirit of great confidence. We are confident that our Churches are determined to reach out to each other in an effort to carry out better the mission God has entrusted to us. We strive to be faithful servants of the tradition which has been handed on to us from the Apostles through the Fathers and great spiritual leaders of this Church. But that tradition is a living one. The efforts at renewal which are going on in the Catholic Church and in the Coptic Church give testimony to this. We are confident therefore that our meetings during these days will strengthen the bonds of brotherly love between us and between our people.

---

* His Holiness, Amba Shendouda III, Pope of Alexandria and Patriarch of the See of St. Mark, is the head of the Coptic Orthodox Church.
** May 5. Extract: SPCU *IS,* 22 (1973), pp. 3–4.

May God enlighten us and guide us and grant us new insights as we strive together to see how we may attain that full unity of the Spirit in the bond of peace which Christ asks of us and which is his gift.

b. Homily of Paul VI*

"This is the day which the Lord has made; let us rejoice and be glad in it". We very willingly repeat this liturgical acclamation, motivated by the feast of Easter, on this present occasion in which the presence of Patriarch Shenouda III—one who is himself honoured by the title of "Pope" of the venerable and most ancient Coptic Church which has its centre at Alexandria in Egypt—evokes in our heart a profound emotion. Here is one who is Head of a Church which is still officially separated from us and which for centuries has been absent from the communal celebration of prayer with this Church of Rome. He is indeed Head of a Church whose origin goes back to the Evangelist Mark, whom Saint Peter calls his son (*1 Pt.* 5:13), and which had in Saint Athanasius—the sixteenth centenary of whose blessed death we are celebrating today—the invincible defender of our common Nicene faith, that is, faith in the divinity of our Lord Jesus Christ, which was proclaimed, under divine inspiration, by Simon, son of John, who was therefore transformed by Christ himself into the unchanging Peter and made by him the foundation of the whole Church. He is here, and he has come expressly and spontaneously to tie again the bonds of love (cf. *Col.* 3:14) in happy anticipation of that perfect unity of the spirit (cf. *Eph.* 3:4) which, after the recent Second Ecumenical Vatican Council, we are striving humbly and sincerely to restore. He is here with us and with this great assembly of faithful at the tomb of the Apostle Peter. How could we not rejoice and invite all of you, sons and daughters of this Roman Catholic Church, to praise the Lord with us on this extraordinary day? Do we not see that the book of the Church's history, in which the mysterious hand of the Lord is the chief guide of men's hands to write there "new things and old" (cf. *Mt.* 13:52), opens before us centuries-old pages and others which are still unused and ready to register events—God willing!—which will be happier ones, the records of the merciful Providence of God in the life of the Church which is still a pilgrim in time? ...

The divinity of Christ is the central point of Saint Athanasius' preaching to the men of his time, who were tempted by the Arian crisis. The definition of the first Ecumenical Council of Nicaea (325)—according to which Jesus Christ is the Son of God, of the same substance as the Father, true God from true God—was the constant point of reference of

---

* Preached in the Eucharistic Liturgy, in commemoration of the 16th centenary of the death of St. Athanasius. May 6, in the Cappella Papale. Extracts: SPCU *IS,* 22 (1973), pp. 4–5.

his teaching. Only if one accepts this doctrine can one speak of redemption, of salvation and of the reestablishment of communion between man and God. Only the Word of God perfectly redeems; without the Incarnation, man would remain in the state of corrupt nature, from which penance itself could not free him (cf. *De Incarnatione, PG,* 25, 144, 119).

Freed by Christ from corruption and saved from death, man is reborn to new life and acquires once more the pristine image of God, in which he had been created in the beginning and which sin had corrupted. "The Word of God", declares Saint Athanasius, "came himself, so that, being the Image of the Father, he might create man anew in the image of God" (*ibid.*).

Saint Athanasius evolves this theology, centering it on the sharing of redeemed man in the very life of God, through baptism and sacramental life. He even declares, in a forceful expression, that the Word of God "became man so that we might be divinized" (*ibid.*).

This new creation restores what sin had compromised: the knowledge of God and a radical change of life.

Jesus Christ reveals the Father to us and makes him knowable: "The Word of God became visible with a body so that we might be able to form an idea of the invisible Father" (*ibid.*).

From this new knowledge of God follows the need for moral renewal. Saint Athanasius calls for it strongly: "Whoever wishes to understand the things of God must purify himself in his way of life and resemble the Saints by the similarity of his own actions, so that united with them in the conduct of his life he may be able to understand what has been revealed to them by God" (*ibid.*).

We are thus brought to the center of the Christian event: redemption by the work of Jesus Christ, the radical renewal of man with his restoration to the image and likeness of God, restored communion of life between man and God, also expressed in a profound change of conduct.

c. Address of Amba Shenouda III to Paul VI*

The Lord Jesus Christ said to the Father: "That they may all be one, even as Thou, Father, art in me and I in Thee, that they also may be one in us" (*Jn.* 17, 21), . . . that they may be one, even as we are one" (*Jn.* 17, 11). Jesus Christ, who so said, undoubtedly leads with His Holy Spirit every action that tends to unity, whether of heart, mind or faith. For the Church is Christ's body; and He has but one body.

We fully believe that He has disposed for this meeting so that we may take a step forward in strengthening the relations between our two apostolic Churches which were two among the four great apostolic Churches of

* May 6. At the main altar of St. Peter's Basilica. Extracts: SPCU *IS,* 22 (1973), pp. 5–6.

early Christianity. We have a responsibility, we believe, to work for the unity of faith, not only between us but all over Christendom.

We dare say our differences were for the sake of Christ's love, through which we love each other regardless of the differences. We meet today so that we may deepen our mutual love. Talks guided by the Holy Spirit in such an atmosphere should lead to unity of heart, mind and faith.

However, we have to declare there are between us many points of agreement in the principles of faith. We all believe in the One God, the Divine Trinity, Father, Son and Holy Ghost. The Lord's Incarnation, act of Redemption, Resurrection, Ascension and Second Coming to judge the living and the dead are our common belief. Yea, we believe that the human soul is everlasting, we believe in the resurrection of the dead and the life hereafter, the intercession of the Virgin Mary, the angels and the saints, the seven sacraments and the work of the Holy Ghost in them. We believe in one way for salvation and we condemn the heresies of Arius, Nestorius, Eutyches, Sabellius, Macedonius and the others.

As for points of difference, there is no doubt that after fifteen centuries of study, examination and controversy both on theological and public levels we are undoubtedly on much nearer grounds than our ancestors of the fifth and sixth centuries. We all are readier and more intensive to reach solutions for the differences and attain simpler and more practical forms of expression for the conceptions of faith that all would welcome. We are mindful that the tension of old philosophic and linguistic understandings together with the political implications connected with the days of schism and the following centuries has been considerably reduced.

Your Holiness, the world of today, suffering from movements of atheistic, materialistic, sceptic or immoral natures, is in drastic need for the cooperation of all Churches so that proper human conscience would find support in the twentieth century. Hence, fully conscious of its duty of witnessing to Christ, the Church is committed to unite so that it would proclaim its spiritual message more effectively. Only through communion in the mystery of the One Christ would it achieve its mission of reconciliation, between God and man, the spirit and the flesh.

The friendly relations between the Roman Catholic Church and the Coptic Orthodox Church have become stronger and more expansive in this generation, particularly through meetings, visits and messages. Coptic delegates attended the sessions of the Vatican Council since 1962. Catholic representatives attended the celebration of the inauguration of St. Mark's Cathedral in Cairo, June 1968. The friendly gift of Your Holiness at that time of the relic of St. Mark now laid in his See in Cairo has met with feelings of deep regard and gratitude on behalf of the Copts. Later we attended the celebrations of St. Mark in Venice. We shared together in many conferences, to mention in particular the theological Consultation in

Vienna, September 1971, between theologians of the Oriental Orthodox Churches and the Roman Catholic Church, where a tentative formula of faith about the nature of Christ was achieved and approved by both sides. This was a positive successful and hopeful step which proved that theological discussions with friendly attitudes lead to proper and useful results.

Through this present personal meeting we are driving on to more promotion of this movement . . .

Your Holiness, as we celebrate the sixteenth Centenary of St. Athanasius the Apostolic, who played the greatest role in editing the Christian Creed at the Council of Nicea and defended the right faith with all power and persistence bestowed upon him by the Almighty, we remember that St. Athanasius the Copt is Father of both of us at the same time. He is father of the Church in the East as well as in the West. In him we meet as we meet at the feet of our Lord. We unite in his dogmas and faith.

In his steps proceeded St. Cyril the Great, the Alexandrian who became a pillar and a hero of Christian faith. As St. Athanasius had struggled against Arianism, so St. Cyril did for the defense of faith against Nestorianism and professed the faith of Western and Eastern Christianity. Like Athanasius he became a point of agreement not only in his faith but also in the proper and definite expression of faith which exemplify clearly the word of truth precisely and effectively.

The common traditional theology of Athanasius and Cyril stands as solid centre for the dialogue that we commit to a considerable number of theologians to go through in a spirit of faithful love. We expect them to agree on proper belief expressed in clear and uncomplicated language that all minds understand and consciences approve with comfort.

d. *Address of Paul VI to Amba Shenouda III**

On this solemn day the Church of Rome greets the Church of Alexandria in a gesture of brotherly love and peace.

Over sixteen hundred years ago, the great Saint Athanasius was welcomed by our predecessor Julius I, who saw in him a champion of that faith which was being compromised and even denied by people who were stronger than he in political power but weaker in faith and understanding. The Church of Rome supported him steadfastly. He in turn recognized in the Church of the West a secure identity of faith despite differences in vocabulary and in the theological approach to a deeper understanding of the mystery of the Triune God. His successor Peter was to find the same brotherly reception and support from our predecessor Damasus. A half century later, the Churches of Alexandria and Rome, in the person of their bishops Cyril and Celestine, were to serve once more as beacons of light when belief in the God-Man, Jesus Christ, was obscured by those who

---

* May 6, in St. Peter's Basilica. Extracts: SPCU *IS,* 22 (1973), pp. 6–7.

refused to render to the holy Mother of God her glorious title of "Theoto-kos". These are our great Fathers, Doctors of the faith and Pastors of men.

Humbly conscious of our own frailties we look to them to strengthen us now as we seek to fulfil the vocation to which God has called us.

For God has truly called us to great things. In a particular way, he wishes us to bring to the world his gift of faith, reconciliation and peace. Men, estranged from him and from each other, are to be reconciled by our humble ministry.

First, however, we must ask ourselves how far we can accomplish this if we Christians are not reconciled with each other. The question is an important one for us. By the grace of God we share with you faith in the one God, Father, Son and Holy Spirit. In Jesus Christ we profess the Incarnate Son of God, who for us and for our salvation was born of the Virgin Mary, suffered, died and rose from the dead. Incorporated into him by baptism, we share his divine life in the sacraments of his Church; we share the Apostolic traditions handed down by our common Fathers; our liturgical, theological, spiritual and devotional life are nourished from the same sources, even though they receive various legitimate expressions. We are particularly mindful of the fact that the principles of the spiritual life propounded by the great fathers of the Egyptian desert, beginning with Saint Anthony, have had an influence upon the entire Christian world.

Yet in humility and sorrow we must recognize that in the history of our Churches we have experienced fierce disputes over doctrinal formulae by which our substantial agreement in the reality they were trying to express was overlooked. Methods alien to the Gospel of Christ were at times used by some to try to impose that Gospel. Reasons of a cultural and political order as well as theological ones have been used to justify and even extend a division which should never have taken place. We cannot ignore this sad legacy. We recognize that a great deal must yet be done to overcome its harmful effects. However, we are determined that we will not let it continue to influence our relations.

A new phenomenon is taking place, of which our meeting today gives eloquent testimony. In mutual fidelity to our common Lord, we are rediscovering the many bonds which already bind us together.

In response to the brotherly invitation extended by our venerable predecessor John XXIII, your own predecessor of happy memory Kyrillos VI sent observers to all sessions of the Second Vatican Council. They were able to experience the efforts made by that great assembly to assist the reform and renewal of the Catholic Church. We are happy to greet two of them as they return to this Basilica with you today as bishops of your Church.

In 1968 we shared in the joy of the return of the relics of the Evangelist Saint Mark, from Venice to the venerable Church of Alexandria.

In 1969 we had the pleasure of greeting a large pilgrimage of Coptic Orthodox clergy and lay people; and more recently our own special delegation assisted at the solemn enthronement of Your Holiness as Father and Head of your Church. We recognize in these events signs coming from God. This is the favourable time which the Lord is granting us and we share with Your Holiness the determination to take advantage of it, knowing full well that there are still obstacles of a theological, psychological and institutional order to be overcome. Not denying them, we refuse to be frightened by them. At one time, the Christian world, torn apart by strife and schism, finally was able to recognize in the faith preached by both Damasus of Rome and Peter of Alexandria the genuine Catholic faith.

Trusting in God's grace and walking in his Spirit, we will strive to overcome the obstacles which still exist, so that once more our Churches can give a common and more perfect witness to the world which has so much need of him.

Venerable Brother, we meet on this solemn and joyful occasion when the Church of Rome celebrates the sixteenth centenary of the death of Saint Athanasius, Bishop of Alexandria. He was a man of constant faith, buoyant hope and generous openheartedness, even to those who opposed him. Because he was constant in his faith, he could hope against hope. And when, after bitter exile, God allowed him to return to his flock, he opened his heart to all men, ever seeking that reconciliation and peace which are God's gifts to us in his Incarnate Son.

May Athanasius, our common Father, intercede for us, that we may be more faithful servants of God in his Church and more effective pastors to those for whose sake Christ has given us the mission of breaking the bread of his Word and of his Body.

e. The Common Declaration *

Paul VI, Bishop of Rome and Pope of the Catholic Church, and Shenouda III, Pope of Alexandria and Patriarch of the See of St. Mark, give thanks in the Holy Spirit to God that, after the great event of the return of relics of St. Mark to Egypt, relations have further developed between the Churches of Rome and Alexandria so that they have now been able to meet personally together. At the end of their meetings and conversations they wish to state together the following:

We have met in the desire to deepen the relations between our Churches and to find concrete ways to overcome the obstacles in the way of our real cooperation in the service of our Lord Jesus Christ who has given us the ministry of reconciliation, to reconcile the world to Himself (*2 Cor.* 5:18-20).

---

* May 10, Vatican City. English Text: *AAS* 65 (1973), pp. 299–301.

In accordance with our apostolic traditions transmitted to our Churches and preserved therein, and in conformity with the early three ecumenical councils, we confess one faith in the One Triune God, the divinity of the Only Begotten Son of God, the Second Person of the Holy Trinity, the Word of God, the effulgence of His glory and the express image of His substance, who for us was incarnate, assuming for Himself a real body with a rational soul, and who shared with us our humanity but without sin. We confess that our Lord and God and Saviour and King of us all, Jesus Christ, is perfect God with respect to His Divinity, perfect man with respect to His humanity. In Him His divinity is united with His humanity in a real, perfect union without mingling, without commixtion, without confusion, without alteration, without division, without separation. His divinity did not separate from His humanity for an instant, not for the twinkling of an eye. He who is God eternal and invisible became visible in the flesh, and took upon Himself the form of a servant. In Him are preserved all the properties of the divinity and all the properties of the humanity, together in a real, perfect, indivisible and inseparable union.

The divine life is given to us and is nourished in us through the seven sacraments of Christ in His Church: Baptism, Chrism (Confirmation), Holy Eucharist, Penance, Anointing of the Sick, Matrimony and Holy Orders.

We venerate the Virgin Mary, Mother of the True Light, and we confess that she is ever Virgin, the God-bearer. She intercedes for us, and, as the Theotokos, excels in her dignity all angelic hosts.

We have, to a large degree, the same understanding of the Church, founded upon the Apostles, and of the important role of ecumenical and local councils. Our spirituality is well and profoundly expressed in our rituals and in the Liturgy of the Mass which comprises the centre of our public prayer and the culmination of our incorporation into Christ in His Church. We keep the fasts and feasts of our faith. We venerate the relics of the saints and ask the intercession of the angels and of the saints, the living and the departed. These compose a cloud of witnesses in the Church. They and we look in hope for the Second Coming of our Lord when His glory will be revealed to judge the living and the dead.

We humbly recognize that our Churches are not able to give more perfect witness to this new life in Christ because of existing divisions which have behind them centuries of difficult history. In fact, since the year 451 A.D., theological differences, nourished and widened by non-theological factors, have sprung up. These differences cannot be ignored. In spite of them, however, we are rediscovering ourselves as Churches with a common inheritance and are reaching out with determination and confidence in the Lord to achieve the fullness and perfection of that unity which is His gift.

As an aid to accomplishing this task, we are setting up a joint commission representing our Churches, whose function will be to guide common study in the fields of Church tradition, patristics, liturgy, theology, history and practical problems, so that by cooperation in common we may seek to resolve, in a spirit of mutual respect, the differences existing between our Churches and be able to proclaim together the Gospel in ways which correspond to the authentic message of the Lord and to the needs and hopes of today's world. At the same time we express our gratitude and encouragement to other groups of Catholic and Orthodox scholars and pastors who devote their efforts to common activity in these and related fields.

With sincerity and urgency we recall that true charity, rooted in total fidelity to the one Lord Jesus Christ and in mutual respect for each one's traditions, is an essential element of this search for perfect communion.

In the name of this charity, we reject all forms of proselytism, in the sense of acts by which persons seek to disturb each other's communities by recruiting new members from each other through methods, or because of attitudes of mind, which are opposed to the exigencies of Christian love or to what should characterize the relationships between Churches. Let it cease, where it may exist. Catholics and Orthodox should strive to deepen charity and cultivate mutual consultation, reflection and cooperation in the social and intellectual fields and should humble themselves before God, supplicating Him who, as He has begun this work in us, will bring it to fruition.

As we rejoice in the Lord who has granted us the blessings of this meeting, our thoughts reach out to the thousands of suffering and homeless Palestinian people. We deplore any misuse of religious arguments for political purposes in this area. We earnestly desire and look for a just solution for the Middle East crisis so that true peace with justice should prevail, especially in that land which was hallowed by the preaching, death and resurrection of our Lord and Saviour Jesus Christ, and by the life of the Blessed Virgin Mary, whom we venerate together as the Theotokos. May God, the giver of all good gifts, hear our prayers and bless our endeavours.

2. John Paul II to Coptic Orthodox Delegation*

I know that one of the fundamental questions of the ecumenical movement is the nature of that full communion we are seeking with each

---

* June 23, 1979, in an audience with a delegation sent by Shenouda III, Pope of Alexandria and Patriarch of St. Mark (Egypt). Extract: *Osservatore Romano,* June 24, 1979, p. 2. The delegation brought a letter from Shenouda, in which he mentions the four official meetings of the Joint Commission since 1974. "It became clear that our two Churches

other and the role that the Bishop of Rome has to play, by God's design, in serving that communion of faith and spiritual life, which is nourished by the sacraments and expressed in fraternal charity. A great deal of progress has been made in deepening our understanding of this question. Much remains to be done. I consider your visit to me and to the See of Rome a significant contribution towards resolving this question definitively.

The Catholic Church bases its dialogue of truth and charity with the Coptic Orthodox Church on the principles proclaimed by the Second Vatican Council, especially in the Constitution on the Church, *Lumen Gentium,* and the Decree on Ecumenism, *Unitatis Redintegratio.* I am happy to make my own the statements of the Common Declaration signed by my venerated predecessor Pope Paul VI with Pope Shenouda III in 1973 and the further encouragement the Holy See has given to this dialogue since that time.

Fundamental to this dialogue is the recognition that the richness of this unity in faith and spiritual life has to be expressed in diversity of forms. Unity—whether on the universal level or the local level—does not mean uniformity or absorption of one group by another. It is rather at the service of all groups to help each live better the proper gifts it has received from God's Spirit. This is an encouragement to move ahead with confidence and reliance upon the guidance of the Holy Spirit. Whatever may be the bitterness inherited from the past, whatever may be the present doubts and tensions that may exist, the Lord calls us to move forward in mutual trust and in mutual love. If true unity is to be achieved, it will be the result of cooperation among pastors on the local level, of the collaboration at all levels of the life of our Churches so that our people may grow in understanding of each other, in trust and love of each other. With no one trying to dominate each other but to serve each other, all together will grow into that perfection of unity for which Our Lord prayed on the night before he died (John 17) and for which the Apostle Paul exhorted us to work with all diligence (Eph. 4, 11–13).

Again, my thanks for your coming. My thoughts and prayers go to my brother Pope Shenouda III, to the bishops, clergy and faithful of your Church, as together with my brothers the bishops and the faithful of the Catholic Churches in Egypt you pray and work for full ecclesial communion which will be God's gift to all of us.

---

confess and profess in essence almost the same teaching that Christ our Lord is incarnate, who is perfect in His Divinity, and perfect in His Humanity. His Godhead and His Manhood are united together inseparably and unconfusedly." But in ecclesiology, "only very little real progress has been reached ... (in) the conception of the future relations between the two Churches and the practical steps to be taken at present and in the near future." Cf. SPCU *IS,* 41(1979), pp. 7–9.

VI

THE ORTHODOX CHURCH OF ALL GEORGIA

1. Visit of Patriarch Ilya II to John Paul II* (Vatican City, June 5–8, 1980)

a. Ilya II's Address to John Paul II
Your Holiness,
Blessed and Beloved Brother in Christ,
First Bishop of the most Ancient Church of Rome.

How marvellous and incomprehensible to human understanding is Divine Providence, by whose will we have come to the Holy City in which once suffered the great Apostles Peter and Paul, as well as many other luminaries of the Universal Christian Church.

We attach great importance to our visit, for this is the very first occasion on which the Chief Pastors of the Roman and Georgian Churches have met.

We have come here from the land in which is preserved the Tunic of Our Lord Jesus Christ; the land in which St Andrew, the first-called, and St Simon the Canaanean preached; the land in which St Nina carried out her work, she who bears the title "Equal to the Apostles"; the land in which the bishop and universal doctor St John Chrysostom died.

We have come to the city in which there is the Chair of St Peter, to reestablish those ancient and brotherly relations which traditionally existed between our two ancient Churches.

Sadly the complexities of history have brought about the division of our Holy Church. Nevertheless we believe that the Lord, with his almighty power, will grant us once again the unity which we have lost and which we desire.

Despite this sad fact, there have always been good mutual relations between our two Churches, and these have found expression in political, spiritual and scientific collaboration.

The Georgian Church and the people of Georgia form the great bridge that links the two great cultures of Europe and Asia.

Today the Christian Churches face many common problems; to resolve these we must draw closer together.

We value greatly the great contribution the Roman Catholic Church is making to mutual understanding between peoples and to the maintenance of peace in the world.

---

* Ilya II is also one of six presidents of the World Council of Churches. Extracts: SPCU *IS*, 44(1980), pp. 95–96.

b. Reply of John Paul II

We meet as brothers. The Church of Georgia treasures the preaching of St Andrew; the Church of Rome is founded on the preaching of St Peter. Andrew and Peter were brothers by blood, but they became brothers in spirit through their response to the call of Jesus Christ, true Son of God and "the first-born among many brethren" (*Rom* 8:29), who, in taking to himself the nature of all men, "was not ashamed to call them brethren" (*Heb* 2:11).

As heirs of Andrew and of Peter we meet today as brothers in Christ.

It is with brotherly love and concern that the Church of Rome has taken a keen interest in the joys and sorrows of the Church of Georgia. In times of peace and in times of persecution alike your Church has borne a faithful and exemplary witness to the Christian faith and the Christian sacraments, a witness borne by many holy men and martyrs from the days of St Nina onwards.

Your Holiness's concern for the renewal of the Church, a renewal firmly rooted in the apostolic tradition and in the particular traditions of the Church of Georgia, is a cause of special joy. You are well aware that the renewal of the Christian life is likewise the concern of the Church of Rome. It is this concern for renewal that has made us so keenly aware of the need and obligation to restore full communion between our Churches. The long course of our history has led to sad, and sometimes bitter, divisions which have led us to lose sight of our brotherhood in Christ; and our concern for renewal is one of the factors that has led us to see more clearly the need there is for unity among all who believe in Christ. The Second Vatican Council said: "Every renewal of the Church essentially consists in an increase of fidelity to her own calling. Undoubtedly this explains the dynamism of the movement towards unity" (*Unitatis Redintegratio*, 6). It went on to remind all the faithful that "the closer their union with the Father, the Word and the Spirit, the more deeply and easily will they be able to grow in mutual brotherly love" (*ibid.*, 7).

Today this task of restoring full communion between divided Christians is a priority for all who believe in Christ. It is our duty to Christ, whose seamless robe is rent by division. It is our duty to our fellowmen, for only with one voice can we effectively proclaim one faith in the Good News of salvation and thus obey our Lord's command to bring his Gospel to all mankind. And it is our duty to each other, for we are brothers and must express our brotherhood.

Chapter Twelve
RELATIONS WITH
THE ANGLICAN COMMUNION

Introduction

As defined by the Lambeth Conference of 1930, the Anglican Communion is "a fellowship, within the One Holy Catholic and Apostolic Church, of those duly constituted Dioceses, Provinces or Regional Churches in communion with the See of Canterbury". They "uphold and propagate the Catholic and Apostolic faith and order as set forth in the Book of Common Prayer," and are "bound together not by central legislative and executive authority, but by mutual loyalty sustained through the common counsel of the Bishops in conference". The latter refers to the decennial Lambeth Conference of all the bishops of the Communion.

I
VISIT OF ARCHBISHOP
MICHAEL RAMSEY TO PAUL VI*

Vatican City and Rome, March 22–24, 1966

1. Archbishop of Canterbury's Address to Paul VI**

Your Holiness, dear Brother in Christ, it is with heartfelt gratitude and brotherly affection in Christ that I greet you as your guest in this

---

* The Archbishop of Canterbury, Primate of all England and President of the Anglican Communion. Michael Ramsey's predecessor, Geoffrey Fisher, had met Pope John XXIII in "a visit of courtesy", on December 2, 1960. The Archbishop's first words to the Pope, "Your Holiness, we are making history!" It was the first time since the Reformation of the sixteenth century that a leader of one of its chief Churches met with a pope. There was, however, no joint communiqué, not even a photograph of the visit. Cf. London *Tablet*, Dec. 10, 1960, p. 1156.

** March 22, at their official meeting in the Sistine Chapel. Text: London *Tablet*, March 26, 1966, p. 372.

Vatican City. I greet you in my office as Archbishop of Canterbury and as President of the Lambeth Conference of Bishops from every part of the Anglican Communion throughout the world. Peace be unto you, and unto all Christians who live and pray within the obedience of the Roman Catholic Church.

I have come with the longing in my heart which I know to be in your heart also, that we may by our meeting together help in the fulfilment of the prayer of our Divine Lord that all his disciples may come to unity in the truth. All Christendom gives thanks to Almighty God for what was done in the service of unity by the greatly loving and greatly loved Pope John XXIII. It is in the same divine inspiration that Your Holiness works and prays for unity, and to that end you met with the Ecumenical Patriarch Athenagoras in Jerusalem and you now receive me here in Rome. May the grace of God enable us to serve His divine purpose by our meeting, and enable Christians everywhere to feel the pain of their divisions, and to seek unity in truth and holiness.

On the road to unity there are formidable difficulties of doctrine. All the more therefore it is my hope, and the hope of Your Holiness too, that there may be increasing dialogue between theologians, Roman Catholic and Anglican, and of other traditions, so as to explore together the divine revelation. On the road to unity there are also difficult practical matters about which the consciences and feelings of Christian people can be hurt. All the more therefore must such matters be discussed together in patience and charity. If the final goal of unity is yet some way ahead, Christians can rejoice already in the fact of their common baptism into the name of the Triune God, Father, Son and Holy Spirit, and they can already pray together, bear witness to God together and together serve humanity in Christ's name.

It is only as the world sees us Christians growing visibly in unity that it will accept through us the divine message of Peace. I would join my voice to the voice of Your Holiness in pleading that the nations agree to abandon weapons of destruction, to settle their quarrels without war, and to find a sovereignty greater than the sovereignty of each separate state. So may the song of the angels be echoed in the wills and actions of men: *Gloria in excelsis Deo, et in terra pax.*

2. Paul VI's Reply to Archbishop Ramsey*

You rebuild a bridge which for centuries has lain fallen between the Church of Rome and the Church of Canterbury: a bridge of respect, of esteem and of charity. You cross over this yet unstable viaduct, still under construction, with spontaneous initiative and sage confidence—may God bless this courage and this piety of yours! . . . Surely from heaven, St.

* March 22. Extracts: London *Tablet*, March 26, 1966, p. 372.

Gregory the Great and St. Augustine look down and bless. . . .We see the ecumenical value of this our meeting, We do not forget the grave and complex problems which it raises, and which it is not intended now to resolve; but these problems are here presented in their essential terms, which are always very difficult, formulated, however, in such a way as to be studied and meditated together—henceforth, without any resentment of human pride, without any shadow of earthly interests, in accordance with the word of Christ and the assistance of the Holy Spirit. . . .In the field of doctrine and ecclesiastical law, we are still respectively distinct and distant; and for now, it must be so, for the reverence due to truth and to freedom; until such a time as we may merit the supreme grace of true and perfect unity in faith and communion.

3. The Common Declaration*

In this city of Rome, from which St. Augustine was sent by St. Gregory to England and there founded the cathedral See of Canterbury, towards which the eyes of all Anglicans now turn as the center of their Christian Communion, His Holiness Pope Paul VI and His Grace Michael Ramsey, Archbishop of Canterbury, representing the Anglican Communion, have met to exchange fraternal greetings.

At the conclusion of their meeting they give thanks to Almighty God who by the action of the Holy Spirit has in these latter years created a new atmosphere of Christian fellowship between the Roman Catholic Church and the Churches of the Anglican Communion.

This encounter of March 23, 1966, marks a new stage in the development of fraternal relations, based upon Christian charity, and of sincere efforts to remove the causes of conflict and to re-establish unity.

In willing obedience to the command of Christ, who bade His disciples love one another, they declare that, with His help, they wish to leave in the hands of the God of mercy all that in the past has been opposed to this precept of charity, and that they make their own the mind of the Apostle which he expressed in these words: "Forgetting those things which are behind, and reaching forth unto those things which are before, I press toward the mark for the prize of the high calling of God in Christ Jesus" (Phil. 3:13–14).

They affirm their desire that all those Christians who belong to these two Communions may be animated by these same sentiments of respect, esteem and fraternal love, and in order to help these develop to the full, they intend to inaugurate between the Roman Catholic Church and the Anglican Communion a serious dialogue which, founded on the Gospels

---

* March 24. Read in Latin and in English at a common prayer service in the Basilica of St. Paul, Rome. *Text: AAS* 58 (1966), pp. 286–288.

and on the ancient common traditions, may lead to that unity in truth, for which Christ prayed.

The dialogue should include not only theological matters such as Scripture, Tradition and the Liturgy, but also matters of practical difficulty felt on either side. His Holiness the Pope and His Grace the Archbishop of Canterbury are, indeed, aware that serious obstacles stand in the way of a restoration of complete communion of faith and sacramental life. Nevertheless, they are of one mind in their determination to promote responsible contacts between their Communions in all those spheres of Church life where collaboration is likely to lead to a greater understanding and a deeper charity, and to strive in common to find solutions for all the great problems that face those who believe in Christ in the world of today.

Through such collaboration, by the grace of God the Father and in the light of the Holy Spirit, may the prayer of our Lord Jesus Christ for unity among His disciples be brought nearer to fulfillment, and with progress toward unity may there be a strengthening of peace in the world, the peace that only He can grant who gives "The peace that passeth all understanding," together with the blessing of Almighty God, Father, Son and Holy Spirit, that it may abide with all men forever.

II
ADDRESS AT THE SHRINE
OF ANGLICAN MARTYRS IN UGANDA*

From its earliest planning, it was Our earnest desire that in the course of this brief visit to Uganda We should come here, to Namugongo. We wished to meet the Anglican Church which flourishes in this country. We wished to pay homage to those sons of whom it is most proud: those who—together with our own Catholic Martyrs—gave the generous witness of their lives to the Gospel of the Lord we have in common, Jesus Christ. For all of them, there is the same inspired word of praise: "These all died in faith, not having received what was promised, but having seen and greeted it from afar, and having acknowledged that they were strangers and exiles on the earth" (*Hebr* 11, 13).

The Uganda martyrs were brought together by suffering, and died in faithful witness and hope. They now see, as we must, much to thank God for, "since God had foreseen something better for us, that apart from us they should not be made perfect" (*Hebr* 11, 40).

Among ecumenical enterprises, the Christian Council in Uganda is particularly flourishing. Since there can be no growth towards unity

---

* August 2, 1969. Anglican and Roman Catholic laity were martyred on Ascension Day, 1886. Extracts: SPCU *IS,* 3 (1969), p.7.

without strong deep local roots, it is Our prayer and, We feel confident, your prayer also, that the spiritual quality of this association may increase as collaboration extends into new fields.

Thus, not only in Uganda, but in all the great African continent, spiritual hunger will intensify to bring healing to that division of which the Second Vatican Council said that it "openly contradicts the will of Christ, scandalizes the world, and damages that most holy cause, the preaching of the Gospel to every creature" (*Unitatis Redintegratio,* No. 1). May the Lord bless the work of the All-Africa Christian Conference, as it bends its efforts towards the unity of all Christians!

A notable achievement in Christian co-operation is the common effort among the various confessions to provide readily accessible translations of Sacred Scripture, that rich source from which the minds and hearts of men receive the life-giving nourishment of divine Revelation. As the Council declared, "in the ecumenical dialogue itself, the Sacred Word is a precious instrument in the mighty hand of God, attaining to that unity which the Saviour holds out to all men" (*ibid*, No. 21)

III

CANONIZATION OF THE
FORTY ENGLISH MARTYRS*

While we are particularly pleased to note the presence of the official representative of the Archbishop of Canterbury, the Rev. Dr. Harry Smythe, we also extend our respectful and affectionate greeting to all members of the Anglican Church who have likewise come to take part in this ceremony. We indeed feel very close to them. We would like them to read in our heart the humility, gratitude and hope with which we welcome them. We wish also to greet the authorities and those personages who have come here to represent Great Britain, and together with them, all the other representatives of the countries and other religions. With all our heart we welcome them, as we celebrate the freedom and the fortitude of men who had, at the same time, spiritual faith and loyal respect for the sovereignty of civil society. . . .

May the blood of these martyrs be able to heal the great wound inflicted upon God's Church by reason of the separation of the Anglican Church from the Catholic Church.

Is it not one—these martyrs say to us—the Church founded by Christ? Is not this their witness? Their devotion to their nation gives us the

---

* October 25, 1970. Address during the solemn canonization ceremonies, in St. Peter's Basilica, for the forty Catholics in England and Wales who were martyred in the 16th and 17th centuries. Extracts: *AAS* 62 (1970), pp. 747–753.

assurance that on the day when—God willing—the unity of the faith and of Christian life is restored, no offence will be inflicted on the honor or the sovereignty of a great country such as England. There will be no seeking to lessen the legitimate prestige and the worthy patrimony of piety and usage proper to the Anglican Church when the Roman Catholic Church—this humble 'Servant of the servants of God'—is able to embrace her ever beloved sister in the one authentic Communion of the family of Christ: a communion of origin and of faith, a communion of priesthood and of rule, a communion of the saints in the freedom of love of the spirit of Jesus.

Perhaps we shall have to go on, waiting and watching in prayer, in order to deserve that blessed day. But already we are strengthened in this hope by the heavenly friendship of the forty martyrs of England and Wales who are canonized today.

IV
CANONIZATION OF ELIZABETH SETON*

Saint Elizabeth Ann Seton was born, brought up and educated in New York in the Episcopalian Communion. To this Church goes the merit of having awakened and fostered the religious sense and Christian sentiment which in the young Elizabeth were naturally predisposed to the most spontaneous and lively manifestations. We willingly recognize this merit, and, knowing well how much it cost Elizabeth to pass over to the Catholic Church, we admire her courage for adhering to the religious truth and divine reality which were manifested to her therein. And we are likewise pleased to see that from this same adherence to the Catholic Church she experienced great peace and security, and found it natural to preserve all the good things which her membership in the fervent Episcopalian community had taught her, in so many beautiful expressions, especially of religious piety, and that she was always faithful in her esteem and affection for those from whom her Catholic profession had sadly separated her. For us it is a motive of hope and a presage of ever better ecumenical relations to note the presence at this ceremony of distinguished Episcopalian dignitaries, to whom—interpreting as it were the heartfelt sentiments of the new Saint—we extend our greeting of devotion and good wishes.

---

* September 15, 1975. Elizabeth Ann Bayley Seton (1774–1821) is the first declared U.S. native-born saint. Born in New York City of an Episcopalian family, later mother of five children, then widowed, she became a Catholic in 1805 and founded the Sisters of Charity of Saint Joseph at Emmitsburg, Maryland. Paul VI refers to her religious background at the solemn canonization ceremony in St. Peter's Basilica. Extract: *AAS* 67 (1975), pp. 539–540.

V
PAUL VI'S AND ARCHBISHOP COGGAN'S
LETTERS ON WOMEN'S ORDINATION*

1. Archbishop Coggan to Pope Paul VI (July 9, 1975)

After our predecessor's visit to Rome in 1966, together with him you inaugurated a 'serious dialogue' between the Roman Catholic Church and the Anglican Communion. The agreed Statements of the consequent Anglican/Roman Catholic International Commission on the Eucharist and the Ministry are not authoritative statements of faith of either the Roman Catholic Church or the Anglican Communion; nevertheless they do bear witness to the steady growth of mutual understanding and trust developing between our two traditions.

It is with this in mind that we write now to inform Your Holiness of the slow but steady growth of a consensus of opinion within the Anglican Communion that there are no fundamental objections in principle to the ordination of women to the priesthood.

At the same time we are aware that action on this matter could be an obstacle to further progress along the path of unity Christ wills for his Church. The central authorities of the Anglican Communion have therefore called for common counsel on this matter, as has the General Synod of the Church of England. Thus in view of our concern, both for the truth as it is understood within the Anglican tradition, and for ecumenical counsel, we are already in correspondence with His Eminence Cardinal Jan Willebrands, President of the Secretariat for Promoting Christian Unity and with the Right Revd. Bishop John Howe, Secretary-General of the Anglican Consultative Council, and we anticipate mutual discussion on this question in the future.

It is our hope that such common counsel may achieve a fulfilment of the Apostle's precept that "Speaking the truth in love", we "may grow up into Him in all things, which is the head, even Christ."

2. Pope Paul VI to Archbishop Coggan (November 30, 1975)

We write in answer to your letter of 9th July last. We have many times had occasion to express to your revered predecessor, and more lately to yourself, our gratitude to God and our consolation at the growth of understanding between the Catholic Church and the Anglican Communion and to acknowledge the devoted work both in theological dialogue

---

* The two letters of Dr. Donald Coggan, Archbishop of Canterbury, were circulated to the members of the General Synod of the Church of England by its Secretary-General, July 26, 1976. Paul VI's letters: *AAS* 68 (1976), pp. 599–601.

and reflection and in Christian collaboration which promotes and witnesses to this growth.

It is indeed within this setting of confidence and candour that we see your presentation of the problem raised by the developments within the Anglican Communion concerning the ordination of women to the priesthood.

Your Grace is of course well aware of the Catholic Church's position on this question. She holds that it is not admissible to ordain women to the priesthood, for very fundamental reasons. These reasons include: the example recorded in the Sacred Scriptures of Christ choosing his Apostles only from among men; the constant practice of the Church, which has imitated Christ in choosing only men; and her living teaching authority which has consistently held that the exclusion of women from the priesthood is in accordance with God's plan for his Church.

The Joint Commission between the Anglican Communion and the Catholic Church, which has been at work since 1966, is charged with presenting in due time a final report. We must regretfully recognise that a new course taken by the Anglican Communion in admitting women to the ordained priesthood cannot fail to introduce into this dialogue an element of grave difficulty which those involved will have to take seriously into account.

Obstacles do not destroy mutual commitment to a search for reconciliation. We learn with satisfaction of a first informal discussion of the question between Anglican representatives and those of our Secretariat for Promoting Christian Unity at which the fundamental theological importance of the question was agreed on. It is our hope that this beginning may lead to further common counsel and growth of understanding.

3. Archbishop Coggan to Pope Paul VI (February 10, 1976)

It is now almost ten years since our beloved predecessor visited the City of Rome. On the 23rd of March 1966, in the Sistine Chapel, Your Holiness and His Grace the Archbishop of Canterbury met to exchange fraternal greetings; this encounter was of profound significance for the future relationship between the Churches of the Anglican Communion and the Roman Catholic Church. For this we thank God.

We also recall with deep gratitude that on the 24th of March, in the Basilica of St. Paul-Without-the-Walls, Your Holiness and His Grace made your Common Declaration announcing your intention to inaugurate the serious dialogue between our respective traditions which has already borne notable fruit in the work of the Anglican/Roman Catholic Commission on Mixed Marriages.

As Your Holiness recalled in your letter of November 30th 1975, which we were most grateful to receive, the goal which we jointly seek is that visible unity of the Church for which Christ prayed. We believe this unity will be manifested within a diversity of legitimate traditions because the Holy Spirit has never ceased to be active within the local churches throughout the world.

Sometimes what seems to one tradition to be a genuine expression of such a diversity in unity will appear to another tradition to go beyond the bounds of legitimacy. Discussion within the Anglican Communion concerning the possibility of the Ordination of Women is at present just such an issue. We are glad that informal discussion between Anglicans and Roman Catholics has already taken place about this matter at the Vatican Secretariat for Promoting Christian Unity. We hope such dialogue will continue in order that our respective traditions may grow in mutual understanding.

While we recognise that there are still many obstacles to be overcome upon that road to the "restoration of complete communion of faith and sacramental life", called for by our predecessor and Your Holiness, we nevertheless believe that in the power of the Spirit Christ's High Priestly prayer for unity will be fulfilled.

We humbly make this prayer our own as we offer Your Holiness our warm greetings and recall that historic meeting in Rome ten years ago. Moreover we look forward to the day when we too shall be able to meet Your Holiness so that together we may take further steps upon the path to unity.

4. Pope Paul VI to Archbishop Coggan (March 23, 1976)

As the tenth anniversary comes round of your revered predecessor's visit to Rome, we write to reciprocate with all sincerity the gratitude and the hope which, in recalling that historic occasion, you express in a letter recently handed to us by Bishop John Howe.

It is good to know that the resolves taken, the dialogue entered upon ten years ago, have continued and spread to many places, and that a new spirit of mutual consideration and trust increasingly pervades our relations.

In such a spirit of candour and trust you allude in your letter of greeting to a problem which has recently loomed large: the likelihood, already very strong it seems in some places, that the Anglican Churches will proceed to admit women to the ordained priesthood. We had already exchanged letters with you on this subject, and we were able to express the Catholic conviction more fully to Bishop John Howe when he brought your greetings. Our affection for the Anglican Communion has for many years been strong, and we have always nourished and often expressed ardent hopes that the Holy Spirit would lead us, in love and in obedience to God's will, along the path of reconciliation. This must be the measure of the sadness with which we encounter so grave a new obstacle and threat on that path.

But it is no part of corresponding to the promptings of the Holy Spirit to fail in the virtue of hope. With all the force of the love which moves us we pray that at this critical time the Spirit of God may shed his light abundantly on all of us, and that his guiding hand may keep us in the way of reconciliation according to his will.

Moreover, we sincerely appreciate the fact that you have expressed a desire to meet us, and we assure you that on our part we would look upon such a meeting as a great blessing and another means of furthering that complete unity willed by Christ for his Church.

VI
VISIT OF ARCHBISHOP
DONALD COGGAN TO PAUL VI*

Vatican City, April 27–30, 1977

1. Address of Paul VI to the Anglican Delegation**

The history of relations between the Catholic Church and the Anglican Communion has been marked by the staunch witness of such men as Charles Brent, Lord Halifax, William Temple and George Bell among the Anglicans; and Abbé Portal, Dom Lambert Beauduin, Cardinal Mercier and Cardinal Bea among the Catholics. The pace of this movement has quickened marvellously in recent years, so that these words of hope "the Anglican Church united not absorbed" are no longer a mere dream.

You yourselves, Brethren, are concerned that the Gospel should be translated into deeds, and renew its significance for a society of Christian tradition. As our predecessor Pius XI put it, "the Church civilizes by evangelizing".

That Gospel is the heart and soul of your Christian living and it is equally our inspiration. The civilization of love is our shared hope—something which is utopia for the worldly-wise, but prophecy for those who live in truth.

With the happiness of that shared hope we greet you and bid you welcome here. May your visit be fruitful and carry us forward along the pilgrim way of love and unity in the Risen Christ.

---

* Archbishop of Canterbury, and successor to Michael Ramsey.
** April 28, at the end of the private audience between the Pope and the Archbishop. Among the delegation: Bishop Alexander Howe, Secretary General of the Anglican Consultative Council; Bishop John Trillo, President of the Church of England's Committee for Relations with the Catholic Church; Rev. Christopher Hill, co-secretary of the International Anglican/Roman Catholic Commission. Extract: SPCU *IS*, 34 (1977), p. 1.

2. Address of Archbishop Coggan to Paul VI*

In this place, hallowed by the prayers of the faithful over so many centuries, meetings have taken place over the last 17 years which have brought together brethren in Christ hitherto separated by the differences and misunderstandings of the centuries. . . . From this place we look out to a world enlightened in large part by the Gospel of Christ, but still dark in larger part where the Gospel has not penetrated.

Even where the Church of Christ is strong, in places such as Uganda, where the members of our Communions work in considerable strength, our brethren suffer greatly. We send to our brethren in Africa and in many other places where the rule of freedom and justice is impeded, the assurance of our united concern and prayers.

As our Lord prayed not only for his immediate disciples but also for those who in the future would believe in him, so together we pray for them, that they may be kept by the power of his Name, in truth, in peace, and in love.

Let us pray also for ourselves, that, as we are united by baptism and by a living faith, so, strengthened by the word of God's grace and by the Body and Blood of Christ, we may reach out in joint evangelistic action to those for whom our Saviour Christ was contented to be betrayed and given up into the hands of sinful men.

3. Address of Paul VI to Archbishop Coggan**

If we examine the list of pioneers in the search for unity, we cannot but be reminded of the majestic survey in the eleventh chapter of the Letter to the Hebrews. It is a survey which puts the Holy Scriptures before us as a record of faith. And we are still "surrounded by so great a cloud of witnesses" (*Heb* 12, 1), for those who in recent years have laboured in the cause of unity have witnessed no less to faith and hope, and to the perseverance which is their outward manifestation.

It is the experience of all of us today that the world desperately needs Christ. The young, in whose aspirations good is often seen most vividly, feel this need most strongly. Secular optimism does not satisfy them. They are waiting for a proclamation of hope. Now is our chance to bear witness together that Christ is indeed the way, and the truth and the life, and that he is communicated through the Holy Spirit.

Here is a task to which the Lord calls everyone who invokes his name. Those who are charged with the care of Christians, and who minister to them, feel especially the responsibility of fidelity to the apostolic faith, its embodiment in the life of the Church today, and its transmission to the

* April 29, in the Sistine Chapel. Extracts: SPCU *IS* 34 (1977), p. 3.
** April 29, in Sistine chapel. Extracts: *AAS* 69 (1977), pp. 284–286.

Church of tomorrow. To discern "the signs of the times" calls for constant refreshment of mind and spirit at the Christian sources, and especially in the Holy Scriptures. In sending all ministers and teachers to the Scriptures, the Vatican Council borrows strong words from Saint Augustine: those ministers and teachers should remain in close contact with the Scriptures by means of reading and accurate study of the text, so as not to become like "one who vainly preaches the word of God externally, while he does not listen to it inwardly". And from Saint Jerome it takes words even more pointed: "Ignorance of the Scriptures is indeed ignorance of Christ."

The supplications we make together this morning to our common Lord are steeped in the Christian love of God's word, and they renew the reality of that pledge made together with us by your revered Predecessor— the pledge to a serious dialogue which, founded on the Gospels and on the ancient common traditions, may lead to that perfect unity in truth for which Christ prayed. What a challenge, what an uplifting ambition is here! It is good that, while our experts continue their work, we should meet humbly to encounter our Lord in prayer. Indeed we might think of the example of Moses, supported by Aaron and Hur, holding up his arms in supplication for Israel (cf. *Ex* 17, 10–13). Today we raise our prayers in support of those who strive for reconciliation and unity in Christ.

To falter in prayer is to falter in hope and to put the cause at risk. We know that a long road remains to be travelled. But does not one of the most moving accounts of the Risen Christ in Saint Luke's Gospel tell us how, as two of the disciples travelled a road together, Christ joined them and "interpreted to them in all the Scriptures the things concerning himself"? (*Lk* 24, 27).

Let us listen as we walk, strong in faith and hope, along the road marked out for us.

4. The Common Declaration*

1. After four hundred years of estrangement, it is now the third time in seventeen years that an archbishop of Canterbury and the Pope embrace in Christian friendship in the city of Rome. Since the visit of Archbishop Ramsey eleven years have passed, and much has happened in that time to fulfil the hopes then expressed and to cause us to thank God.

2. As the Roman Catholic Church and the constituent Churches of the Anglican Communion have sought to grow in mutual understanding and Christian love, they have come to recognise, to value and to give thanks for a common faith in God our Father, in our Lord Jesus Christ, and in the Holy Spirit; our common baptism into Christ; our sharing of the

---

* April 19, read in the Pauline Chapel. Text: *AAS* 69 (1977), pp. 286–289.

Holy Scriptures, of the Apostles' and Nicene Creeds, the Chalcedonian definition, and the teaching of the Fathers; our common Christian inheritance for many centuries with its living traditions of liturgy, theology, spirituality and mission.

3. At the same time in fulfilment of the pledge of eleven years ago to "a serious dialogue which, founded on the Gospels and on the ancient common traditions, may lead to that unity in truth, for which Christ prayed" (Common Declaration PPVI/ABC 1966) Anglican and Roman Catholic theologians have faced calmly and objectively the historical and doctrinal differences which have divided us. Without compromising their respective allegiances, they have addressed these problems together, and in the process they have discovered theological convergences often as unexpected as they were happy.

4. The Anglican/Roman Catholic International Commission has produced three documents: on the Eucharist, on Ministry and Ordination and on Church and Authority. We now recommend that the work it has begun be pursued, through procedures appropriate to our respective Communions, so that both of them may be led along the path towards unity.

The moment will shortly come when the respective Authorities must evaluate the conclusions.

5. The response of both communions to the work and fruits of theological dialogue will be measured by the practical response of the faithful to the task of restoring unity, which as the Second Vatican Council says "involves the whole Church, faithful and clergy alike" and "extends to everyone according to the talents of each" (*Unitatis Redintegratio*, n. 5). We rejoice that this practical response has manifested itself in so many forms of pastoral cooperation in many parts of the world; in meetings of bishops, clergy and faithful.

6. In mixed marriages between Anglicans and Roman Catholics, where the tragedy of our separation at the sacrament of union is seen most starkly, cooperation in pastoral care (*Matrimonia Mixta*, par. 14) in many places has borne fruit in increased understanding. Serious dialogue has cleared away many misconceptions and shown that we still share much that is deep-rooted in the Christian tradition and ideal of marriage, though important differences persist, particularly regarding remarriage after divorce. We are following attentively the work thus far accomplished in this dialogue by the Joint Commission on the Theology of Marriage and its Application to Mixed Marriages. It has stressed the need for fidelity and witness to the ideal of marriage, set forth in the New Testament and constantly taught in Christian tradition. We have a common duty to defend this tradition and ideal and the moral values which derive from it.

7. All such cooperation, which must continue to grow and spread, is the true setting for continued dialogue and for the general extension and appreciation of its fruits, and so for progress towards that goal which is

Christ's will—the restoration of complete communion in faith and sacramental life.

8. Our call to this is one with the sublime Christian vocation itself which is a call to communion; as St. John says "that which we have seen and heard we proclaim also to you, so that you may have fellowship with us; and our fellowship is with the Father and His Son Jesus Christ" (*I John* 1, 3). If we are to maintain progress in doctrinal convergence and move forward resolutely to the communion of mind and heart for which Christ prayed we must ponder still further his intentions in founding the Church and face courageously their requirements.

9. It is their communion with God in Christ through faith and through baptism and self-giving to Him that stands at the centre of our witness to the world, even while between us communion remains imperfect. Our divisions hinder this witness, hinder the work of Christ (*Evangelii Nuntiandi, 77*) but they do not close all roads we may travel together. In a spirit of prayer and of submission to God's will we must collaborate more earnestly in a "greater common witness to Christ before the world in the very work of evangelisation" (*Evangelii Nuntiandi*, ibid.). It is our desire that the means of this collaboration be sought: the increasing spiritual hunger in all parts of God's world invites us to such a common pilgrimage.

This collaboration pursued to the limit allowed by truth and loyalty, will create the climate in which dialogue and doctrinal convergence can bear fruit. While this fruit is ripening, serious obstacles remain both of the past and of recent origin. Many in both communions are asking themselves whether they have a common faith sufficient to be translated into communion of life, worship and mission. Only the communions themselves through their pastoral authorities can give that answer. When the moment comes to do so, may the answer shine through in spirit and truth, not obscured by the enmities, the prejudices and the suspicions of the past.

10. To this we are bound to look forward and to spare no effort to bring it closer: to be baptised into Christ is to be baptised into hope—"and hope does not disappoint us because God's love has been poured into our hearts through the Holy Spirit which has been given us" (*Rom* 5, 5).

11. Christian hope manifests itself in prayer and action—in prudence but also in courage. We pledge ourselves and exhort the faithful of the Roman Catholic Church and of the Anglican Communion to live and work courageously in this hope of reconciliation and unity in our common Lord.

VII
MESSAGE OF PAUL VI
TO THE LAMBETH CONFERENCE*

We have learnt with deep interest of the forthcoming eleventh Lambeth Conference of the Bishops of the Anglican Communion, to be held this year in the historic city of Canterbury.

Vivid memories of the Second Vatican Council enable us to appreciate the value of such a period of common reflection by Christian pastors, and we note with happiness that the theme which is to dominate the Conference is the place and function of the Bishop in the world of today. This theme has already been the subject of fruitful dialogue between Anglican and Catholic scholars, and we hope that the Conference on its part may serve to lead us closer together in fellowship.

We assure you of our prayers for the Conference and invoke God's abundant blessings upon it.

VIII
MEETING OF JOHN PAUL II AND ARCHBISHOP ROBERT RUNCIE**

The first meeting of Pope John Paul II and the Archbishop of Canterbury, Robert Runcie, though a brief encounter in the midst of full programmes, has been a joyful and moving occasion. They were glad that it took place in Africa where the rapid expansion and the self-sacrificing zeal of the Church and the visible enthusiasm and love for Our Lord Jesus Christ has many lessons for Christians in Europe. They recognize the immense opportunities for the Christian Church in the countries of Africa to proclaim Christ in worship and in service and to make a contribution to the search for peace and justice. They believe that the time is too short and the need too pressing to waste Christian energy on old rivalries and that the talents and resources of all the Churches must be shared if Christ is to be seen and heard effectively.

Their much loved predecessors, Paul VI and Archbishop Donald Coggan, saw the urgent need for this common action and solemnly committed themselves to work for it in the common declaration of 1977. Pope John Paul II and Archbishop Robert Runcie endorse that commit-

---

* On July 18, 1978, shortly before Paul VI died (August 6), he sent this message to the 11th Lambeth Conference, involving nearly all the diocesan bishops of the Anglican Communion (July 22–Aug. 13). Text: SPCU *IS,* 40 (1979), pp. 20–21.

** May 9, 1980, in Accra, Ghana, West Africa. On March 25, 1980 Dr. Runcie succeeded Dr. Donald Coggan as Anglican Primate. This official communiqué: SPCU *IS,* 44 (1980), p. 90.

ment to "collaborate more earnesly in a greater common witness to Christ", and they share the recognition that common action depends on progress in the "serious dialogue", now nearly fourteen years established, by which Roman Catholics and Anglicans have been seeking the way to that unity of faith and communion which Christ wills for his Church.

Chapter Thirteen
EXTRACTS FROM PAPAL LETTERS, SERMONS, ADDRESSES, ETC.

I
POPE PAUL VI

1. Ecclesiam Suam*

The dialogue, which has come to be called ecumenical, has already begun. In some areas it is making real headway. There is much to be said on this complex and delicate subject, but our discourse does not end here. For the moment we limit ourself to a few remarks—none of them new.

The principle that we are happy to make our own is this: Let us stress what we have in common rather than what divides us. This provides a good and fruitful subject for our dialogue. We are ready to carry it out wholeheartedly. We will say more: On many points of difference regarding tradition, spirituality, canon law, and worship, we are ready to study how we can satisfy the legitimate desires of our Christian brothers, still separated from us. It is our dearest wish to embrace them in a perfect union of faith and charity.

But we must add that it is not in our power to compromise with the integrity of the faith or the requirements of charity. We foresee that this will cause misgiving and opposition, but now that the Catholic Church has

---

* Paul VI published his first encyclical on August 6, 1964, shortly before the third Council session, "in order to communicate some of the dominant thoughts in our heart which seem useful as practical guidelines at the beginning of our service of Pope". He describes "the actual relations of humankind with the Catholic Church in concentric circles". The circle "which is nearest to us contains those who bear the name of Christ". *Ecclesiam Suam* extract: *AAS* 56 (1964), pp. 655–657.

taken the initiative in restoring the unity of Christ's fold, it will not cease to go forward with all patience and consideration.

It will not cease to show that the prerogatives, which keep the separated brothers at a distance, are not the fruits of historic ambition or of fanciful theological speculation, but derive from the will of Christ and that, rightly understood, they are for the good of all and make for common unity, freedom and Christian perfection. The Catholic Church will not cease, by prayer and penance, to prepare herself worthily for the longed-for reconciliation.

In reflecting on this subject, it distresses us to see how we, the promoter of such reconciliation, are regarded by many of the separated brethren as being its stumbling-block, because of the primacy of honor and jurisdiction which Christ bestowed upon the Apostle Peter, and which we have inherited from him.

Do not some of them say that if it were not for the primacy of the Pope, the reunion of the separated churches with the Catholic Church would be easy?

We beg the separated brethren to consider the inconsistency of this position, not only in that, without the Pope the Catholic Church would no longer be Catholic, but also because, without the supreme, efficacious and decisive pastoral office of Peter the unity of the Church of Christ would utterly collapse.

It would be vain to look for other principles of unity in place of the one established by Christ Himself. As St. Jerome justly wrote: "There would arise in the Church as many sects as there are priests." We should also like to observe that this fundamental principle of Holy Church has not as its objective a supremacy of spiritual pride and human domination. It is a primacy of service, of ministration, of love. It is not empty rhetoric which confers upon the Vicar of Christ the title of "Servant of the Servants of God."

111. It is along these lines that our dialogue is alert, and, even before entering into fraternal conversation, it speaks in prayer and hope with the heavenly Father.

112. We must observe, Venerable Brethren, with joy and confidence, that the vast and varied circle of separated Christians is pervaded by spiritual activities which seem to promise consoling developments in regard to their reunion in the one Church of Christ. We beg that the Holy Spirit will breathe upon the "ecumenical movement," and we recall the emotion and joy we felt at Jerusalem in our meeting, full of charity and new hope, with the Patriarch Athenagoras.

We wish to greet with gratitude and respect the participation of so many representatives of separated churches in the Second Vatican Ecumenical Council.

We want to give our assurance, once again, that we have an attentive, reverent interest in the spiritual movements connected with the problem of unity, which are stirring up vital and noble religious sentiments in various individuals, groups and communities. With love and reverence we greet all these Christians, in the hope that we may promote together, even more effectively, the cause of Christ and the unity which He desired for His Church, in the dialogue of sincerity and love.

2. Address to the Secretariat for Promoting Christian Unity*

We propose to review with you, beloved sons, some of the points which seem to us the most significant among those which are raised today in the Catholic world by the question of ecumenism. . . .

First of all, the ecumenical question has been raised by Rome in all its gravity, its breadth, and its innumerable doctrinal and practical implications. It has not been considered with an occasional and passing glance, but has become the object of permanent interest, of systematic study and of unceasing charity.

It remains such, in accordance with a line which has by now become part of our apostolic ministry. The council makes this an obligation for us and traces the way for us.

The conciliar documents which deal expressly or incidentally with the question of the recomposition of the unity of the one Church by all those who bear the name of Christian are so authoritative and so explicit, they have such a force of orientation and obligation, that they offer Catholic ecumenism a doctrinal and pastoral basis that it never had before.

We must admit that we have here a fact in which the Holy Spirit, who guides and animates the Church, plays the principal and decisive part. We will be docile and faithful to Him. We are happy in this respect to comply with the wish that had been expressed to us and to announce that the first part of the "Ecumenical Directory" will be published within the very near future.

Secondly: an ecumenical spirit has been created and is developing. This is a merit of the council, and also the merit of the undertaking, which had already spread and become known everywhere, of celebrating a "week of prayer" for the recomposition of the unity of the Christians in the one Church of Christ. It is the merit of the diligent activity of the Secretariat and finally, the merit of the innumerable undertakings, organized by the bishops with the support of the clergy, the faithful, scholars and public

---

* April 28, 1967, at the SPCU's General Meeting *(Plenarium)* of bishop members, consultors and staff. French Text: *AAS* 59(1967), 493–498. English Extracts: SPCU *IS,* 2 (1967), pp. 3–5.

opinion, in noble competition with the separated brethren, to promote the cause of ecumenism by means of speech, writings, and meetings.

The conviction that unity is willed by Christ, that it is an important and urgent question not only for Christianity but also for the spiritual destinies of the world, the conviction that it is no longer a matter of dwelling on discussion of the historical causes from which present divisions originate but that it is necessary to form friendly and loyal relations between the Catholic Church and all other Christian communities which sincerely pursue ecumenical aims, that a fundamental unity between all baptized Christians already exists in the faith in Christ and in the invocation of the Most Blessed Trinity, this conviction—we were saying—already full of so many factors favorable to ecumenism, is by now present and active in every vigilant Christian heart and this seems to us a great achievement.

Charity inspires the entire spiritual process and aims at expressing itself in external forms. Respect, loyalty, esteem, trust mark with a Christian seal the friendly and practical relations which are being established in determined fields between Catholics and Christians of other confessions.

They prepare, God willing, for agreements which may still at this stage seem delicate and difficult but promise already to be full of truth and of joy in the spirit of the Lord.

Thirdly: the series of meetings to which we have referred must be attributed to the mysterious inspiration of the Holy Spirit: significant and moving meetings which not only we ourself but also members of your Secretariat have had the honor and the opportunity to have with illustrious representatives of Churches, communities and cultural trends which are close to us through the common reference to the name of Christ but are still separated from us in one way or another. . . .

These visits, conversations and promises are carved in our memory as so many dazzling signs, as the mysterious prelude of the forthcoming apparition of the Christ among us, announcing His ineffable peace and manifesting His unfailing presence there where it is truly in His name that we have gathered.

These are not signs of the aging of Christianity, as some have insinuated, but are further proofs, instead, of its ever renewed youth.

These rapprochements are not based on an equivocal irenicism aiming at the elimination of doctrinal and canonical difficulties. No, they are the fruit, rather, of a mutual and spontaneous effort of reciprocal understanding, aiming at the discovery of the truths of the faith and of the concrete demands of ecclesial charity—the sole bases of an authentic and perfect unity.

The symphony of the dialogue thus begins to spread in various forms and in various groups and seems to be a prelude to the final harmony of the Church which was at its beginning—do not let us forget—"one heart and one soul" (*Acts* 4, 32).

Fourthly: this ecumenical progress is not without difficulties. No one is more aware of it than you are. Incomprehension and opposition which has lasted for centuries cannot be dispelled in a few years. Patience is an ecumenical virtue. Psychological maturing is no less slow nor less difficult than theological discussion.

The possibility alone of having to abandon old positions, stiffened by bitter memories and mixed up with questions of prestige and subtle controversies, reawakens reactions of principle on which it would seem impossible to compromise.

The habit of being resigned to a Christianity torn within itself might lead one to fear the prospect of a reconciliation which would restore to it its primitive hierarchical and community features, presenting it to the world without those aspects to which we have become accustomed—incomprehensible sectarian exclusiveness, and pluralism which extends to essentials and is therefore intolerable. In face of such a fear, each turns in afresh on himself, resists and rebels. Ecumenism comes to a standstill.

It comes to a standstill before particular problems, such, for instance, as the problem of proselytism. Nevertheless, if presented in its true light and conducted according to practical criteria—not those of a vain emulation but reasonable and always brotherly—proselytism, or rather, the missionary effort, should not frighten anyone, but should rather appear as the peaceful, legitimate and rightful exercise of an indisputable religious liberty.

Likewise, ecumenism comes to a standstill before the canonical discipline of mixed marriages and before many other problems which are certainly very complicated and delicate and to which, for our part, we will endeavor to give the most sympathetic attention.

There is, on the other hand, a certain ecumenism which would be too precipitate, on other points, and go beyond the confines marked by theological reality and established rules—as sometimes in the 'communio in sacris'. Excesses too can harm the frank and loyal progress of true ecumenism.

And what should we say of the difficulty to which our separated brothers are always so sensitive? That which comes from the function that God has assigned to us in the Church of God and which our tradition has sanctioned with such authority?

The Pope, as we well know, is undoubtedly the gravest obstacle in the path of ecumenism. What shall we say? Should we refer once more to titles which justify our mission? Should we once more attempt to present it in its exact terms such as it is really intended to be—the indispensable principle of truth, charity, and unity? A pastoral mission of guidance, of service and of brotherhood which does not challenge the liberty and honor of anyone who has a legitimate position in the Church of God, but instead protects the rights of all and demands no other obedience than that which is demanded from the sons of a family?

It is not easy for us to make our apologia. It is you who with words of sincerity and mildness will know how to make it when the occasion and the possibility arises. As far as we are concerned, in all serenity we prefer to remain silent and pray.

If there is a cause in which our human efforts prove unable to attain any good results and show themselves to be essentially dependent on the mysterious and powerful action of the Holy Spirit, it is precisely this one of ecumenism. This awareness of our weakness, of the disproportion between our forces and the results to be obtained make us humble to the point where we are tempted to believe that our plans are naive, that our undertakings are in vain, that it is all a matter of the dreams of people who do not know the laws of history and of human psychology.

3. Address to the National Council of Churches U.S.A. Delegation*

In 1964, We stated to the representatives of the various Christian churches and communities gathered in Bombay: "It is Our hope that Our efforts can accompany yours, can mingle with yours so that together, in humility and charity and mutual understanding, we can seek out the ways by which Christ's will 'that all may be one' can one day be fully realized" (cf. *Il viaggio di Paolo VI in India,* p. 74). More recently We affirmed that "the ecumenical question has been raised by Rome in all its gravity, its breadth, and its innumerable doctrinal and practical implications. It has not been considered with an occasional and passing glance, but has become the object of permanent interest, of systematic study and of unceasing charity. It remains such, in accordance with a line which has now become part of Our apostolic ministry. The Council makes this an obligation for us and traces the way for us" (cf. *Oss. Rom.,* 28 April, 1967).

Your distinguished spokesman** had mentioned the common initiatives which you are making as Christians to help resolve the pressing problems of war and violence, of conflict between races and between the rich and the poor, of the gap between the generations. Indeed, "not everyone who cries, 'Lord, Lord' will enter into the kingdom of heaven,

---

* March 28, 1969. Six representatives of the National Council of Churches of Christ in the U.S.A. were in Rome to confer with Paul VI, the SPCU staff and consultors, and representatives of the Roman Curia. The Chairman of the delegation was Bishop James K. Mathews, United Methodist Church. Accompanying the delegation as its guests were two representatives of the U.S. Bishops' Committee for Ecumenical and Interreligious Affairs. Extracts: SPCU *IS,* 7 (1969), pp. 15–16.

** Rev. Dr. Robert J. Marshall, President, Lutheran Church in America. Text of his opening statement: *ibid.,* pp. 13–14.

but those who do the Father's will and take a strong grip on the world at hand" (*Gaudium et Spes,* n. 93). We are happy to know that while you are endeavoring to carry out these activities, you are together reflecting on the biblical message itself.

For We are convinced that doctrine and practice are inextricably intertwined in the common effort towards that unity through which Christ will truly be a sign to the world. Doctrine animates action; it guides it, gives it deeper inspiration and ensures that action is truly christian. On the other hand, action gives a new and dynamic dimension to reflection upon the doctrine of Christ and its meaningful application to the concrete problems of today's world.

This dialectic between truth and love, doctrine and action, experience and reflection, is the fulfilment of those words of St. Paul which form, what could be called, "the great ecumenical commandment": "Veritatem facientes in caritate: Speaking the truth in love, we are to grow up in every way into him who is the head, into Christ" (Eph. 4:15).

Fidelity to that Pauline "commandment" will help us to search out, understand and exploit those many bonds which already unite us as brothers in Christ, so that both in our teaching and in our common activity, the Good News of the Resurrected Lord may become more visible in the living practice of Christians. Such fidelity will indeed more clearly reveal the painful differences which still exist among brothers in Christ, but will help us discern better those ways of activity which can make an authentic contribution towards resolving those differences, and distinguish them from others which, though often inspired by sincere good will and love, in the final analysis impede rather than assist the search for that restoration of christian unity which will make more vivid our common witness to the world.

You no doubt are aware that the witness of your ecumenical spirit, attitudes and activities is not confined to your own country. The relations between Roman Catholics and Protestants in the United States have, in many ways, implications for the general ecumenical and—We would add—missionary movements throughout the world.

We wish to assure you that We are deeply sensitive to the seriousness and the loyalty to our common Lord Jesus Christ which marks the work of your Council itself, and the various types of collaboration you have already undertaken and propose to undertake with the Roman Catholic Church.

In a particular way, then, may Christians in the United States, "being rooted and grounded in love" (Eph. 3:17), realize in themselves and for the world "the immeasurable greatness of his power in us who believe, according to the working of his great might which he accomplished in Christ when he raised him from the dead and made him sit at his right hand in the heavenly places" (Eph. 2:19–20).

4. Address to a Delegation from the Lutheran World Federation*

We hold in living memory the openness with which the Lutheran World Federation participated in the Council through representatives of quality. A series of publications testifies to the interest and the care with which your observers and other Lutheran theologians have followed the Council and studied its decrees. We remember particularly the second Conciliar session where Prof. Skydsgaard, representing your federation, spoke on behalf of all observers of the Council and underlined the fundamental importance for the ecumenical movement of a theology of the history of salvation. This task will be assumed, particularly, through the new Ecumenical Institute of Jerusalem.

We have recognized with great interest to what extent the collaboration with the Lutheran World Federation has been intensified after the Council. We think especially of the mixed working group between the Lutheran World Federation and the Roman Catholic Church which met first in 1965 and has met every year since.

We rejoice in seeing that for three years the problems of Gospel and Church have been examined by this study commission between evangelical Lutherans and Roman Catholics and we are convinced this question is one of the most central which still stands between us and without solution since the unhappy rupture of the time of the Reformation.

We are aware that the cooperation between the Lutheran World Federation and the Roman Catholic Church is not limited to just the theological field but has led to a number of ecumenical contacts during the past years. Your visit is a cause of joy for us because it opens new perspectives of cooperation and dialogue with the Roman Catholic Church in order to achieve to an ever-increasing degree our fundamental unity with Christ.

5. Address to the World Council of Churches**

Is not the World Council a marvelous movement of Christians, of "children of God who are scattered abroad" (John 11:52), who are now searching for a recomposition in unity? Is not the meaning of our coming here, at the threshold of your house, found in that joyous obedience to an unseen impulse which, by the merciful command of Christ, makes our ministry and mission what it is? Truly a blessed encounter, a prophetic moment, dawn of a day to come and yet awaited for centuries!

---

* May 31, 1969. A seven-member L.W.F. staff delegation, headed by Dr. André Appel, General Secretary. Extracts: SPCU *IS,* 8 (1969), p. 11.
** June 10, 1969, on the occasion of the Pope's visit to the W.C.C. headquarters in Geneva, Switzerland. Extract: SPCU *IS,* 8 (1969), pp. 20–23

We are here among you. Our name is Peter. Scripture tells us which meaning Christ has willed to attribute to this name, what duties He lays upon us: the responsibilities of the Apostle and his successors. But permit us to recall other titles which the Lord wishes to give to Peter in order to signify other charisms. Peter is fisher of of men. Peter is shepherd. In what concerns our persons, we are convinced that without merit on our part, the Lord has given us a ministry of communion. This charisma has been given to us not indeed to isolate us from you or to exclude among us understanding, collaboration, fellowship and ultimately, the recomposition of unity, but to allow us to carry out the command and the gift of love in truth and humility (cf. Ephesians 4, 15: John 13, 14). And the name Paul which we have assumed sufficiently points out the orientation which we have wanted to give to our apostolic ministry.

You have placed the visit this afternoon in the historical context of our relations. We also see in this gesture a clear sign of the Christian fellowship which already exists between all the baptized, and thus between the member churches of the World Council and the Catholic Church. The present communion between the Christian Churches and communities is regretfully only imperfect: but, as we believe, the Father of mercies, in His spirit, is leading and inspiring us. He is guiding all Christians in the search for the fullness of that unity which Christ wills for His one and only church in order that it may better reflect the ineffable union of the Father and the Son and fulfil its mission in the world of which Jesus is the Lord: "In order that the world may believe" (John 17, 21).

This supreme desire of Christ, and the deep need of men who believe in Him and have been redeemed by Him, keep our spirit in a constant tension of humility, of regret for the present divisions among the followers of Christ: of a hope-filled desire for the restoration of unity among all Christians: of prayer and reflection on the mystery of the Church which is committed, for its sake and that of the world, to give witness to the revelation made by God the Father, through the Son and in the Holy Spirit. You may understand how at this moment this tension reaches a high degree of emotion in us, but far from troubling us, it rather makes our conscience clearer than ever.

You* have also referred to the visit of this same center in February, 1965, of the beloved Cardinal Bea, and to the setting up of a joint working group. Since the creation of this group, we have followed its work with interest, and we wish to express, without hesitation, our profound appreciation for the development of these relations between the World Council

---

* I.e., Dr. Eugene Carson Blake, General Secretary, in his welcome talk.

and the Catholic Church, two bodies indeed very different in nature, but whose collaboration has proved to be fruitful.

In common accord with our Secretariat for Promoting Christian Unity, competent Catholics have been invited to participate in your activities in various ways. The ideological, the theological reflection on the unity of the Church, the search for a better understanding of Christian worship, the deep formation of the laity, the consciousness of our common responsibilities and the coordination of our efforts for social and economic development and for peace among the nations—these are some examples of areas where this cooperation has taken shape. There are plans also to find the possibilities of a common Christian approach to the phenomenon of unbelief, to the tensions between the generations, and to relations with the non-Christian religions.

These realizations witness our desire to see the present undertaking develop according to our future possibilities in men and in resources. Such development supposes that at the local level the Christian people are prepared for dialogue and for ecumenical collaboration. Is it not for this that in the Catholic Church the promotion of the ecumenical effort has been confided to the bishops for their diligent promotion and prudent guidance (cf. Decree on Ecumenism, n. 4), according to the norms set down by the Vatican Council and given precision in the ecumenical directory?

Our primary concern, of course, is more the quality of this manifold cooperation than the mere multiplication of activities. "There can be no ecumenism worthy of the name without conversion. For it is from newness of attitudes of mind (cf. Ephesians 4, 23), from self-denial and unstinted love, that desires of unity take their rise and develop in a mature way" (*Decree on Ecumenism*, n. 7). Fidelity to Christ and to His word, humility before the workings of His spirit in us, service to one another and to all men—these virtues will give a Christian quality to our reflection and work. Only then will collaboration among all Christians vividly express that union which already exists among them and set in clearer relief the features of Christ the servant (cf. *ibid.*, n. 12).

Because of this growing cooperation in so many areas of common concern, the question is sometimes asked: Should the Catholic Church become a member of the World Council? What can we answer at this moment? In fraternal frankness we do not consider that the question of the membership of the Catholic Church in the World Council is so mature that a positive answer could or should be given. The question still remains a hypothesis. It contains serious theological and pastoral implications. It thus requires profound study and commits us to a way that honesty recognizes could be long and difficult. But this does not prevent us from assuring you of our great respect and deep affection. The determination which animates us and the principles which guide us will always be the search, filled with hope and pastoral realism, for the unity willed by Christ.

6. Address to Leaders of Other Christian Communities in the Philippines*

At this moment one cannot but think of the important calling of the peoples of the Philippine Islands. This land has a special vocation to be the city set on the hill, the lamp standing on high (cf. Mt. 5:14–16) giving shining witness amid the ancient and noble cultures of Asia. Both as individuals and as a nation you are to show forth the light of Christ by the quality of your lives.

And indeed it is in God's goodness that we have become aware again in these times of the very real bonds already existing between us. We have rediscovered what is common in our heritage and therefore now we are able to pray together. Now we are able to engage in dialogue and in study of theological problems.

Moreover, in a way that is particularly needed at this time, we can now pledge ourselves to work together to promote justice for all, in our own lands as well as among the family of nations. And you have many opportunities to do this here in the Philippine Islands.

There is the boundless desire of your young people to achieve a society in which honesty and integrity are paramount. There is the desire of Christians, both of the Catholic Church and of the communions to which you belong, to be the new leaven that will help purge out all corruption (cf. 1 Cor. 5:7–8), in particular that which proliferates when all the concern of men's hearts is set on power and wealth. And in this happy moment of encounter we would like to stress what we have already said: "We are sure that all Christians, our brethren, will wish to expand their common cooperative effort in order to help mankind vanquish selfishness, pride and rivalries, to overcome ambitions and injustices, to open up to all the road to a more human life, where each man will be loved and helped as his brother, as his neighbor" (Encycl. *Populorum progressio,* n. 82).

This is the direction to which the Catholic Church is committed. The task of assisting the whole development of human beings is to be served by Catholics working together with their fellow Christians, and indeed with all men of goodwill.

As you thus proclaim the Good News of Christ by the quality of your lives and by the integrity of your social order, may it also become increasingly possible for you and for the sons of the Catholic Church "to make together before the nations a common profession of faith in God and in Jesus Christ" (Vat. II *Decree on Church's Missionary Activity,* n. 15).

* November 29, 1970, in Manila. Extracts: *AAS* 63(1971), pp. 44–46.

7. Address to Christian Leaders in Australia*

In these days it is clear that ecumenical work is a continuing and costly task. It demands honest facing of the fact "that in content, development and expression of faith ... there exist certain differences" (SPCU, Sept. 18, 1970, *Reflections and Suggestions concerning Ecumenical Dialogue,* IV,2,b), that doctrinal indifferentism is to be rejected (*ibid.,* a), and at the same time that "confessional triumphalism or the appearance of it" (*ibid.,* 6) must be avoided. History cannot be written off overnight, and the honest hesitations of sensitive consciences always demand our respect and understanding. There is no easy way. The reconciling work of our Lord was achieved through suffering and the Cross. The unity which the ecumenical movement strives to serve has to be bought at a similar price.

Because bonds of unity exist between Christians, it is possible to act together as well as to speak together. Through such efforts undertaken by Christians the world is better able to see the countenance of him "who emptied himself to assume the condition of a slave" (Phil. 2:7). This is our common calling, to glorify the Father through his Son, by bringing to the world evidence of the redeeming love with which God has enfolded the world from the beginning.

We rejoice to be with you, dear brothers, on this occasion when you have gathered to renew your intention of continuing on the ecumenical way, "to seek in order to find, to find in order to seek still further". May God bless us all and lead us "to a deeper realization and clearer expression of the unfathomable riches of Christ".

8. Address During the Week of Prayer for Unity**

Today we have to call to mind the fact that we are celebrating "The Week of Unity", that period when we are all encouraged to meditate on the profound mystery of an essential property and outward mark of the Church of Christ, that is, of mankind living by the faith and the grace of Christ. That property and characteristic mark of the Catholic Church is that it is intimately united in one single body (cf. *1 Cor.* 10, 17). It forms one single thing, is animated by one sole spirit (*2 Cor.* 13, 13), is all one (cf. *Jn.* 17, 21–22), today, in time, through the visible and social union in the one Catholic Church, the unique and universal Church; tomorrow, in eternity, in the mystical body of the risen Christ, always conscious of our individual personalities, but participating in the totality of the one Man-

---

* November 29, 1970, at an ecumenical prayer service in Sydney, in which participated, among others, representatives from the Australian Council of Churches and from the Catholic National Commission on Ecumenism. Extract: *AAS* 63 (1971), p. 70.

** January 20, 1971, at the Pope's General Audience, Vatican City. Extracts: SPCU *IS,* 13 (1971), pp.14–15.

God, our Saviour, *Christus-totus,* as Saint Augustine said, head and body together (*In Ep. Jn.* 1; *PL, III,* 1979).

It is a sublime vision, which comprises the whole panorama of mankind and its history. It touches essentially upon the destiny of each one of us and of all of us together; it obliges us to define the living relationship existing between Christ and the Church. This relationship cannot be uncertain, ambiguous or multiple; it is one, just as Christ instituted and willed it, and it involves a demand upon us, one that is rendered dramatic by tremendous historical events. It is a demand that cannot be suppressed for union among those who are the followers of Christ, that is, the Church. We realize, we Christians, believers in Christ, baptized, members of communities adorned with the name of Christian, all equally threatened by the modern spirit of irreligion, and awaiting the same eschatological destiny, we realize that we find ourselves in a strange situation, we might call it an absurd one. We are still separated, we are disunited, we often distrust and rival each other and until yesterday were engaged in fierce polemics. Today perhaps we desire to understand one another, to forgive one another, to comprehend one another, to work together. But we are still far from each other, still lack certain principles which are essential for perfect union. Some such principles are: complete accord in the same profession of faith and the same bond of charity. This means to say that we are still only partially in communion, even though our communion is deep, and, as regards the venerable Eastern Orthodox Churches, it is almost full, but not yet perfect. This is one of Christianity's gravest problems, and we might say, of humanity. We fortunate, responsible ones are finally aware of this today.

It is quite a difficult problem—woe to them who believe they can find fast and easy solutions to it by disregarding the facts which make it what it is, that is, by disregarding truth, to which we must cleave, and Church unity, in which Christ wishes us to share.

We will now confine Ourself to a word to Catholics. They are in a strange position, for they must above all remain faithful and steadfast; they ought not doubt their Church, the Catholic Church, even though many of its features are blameworthy when we look at it in history and also in the present. But its creed, its relationship with Christ, its worship, its sacramental and moral treasures, its institutional structure, in a word, its doctrinal and practical definition, must not be called in question. We have no right to do so. We should fail in our unrenounceable responsibility to Christ, and to our separated Brethren themselves, if we were to cast doubt upon our authentic Catholic profession of faith or repudiate its binding requirements in order to find common ground.

Irenicism, purely pragmatic and superficial agreement, simplifications of doctrine and discipline, acceptance of criteria which were once the cause of separations we now deplore, all these things would produce only illusions and confusion; only a ghost of our Catholicism would remain, not its real life, not the living Christ whom it bears within itself.

Might not such clarity and firmness hinder dialogue even before it begins? Not at all—on the contrary, they make it a duty and possible. A duty, because only posession of a faith which we believe to be true and indispensable can make us suited for dialogue, and constitutes the condition of faithful dialogue; possible, because this zeal for the faith provides endless means for the dialogue that we are concerned with. We will not say much about this now. But, first, we can sometimes learn from others how to understand and live aspects of our faith better, and so modify our old state of mind, which was closed, and distrustful of our separated Brethren. And we ought to make a loving effort to understand them—an effort that we have not always made in due measure. We should recognize the good in them, and in not a few cases we should learn from them how to perfect our religious and human culture, our education in rightful tolerance, true liberty, and prompt generosity. We should seek to dissipate the instinctive fears which many of them have towards the Catholic Church. Take the fear about our creed, for example. We should show them, more perhaps by the example and naturalness of our psychology as faithful Catholics, how objective assent to the truths which the Church proposes for our belief is not a supine acquiescence in arbitrary formulas which alter God's Word. Rather, it is an acceptance of authentic and univocal propositions of that same Word and of its original totality, together with its logical deductions inspired by tradition ever vigilant and living down the ages. And the subjective effect of the light, of the certainty, of the peace of that Word is that our faith is deepened every day in our soul and makes us more than ever desirous to seek God and Christ.

Another characteristic fear of our separated Brethren concerns the authority existing in the Catholic Church, as if this authority, which is exercised in great and fraternal collaboration with all the Bishops established by God to feed his flock (cf. *Acts*, 20, 28), were not aware, today more than ever, of being service, not dominion; as if it did not allow (whereas in fact it protects) various rightful forms of spiritual expression on the part of souls and of ecclesial communities; as if authority in the Church were not of divine institution, and were not necessary for maintaining unity therein, and nourishing charity, in that obedience which is love.

It is a hard road, we said, the road of ecumenism, that is, the road towards the restoration of unity among Christians; but is it not a fine one? Does it not perhaps foster in Catholicism itself a process of thoughtful purification, a testing of identity, a study in depth, an exercise of humility, a more active and broader love? Do there not open up before us hopes based on the promises of the Holy Spirit, more joyful than any dream?

9. Address to Delegates of Catholic Ecumenical Commissions*

Is it not the primary mission of the Church to call men to enter into communion with God, through Christ, in the Holy Spirit, and then to help them to live in this communion which saves them and establishes among them a unity as deep and mysterious as the unity of the Father and the Son (cf. *Jn.* 17, 21–23)?

In these perspectives, this unity appears as a gratuitous gift from God and we must continually grow in this unity, at the same time as we must continually grow in this divine life. Throughout our lives, like the Church throughout her earthly pilgrimage, we must progress in unity, manifest it, defend it. Unity of lived and proclaimed faith; unity of worship which, in the diversity of its forms, is centred on the celebration of Holy Eucharist, making present among us and for us the unique sacrifice of Christ. It is a unity nourished and deepened by the sacraments which make our union with Christ closer or restore it; a unity of common life under the guidance of the bishops grouped round the bishop of Rome, each one being charged, according to his own responsibility, with ensuring faithfulness to God's gift bringing about the reign of charity. This Catholic unity is strengthened and highlighted by the diversity of charisms, cultures, mentalities, traditions, customs and disciplines which, in the same body, by the action of the same Spirit, become, as it were, an immense symphony in praise of the glory of God.

We have received this ministry of reconciliation. The unbelief of many of our contemporaries must give us a new awareness of the urgency of curing our present division. Is not the unity of the disciples of Christ the great sign that is to bring about the faith of the world? Is it not the reason for which the Second Vatican Council asked that ecumenical action should be promoted in such a way that the cooperation between Catholics and other Christians, in social and technical, cultural and religious matters, "should be undertaken not only among private persons, but also, according to the judgment of the local Ordinary, among Churches or ecclesial communities and their enterprises" (*Ad Gentes,* n. 15)?

We cannot shirk our responsibility before unbelief; we must all assume it, clear-sightedly and courageously. Unfortunately, in the present divided situation of Christians, our divergences on the content of the testimony we must give prevent this common responsibility from always being expressed in joint actions. The greater our agreement is, the more this collaboration can be developed. With the Orthodox Churches, for example, we are in almost complete communion, and the possibilities of pastoral collaboration are in proportion to the close bonds uniting us.

---

* November 22, 1972, during a SPCU meeting of delegates from the Commissions for Ecumenism of episcopal conferences and of the synods of Catholic Eastern patriarchates, Rome. Extracts: *AAS* 64(1972), pp. 760–763. SPCU *IS,* 20 (1973), pp. 22–23.

In all cases care must be taken that, in the exercise of this common responsibility, there should be the spiritual emulation that befits brothers animated by real charity and anxious, not only to avoid all vain competition, but above all to promote what can extend the kingdom of Christ, their one Master and Lord. Among Christians eagerly concerned with the truth, there are no rivals, there can be only emulators and friends.

10. Address during the 1973 Week of Prayer for Christian Unity*

Today, beloved Brothers and Sons, a thought—an idea, a Truth, a Reality—lights up before the eyes of our mind, attracts our gaze, absorbs us, fills us both with enthusiasm and worry, as do things that gain our love. What is this thought? It is the unity of the Church.

As soon as this thought is grasped in its general significance, it takes hold of us, dominates us. Unity: immediately it imposes itself on account of its logical and metaphysical force. It refers to the Church, that is, to mankind called by Christ to be one thing only with Him and in Him. It holds us spellbound because of its theological depth. Then it torments us because of its historic aspect, yesterday and still today, bleeding and suffering like that of Christ crucified. It reproves us and awakens us, like the sound of a trumpet, calling us with the urgency of a vocation, which becomes relevant and characteristic in our times. The thought of unity irradiates over the world scene, scattered with the magnificent rent limbs and the ruins of so many Churches, some of them isolated as if self-sufficient, others broken into hundreds of sects. All of them are now invaded by two conflicting forces, in a moving tension; one centrifugal, fleeing, in its pursuit of autonomy, towards schismatic and heretical goals; the other centripetal, demanding with reborn nostalgia the recomposition of unity. Motherly and fearless, Rome, certainly not faultless, and burdened on her own account with immense responsibility, stubbornly affirms and promotes this unity as her own duty, smacking of witness and martyrdom. It is the authentically ecumenical and unitarian force, which is seeking its principle and its centre, the base, which Christ, the real cornerstone of the ecclesial edifice, chose and fixed, in his stead, to signify and perpetuate the foundations of his kingdom.

The epistles of St. Paul contain a deep theology, but they do not constitute a theoretical treatise. They had in mind the concrete situation in the churches of Ephesus, Corinth, Colossae. In the priestly prayer for unity Jesus was speaking in the intimate circle of his Apostles, referring, however, to all those who will believe in Him through the word of the Apostles (cf. *Jn.* 17, 20).

Therefore if the principles enunciated by Jesus and the Apostle have a

---

* January 24, 1973, at the Pope's General Audience, Vatican City. Extracts: SPCU *IS,* 21 (1973), pp. 3–4.

universal value, for all Christians of all times, they are put into practice concretely in particular communities and through these communities.

Unity, which is a real gift from Christ, develops and grows in the concrete situation represented by the lives of the Christian communities. Understanding of the important role of the particular communities, of the particular churches, was clearly formulated by the Council: "The individual bishop is the visible principle and foundation of unity in his particular church, fashioned after the model of the universal Church. In and from such individual churches there comes into being the one and only Catholic Church" *(Lumen gentium,* 23; cf. Bossuet, *Oeuvres* vol. **XI**, lettre **IV**, pp. 114ff.).

In fact the unity of the Church, which, as we said, in the historical charism of the whole Catholic Church and the Roman Church particularly, is already a reality, in spite of the deficiencies of the men composing it, is not, however, complete. It is not perfect in the statistical and social framework of the world, it is not universal. Unity and catholicity are not equal, either in the sphere that calls for this correspondence most, the sphere of the baptized and believers in Christ, or, even less, in that of the whole of mankind on earth, where most do not yet adhere to the Gospel. These are the two great problems of the Church, the ecumenical and the missionary, both dramatic.

Today we are speaking of the first one, that is, the union of Christians in one Church.

We would like to indicate as one of the ways to the solution, even though it is a way that is already known, long, delicate and difficult, the duty and the possibility of interesting the local churches in the ecumenical question, in harmony, of course with the universal and central Church (if we do not want to make the situation worse instead of better).

We see how important it is that the particular churches of the Catholic communion should keep in mind their tasks and their characteristic ecumenical responsibilities.

Through the particular church the Catholic Church is present in the same local and regional environment in which other Christian Churches and Communities also live and work. The establishment of contacts and brotherly relations often turns out to be easier in this context.

We therefore exhort all our Brothers and Sons wholeheartedly to bring it about that the commitment for the unity of Christians will become an integral part of the life also of the particular churches.

"The dialogue of charity", the expression so dear to our brother of venerated memory, the Ecumenical Patriarch of Constantinople, Athenagoras, can be fully realized between persons and communities that have frequent mutual contacts, share sufferings and, together, to the Spirit operating in them in the course of the concrete experiences of their lives.

The catholicity and the unity of the Church are manifested in the capacity of the particular churches and of the whole to take root in different worlds, times and places; to find themselves in reciprocal fellowship in every world, time and place.

Unity at the local level is always a sign and manifestation of the mystery of the unity which is the Lord's gift to the Church. The particular churches can enrich the ecumenical movement as a whole with their experiences, can make a contribution fruitful for the whole Church. At the same time they will receive suggestions and directives coming from the centre of unity, that is the Apostolic See, "universo caritatis coetui praesidens" (St. Ignatius, *Ad Rom.,* Inscrip.), to be helped in their problems and to be able to judge the validity and fruitfulness of their own experiences.

"I believe in the One Church . . ."—this profession of faith urges us, therefore, to dedicate ourselves to the cause of the unity of Christians, with all the ardour of which we are capable, and with all the possibilities that the life of the Church offers us at many levels.

Dear Sons, in this week of prayer for the unity common to all Christians, we all ask for forgiveness for the faults committed against this great gift, greater than any merits of ours.

11. Letter to W.C.C. General Secretary*

The World Council of Churches has been created in order, by the grace of God, to serve the Churches and ecclesial Communities in their endeavours to restore and to manifest to all that perfect communion in faith and love which is the gift of Christ to his Church. We earnestly pray that the Spirit of the Lord, the Spirit of wisdom, may enlighten and strengthen you and that in the obedience of faith you may make progress towards achieving the one hope which belongs to our call (cf. Eph 4:4).

On the occasion of our visit to the World Council of Churches in Geneva in 1969, we expressed our deep appreciation for the development of the relations between the World Council of Churches and the Catholic Church, two bodies indeed very different in nature, but whose collaboration has proved fruitful (cf. *AAS,* 61, 1969, p. 504). It is our sincere desire that this collaboration may be pursued and intensified, according to the spirit of the Second Vatican Council.

12. Message for the Day of Peace, January 1, 1975**

The Holy Year which we are about to begin wishes to involve us in this first and happy reconciliation: Christ is Our Peace; he is the principle of reconciliation in the unity of the Mystical Body (cf. Eph 2:14–16). . . .

---

* Dr. Philip Potter. August 6, 1973, on the occasion of the meeting of the WCC. Central Committee, and the celebration of the WCC's 25th anniversary. Extract: SPCU *IS,* 22 (1973), p. 26.
** Excerpt: Vatican Polyglot Press booklet, p. 16.

Hence a logical and necessary consequence—one that is also easy if we are truly in Christ: we must perfect the sense of our unity—unity *in* the Church, unity *of* the Church. Mystical, constitutive communion, the former (cf. 1 Cor 1:10; 12:12–27); ecumenical restoration of the unity of all Christians, the latter. One and the other demand their own proper reconciliation, which must bring to the Christian collectivity that Peace which is the fruit of the Spirit, following upon love and its joy (cf. Gal 5:22).

13. Address during the Week of Prayer for Christian Unity*

The present feast makes us still celebrate, after so many centuries, the conversion of Saint Paul, which was a decisive turning point in the history of the spreading of the faith and in the organic formation of the infant Church.

A theme that draws inspiration and comfort from that veneration we pay to Saint Paul is that of Christian unity—true and complete unity—which especially since the Council we have in our thoughts and are trying to reestablish, so that all may rejoice in its fullness. We confide to you the two fundamental feelings that the theme evokes in our hearts: one of sadness, and one of hope.

Why sadness? How can the thought of the restoration of unity among all Christ's followers inspire such a sentiment? The reason for this sadness is all too obvious.

And it is a many-sided reason.

First, because that unity has not yet been restored. This brings to our mind an obvious and painful memory, the memory of history. Christ founded one Church. Saint Paul has left us in heritage, as it were, his commitment: "Do all you can to preserve the unity of the Spirit by the peace that binds you together. There is one Body, one Spirit, just as you were all called into one and the same hope, when you were called. There is one Lord, one faith, one baptism, and one God who is Father of all, over all, through all and within all" (Eph 4, 3–6). How have we been able to become divided in such a serious, many-sided and enduring manner? And how can we fail to suffer at such a state of things, which in so many concrete ways still endures? In this, we Catholics certainly have our share of blame, which also is many-sided and enduring. How can we fail to feel pain and remorse for this?

Secondly, how can the difficulties standing in the way of reconciliation be overcome? Another reason for our reflection. We see the great obstacles, and they seem insuperable.

This is a grave state of affairs that even militates against the very

---

* January 25, 1975, Feast of the Conversion of St. Paul. A homily during the Eucharistic concelebration at St. Paul's Basilica, Rome, to mark the closing of the Week of Prayer for Christian Unity. Extracts: *AAS* 66 (1975), pp. 112–116. In Italian. TFS trans.

work of Christ. The Second Vatican Council affirms clearly and firmly that the division of Christians "inflicts damage on the most holy cause of proclaiming the good news to every creature" (*Unitatis Redintegratio,* 1), and thus damages the work of reconciliation of all men.

The division among Christians thus succeeds in damaging and even sometimes nullifying the fruitfulness of Christian preaching, in rendering ineffective the action of reconciliation with God which it is the Church's mission to continue until the end of time. For this reason, in proclaiming the Holy Year we considered it necessary to remind all the faithful of the Catholic world that "before all men can be brought together and restored to the grace of God our Father, communion must be reestablished between those who by faith have acknowledged and accepted Jesus Christ as the Lord of mercy who sets men free and unites them in the Spirit of love and truth" (*Apostolorum Limina,* VII).

How in fact can we consistently bear witness to the fact that God has reconciled us to himself if we who believe and have been baptized in his name do not show that we are reconciled among ourselves? And it is also for this reason that "it is in fact the task and duty of the whole Church to reestablish this unity in full ecclesial communion" (*Apostolorum Limina,* VII; cf. *Unitatis Redintegratio,* 5).

Thirdly, in these last few years marvellous strides have been made in different ways toward reconciliation. This is known and seen by everyone, and certainly we all rejoice at it. But so far no stride has reached the goal. The heart that loves is always hasty. If our haste is not heeded, love itself makes us suffer. We are conscious of the inadequacy of our efforts. We are aware of the laws of history, which call for a longer period of time than that of our human existence; and it is understandable that the slowness in reaching solutions should seem to make our desires, our attempts, our efforts and our prayers vain. Let us accept this economy of the divine plan, and let us resolve humbly to persevere. But is not perseverance also suffering? Is it not understandable that we should feel a sentiment which consumes itself in expectancy, whose duration is unknown? Ecumenism is a most difficult undertaking. It cannot be simplified to the detriment of faith and of the plan of Christ and of God for the authentic salvation of mankind. Does not Scripture say: "Hope deferred makes the heart sick" (Proverbs 13, 12)? Share, therefore, brethren, in our sadness. It is the expression of our desire and of our love.

But there is another sentiment that fills our heart with its life-giving breath in regard to ecumenism, that ecumenism which really strives for the reestablishment of unity among all Christians. It is hope. Is it not prayer that nourishes hope? And does not Saint Paul assure us that "hope is not deceptive" (Rom 5, 5)?

We too have wished to celebrate the week of prayer for Christian Unity, particularly this time on the occasion of the Holy Year. We had in fact proclaimed that reconciliation among Christians is one of the central aims of this year of grace (cf. *Apostolorum Limina,* VII).

To "bring everything together under Christ, as head, everything in the heavens and everything on earth" (Eph 1, 10). This theme which has been proposed for the reflection of all Christians during this year's week of prayer concentrates our meditation upon the salvific plan of God for man and for the whole of creation.

God has made known to us the mystery of his will in order to bring it to realization in the fullness of time. In Jesus Christ, his beloved Son, we have redemption, through his blood, the forgiveness of sins according to the richness of his grace (cf. Eph 1, 7). "God wanted all perfection to be found in him and all things to be reconciled through him and for him" (Col 1, 19–20). Jesus Christ is thus our true reconciliation: he is God's mercy for men, our great and living indulgence. He has "made purification for sins" (Heb 1, 3) and has brought us into communion with the Father in the Holy Spirit.

This salvific act embraces not only all men but in a vision surpassing the human dimension it extends to all creation, to the entire universe, opening wide to us the threshold of a new creation, with mankind renewed, on pilgrimage towards "a new heaven and a new earth" (Rev 21, 1).

Christ continues this ministry of reconciliation through his Church, the sacrament of salvation.

"For this the Church was founded: that by spreading the kingdom of Christ everywhere for the glory of God the Father, she might bring all men to share in Christ's saving redemption; and that through them the whole world might in actual fact be brought into relationship with him" (*Apostolicam Actuositatem,* 2).

But today we give thanks with you to the Lord for having permitted us to see the relations between Christians strengthened and deepened. The quest for reconciliation among Christians, which is the work of the Holy Spirit and an expression of that "wisdom and patience" with which the Lord "follows out the plan of his grace on behalf of us sinners" (*Unitatis Redintegratio,* 1), is becoming more and more a subject of increasing care and attention for the Catholic Church and for the other Christian Communions. We note with joy the efforts being made everywhere by bishops, theologians, priests and laity to bring about reconciliation. We know too that the members of that chosen category of persons who, in the silence of contemplation, achieve through prayer and penance an ever closer and more perfect union with God, are likewise deeply sensitive to this task.

With the Council, we are fully aware that "the holy task of reconciling all Christians in the unity of the one and only Church of Christ transcends human energies and inabilities" (*Unitatis Redintegratio,* 24). For this reason we resume our prayer, asking the Lord to make us more attentive to his word and more obedient to his will, so that we may continue our task with confidence and dedication, with perseverance and courage, and be enabled by him to make our effective contribution to reconciliation among all Christians and to the reconciliation of all men, so that, as Saint Paul exhorts us, every tongue may "proclaim to the glory of God the Father: Jesus Christ is Lord!" (Phil 2, 11). So be it!

14. Message to the W.C.C. General Assembly at Nairobi*

We hope that the Assembly will indeed have an important influence on the life of the World Council of Churches, on the member Churches and on all who are committed to the ecumenical movement.

We trust that the efforts which the Catholic Church has made and will continue to make to promote the ecumenical movement and, wherever possible, to collaborate with the World Council of Churches will continue and grow ever greater with God's help. May the assurance of our fraternal solidarity hearten you for the years ahead.**

The year of the Lord 1975 is undoubtedly most significant in the history of the Church because of several great spiritual events which it is witnessing. A major one is the Fifth Assembly of the World Council of Churches, called together in order to consider in the light of Christ, who illumines all nations and is the good news for all men, the problems and pains and sorrows of the contemporary world. Above all it seeks to further ecclesial unity among all Christians. From the beginning this goal has inspired the World Council of Churches in its studies and activities so that a common witness to Jesus Christ as God and Saviour may be given to the world and his prayer may be fulfilled: "May they all be one. Father, may they be one in us, as you are in me and I am in you, so that the world may believe it was you who sent me"(*Jn* 17, 21).

This year the Catholic Church is celebrating a Jubilee or Holy Year which "provides a special opportunity of repentance for the divisions which exist among Christians; it offers an occasion for renewal in the sense of a heightened experience of holiness of life in Christ; it allows progress towards the reconciliation we hope for by intensified dialogue and by concrete Christian collaboration for the salvation of the world" (*Apostolorum Limina*, VII).

As this same year ends, we are celebrating the tenth anniversary of the Second Vatican Council during which the Catholic Church responded in a new way to the longing "for the one visible Church of God, a Church

---

* November 20, 1975, in a letter addressed to Dr. Philip Potter, WCC General Secretary. The Pope had delegated sixteen official Roman Catholic observers to the Assembly in Nairobi, Kenya (Nov. 23–Dec. 10, 1975). The RCC/WCC Joint Working Group had been established in 1965. Text: SPCU *IS* 30 (1976), p. 1.

** Accompanying this message was a letter from the SPCU President, John Cardinal Willebrands, charged by the Pope to so write. Extracts: SPCU *IS*, 30 (1976), p. 1.

truly universal and sent forth to the whole world" (*Unitatis Redintegratio,* 1) and committed itself to take part in that ecumenical movement which is "fostered by the grace of the Holy Spirit for the restoration of unity among all Christians" (*Unitatis Redintegratio,* 1).

Now as the World Council of Churches assembles the delegates of its member Churches in Nairobi to celebrate the Fifth Assembly, the opportuneness and importance of this moment move us to address ourselves to you.

More striking than the events in themselves and their coincidence is the similarity of the themes chosen for these celebrations: the theme "Jesus Christ frees and unites" is the inspiring motive of the Assembly; the theme "Renewal and Reconciliation" is the goal of the Holy Year. Jesus Christ came to loose the bonds of sin and death, to free from oppression and the limitation of our mortal condition all men and women in their individual lives, in their life in society, and in their membership in the human family as a whole. Jesus Christ is the source and centre of communion for all who are Christians, their only and firm hope of being able "to fulfill together their common calling to the glory of the one God, Father, Son and Holy Spirit" (Basis WCC; cfr. *Unitatis Redintegratio,* 2) to be "a lasting and sure seed of unity, hope and salvation for the whole human race" (*Lumen Gentium,* 9). Here surely is a point of contact with the content and perspective of renewal and reconciliation as it was described in the Bull of Indiction of the Holy Year: "It is in the depths of the heart therefore that there must take place conversion or 'metanoia', that is, a change of direction, of attitude, of option, of one's way of life", and, "For the whole world: . . . liberty, justice, unity and peace" (*Apostolorum Limina,* 1).

As Catholics our best ecumenical efforts are directed both to removing the causes of separation that still remain, as well as to giving adequate expression to the communion which already exists among all Christians. We are sustained and encouraged in this task because so many of the most significant elements and endowments "that are Christ's gifts to his Church are the common source of our strength" (*Unitatis Redintegratio,* 3). In this context we acknowledge gratefully the work done by the Joint Working Group between the Catholic Church and the World Council of Churches. With complete loyalty to the principles and methods of both partners it is an instrument of reflection and of planning that has promoted authentic ecumenical activity.

For these reasons, then, as we Catholics give thanks for the ecumenical emphasis given by the Second Vatican Council and the ten subsequent arduous years of implementing its decrees, I address this brotherly word of hope and encouragement to you our Christian brethren and to the Churches and Communities which gather in the fellowship of the World Council of Churches. For us in the Catholic Church it is a moment of rededication to the task of enabling the spirit and principles of the Vatican

Council to penetrate the structures and the living tissue of the Church's life. So that an important part of our concern meets yours as you gather in Nairobi—to renew commitment to the principles by which ecumenical activity is guided, looking to the future, joining, wherever possible our initiatives with those undertaken by you, our brethren (vid. *Unitatis Redintegratio,* 24), intent on going forward "without obstructing the ways of divine Providence, and without prejudging the future inspirations of the Holy Spirit" (*Unitatis Redintegratio,* 24).

15. Apostolic Exhortation on Evangelization in the Modern World*

The power of evangelization will find itself considerably diminished if those who proclaim the Gospel are divided among themselves in all sorts of ways. Is this not perhaps one of the great sicknesses of evangelization today? Indeed, if the Gospel that we proclaim is seen to be rent by doctrinal disputes, ideological polarizations or mutual condemnations among Christians, at the mercy of the latter's differing views on Christ and the Church and even because of their different concepts of society and human institutions, how can those to whom we address our preaching fail to be disturbed, disoriented, even scandalized?

The Lord's spiritual testament tells us that unity among His followers is not only the proof that we are His but also the proof that He is sent by the Father. It is the test of the credibility of Christians and of Christ Himself. As evangelizers, we must offer Christ's faithful not the image of people divided and separated by unedifying quarrels, but the image of people who are mature in faith and capable of finding a meeting-point beyond the real tensions, thanks to a shared, sincere and disinterested search for truth. Yes, the destiny of evangelization is certainly bound up with the witness of unity given by the Church. This is a source of responsibility and also of comfort.

At this point we wish to emphasize the sign of unity among all Christians as the way and instrument of evangelization. The division among Christians is a serious reality which impedes the very work of Christ. The Second Vatican Council states clearly and emphatically that this division "damages the most holy cause of preaching the Gospel to all men, and it impedes many from embracing the faith" (*Ad Gentes,* n. 6; *U. Redintegratio,* n. 1). For this reason, in proclaiming the Holy Year we considered it necessary to recall to all the faithful of the Catholic world that "before all men can be brought together and restored to the grace of

---

* December 8, 1975. Following the third Synod of Bishops, in October 1974, which had treated the theme of evangelization, Paul VI refined and enlarged the synodal discussions and conclusions in this encyclical "to the Episcopate, to the Clergy and to all the Faithful of the entire world". The extract is Paragraph 77. *Evangelii Nuntiandi: AAS* 68 (1976), pp. 69–70.

God our Father, communion must be reestablished between those who by faith have acknowledged and accepted Jesus Christ as the Lord of mercy who sets men free and unites them in the Spirit of love and truth" (Bull *Apostolorum Limina* VII: *AAS* 66 (1971), p. 305).

And it is with a strong feeling of Christian hope that we look to the efforts being made in the Christian world for this restoration of the full unity willed by Christ. St. Paul assures us that "hope does not disappoint us" (Rom. 5:5). While we still work to obtain full unity from the Lord, we wish to see prayer intensified. Moreover we make our own the desire of the Fathers of the Third General Assembly of the Synod of Bishops, for a collaboration marked by greater commitment with the Christian brethren with whom we are not yet united in perfect unity, taking as a basis the foundation of Baptism and the patrimony of faith which is common to us. By doing this we can already give a greater common witness to Christ before the world in the very work of evangelization. Christ's command urges us to do this; the duty of preaching and of giving witness to the Gospel requires this.

16. Address to Non-Catholic Pentecostals*

You have come from certain Pentecostal Churches and from Pentecostal movements in other confessions to meet with our Secretariat for Promoting Christian Unity and its collaborators, in order to reflect together on prayer, on spirituality and on related aspects of theology. In doing so, you have been dealing with spiritual resources of which the whole human family has urgent need. Your exchanges have been a testimony to the living power of the Spirit of God experienced in the lives of Christians and offered to all who will accept it. You have spoken together of how faithful souls participate in the reality of God. We believe this is a reality which establishes itself among the faithful as a visible communion, so that they are united not only by a spiritual relationship on the level of mystery and the invisible, but also on the visible level of human realities transformed by the Spirit. It is a communion expressed in the fellowship of the Church which seeks always, according to our Lord's will, to become perfect in unity. How untiring all who love this Lord of ours must be in working to overcome all the causes of division and separation that still impede the fullness of this communion.

As you come to the conclusion of the present phase of your work, we shall learn with great interest the outcome of your studies and give attentive consideration to what they indicate for the future of our relationship.

Let us continue to walk together in the paths of understanding and

---

* May 26, 1976. The SPCU Roman Catholic/Pentecostal dialogue group had just finished its five years of conversations. Text: SPCU *IS* 32(1976), p. 32

growing Christian love, listening with docility and care to what the Spirit
is saying today, and ready to move into his future with joy and trust.

17. Address to the Secretariat for Promoting Christian Unity*

You come at a moment when, in this field of ecumenism as in so
many other things, it is fashionable to speak of a crisis. As a matter of fact,
the Council and the years that followed it were marked by deep and rapid
changes in the relations between the Catholic Church and other Christian
Churches.

Mutual lack of appreciation rapidly melted away with the rediscovery
of the bonds of communion that united us in spite of our divergences (cf.
Decree *Unitatis Redintegratio,* 3). We have rediscovered one another as
brothers, brothers still disunited, it is true, but really brothers who "justified by faith in baptism are incorporated into Christ; they therefore have a
right to be called Christians" (*ibid.,* 3).

The joy of meeting again in this way made many people think,
perhaps, that we were on the eve of reaching the goal of refound full
communion. Hence their disappointment, their impression of marking
time when the theological dialogue was started and developed. Wishing to
cure ourselves of the disease of our divisions, it was necessary for us, in a
common effort of brotherly lucidity, to discern its real causes and discover
its roots. It is inevitable that the progress made in this field should be less
perceptible to the general public. It is a question of an effort of renewed
and deepened faithfulness to the Word of God, understood and lived in the
great multiform tradition of the Church, One, Holy, Catholic and Apostolic.

Convergences assert themselves; agreements are outlined on the fundamental realities of baptism, the Eucharist, the ministry of unity in the
Church. Studies begin or are continued on the authority of the Church in
her teaching. The Catholic Church is determined to continue and intensify
her contribution to this common effort of all Christians. It is furthermore
"a requirement of the work of preaching and of the witness to be borne to
the Gospel", as we stated in our recent Exhortation on Evangelization in
the modern world (cf. n. 77), taking up again the wish expressed by the
Fathers at the third general Assembly of the Synod of Bishops. And we
must all collaborate in promoting this "civilization of love", which seems
to us to be more and more a necessity of the action of Christians in this
world.

The fact that we have not yet arrived at the goal, that serious
obstacles are still to be overcome, must not discourage us or stop us; on the
contrary, we must intensify our effort to put into practice the conciliar

---

* November 13, 1976, at the SPCU's General Meeting *(Plenarium)* of bishop members,
consultors and staff. Extracts: SPCU *IS,* 33 (1977), pp. 1–2. *AAS* 68 (1977), pp. 721–724.

decree, the directives we have given since then, and the guidelines published by this Secretariat for ecumenical collaboration on the national plane and on the local plane.

We would also like to recall emphatically the fundamental importance of spiritual ecumenism. Change of heart, renewal of the spirit, renunciation of self, the free outpouring of charity (cf. *UR,* 7), that is the soul of the ecumenical movement (cf. *UR,* 8) for which, under this aspect, one and all of the faithful are responsible. A real change of heart instills in us a deep attitude of offering our whole selves to the Father through the Son in the Holy Spirit. It is the mysterious source of the desire for unity. It produces rich results not only in supplication to the One who alone can take us where we are trying to go, but also in fervent and brotherly prayers for one another.

The seeking of unity also calls for complete loyalty to all the demands of truth. This loyalty does not oppose the effort, here and now, to bear witness together with our brothers, to all that we profess in common. But what we must avoid is acting now "as if" we had reached the goal. This would be to render a very bad service to our march forward. It would delay it considerably by leading it into blind alleys.

It is necessary to go on prudently, but without hesitating, moved by a love strong enough to bear witness to the whole truth, holding firmly the anchor of our hope (cf *Heb* 6, 18–19) and docile to the Holy Spirit who guides us unceasingly towards the whole truth (cf. *Jn* 16, 13), towards this truth which is inseparably the way and the life, towards this truth which is Christ (cf. *Jn* 14, 6).

18. Address During the 1977 Week of Prayer for Unity*

The subject proposed to the reflection and prayer of us all this year is taken from St. Paul: "hope does not disappoint us" (*Rom* 5, 5). How opportune this appeal is, so that we do not fall into disappointment, so that we do not remain caught up in the web of habit and stop half way. Hope is the moving spirit of the ecumenical cause. It is the star that directs our steps towards the place where the Lord certainly is. St. Paul reminds those who, from the first hour, have committed themselves to the search for unity and who, perhaps with a touch of sadness, observe that the desired unity is not yet reached, that "hope does not disappoint us" and that perseverance is necessary. He reminds those whose interest in this work may now be a matter of routine, no longer creative, that "hope does not disappoint us" and that it is necessary to strain towards the future and race towards the goal (cf. *Phil* 3, 13). He reminds those who are tempted to be satisfied with the positive results already reached in the relations between Christians and who therefore run the risk of stopping at a stage of

---

* January 19, 1977, at the Pope's General Audience, Vatican City. Extracts: SPCU *IS,* 33 (1977), pp. 31–32.

peaceful coexistence, but not of complete unity, that it is necessary to carry out the work right to the end, attaining finally the goal indicated by the Lord himself, which is that of being "consecrated in truth" (*Jn* 17, 19) and "perfect in unity" (*ibid.*, 17, 23). And to those who, at the last minute, are in doubt whether to take their place in this movement, St Paul announces with ardent conviction that "hope does not disappoint us" and that, united with the Lord, it is possible to defeat all resistance and overcome every difficulty.

Our hope, in fact, is based on God and on his plan of salvation. God is omnipotent and faithful, and always keeps his promise. His Word does not return to him without having worked wonders. As the Psalmist sings, the Lord is "my strength, my rock, my deliverer, my shield, and the horn of my salvation, my stronghold" (*Ps* 18, 2–3, cf. 17, 2; 17, 27–31; etc.). Therefore we do not rely presumptuously on our works and our aspirations but "we rejoice in our hope of sharing the glory of God", as the Apostle admonishes further (*Rom* 5, 2). This word is certain: God will finally make his glory shine forth and will communicate his holiness to everyone. He will be "everything to everyone" (*1 Cor* 15, 28) and will place his seal on the definitive triumph over every expression of the "mystery of lawlessness" (*2 Thess* 2, 7), especially mutual violent destruction, polemics, violence, tyranny, division, envy and every form of hatred. This is the Christian's supreme hope, which he knows "will not disappoint" him, having in himself the active presence of the Holy Spirit which has been given to us (cf. *Rom* 5, 5). In fact the outpouring of the Spirit in our hearts brings about in Christians a change which is slow and hard won, but certain. It is a change which leads towards the formation of the new man, "until we all attain to the unity of the faith and of the knowledge of the Son of God, to mature manhood, to the measure of the stature of the fullness of Christ" (*Eph* 4, 4, 13).

The search for the unity of Christians is placed precisely in this perspective: growth of faith, maturity in Christ, striving towards full communion in God. All Christians, because of their baptism, are individually "justified by faith and have peace with God through our Lord Jesus Christ" (*Rom* 5, 1); but they are also called to draw the due ecclesial consequences from the requirements of common baptism, so that Christ may also become "our peace", in a mutual and ecumenical way (*Eph* 2, 14). The Second Vatican Council explicitly indicated this in the following forceful terms: "Baptism constitutes the sacramental bond of unity existing among all who through it are reborn. But baptism, of itself, is only a beginning, a point of departure, for it is wholly directed toward the acquiring of fullness of life in Christ. Baptism is thus ordained toward a complete profession of faith, a complete incorporation into the system of salvation such as Christ himself willed it to be, and finally, towards a complete integration into eucharistic communion" (*Unitatis Redintegratio,*

22). So there is still a path of faith to be traversed, before we can find ourselves united at last in joint participation in the one Eucharist, which we cannot realize today owing to the lack of full unity in faith. But once more, our stimulus is hope. Objective difficulties themselves must not prevent us from going on. On the contrary, we must draw spiritual advantage from these very painful experiences, since, as St Paul explains again "suffering produces endurance, and endurance produces character, and character produces hope" (*Rom* 5, 4).

Our hope is also based on, and sustained by, the positive results which the search for unity among Christians is obtaining. A new atmosphere, in fact, has been established and the spirit of true brotherhood is becoming more and more solid and fruitful. We ourself are experiencing this in our more and more frequent and personal meetings with so many Venerated Brethren, who honour us with their visits here in Rome. In the same way, we experienced this proof in our pilgrimages to Jerusalem, Istanbul and Geneva. We thank the Lord who has deigned to make us the instrument of this meeting between Christians of various denominations, and so being able to make our contribution towards this mysterious work of the Holy Spirit, who is bringing new vitality to the Church of our time. Moreover, we do not look on Peter's See in any other way than as a particular form of service for the unity of the Church. The search for unity also leads to a progressive coming closer on the doctrinal plane. Positive convergences are taking shape more and more, even on questions on which Christians were greatly divided in the past, such as the fundamental ones concerning the reality of the Eucharist, and concerning the ministry and authority in the Church. The dialogue between the Catholic Church and the other Churches and ecclesial Communities, sustained by prayer, is progressing in its delicate work, which we hope will lead to full clarification of all the controversial questions of faith and to complete agreement in the whole truth.

19. Address to the Bishops of Scandinavia*

You come from countries in which almost the entire population is of the Lutheran confession, and therefore you represent a Catholic Church very much in diaspora: that is, a dispersed minority, like a drop of oil emulsified in a basin of water.

We recognize with you, therefore, that the situation of Catholics in Finland, Sweden, Norway, Denmark and Iceland is really that of the "little flock" of the Gospel, which has with it, however, the radiant assurance of Jesus: "Fear not, for it is your Father's good pleasure to give you the kingdom" (*Lk* 12, 32).

Your Regions are characterized, not only by the different Christian

* May 2, 1977, on the occasion of the bishops' visit "ad limina" to the Holy See. Extracts: SPCU *IS,* 36 (1978), pp. 10–11.

confessions, but also by a particular historico-social condition: their extraordinary cultural and political tradition has reached very high points of human, civil, social and economic progress, which deservedly do honour to your hard-working populations, and rightly draw to them the admiration and emulation of other peoples. Though it is true that this noble level of life is not unaccompanied by dangerous forms of a secularism and a practical materialism which are inherent in every expression of advanced progress, there can be noted, on the other hand, comforting signs of spiritual and moral awakening, of an appeal to higher values and often of an anxious seeking of the "why" that underlie human existence and find no explanation in the mere certainty of progress and of civilization as an end in itself.

Above all, however, you with your communities are faced with the delicate problem of religious relations with Christian brothers separated from us. The fact of finding yourselves side by side with them cannot prevent you, but on the contrary urges you, to form ties of sincere friendship in the name of our one Saviour and Lord Jesus Christ; this is possible, without, however, going too far, adopting an ambiguous ecumenism which renounces its own original context and is passively ready to let itself be absorbed. Catholics, in your countries, have values of their own to guard: the riches of the doctrinal deposit, faithfulness to it while duly updating it as the Council desired, the duty of evangelization in conviction and joy, communion with the universal Church, obedience to the successor of Peter and union with his ministry which guarantees ecclesial unity, respect for the wholesome values of culture and progress, sincere and constructive brotherhood. They are all *tesserae* of a splendid mosaic, which gives an extraordinarily beautiful and persuasive image of Catholicism in your lands. This may lead to a fruitful rapprochement with other brothers of Christian denomination on the way to the recomposition of unity in the Lord Jesus. Whatever may be the sociological background in which the Church is called to operate among the various peoples, her vocation, her incentive, her vaunt is that of being in the service of society, as it is. In Scandinavia, the Church is therefore in the service of that precise, concrete, existential society, with all its limits, it is true, but also with all its riches. And there she wishes to contribute, willingly, to the growth of man's eternal values, in his relationship with God, serving in humility and joy, content just to fulfil her own vocation in this way.

20. Address to the Bishops of Greece*

Your Catholic communities in Greece are certainly scattered and reduced in number, but they have an appreciable role. In the first place

* November 7, 1977, on the occasion of the Episcopal Conference of Greece's visit "ad limina" to the Holy See. Extracts: SPCU *IS*, 36 (1978), pp. 9–10.

they correspond to the right of Catholic faithful, whether they be of the Latin, Byzantine or Armenian rite, to live and to assemble according to their faith. They bear witness to the Gospel of Christ with this specific note of an organic link with the Church of Rome. They manifest the riches of the pluralism of rites in the unity of the Church. And we know that their educational and welfare works carry out an important service, the value of which is esteemed by authorities and the people.

Ecumenism is a crucial problem for you, in view of your daily relations with your fellow-countrymen who are nearly all Orthodox. You have nominated—we are very happy to hear it—a Commission in charge of contacts with a Greek Orthodox Commission, for preparation of the dialogue between the two Churches. There are difficult questions, which must be solved in an atmosphere of truth and peace, such as that of marriages between Catholics and Orthodox.

In the whole of the Church today, the reestablishment of brotherly charity now makes possible a sincere theological dialogue on all questions that still separate us. How we would like the dialogue to make progress, in order to arrive at full communion as soon as possible!

On your side, we venture to say that you are in the best position to bear witness concretely to the following: that your deep communion with the Successor of Peter, the guarantor of unity—which you do not intend to question at any cost, for it characterizes fundamentally your faithfulness to Christ—is united with sincere esteem and real acceptance of the venerable liturgical, spiritual, theological and disciplinary traditions, legitimate in their diversity since they are compatible with the one faith of the Church: "One Lord, one faith, one baptism, one God and Father" (*Eph* 4, 5–6; *Cf. Unitatis Redintegratio,* n. 17–18). Thus your presence in Greece, far from causing tension and rivalry, should constitute an appeal and a stimulus for true ecumenism.

Then, too, the real problem that all Christians must tackle today, is that of the evangelization of the rising generations. How many young people, of all rites, let themselves be captivated by non-Christian ideologies and by a materialistic atmosphere, which drive them to religious indifference and violence! This is a reality which partly escapes us, which depends on a certain civilization, but it is up to the Churches to help to form this civilization.

Do these young people find in our Churches the evangelical testimony they are entitled to expect, that of God's absoluteness and charity? It is a question of the quality of our liturgical assemblies, the scope and depth of our catechetical efforts and our real concern to construct a more just and brotherly world. This evangelization merely increases the urgency of the pursuit of full communion: "That they may become perfectly one, so that the world may know that thou hast sent me!" (*Jn* 17, 21).

21. Address to the Bishops of England*

The ministry that we are called upon to perform is indeed a service of love: the love of Christ for his Father and his brethren becoming the pattern of our own pastoral charity. This love must find constant expression in our giving to our people the word of God, and in fulfilling their deepest needs for Christ, who is "the way, and the truth, and the life" (*Jn* 14, 6). In particular we owe this love to the poor and suffering.

And because love reaches its perfection in unity, we are called to promote that unity for which Christ prayed, for which he died. Our whole ministry is directed to building up the Church in truth and love. United with us and in the communion of the universal Church, you will find the guarantee of the authenticity of your pastoral initiatives, and the assurance of their supernatural effectiveness for the Kingdom of God. With charity and humility, without anxiety, without compromise in truth, do all you can to advance Christ's plan: "to gather into one the children of God" (*Jn* 11, 52). To each of you we repeat the words Ignatius wrote in his Letter to Polycarp: "Devote yourself to unity, the greatest of blessings".

22. Address to the Bishops of Eastern France**

You are called to construct unity. We ourself have recognized, on certain conditions, the benefit of basic ecclesial communities with more human dimensions (cf. Apostolic Exhortation *Evangelii Nuntiandi,* n. 58). But at present Catholic families tend to set up clans in the Church, which hesitate to communicate and commune on essential matters. At the same time, projects of ecumenism are rightly cherished and it is desired to work at the *rapprochement* and unity of peoples. "Doctor, cure yourself". This unity must begin among Catholics, among the priestly and apostolic forces of the parish, the diocese and the region. And it must be formed around the Bishops. We know the zeal you dedicate to this.

Already among yourselves, you are carrying out intense community work, on the planes of the region and of the Episcopal Conference. Every year the Lourdes Assembly is an occasion for brotherly revision of life and common commitments on the great pastoral objectives. May it be for all your faithful, in search of truth and unity, a source of commitments on the great pastoral objectives. May it be for your faithful, in search of truth and unity a source of comfort and light!

---

* November 10, 1977, on the occasion of the bishops' visit "ad limina" to the Holy See. Extract: SPCU *IS,* 36 (1978), p. 12.
** December 5, 1977, on the occasion of the bishops' visit "ad limina" to the Holy See. Extract: SPCU *IS,* 36 (1978), p. 13.

23. Last Testament of Paul VI*

As regards ecumenism: the approach to the separated Brethren must go on, with great understanding and patience, with great love; but without deflecting from the true Catholic doctrine.

II
POPE JOHN PAUL I**

Inaugural Sermon†

Our presidence in charity is a service and, in affirming it, we think not only of our Catholic brothers and sisters, but also of those who also are trying to be disciples of Jesus Christ, to honor God, to work for the good of humanity.

In this way, we greet affectionately and gratefully the Delegations from other Churches and Ecclesial Communities who are present here. Brethren not yet in full communion, we turn together to Christ our Savior, advancing all of us in the holiness in which He wishes us to be, and also in the mutual love without which there is no Christianity, preparing the paths of unity in faith, with respect for His truth and for the ministry that He entrusted, for His Church's sake, to His apostles and their successors.

III
POPE JOHN PAUL II

1. Address to Christian Delegations at Papal Inauguration Mass††

We wish first of all to thank you from the bottom of our heart for having come here today. Your presence, in fact, bears witness to our

---

* From his handwritten *Testamento,* dated September 16, 1972, and made public after his death on August 6, 1978. Italian Text: *AAS* 70 (1978), p. 561. The entire 56 page issue of SPCU Information Service, 38(1978), contains messages to the Holy See from Orthodox, Anglican, Protestant and Jewish leaders concerning the death of Paul VI, the election of his successor John Paul I (August 26) and his death (September 28), and the election of John Paul II.

** From his election to the See of Rome on August 26, 1978, until his sudden death on September 28, only eighteen letters, sermons and addresses are officially recorded in the *Acta,* 70 (1978).

† September 3, 1978, during the liturgy. French Extract: *AAS* 70 (1978), p. 711. TFS trans.

†† October 22, 1978. Delegations from the Orthodox Churches of Constantinople, Moscow, Rumania, Bulgaria, Cyprus, Georgia, Greece, America, Coptic Patriarchate of Alexandria; Armenian Orthodox; Assyrian; Old Catholics; Anglican Communion (Archbishop of Canterbury); World Lutheran Federation; World Alliance of the Reformed Churches; World Methodist Council; World Council of Churches; Church of Scotland; Lutheran Church of Italy. Names in SPCU *IS,* 38(1978), pp. 55–56. Text: p. 56.

common will to establish closer and closer ties among us and to overcome the divisions inherited from the past. These divisions are, we have already said, an intolerable scandal, hindering the proclamation of the good news of salvation given in Jesus Christ, and the announcement of this great hope of liberation which the world needs so much today.

At this first meeting, we are anxious to tell you of our firm resolution to go forward along the way to unity in the spirit of the Second Vatican Council and following the example of our predecessors. A fine stretch has already been covered, but we must not stop before arriving at the goal, before realizing this unity which Christ wishes for his Church and for which he prayed.

The will of Christ, the witness to be borne to Christ, that is the motive that incites one and all of us not to tire or become discouraged in this effort. We are confident that he who began this work among us, will give us abundantly the strength to persevere and carry it out successfully.

Please say to those whom you represent, and to everyone, that the commitment of the Catholic Church to the ecumenical movement, such as it was solemnly expressed in the Second Vatican Council, is irreversible.

We rejoice at your relations of brotherly trust and collaboration with our Secretariat for Unity. We know that you are searching patiently, along with it, for the solution of the differences that still separate us, and the means of progressing together in more and more complete faithfulness to all aspects of the truth revealed in Jesus Christ. We assure you that we will do everything to help you.

May the Spirit of love and truth grant that we may meet often and in increasing closeness, more and more in deep communion in the mystery of Christ our one Savior, our one Lord. May the Virgin Mary be for us an example of this docility to the Holy Spirit which is the deepest centre of the ecumenical attitude; may our answer always be like hers: I am your servant, let it be to me according to your word (cf. *Lk* 1:10).

2. Address to the Secretariat for Promoting Christian Unity*

The restoration of unity among all Christians was indeed one of the principal aims of the Second Vatican Council (cf. *Unitatis Redintegratio,* 1) and since the moment of my election I have formally engaged myself to promote the carrying out of its guiding principles and directions, seeing this as one of my first duties. Hence your presence here today has a symbolic value. It shows that the Catholic Church, faithful to the direction taken at the Council not only wants to go forward on the way that leads to the restoration of unity, but is anxious, according to its means and in full submission to the promptings of the Holy Spirit (cf. *UR,* 24) to strengthen

---

* November 18, 1978, at the SPCU's General Meeting *(Plenarium)* of bishop members, consultors and staff. Extract: *AAS* 71(1979), pp. 37–40.

at every level its contribution to this great movement of all Christians (cf. *UR,* 4).

A movement does not stop, should not stop before reaching its goal. We have not reached it, even though we have to thank God for the road we have covered since the Council. You have been meeting precisely to take stock, to look where we are. After these years of many-sided efforts animated by immense good will and untiring generosity, nourished by so many prayers and sacrifices, it is good to survey the ground so as to assess the results obtained and make out the best routes for further progress. For it is this we are concerned with. As the apostle tells us, we should be "straining forward to what lies ahead" (*Phil* 3, 13) with a faith which knows no fear because it knows what it believes in and who it counts on. But our haste to get there, the eagerness to put an end to the intolerable scandal of Christian divisions, means that we must avoid "all superficiality, all rash enthusiasms which might hinder the progress towards unity" (*UR,* 24). You do not heal a sickness by giving painkillers but by attacking its causes. In particular I would like to remind you here that the Council was persuaded that the Church is chiefly manifest in the assembly of all its members for the celebration of the same eucharist at the one altar where the bishop presides surrounded by his *presbyterium* and his ministers (cf. *Sacrosanctum Concilium,* 41). Even if it is rarely that we can have such a solemn eucharistic celebration in our modern world, it remains true that in every eucharist it is the whole faith of the Church that comes into play; it is ecclesial communion in all its dimensions that is manifested and realised. We cannot arbitrarily separate its component parts. To do so would be to fall into that superficiality the Council tells us to guard against. It would be a failure to perceive the close relations between eucharist and church unity, their richness, the demands they make on us. I know that the more we find how we are brothers in the charity of Christ, the more painful it is for us not to be able to take part together in this great mystery. Have I not said that the divisions between Christians are becoming intolerable? This suffering should incite us to overcome the obstacles which still hold us back from unanimous profession of the same faith, from the reunification of our divided communities by means of the same sacramental ministry. We cannot escape the obligations of solving together those questions which have divided Christians. It would be a very unenlightened charity that expressed itself at the expense of truth. The first president of the Secretariat, the venerated Cardinal Bea, whose tenth anniversary you have celebrated this week, was fond of repeating the principle: seek the truth in charity.

For thirteen years, in close and trusting collaboration with our brethren of other Churches, the Secretariat has been devoting itself to this search for agreement on points which still divide us, at the same time trying to promote throughout the Catholic Church a mind and spirit loyally at one with the wishes of the Council—something without which the positive results achieved in the various dialogues could not be received by the faithful. Here it should be remembered that the Council demanded a particular effort in teaching theology and forming the outlook of future priests (cf. *UR*, 10). This is especially important now, when this teaching must take account of the work of the dialogues which are in progress. Once they are engaged in the ministry, how will priests be able under their bishops' direction to find judicious and pastorally responsible ways of informing the faithful about the dialogues and their progress, if they have not been initiated into them during their training? Indeed there should be no loosening of the bond, still less opposition, between the deepening of the Church's unity by renewal and the search for restoration of unity among divided Christians. Both are aspects of the same unity for which Christ prayed and which is brought about by the Holy Spirit; there should therefore be an unceasing interaction between them as between two manifestations of a single pastoral effort which must come from the whole Church. You know this, you who come from your dioceses to help us work out, in the light of your experience, all that is implicit in the Council about unity, and to face up to the demands created by new circumstances and the progress of the ecumenical movement itself.

3. Address for the 1979 Week of Prayer for Christian Unity*

This year, the subject of the Week of Prayer for Unity calls our attention precisely to the exercise of some fundamental virtues of Christian life. "Be in one another's service for the glory of God." This subject is taken from a passage of the First Letter of Peter (1 *Pt* 4:7–11). The apostle addresses some communities of the diaspora, of Pontus, Galatia, Cappadocia, Bithynia, Asia, at a moment of particular difficulty. He recalls these communities to Christian faith and affirms that "the end of all things is at hand" (1 *Pt* 4:7). The time in which we are living is eschatological time, the time, that is, which goes from the redemption operated by Christ to his glorious return. We must therefore live in active expectation. In this context the apostle Peter calls them to keep sober in order to dedicate themselves to prayer; he asks them to keep love "unfailing", to practise hospitality, that is openness and generous giving to the brethren, in particular to the under-privileged and emigrants. He asks them to live according to the grace received and to put this grace in the service of others, as good stewards of God's varied grace.

Faithful listening to this advice and its practical application purifies, on the one hand, the relations between persons, because "love covers a multitude of sins" (1 *Pt* 4:8), on the other hand it consolidates the

---

* January 17, 1979, at the Pope's General Audience, Vatican City. Extracts: SPCU *IS*, 40 (1979), pp. 1–2.

community, strengthens it and makes it grow. It is a question of a real exercise of the pursuit of unity. The subject proposes to us to live together as much as possible the common heritage of Christians. Contacts, cooperation, mutual love, reciprocal service, make us get to know one another better, make us rediscover what we have in common, and make us also see how much is still divergent between us. These contacts also urge us to find ways to overcome these divergences.

In recent times the Catholic Church has set up brotherly relations with all the other Churches and ecclesial Communities, relations which we wish to continue and deepen with trust and hope. With the Orthodox Churches of the East the dialogue of charity has made us rediscover a communion that is almost full, even if still imperfect. It is consoling to see how this new attitude of understanding is not limited only to the leaders of the Churches, but is gradually penetrating into the local Churches; for a change of relations on the local plane is indispensable for all further progress.

I wish to recall that a theological dialogue is about to open between the Catholic Church and the Eastern Churches of Byzantine tradition in order to eliminate those difficulties which still prevent eucharistic concelebration and full unity. This is an important moment and we implore God's help for it.

4. Letter to the WCC/RCC Joint Working Group*

Since the Joint Working Group of the World Council of Churches and our Secretariat for Unity is about to hold its first meeting since my election to the See of Rome, I wish to convey to it, through you, my desire that efforts to hasten the reestablishment of unity among all Christians should be intensified. For it is a matter of urgency that we should be able to bear witness to our faith in Christ and his saving work with complete accord. Yet even now, even before this unity of faith, sacramental life and hierarchical bonds is re-established, it is our duty, while honestly recognizing our actual situation today, to find ways whereby we may bear witness to the faith we already share and to the real though incomplete fellowship which already unites us in Christ and in the mystery of his Church. To this end, I hope that you will be able to find ways of ensuring increased cooperation between the Catholic Church and the World Council of Churches in all the fields where this is now possible.

May the Holy Spirit grant you the necessary lucidity, imagination, prudence and courage to forge ahead.

---

* February 23, 1979, addressed to Bishop Ramon Torrella Cascante, SPCU Vice-President, on the occasion of the JWG's meeting in Neuchâtel, Switzerland, Feb.26–March 2. Text: SPCU *IS,* 40 (1979), p. 15.

5. Redemptor Hominis*

Have we gone far along that road? Without wishing to give a detailed reply, we can say that we have made real and important advances. And one thing is certain: We have worked with perseverance and consistency, and the representatives of other Christian churches and communities have also committed themselves together with us, for which we are heartily grateful to them. It is also certain that in the present historical situation of Christianity and the world the only possibility we see of fulfilling the church's universal mission, with regard to ecumenical questions, is that of seeking sincerely, perseveringly, humbly and also courageously the ways of drawing closer and of union. Pope Paul VI gave us his personal example for this. We must therefore seek unity without being discouraged at the difficulties that can appear or accumulate along that road; otherwise we would be unfaithful to the word of Christ, we would fail to accomplish his testament. Have we the right to run this risk?

There are people who in the face of the difficulties or because they consider that the first ecumenical endeavors have brought negative results would have liked to turn back. Some even express the opinion that these efforts are harmful to the cause of the Gospel, are leading to a further rupture in the church, are causing confusion of ideas in questions of faith and morals and are ending up with a specific indifferentism. It is perhaps a good thing that the spokesmen for these opinions should express their fears. However, in this respect also, correct limits must be maintained. It is obvious that this new stage in the church's life demands of us a faith that is particularly aware, profound and responsible. True ecumenical activity means openness, drawing closer, availability for dialogue, and a shared investigation of the truth in the full evangelical and Christian sense; but in no way does it or can it mean giving up or in any way diminishing the treasures of divine truth that the church has constantly confessed and taught. To all who, for whatever motive, would wish to dissuade the church from seeking the universal unity of Christians the question must once again be put: Have we the right not to do it? Can we fail to have trust—in spite of all human weakness and all the faults of past centuries—in our Lord's grace as revealed recently through what the Holy Spirit said

---

* In his first encyclical, *The Redeemer of Man,* released on March 15, 1979 John Paul II observes, "While the ways the Council of this century has set the Church going . . . will continue to be for a long time the ways that all of us must follow, we can at the same time rightly ask at this new stage: How, in what manner should we continue?" The Pope mentions "All of the initiatives that have sprung up from the new ecumenical orientation". Paul VI, "availing himself of the activities of the Secretariat for Promoting Christian Unity, began the first difficult steps on the attainment of unity", as outlined in the *Decree on Ecumenism*. John Paul II then continues in this first extract (n.6). The second extract (n.11) deals with the mystery of Christ as the basis of the Church's mission and of Christianity. The Vatican English translation appeared in *Origins,* March 22, 1979. *AAS* 71 (1979), pp. 266–268: 275–278.

and we heard during the council? If we were to do so, we would deny the truth concerning ourselves that was so eloquently expressed by the apostle: "By the grace of God I am what I am, and his grace toward me was not in vain." (I Cor 15:10)

What we have just said must also be applied—although in another way and with the due differences—to activity for coming closer together with the representatives of the non-Christian religions, an activity expressed through dialogue, contacts, prayer in common, investigation of the treasures of human spirituality, in which, as we know well, the members of these religions also are not lacking. Does it not sometimes happen that the firm belief of the followers of the non-Christian religions—a belief that is also an effect of the Spirit of truth operating outside the visible confines of the mystical body—can make Christians ashamed at being often themselves so disposed to doubt concerning the truths revealed by God and proclaimed by the church and so prone to relax moral principles and open the way to ethical permissiveness. It is a noble thing to have a predisposition for understanding every person, analyzing every system and recognizing what is right; this does not at all mean losing certitude about one's own faith[1] or weakening the principles of morality, the lack of which will soon make itself felt in the life of whole societies, with deplorable consequences besides.

(N. 11). The Second Vatican Council did immense work to form that full and universal awareness by the Church of which Pope Paul VI wrote in his first Encyclical. This awareness—or rather self-awareness—by the Church is formed "in dialogue"; and before this dialogue becomes a conversation, attention must be directed to "the other", that is to say: the person with whom we wish to speak. The Ecumenical Council gave a fundamental impulse to forming the Church's self-awareness by so adequately and competently presenting to us a view of the terrestrial globe as a map of various religions. It showed furthermore that this map of the world's religions has superimposed on it, in previously unknown layers typical of our time, the phenomenon of atheism in its various forms, beginning with the atheism that is programmed, organized and structured as a political system.

With regard to religion, what is dealt with is in the first place religion, as a universal phenomenon linked with man's history from the beginning, then the various non-Christian religions, and finally Christianity itself. The Council document on non-Christian religions, in particular, is filled with deep esteem for the great spiritual values, indeed for the primacy of the spiritual, which in the life of mankind finds expression in religion and then in morality, with direct effects on the whole of culture. The Fathers of the Church rightly saw in the various religions as it were so many reflections of the one truth, "seeds of the Word",[2] attesting that, though the routes taken may be different, there is but a single goal to which is directed the deepest aspiration of the human spirit as expressed in its quest for God and also in its quest, through its tending towards God, for the full dimension of its humanity, or in other words for the full meaning of human life. The Council gave particular attention to the Jewish religion, recalling the great spiritual heritage common to Christians and Jews. It also expressed its esteem for the believers of Islam, whose faith also looks to Abraham.[3]

The opening made by the Second Vatican Council has enabled the Church and all Christians to reach a more complete awareness of the mystery of Christ, "the mystery hidden for ages" (Col 1:26) in God, to be revealed in time in the Man Jesus Christ, and to be revealed continually in every time. In Christ and through Christ God has revealed himself fully to mankind and has definitively drawn close to it; at the same time, in Christ and through Christ man has acquired full awareness of his dignity, of the heights to which he is raised, of the surpassing worth of his own humanity, and of the meaning of his existence.

All of us who are Christ's followers must therefore meet and unite around him. This unity in the various fields of the life, tradition, structures and discipline of the individual Christian Churches and ecclesial Communities cannot be brought about without effective work aimed at getting to know each other and removing the obstacles blocking the way to perfect unity. However, we can and must immediately reach and display to the world our unity in proclaiming the mystery of Christ, in revealing the divine dimension and also the human dimension of the Redemption, and in struggling with unwearying perseverance for the dignity that each human being has reached and can continually reach in Christ, namely the dignity of both the grace of divine adoption and the inner truth of humanity, a truth which—if in the common awareness of the modern world it has been given such fundamental importance—for us is still clearer in the light of the reality that is Jesus Christ.

Jesus Christ is the stable principle and fixed centre of the mission that God himself has entrusted to man. We must all share in this mission and concentrate all our forces on it, since it is more necessary than ever for modern mankind. If this mission seems to encounter greater opposition nowadays than ever before, this shows that today it is more necessary than ever and, in spite of the opposition, more awaited than ever. Here we touch indirectly on the mystery of the divine "economy" which linked salvation and grave with the Cross. It was not without reason that Christ said that "the kingdom of heaven has suffered violence, and men of violence take it by force" (Mt 11:12) and moreover that "the children of this world are more astute . . . than are the children of light" (Lk 16:8). We gladly accept this rebuke, that we may be like those "violent people of God" that we have so often seen in the history of the Church and still see today, and that we may consciously join in the great mission of revealing Christ to the world, helping each person to find himself in Christ, and helping the contemporary generations of our brothers and sisters, the peoples, nations, States, mankind, developing countries and countries of opulence—in short, helping everyone to get to know "the unsearchable riches of Christ" (Eph 3:8), since these riches are for every individual and are everybody's property.

Notes

1. Cf. VATICAN COUNCIL I: Dogmatic Constitution *Dei Filius,* Cap. III *De fide,* can. 6: *Conciliorum Oecumenicorum Decreta,* Ed. Istituto per le Scienze Religiose, Bologna 1973[3], p. 811.

2. Cf. SAINT JUSTIN, *I Apologia,* 46, 1–4; *II Apologia,* 7 (8), 1–4; 10, 1–3; 13, 3–4: *Florilegium Patristicum,* II, Bonn 1911[2] pp. 81, 125, 129, 133; CLEMENT OF ALEXANDRIA, *Stromata,* I, 19, 91 and 94: *Sources Chrétiennes,* 30, pp. 117–118; 119–120; VATICAN COUNCIL II: Decree on the Church's Missionary Activity *Ad Gentes,* II: *AAS* 58 (1966) 960; Dogmatic Constitution on the Church *Lumen Gentium,* 17: *AAS* 57 (1965) 21.

3. Cf. VATICAN COUNCIL II: Declaration on the Church's Relations with Non-Christian Religions *Nostra Aetate,* 3–4: *AAS* 58 (1966) 741–743.

6. Address to Orthodox Students*

Theologians engaged in various ways in service of your Church, you have come to this City to specialize and, at the same time, to get to know directly the great effort of theological reflection and pastoral renewal carried out at all levels of the life of the Catholic Church, especially after the recent Council. An effort of spiritual deepening, purifying tension towards what is essential, increasingly dynamic and consistent faithfulness to our one Lord and to all aspects of his message of salvation, which we must announce to the men and women of today.

In this vast field of the mission of the Church in the modern world, the possibilities of collaboration between the Catholic Church and the venerable Orthodox Churches, to which you belong, are vast, since they spring from the communion which, although not yet full, already unites us. Then, too, it is just by endeavoring to live and present together the whole reality of the Gospel given to the Church and handed down to us, from generation to generation, that we will be able to dispel and overcome better the divergences inherited from the incomprehension of the past.

This collaboration is not only possible immediately, but it is necessary, if we really wish to be faithful to Christ. He wants our unity. He prayed for our unity. Today more than ever, in a world that demands authenticity and consistency, our division is an intolerable counter-testimony. It is as though we denied in our lives what we profess and proclaim.

---

* May 19, 1979, in an audience with Orthodox students, sponsored by the Catholic Committee for Cultural Collaboration, and sent by their Churches to attend courses in Rome at Catholic cultural institutions. Extracts: SPCU *IS,* 40 (1979), p. 8.

A strong personal spiritual life is the indispensable condition for all theological work and the spring at which every true ecclesial service must continually be nourished and renewed. And may this stay be fruitful also for your preparation for the tasks that will be entrusted to you in the future.

7. Address to the Bishops of the Antilles*

It is inevitable, and indeed salutary, that as Christians strive towards the restoration of unity they should feel the pain of existing divisions. As I have pointed out, "A sickness is not healed by giving painkillers but by attacking its causes". We must continue to work humbly and resolutely to remove the real divisions, to restore that full unity in faith which is the condition for sharing in the Eucharist. Of great importance is the fact that "in every Eucharistic celebration it is the whole faith of the Church that comes into play; it is ecclesial communion in all its dimensions that is manifested and realized" *(ibid.)*. Sharing in the Eucharist therefore presupposes unity in faith. Intercommunion between divided Christians is not the answer to Christ's appeal for perfect unity. God has set an hour for the realization of his salvific design for Christian unity. As we yearn for this hour, in common prayer and dialogue, and endeavour to offer an ever more purified heart to the Lord, we must also wait for the Lord's action. It must be said and said again that the restoration of Christian unity is above all a gift of God's love. Meanwhile, on the basis of our common Baptism and the patrimony of faith that we already share, we must intensify our common witness to the gospel and our common service to humanity.

8. Address to Non-Catholic Religious Superiors**

The Second Vatican Council looks upon religious life as being ordered to the greater holiness of the Church and to the greater glory of the Blessed Trinity, which in Christ and through Christ is the source and origin of all holiness (cf. *Lumen Gentium,* 47). It sees all the fruitful ecclesial service of religious as resulting from intimate union with Christ (cf. *Perfectae Caritatis,* 8).

Any consideration of religious life as a new and special title of fulfilling the universal call of all God's people to holiness brings us, moreover, of necessity to the ecclesial aspect of religious life. In the history of the Church, the ecclesiastical authority has guaranteed the authenticity of this life, and this life has constantly been viewed in its relationship to the

---

* May 4, 1979, on the occasion of the bishops' visit "ad limina" to the Holy See. Extract: SPCU *IS,* 40 (1979), p. 5.
** May 21, 1979, to a group of Superiors General of Non-Catholic religious orders of men and women who were in Rome for a series of ecumenical meetings on the religious life. Extracts: SPCU *IS,* 40 (1979), pp. 8–9.

entire Body of Christ, in which the activities of each member and of communities are advantageous to the whole Body by reason of the principle of dynamic union with Christ the Head.

Who more than religious should experience in prayer the urgency, not only of manifesting unity, but also of living it in the fullness of truth and charity? And as we experience this urgency—an experience which is itself a gift of God—do we not likewise experience the need for that increased personal purification, for that ever greater conversion of heart that God seems to be requiring as a prerequisite for the restoration of the corporate unity of all Christians? And does not the spiritual freedom that religious endeavor to acquire in adhering totally to the Lord Jesus bind them ever more closely, in love, to pursue to the end the will of Christ for his Church? Are religious not called in a special way to give expression to the yearning of Christians that the ecumenical dialogue—which by its nature is temporary—should be brought to term in that full ecclesial fellowship which is "with the Father and with his Son Jesus Christ" (1 *Jn* 1–3)? Should religious not be the first to pledge the fullness of their generosity before God's salvific plan, each one repeating with Saint Paul. "What am I to do, Lord?" (*Acts* 22:10).

9. A Plea for Peace in Ireland*

This truly fraternal and ecumenical act on the part of representatives of the churches is also a testimony that the tragic events taking place in Northern Ireland do not have their source in the fact of belonging to different churches and confessions; that this is not—despite what is so often repeated before world opinion—a religious war, a struggle between Catholics and Protestants. On the contrary, Catholics and Protestants, as people who confess Christ, taking inspiration from their faith and the Gospel, are seeking to draw closer to one another in unity and peace. When they recall the greatest commandment of Christ, the commandment of love, they cannot behave otherwise.

But Christianity does not command us to close our eyes to difficult human problems. It does not permit us to neglect and refuse to see unjust social or international situations. What Christianity does forbid is to seek solutions to these situations by the ways of hatred, by the murdering of defenseless people, by the methods of terrorism. Let me say more: Christianity understands and recognizes the noble and just struggle for justice; but Christianity is decisively opposed to fomenting hatred and to promot-

---

* September 29, 1979, during a liturgy of the word service in Drogheda, near the border of Northern Ireland. Present were many representatives of the Church of Ireland and of other Churches, including those from Northern Ireland. Extracts: *AAS* 71(1971), pp. 1078–1085.

ing or provoking violence or struggle for the sake of "struggle." The command, "Thou shalt not kill," must be binding on the conscience of humanity, if the terrible tragedy and destiny of Cain is not to be repeated.

There is another word that must be part of the vocabulary of every Christian, especially when barriers of hate and mistrust have been constructed. This word is reconciliation. "So if you are offering your gift at the altar, and there remember that your brother has something against you, leave your gift there before the altar and go; be reconciled with your brother, and then come and offer your gift" (Mt. 5:23–24). This command of Jesus is stronger than any barrier that human inadequacy or malice can build. Even when our belief in the fundamental goodness of every human being has been shaken or undermined, even if long-held convictions and attitudes have hardened our hearts, there is one source of power that is stronger than every disappointment, bitterness or ingrained mistrust, and that power is Jesus Christ, who brought forgiveness and reconciliation to the world.

I appeal to all who listen to me; to all who are discouraged after the many years of strife, violence and alienation—that they attempt the seemingly impossible to put an end to the intolerable. I pay homage to the many efforts that have been made by countless men and women in Northern Ireland to walk the path of reconciliation and peace. The courage, the patience, the indomitable hope for the men and women of peace have lighted up the darkness of these years of trial. The spirit of Christian forgiveness shown by so many who have suffered in their persons or through their loved ones have given inspiration to multitudes. In the years to come, when the words of hatred and the deeds of violence are forgotten, it is the words of love and the acts of peace and forgiveness which will be remembered. It is these which will inspire the generations to come.

To all of you who are listening I say: Do not believe in violence; do not support violence. It is not the Christian way. It is not the way of the Catholic Church. Believe in peace and forgiveness and love; for they are of Christ.

I came to Drogheda today on a great mission of peace and reconciliation. I come as a pilgrim of peace, Christ's peace. To Catholics, to Protestants, my message is peace and love. May no Irish Protestant think that the pope is an enemy, a danger or a threat. My desire is that instead Protestants would see in me a friend and a brother in Christ. Do not lose trust that this visit of mine may be fruitful, that this voice of mine may be listened to. And even if it were not listened to, let history record that at a difficult moment in the experience of the people of Ireland, the bishop of Rome set foot in your land, that he was with you and prayed with you for peace and reconciliation, for the victory of justice and love over hatred and violence.

10. Address to Irish Ecumenical Leaders*

Let no one ever doubt the commitment of the Catholic Church and of the Apostolic See of Rome to the pursuit of the unity of Christians. Last November, when I met the members of the Secretariat for Promoting Christian Unity, I spoke of the 'intolerable scandal of division between Christians'. I said that the movement towards unity must not stop until it has reached its goal; and I called for an energetic commitment by Catholic bishops, priests and people to forward this movement. I said on that occasion:

The Catholic Church, faithful to the direction taken at the Council, not only wants to go forward on the way that leads to the restoration of unity, but is anxious, according to its means and in full submission to the promptings of the Holy Spirit, to strengthen at every level its contribution to this great movement of all Christians (Address of 18 November 1978).

I renew that commitment and that pledge today here in Ireland, where reconciliation between Christians takes on a special urgency, but where it also has special resources in the tradition of Christian faith and fidelity to religion which marks both the Catholic and Protestant communities.

The work of reconciliation, the road to unity, may be long and difficult. But, as on the way to Emmaus, the Lord himself is with us on the way, always making 'as if to go on' (Luke 24:28). He will stay with us until the longed-for moment comes, when we can join together in recognizing him in the holy scriptures and 'in the breaking of the bread' (Luke 24:35).

Meanwhile, the internal renewal of the Catholic Church, in total fidelity to the Second Vatican Council, to which I pledged all my energies at the beginning of my papal ministry, must continue with undiminished vigour. This renewal is itself an indispensable contribution to the work of unity between Christians. As we each, in our respective Churches, grow in our searching of the Holy Scriptures, in our fidelity to and continuity with the age-old tradition of the Christian Church, in our search for holiness and for authenticity of Christian living, we shall also be coming closer to Christ, and therefore closer to one another in Christ.

It is he alone, through the action of his Holy Spirit, who can bring our hopes to fulfilment. In him we place all our trust: in 'Jesus Christ our hope' (1 Tim. 1:2). Despite our human weakness and our sins, despite all obstacles, we accept in humility and faith the great principle enunciated by our Saviour: 'What is impossible with men is possible with God' (Luke 18:27).

May this day truly mark, for all of us and for those whom we serve in Christ, the occasion for ever greater fidelity, in prayer and penance, to the

---

* September 29, 1979, at the Apostolic Nunciature, Dublin. Extracts: *AAS* 71(1979), pp. 1090–1093.

cause of Jesus Christ, and to his message of truth and love, of justice and peace. May our common esteem and love for the holy and inspired word of God unite us ever more, as we continue to study and examine together the important issues affecting ecclesial unity in all its aspects, as well as the necessity for a united service to a world in need.

Ireland, dear brothers in Christ, has special and urgent need for the united service of Christians. All Irish Christians must stand together to defend spiritual and moral values against the inroads of materialism and moral permissiveness. Christians must unite together to promote justice and defend the rights and dignity of every human person. All Christians in Ireland must join together in opposing all violence and all assaults against the human person—from whatever quarter they come—and in finding Christian answers to the grave problems of Northern Ireland. We must all be ministers of reconciliation. We must by example as well as by word try to move citizens, communities and politicians towards the ways of tolerance, co-operation and love. No fear of criticism, no risk of resentment, must deter us from this task. The charity of Christ compels us. Precisely because we have one common Lord, Jesus Christ, we must accept together the responsibility of the vocation we have received from him.

Dear brothers: with a conviction linked to our faith, we realize that the destiny of the world is at stake, because the credibility of the Gospel has been challenged. Only in perfect unity can we Christians adequately give witness to the truth. And so our fidelity to Jesus Christ urges us to do more, to pray more, to love more.

11. Address to U.S.A. Ecumenical Leaders*

With great satisfaction and joy I welcome the opportunity to embrace you, in the charity of Christ, as beloved Christian brethren and fellow disciples of the Lord Jesus. It is a privilege to be able, in your presence and together with you, to give expression to the testimony of John, that "Jesus Christ is the Son of God" (1 Jn. 4:15), and to proclaim that "there is one mediator between God and men, the man Christ Jesus" (1 Tim 2:5).

In the united confession of faith in the divinity of Jesus Christ, we feel great love for each other and great hope for all humanity. We experience immense gratitude to the Father, who has sent his Son to be our savior, "the expiation for our sins, and not for ours only but for the sins of the whole world" (1 Jn 2:2).

By divine grace we are united in esteem and love for sacred scripture, which we recognize as the inspired word of God. And it is precisely in this word of God that we learn how much he wants us to be fully one in him

---

* October 7, 1979, during a prayer service at Trinity College chapel, Washington, D.C. Extract: *AAS* 71(1979), pp. 1264–1267.

and in his Father. Jesus prays that his followers may be one "so that the world may believe . . ." (Jn 17:21). That the credibility of evangelization should, by God's plan, depend on the unity of his followers is a subject of inexhaustible meditation for all of us.

I wish to pay homage here to the many splendid ecumenical initiatives that have been realized in this country through the action of the Holy Spirit. In the last 15 years there has been a positive response to ecumenism by the bishops of the United States. Through their Committee for Ecumenical and Interreligious Affairs, they have established a fraternal relationship with other churches and ecclesial communities—a relationship which, I pray, will continue to deepen in the coming years. Conversations are in progress with our brothers from the East, the Orthodox. Here I wish to note that this relationship has been strong in the United States and that soon a theological dialogue will begin on a worldwide basis in an attempt to resolve those difficulties which hinder full unity.

There are also American dialogues with the Anglicans, the Lutherans, the Reformed churches, the Methodists and the Disciples of Christ—all having a counterpart on the international level. A fraternal exchange exists likewise between the Southern Baptists and American theologians.

My gratitude goes to all who collaborate in the matter of joint theological investigation, the aim of which is always the full evangelical and Christian dimension of truth. It is to be hoped that, through such investigation, persons who are well-prepared by a solid grounding in their own traditions will contribute to a deepening of the full historical and doctrinal understanding of the issues.

The particular climate and traditions of the United States have been conducive to joint witness in the defense of the rights of the human person, in the pursuit of goals of social justice and peace and in questions of public morality. These areas of concern must continue to benefit from creative ecumenical action, as must the fostering of esteem for the sacredness of marriage and the support of a healthy family life as a major contribution to the well-being of the nation. In this context, recognition must be given to the deep division which still exists over moral and ethical matters. The moral life and the life of faith are so deeply united that it is impossible to divide them.

Much has been accomplished but there is still much to be done. We must go forward, however, with a spirit of hope. Even the very desire for the complete unity in faith—which is lacking between us, and which must be achieved before we can lovingly celebrate the eucharist together in truth—is itself a gift of the Holy Spirit, for which we offer humble praise to God. We are confident that through our common prayer the Lord Jesus will lead us, at the moment dependent on the sovereign action of his Holy Spirit, to the fullness of ecclesial unity.

Doing The Truth In Charity

12. Ecumenism in Catechesis*

Catechesis cannot remain aloof from this ecumenical dimension, since all the faithful are called to share, according to their capacity and place in the church, in the movement toward unity.[1]

Catechesis will have an ecumenical dimension if, while not ceasing to teach that the fullness of the revealed truths and of the means of salvation instituted by Christ is found in the Catholic Church,[2] it does so with sincere respect, in words and in deeds, for the ecclesial communities that are not in perfect communion with this church.

In this context, it is extremely important to give a correct and fair presentation of the other churches and ecclesial communities that the Spirit of Christ does not refrain from using as means of salvation; "moreover, some, even very many, of the outstanding elements and endowments which together go to build up and give life to the church herself, can exist outside the visible boundaries of the Catholic Church."[3]

Among other things, this presentation will help Catholics to have both a deeper understanding of their own faith and a better acquaintance with and esteem for their other Christian brethren, thus facilitating the shared search for the way toward full unity in the whole truth. It should also help non-Catholics to have a better knowledge and appreciation of the Catholic Church and her conviction of being the "universal help toward salvation."

Catechesis will have an ecumenical dimension if, in addition, it creates and fosters a true desire for unity. This will be true all the more if it inspires serious efforts—including the effort of self-purification in the humility and the fervor of the Spirit in order to clear the ways—with a view not to facile irenics made up of omissions and concessions on the level of doctrine, but to perfect unity, when and by what means the Lord will wish.

Finally, catechesis will have an ecumenical dimension if it tries to prepare Catholic children and young people, as well as adults, for living in contact with non-Catholics, affirming their Catholic identity while respecting the faith of others.

In situations of religious plurality, the bishops can consider it opportune or even necessary to have certain experiences of collaboration in the field of catechesis between Catholics and other Christians, complementing the normal catechesis that must in any case be given to Catholics. Such experiences have a theological foundation in the elements shared by all Christians.[4]

---

* Extract from John Paul II's Apostolic Exhortation on Catechetics *(Catechesi Tradendae)*, released October 25, 1979. The document is a reflection on the 1977 Synod of Bishops which had catechetics as its theme. Full English translation in *Origins,* November 8, 1979. *AAS* 71(1979), pp. 1304–1305.

But the communion of faith between Catholics and other Christians is not complete and perfect; in certain cases there are even profound divergences. Consequently, this ecumenical collaboration is by its very nature limited: It must never mean a "reduction" to a common minimum. Furthermore, catechesis does not consist merely in the teaching of doctrine. It also means initiating into the whole of Christian life, bringing full participation in the sacraments of the church.

Therefore, where there is an experience of ecumenical collaboration in the field of catechesis, care must be taken that the education of Catholics in the Catholic Church should be well ensured in matters of doctrine and of Christian living.

During the synod, a certain number of bishops drew attention to what they referred to as the increasingly frequent cases in which the civil authority or other circumstances impose on the schools in some countries a common instruction in the Christian religion, with common textbooks, class periods, etc., for Catholics and non-Catholics alike. Needless to say, this is not true catechesis. But this teaching also has ecumenical importance when it presents Christian doctrine fairly and honestly. In cases where circumstances impose it, it is important that in addition a specifically Catholic catechesis should be ensured with all the greater care.

At this point another observation must be made on the same lines, but from a different point of view. State schools sometimes provide their pupils with books that for cultural reasons (history, morals or literature) present the various religions, including the Catholic religion. An objective presentation of historical events, of the different religions and of the various Christian confessions can make a contribution here to better mutual understanding. Care will then be taken that every effort is made to ensure that the presentation is truly objective and free from the distorting influence of ideological and political systems or of prejudices with claims to be scientific. In any case, such schoolbooks can obviously not be considered catechetical works. They lack both the witness of believers stating their faith to other believers and an understanding of the Christian mysteries and of what is specific about Catholicism, as these are understood within the faith.

Notes
1. Cf. *Decree on Ecumenism,* n.5. *Decree on the Missionary Activity of the Church,* n. 15. Congregation of the Clergy, *General Catechetical Directory,* n. 27: *AAS* 64 (1972), p.115.
2. Cf. *Decree on Ecumenism,* nn. 3–4.
3. *Ibid.,* n. 3.
4. *Constitution on the Church,* n. 15.

13. Address to Delegates of Catholic Ecumenical Commissions*

You are here to discuss ecumenism. This word should not evoke that false fear of the adjustments necessary to any genuine renewal of the church (cf. *Ecumenical Directory* 1, 2). But still less is ecumenism a passport to indifferentism or to neglect of all that is essential to our sacred tradition. Rather it is a challenge, a vocation to work under the guidance of the Holy Spirit for the visible and perfect oneness in faith and love, in life and work, of all who profess faith in our one Lord Jesus Christ. Despite the rapid progress of recent years, much remains to be done.

In this regard the task of furthering theological dialogue and cooperation with other churches and communities must go on. Moreover, there is hardly a country in which the Catholic Church is not cooperating with other Christians in work for social justice, human rights, development and the relief of need. Such work already bears a common witness to Christ, for "cooperation among Christians vividly expresses the bond that already unites them, and it sets in clearer relief the features of Christ the servant." (*Unitatis Redintegratio,* 12)

Your work has another, and equally vital, aspect. "Concern for restoring unity involves the whole church, faithful and clergy alike." (*ibid.,* 5)

One of the principal tasks of ecumenical commissions at every level is to promote unity by placing before the Catholic people the aims of ecumenism, aiding them to respond to this urgent vocation which they should see as integral to their baptismal calling. This vocation is a call to renewal, to conversion, to that prayer which can alone bring us nearer to Christ and to each other, which the council so rightly calls "spiritual ecumenism" and "the soul of the ecumenical movement" (*ibid.,* 8). Every Christian is called to serve the unity of the church. Two tasks are particularly urgent today. One is that of aiding priests and students for the priesthood to appreciate this ecumenical dimension of their mission and to convey it to the people entrusted to their care. The other, as I said last month in my exhortation *Catechesi Tradendae,* concerns the ecumenical dimension of catechesis: "Catechesis will have an ecumenical dimension . . . if it creates and fosters a true desire for unity. This will be true all the more if it inspires serious efforts—including the effort of self-purification in the humility and the fervor of the spirit in order to clear the ways—with a view not to facile irenics . . . but to perfect unity when and by what means the Lord will wish" (*ibid.,* 32).

For these very reasons the task of promoting unity must be seen as an essentially pastoral task. It is pastoral in that the bishops are the principal

---

* November 23, 1979, during a SPCU meeting of 62 delegates from the Commissions for Ecumenism of episcopal conferences and of the synods of Catholic Eastern patriarchates, Rome. Extract: *AAS* 71(1979), pp. 1518–1522.

ministers of unity within the local churches and therefore "have a special responsibility for promoting the ecumenical movement" (Ecumenical Directory II, 65). It is pastoral also in that all who are entrusted with this work must see it as primarily ordered to the building up of the body of Christ and the salvation of the world. As long as Christians are divided, so long will the work of preaching the Gospel be hampered: Divisions among Christians impair the credibility of the Gospel, the credibility of Christ himself (cf. *Evangelii Nuntiandi,* 77). This service of unity is a service of Christ, of the Gospel, and of all humanity. It is, then, a truly pastoral service.

A high priority attaches to this truly pastoral work. The Vatican Council clearly stated the urgency of the ecumenical task. Disunity is a scandal, a hindrance to the spread of the Gospel; it is our duty to strive by God's grace to overcome it as soon as we can. The inner renewal of the Catholic Church is an indispensable contribution to the work of Christian unity. We must therefore present this call to holiness and renewal as central to the church's life. Let no one delude himself that work for perfect unity in faith is somehow secondary, optional, peripheral, something that can be indefinitely postponed. Our fidelity to Jesus Christ urges us to do more, to pray more, to love more. The way may be long and demands patience, and we have to pray that this "genuine need for patience to await God's hour will never occasion complacency in the status quo of division in faith" (Ecumenical address given in the United States, 7 October 1979). You, then, who are charged with particular responsibility for the Catholic Church's ecumenical work in your own lands must always look upon this as one of the main priorities in the church's mission today.

For it is the work of the Church. The Vatican Council's commitment of the Catholic Church to work for ecumenism has been frequently reaffirmed by both Paul VI and myself. To work for unity is not simply to follow one's own fancy, one's personal preference; it means being faithful to and truly representative of the position of the Catholic Church. The council reminded us that "this ecumenical activity cannot be other than truly Catholic, that is, loyal to the truth we have received from the apostles and the fathers, and at the same time tending toward that fullness in which our Lord wants his body to grow in the course of time" (*Unitatis Redintegratio,* 24). This places on you a heavy responsibility. But always remember that it also assures you of a great grace.

You know well that your vocation calls for work, and I hope that during this week you have been encouraged to learn how much work is being done in so many parts of the world, and how much is being done each day by the secretariat here in Rome. But in the end this work is God's work. He looks for our cooperation, and we must put our whole trust in him, for he alone can bring us to the unity he wills, a unity that is the created reflection of the oneness between the divine persons. For is not the church of Christ "a people made one with the unity of the Father, the Son and the Holy Spirit"? (Cf. St. Cyprian, *De Oratione Dominica,* 23, pl 4, 553, quoted in *Lumen Gentium,* 4)

It is in the light of this deep and prayerful confidence in the power of God that I urge you to face with courage, faith and perseverance the difficulties and obstacles inevitable in your work. No difficulty should ever deter us from the work of God. The way of truth and fidelity will always bear the mark of the cross: As the apostle said, "through many tribulations we must enter the kingdom of God." (Acts 14:22)

14. Address to the Secretariat for Promoting Christian Unity*

Unity calls for a fidelity that is continually deepened through listening to one another. With brotherly freedom partners in a true dialogue challenge one another to a more and more exacting faithfulness to God's plan in its entirety.

In faithfulness to Christ the Lord who asked for unity, prayed for it and sacrificed Himself for it, and in docility to the Holy Spirit who guides believers towards the whole truth (cf. Jn 16:13), they continually oblige themselves to go beyond the limits that the religious history of each one may have entailed in order to open up more and more to the "breadth and length and height and depth" of God's mysterious plan which surpasses all knowledge (cf. Eph 3:18–19). Moreover, let us say so incidentally, this spirit of brotherly dialogue which must exist, and I would even say must exist in the first place among the theologians who in the Catholic Church are engaged in the effort of theological renewal, evidently implies also that this dialogue should be carried out in truth and faithfulness. It then becomes an indispensable means of balance which should make it unnecessary for the authority of the Church to be obliged to declare that certain members have embarked on a way that is not the real way to renewal. If the authority is obliged to intervene, it does not act against the ecumenical movement but makes its contribution to this movement by letting it be known that certain paths or certain short cuts do not lead to the goal sought. . . .

This year will be marked by the beginning of the theological dialogue with the Orthodox Church. This theological dialogue is a development of the dialogue of charity which started during the Council, and which must continue and be intensified, for it is the vital atmosphere necessary for this effort of lucidity that will make it possible to rediscover, beyond the divergences and misunderstandings inherited from history, the ways which

* February 8, 1980, at the SPCU's General Meeting *(Plenarium)* of bishop members, consultors and staff. Extracts: *AAS* 72(1980), pp. 178–183.

will finally lead us to a common profession of faith within eucharistic concelebration. The second millennium witnessed our progressive separation. The opposite movement has begun everywhere. It is necessary, and I beseech the "Father of lights" from whom every perfect gift comes down (cf. Jas 1:17) to grant it, that the dawn of the third millennium should rise on our full refound communion.

I hope that this first meeting will soon be followed by other meetings with Patriarch Dimitrios but also with other leaders of Churches and ecclesial Communities in the West.

I am convinced, moreover, that a rearticulation of the ancient Eastern and Western traditions and the balancing exchange that will result when full communion is found again, may be of great importance to heal the divisions that came about in the West in the 16th century.

The various dialogues that have been developing since the end of the Council, have already made good progress. With the Anglican Communion, the joint commission is finishing its work and should present its final report next year. The Catholic Church will then be able to make an official pronouncement and draw the consequences for the stage that will follow.

This year is the 450th anniversary of the Augsburg Confession. In our dialogue with the Lutheran World Federation we have begun to rediscover the deep bonds which unite us in faith and which were masked by the polemics of the past. If, after 450 years, Catholics and Lutherans could arrive at a more exact historical evaluation of this document and establish better its role in the development of ecclesiastical history, it would be a considerable step forward in the march towards unity.

With lucidity, openness, humility and charity, it is necessary to continue to study the principal doctrinal divergences which were, in the past, at the origin of the divisions which still separate Christians today.

These various dialogues are so many efforts aiming at the same goal while taking into consideration the variety of the obstacles to be overcome. It is the same for those in which the Catholic Church is not directly involved. There is no opposition between these various types of dialogue, and nothing must be neglected that may hasten the progress towards unity.

This pursuit of unity, both through dialogue and through collaboration wherever it is possible, has as its purpose the witness to be borne to Christ today. This common witness is limited and incomplete as long as we disagree about the content of the faith we have to proclaim. Hence the importance of unity for evangelization today. In fact Christians must be concerned straightaway to bear witness together to these gifts of faith and life that they have received from God (cf. *Redemptor Hominis,* n. 11). The principal theme of your plenary meeting is precisely common witness. The problem is not only that it should be common, but that it should be true witness to the Gospel, witness borne to Jesus Christ living in the fullness of his Church today. In that direction, Christians—and I am thinking here especially of Catholics—must deepen their faithfulness to Christ and to his Church. Yes, the urgent duty of Catholics is to understand what this witness must be, what it implies and requires in the life of the Church.

I hope that this reflection and this effort will take place everywhere in the Church under the direction of the bishops and Episcopal Conferences. In all situations, according to circumstances, it would be necessary to endeavour, with great pastoral wisdom, to discover the possibilities of joint witness of Christians. Doing so, we will come up against the limits that our divergences still impose on this witness and this painful experience will stimulate us to intensify the effort towards a real agreement in faith. I hope that the results of your plenary meeting will encourage the initiatives of the local Churches in this direction, which is the one indicated by the Vatican Council (cf. Decree *Unitatis Redintegratio,* nos. 12 and 24). It is necessary to advance in this direction with prudence and courage. Nowadays more than ever, is not courage often a requirement of prudence for us who know in whom we believe?

15. Address to Leaders of Other Churches in Zaire*

All initiatives in view of unity would be vain if they were not based on the constant and sometimes painful pursuit of the full truth and of holiness. This pursuit, in fact, brings us closer to Christ and, through him, really brings us nearer to one another.

I know, and it makes me very happy, that various forms of collaboration in the service of the Gospel already exist between the different Christian Churches and Communities in your country. This commitment is a sign of the witness that all those who act in Christ's name wish to bear to God's salvific action, at work in the world; it is also a real step towards the unity that we ask for in our prayer.

Since my election as Bishop of Rome, I have reaffirmed several times, as you know, my ardent desire to see the Catholic Church fully enter the holy work which has its aim the restoration of unity. I hope that my presence among you today will be considered a sign of this commitment. Certainly, the different countries and the different regions have each their religious history; that is why the methods of the ecumenical movement may differ, but its essential imperative always remains identical: the search for the truth in its very center, Christ. It is he whom we seek above all, in order to find real unity in him.

* May 3, 1980, in Kinshasa. Extract: SPCU *IS,* 44 (1980), p. 82

16. Address to Leaders of Other Churches in Kenya*

Because of this one Baptism, in which we profess one basic faith that Jesus is Lord and that God raised him from the dead (cf. *Rom* 10:9), we stand together before the world of today with a common responsibility which stems from obedience to Christ. This common responsibility is so real and so important that it must impel us to do all we can, as a matter of urgency, to resolve the divisions that still exist between us, so that we may fulfill the will of Christ for the perfect unity of his followers.

Without full organic unity, Christians are unable to give a satisfactory witness to Christ, and their division remains a scandal to the world, and especially to the young Churches in mission lands. Your presence here testifies to a deep insight: that especially in the young Churches of Africa, in a continent that hungers and thirsts for God—a longing that can be fulfilled only in Christ—the common apostolic faith in Christ the Savior must be held and manifested, for in Christ there can be no division. Your presence, together with the sincere ecumenical efforts which are developing, shows our common desire for full unity. For truly the credibility of the Gospel message and of Christ himself is linked to Christian unity.

Our divisions impair that vitality and prevent our neighbours from hearing the Gospel as they should. And yet, even now, thanks to what we already have in common, it is possible for us, despite those divisions, to give a sincere even if limited witness together before a world that so sorely needs to hear that message of love and hope which is the Good News of the salvation won for all mankind by Jesus Christ, who "was crucified in weakness but lives by the power of God" (*2 Cor* 13:4). It is possible for us to collaborate frequently in the cause of the Gospel. Although we cannot yet do everything together—especially the fullness of Eucharistic worship—we can still accomplish much together.

Wherever possible, then, let us find ways of engaging in acts of common witness, be it in joint Bible work, in promoting human rights and meeting human needs, in theological dialogue, in praying together when opportunity allows—as it does so beautifully today—or in speaking to others about Jesus Christ and his salvation. As we do these things we must continue to ask the Holy Spirit for light and strength to conform perfectly to God's holy will for his Church.

17. Letter to the German Episcopal Conference**

Anyone who participates in the history of our century and is not unfamiliar with the various trials which the Church lives in its midst, in the march of these first post-conciliar years, is conscious of these tempests.

---

* May 7, 1980, in Nairobi. Extracts: *AAS* 72 (1980), pp. 500–501
** May 15, 1980. Extracts: *L'Oss. Rom.*, May 23, 1980. TFS trans.

The Church which must confront them cannot be affected by uncertainty in faith and by relativism of truth and morals. Only a Church deeply consolidated in its faith can be a Church of authentic dialogue.

Dialogue requires, in fact, a particular maturity in proclaimed and professed truth. Only such maturity that is certainty in faith is able to oppose the radical negations of our time, even when they are aided by various means of propaganda and pressure. Only such a mature faith can become an effective advocate of true religious liberty, liberty of conscience and all the rights of man.

From the ecumenical point of view of the union of Christians, one cannot in any way pretend that the Church renounces certain truths it professes. It would be in contrast with the way indicated by the Council. If to achieve such an end that Council affirms that "Catholic faith must be explained with more profundity and exactness," it is indicating also the duty of theologians. Most significant is the section of the *Decree on Ecumenism* which deals directly with Catholic theologians, emphasizing that "in searching together with separated brethren into the divine mysteries," they must remain "faithful to the doctrine of the church" (n. 11).

I already pointed to the "hierarchy" or order of truths of Catholic doctrine, of which theologians must be reminded, particularly "when comparing doctrines." The Council evokes such a hierarchy, given that "they vary in their relation to the foundation of the Christian faith." (ibid.)

In this way ecumenism, this great inheritance of the Council, can become an always more mature reality—that is, only on the road of a greater commitment of the Church, inspired by certainty of faith and by a confidence in the power of Christ, in which, since the beginning, the pioneers of this work have distinguished themselves.

18. Address to Christian Leaders in France*

First and foremost, and in the dynamics of the movement towards unity, our personal and community memory must be purified of the memory of all the conflicts, injustice and hatred of the past. This purification is carried out through mutual forgiveness, from the depths of our hearts, which is the condition of the blossoming of real fraternal charity, a charity that is not resentful and that excuses everything (cf. *1 Cor* 13:5 and 7). I say so here for I know the cruel events which, in the past, have marked the relations of Catholics with Protestants in this country. To be a Christian today requires us to forget this past in order to be wholly available for the task to which the Lord calls us now (cf. *Phil* 3:13). You are facing this task and I rejoice particularly at the quality of the collaboration that exists among you, especially as regards the service of man, a

---

* May 31, 1980, in Paris. Extracts: *AAS* 72 (1980), pp. 702–705.

service understood in its whole dimension and which requires urgently and immediately the testimony of all Christians.

But, today more than ever perhaps, the first service to render to man is to bear witness to the truth, the whole truth, "aletheuontes en agape", "speaking the truth in love" (*Eph* 4:15). We must not cease until we are once more able to confess together the whole truth, this whole truth in which the Spirit guides us (cf. *Jn* 16:13). . . . We must be able to confess the whole truth together in order to be able really to bear witness in common to Jesus Christ, the only one in whom and through whom man can be saved (cf. *Acts* 4:12).

I should say that I am living in a very profound way the anniversary you are living this year, I mean the 450th anniversary of the 'Confession of Augsburg'—yes, in a very profound way. I am living it in a way that I find almost beyond my comprehension, for there is someone who is living it in me. "Someone will lead you!" I think that these words the Lord spoke to Peter are, perhaps, the most important of all the words he heard: "Someone will lead you!"

I must also say that my fraternal visit to (the Patriarchate of) Constantinople gave me great hope. I felt very much at ease in that atmosphere, that milieu which so clearly constitutes a great spiritual reality. A complementary reality; one cannot breathe as a Christian, indeed I would say as a Catholic, with only one lung; you need to have two lungs, that is the Eastern and the Western.

I think that in this great question of rediscovering unity there is clearly an historic moment; and if we are putting questions to one another, there is another who is questioning us much more, for clearly we are faced with a radical denial of all that we are, of what we believe, of what we preach, of what we witness to. This radical questioning cannot be answered except by witness: witness of the faith, witness of unity, witness in Christ. That is the historical moment to which we have come, and this moment is matched by our efforts.

I think that here we are on the right lines: we have recognised the signs of the times and we are seeking to respond to them, in ourselves, with our powers, our human powers, we are all seeking to respond to them. But there is another element that is much more important than our efforts, and that is time. To say time is to say hope. We hope that the Lord will grant us the day when we shall find ourselves united and perhaps on that day we shall have—we can be sure we shall have—a different view of the difficulties which we see as such today. A vision of different approaches to the same source, the same truth, the same Jesus Christ, the same Gospel. I am convinced that the Lord is preparing this for us, and that it was for this that he inspired the spirit of our predecessors—I mean our predecessors in the ecumenical sense—and clearly I am speaking especially of John XXIII who was here as Nuncio and who continues to be present in our spirits.

19. 450th Anniversary of the Confession of Augsburg*

My thoughts turn today to a memorable date in the history of Western Christianity. Four hundred and fifty years ago the forerunners of our brothers and sisters of the Evangelical Lutheran Confession submitted a document to the Emperor (Charles V) and the Imperial Diet at Augsburg, with the intention of witnessing to their faith "in the one, holy, catholic and apostolic Church". This document has become a part of the history of Christianity under the title of "the Confession of Augsburg". As a "confessional text" it remains today a fundamental document for the confession of faith and the ecclesial life of Lutheran Christians and others.

To look back at the historical events of 450 years ago and, still more, at the developments that followed, fills us with sadness and sorrow. We must recognize that despite the honest desire and the serious effort of all concerned, they did not then succeed in avoiding the tensions that threatened between the Roman Catholic Church and the evangelical reform. The last real attempt to restore peace at the Diet of Augsburg floundered. Soon afterwards the point of clear division was reached.

We are all the more grateful that today we see with even greater clearness that at that time, even if there was no success in building a bridge, the storms of that age spared important piers of that bridge. The intense and long-standing dialogue with the Lutheran Church, called for and made possible by the Second Vatican Council, has enabled us to discover how great and solid are the common foundations of our Christian faith.

Today as we look at the history of the divisions of Christianity, we are more aware than ever what tragic and scandalous consequences human failure and human guilt have over a long period, and how they can obscure Christ's will and damage the dignity of faith in the Good News. The Second Vatican Council has reminded us that there is an intimate relationship between the constant renewal of the Church in the power of the Gospel and the safeguarding of its unity and also the restoration of its unity.

I want to urge all the faithful, and particularly theologians, and to beg them unceasingly that, faithful to Christ and to the Gospel, faithful to the "primitive Church", faithful to our common fathers of the Church and to our common Ecumenical Councils, we may seek all there is in the apostolic heritage that unites us with our brothers and sisters, in order that we may discover anew the treasure of one common creed. The world of the late twentieth century in which we live is marked by an indescribable hunger. The world is hungry and thirsty for the confession of Christ and

---

* June 25, 1980, at a General Audience in the Vatican. Extract: SPCU *IS*, 44 (1980), p. 91.

for witness to Christ by word and deed, Christ who alone can satisfy this hunger and thirst.

With all my heart I greet all the Christians who, today and in the next few days, will be gathering at Augsburg to confirm, in the face of the fears and pessimism of a troubled humanity, that Jesus Christ is the salvation of the world, the Alpha and the Omega of everything that exists. I greet also all Christians who are gathering in many other places all over the world on the occasion of this 450th anniversary of the "Confession of Augsburg", so that from the Gospel of creation by God, of Redemption in Jesus Christ, and of the call to one People of God, there may develop a new force for a confession of faith full of hope, today and tomorrow. The will of Christ and the signs of the times are leading us to a common witness in a growing fullness of truth and love.

20. Address to the Roman Curia*

The special task of the way that concerns the mission of the Church is ecumenism: the trend to the union of Christians. It is a priority that is imposed on our action, in the first place because it corresponds to the very vocation of the Church. The ecumenical effort is not engaged in for reasons of opportuneness. It is not dictated by contingent situations or conditions. It is based on God's will.

On the strength of this conviction, I visited the Ecumenical Patriarch, His Holiness Dimitrios I, in Istanbul. It was necessary for me to visit the first see of the Orthodox Church, with which we are united by deep communion. We have become newly aware of this communion in the last few years, during which there developed the dialogue of charity, which led to the theological dialogue. The latter has just started in Patmos with a spiritual dynamism that arouses in me joy and hope. The dawn of the century that is approaching must find us united in full communion. The theological dialogue will have to overcome the disagreements that still exist, but, as I had occasion to say elsewhere, it will be necessary to learn again to breathe fully with two lungs, the Western and the Eastern.

I recently received, here in Rome, delegations from the Patriarchates of Moscow and Bulgaria. But above all, I had the joy to have the visit of the Catholicos-Patriarch of Georgia, Ilya II. I am not forgetting the Ancient Eastern Churches. My meeting in Istanbul with Patriarch Snork Kaloustian marks the determination to carry on what has been undertaken by my venerated predecessor and by the Catholicos of the Armenian Church. With the Coptic Church, a document is being completed. Its preparation started with the visit I received last year from an important delegation of that Church. I have also recently received the visit of a

* June 28, 1980. Extract: *AAS* 72 (1980), pp. 653–656.

metropolitan of the Syrian Church in India, and of a delegation of the Church of Ethiopia, whose Patriarch I hope to meet. But above all, last May Mar Ignatius Jacob III, the Patriarch of the Syrian Church, who died just a few days ago, led an important delegation to renew the visit he paid to the Church of Rome in 1971.

I also like to hope that those who are most directly charged with promoting unity—those who are responsible for ecumenism in the dioceses, ecumenical commissions in the episcopal conferences, the Secretariat for Promoting Christian Unity within the Roman Curia, which I wish to thank publicly here—are closely associated in fruitful collaboration.

The effort to re-establish full communion with the Churches that are heirs to the various Eastern traditions does not make us neglect, however, the concern to overcome the divisions that came into being in the 16th century in the West. In less than two years, and in a spirit of Christian friendship, I have had exchanges with two Archbishops of Canterbury: Dr. Coggan, who kindly attended the solemn inauguration of my pontificate, and Dr. Runcie, who met me in Africa. At these meetings I saw reflected the intentions of so many Anglicans for the restoration of unity.

This intention instils strength in so many dialogues and so much collaboration in progress in the English-speaking world. This experience must lead us to follow in prayer the work carried out by the joint Commission between the Catholic Church and the Anglican Communion. The very important results will be presented at the end of next year.

The Methodists followed the Second Vatican Council closely. They found in the renewal that it has produced many inspirations close to their ideals of holiness life.

In the official dialogue with the Lutheran World Federation, the numerous controversies of the 16th century, still not without effect today, have been studied in a joint theological effort.

In the framework of these contacts with the Lutheran Christians, the discussion on the *Confessio Augustana* has assumed particular significance in these times. The 450th anniversary of this fundamental document, which dates back to 1530, occurs at this time.

Also in the dialogue with the World Alliance of Reformed Churches, reflection has been carried out on our common origins and we have reached agreement in reflecting on Christian responsibility in the world of today.

A dialogue is being carried on with the Pentecostal Churches, and many misunderstandings are being removed.

Parallel to "bilateral" contacts and dialogues with the different Churches, collaboration has been developed at the same time with the World Council of Churches and its various departments. I have asked for this collaboration to be increased, since I am convinced—in spite of the difficulties—of the importance of this multilateral dialogue and of the benefits it may have. In this connection I had useful conversations with the General Secretary of that organization, Pastor Philip Potter, at the beginning of last year.

During each of my journeys I endeavoured to meet my brothers of other Churches and ecclesial communities. This happened particularly in Ireland, in the United States of America, in various African countries, and in Paris. These meetings made it possible, with the help of experience, to carry out brotherly exchanges progressively. They permitted mutual listening and mutual understanding. I hope they will grow and develop in this direction during future journeys.

But since only God allows us to advance in fulfilment of Christ's supreme desire *ut unum sint* (*Jn* 17:21ff.), the essential importance of prayer can be understood, as the Second Vatican Council stressed (cf. *Unitatis Redintegratio*, n. 8). Once more and insistently, I urge the Catholic faithful, especially those called to the contemplative life, to raise incessant supplication for the real and complete unity of all disciples of Christ. The Week of Prayer for the Unity of Christians must be, every year, the very special time, the heart, of this supplication. In this way the Catholic principles of ecumenism, established by the Second Vatican Council, will be able to be fully realized. In this way we shall be able to follow the present and future impulses of the Holy Spirit with discernment, in complete docility and generosity (cf. n. 24).

However, as I stressed in my recent letter to the German Episcopate, according to the *Decree on Ecumenism*, the union of Christians cannot be sought in a "compromise" between the various theological positions, but only in a common meeting in the most ample and mature fullness of Christian truth. This is our wish and theirs. It is a duty of mutual loyalty. The Second Vatican Council stated: "Nothing is so foreign to the spirit of ecumenism as a false irenicism which harms the purity of Catholic doctrine and obscures its genuine and certain meaning" (n. 11).

True ecumenical dialogue demands, therefore, on the part of theologians particular maturity and certainty in the truth professed by the Church; it demands particular faithfulness on their part to the teaching of the Magisterium. Only by means of such a dialogue "can ecumenism, this great heir of the Council, become an ever more mature reality, that is, only along the way of a great commitment of the Church, inspired by the certainty of faith and by confidence in the power of Christ, in which, since the beginning, the pioneers of this work distinguished themselves" (Letter to the German Episcopate, *L'Osservatore Romano*, 23 May 1980). In this effort we take as our basis solely the doctrine of the Council and we wish to see verified the programmatic words of its Decree on Ecumenism: *Unitatis Redintegratio*, the "restoration of unity".

21. Address to Christian Leaders in Brazil*

I cannot refrain from mentioning here what has been done in the area of collaboration among Christians on behalf of human rights and the complete respect for them. In saying this, I refer not only to some important initiatives on the level of the explanation and research of the evangelical bases for these rights, but also to the daily work, in such diverse places and circumstances, for the defence and advancement of men and women, especially the poorest and most forgotten, whom present-day society often tends to abandon to themselves and to exclude, as if they did not exist, or as if their existence did not count. "Man is in fact the way for the Church", as I wished to explain in my first encyclical *Redemptor Hominis* (n. 14). In this way, various fundamental guidelines of the Puebla Document, gathered in the chapter on dialogue and in other texts, are also put into practice. **

22. Address to Working Group of Faith and Order Commission†

In studying together baptism, the Eucharist and the ministry, not only are you dealing with realities that are at the heart of the mystery of the Church and her structure, but you are also tackling questions which were, if not the cause of our divisions, at least among the main subjects about which opposition arose. Now there cannot be a true and lasting re-establishment of unity without our succeeding in expressing our faith clearly together in these aspects of the mystery on which we opposed one another. The question of the ministry certainly remains a key question for the re-establishment of full communion.

In this work, you have to examine the Scriptures thoroughly; you have to consider how the Christians, from the beginning, with their pastors, received this teaching and interpreted it, not only on the intellectual plane, but on the existential plane, in their everyday life, in their profession of faith, in their institutions; how this teaching brought forth a more intense spiritual life.

23. Address to Council of the German Evangelical Church††

I recall at this moment that in 1510–1511 Martin Luther came to Rome as a pilgrim to the tombs of the Princes of the Apostles, but also as

---

* July 4, 1980, in Porto Alegre. Extract: SPCU *IS*, 44 (1980), p. 87.

** Cf. *The Puebla Conclusions*, Washington, DC: National Conference of Catholic Bishops' Committee for the Church in Latin America, 1979, pp. 173–176.

† November 3, 1980, Vatican City. Since 1968 ten to twelve Catholic theologians have been members of this commission of the World Council of Churches. This meeting in Rome concerned progress on the study, "Baptism, Eucharist and Ministry." Extracts: SPCU *IS*, 45 (1981).

†† November 17, 1980, in Mainz, Federal Republic of Germany. Extracts: *AAS* 73 (1981), pp. 72–75. TFS trans.

one seeking and questioning. Today I come to you, the spiritual heirs of Martin Luther. I come as a pilgrim. By this pilgrimage in a changed world, I come to set up a sign of union in the central mystery of our faith. Allow me to express right at the beginning of our talk what particularly moves me. I do so in connection with the testimony of the Letter to the Romans, that writing which was absolutely decisive for Martin Luther. "This letter is the real masterpiece of the New Testament and the purest Gospel", he wrote in 1522.

In the school of the Apostle of the Gentiles we can become aware that we all need conversion. There is no Christian life without repentance. "There can be no ecumenism worthy of the name without interior conversion" (*U. Redintegratio*, n. 7). "Let us no more pass judgment on one another" (Rom 14:13). Let us rather recognize our guilt. "All have sinned" (Rom 3:23) applies also to the grace of unity. We must see and say this in all earnestness and draw our conclusions from it. Most important is to recognize more and more deeply what consequences the Lord draws from human failing. Paul reduces it to the same denominator: "where sin increased, grace abounded all the more" (Rom 5:20). God does not cease to "have mercy upon all" (Rom 11:32). He gives his Son, he gives himself, he gives forgiveness, justification, grace, eternal life. Together we can recognize all this.

Decades of my life have been marked by the experience of the challenging of Christianity by atheism and non-belief. It appears to me all the more clearly how important is our common profession of Jesus Christ, of his word and work in this world, and how we are driven by the urgency of the hour to overcome the differences that divide us, and bear witness to our growing union.

Jesus Christ is the salvation of us all. He is the only mediator, "whom God put forward as an expiation by his blood, to be received by faith" (Rom 3:25). "We have peace with God through our Lord Jesus Christ" (Rom 5:1) and among ourselves. By virtue of the Holy Spirit we are his brothers and sisters, really and essentially sons and daughters of God. "If children, then heirs, heirs of God and fellow heirs with Christ" (Rom 8:17).

All the gratitude for what remains to us in common and unites us cannot make us blind to what still divides us. We must examine it together as far as possible, not to widen the gaps but to bridge them. We cannot stop at the acknowledgement: "We are and remain divided for ever and against each other". We are called to strive together, in the dialogue of truth and love, to full unity in faith. Only full unity gives us the possibility of gathering with the same sentiments and the same faith at the Lord's one table. The lectures given by Luther on the Letter to the Romans in the years 1516–1517 tell us what this effort above all consists of. Luther teaches that "faith in Christ through which we are justified, is not just belief in Christ, or more exactly in the person of Christ, but belief in what is Christ's". "We must believe in him and in what is his". To the question; "What is this, then?", Luther refers to the Church and to her authentic teaching. If the difficulties that exist between us were only a question of "ecclesiastical structures set up by men" (cf. *Confessio Augustana*, VIII), we could and should eliminate them immediately. According to the conviction of Catholics, disagreement revolves around "what is Christ's", around "what is his": his Church and its mission, its message, its sacraments, and the ministries placed in the service of the Word and the Sacrament.

We must leave no stone unturned. We must do what unites. We owe it to God and to the world. "Let us then pursue what makes for peace and for mutual upbuilding" (Rom 14:19). Each of us must say to himself with St Paul: "Woe to me if I do not preach the Gospel" (1 Cor 9:16). We are called to be witnesses of the Gospel, witnesses of Christ. His message requires us to bear witness together. . . .

The tasks that await us are great and difficult. If we could count only on our own strength, we would despair. "Likewise the Spirit helps us in our weakness" (Rom 8:26). Trusting in him, we can continue our dialogue, we can tackle the acts required of us. Let us begin with the most important dialogue, with the most important act: let us pray!

24. Address to Leaders of Other Christian Communities in Germany*

Our being together in your German homeland confronts us with the event of the Reformation. We must think of what preceded it and of what since has happened. If we do not evade the facts, we realize that the faults of men led to the unhappy division of Christians, and that our faults again hinder the possible and necessary steps towards unity. I emphatically make my own what my predecessor Hadrian VI said in 1523 at the Diet of Nuremberg: "Certainly the Lord's hand has not been shortened so much that he cannot save us, but sin separates us from him . . . All of us, prelates and priests, have strayed from the right path and there is not anyone who does good (cf. Ps 14:3). Therefore we must all render honour to God and humble ourselves before him. Each of us must consider why he has fallen and judge himself rather than be judged by God on the day of wrath". With the last German or Dutch Pope, I say: "The disease is deep-rooted and developed; we must therefore proceed step by step, and first of all treat the most serious and dangerous ills with suitable medicines, so as not to make things even more confused with a hasty reform". Today, as then, the first and most important step towards unity is the renewal of Christian life. "There can be no ecumenism worthy of the name without interior conversion" (*Unitatis Redintegratio*, 7).

* November 17, 1980, in Mainz, FDR. Extract: *AAS* 73(1981), p. 76.

25. Address to the German Episcopal Conference*

You live in the country in which the Reformation originated. Your ecclesiastical life and your social life are deeply marked by the scission of the Church, which has now lasted for over four and a half centuries. You must not resign yourselves to the fact that disciples of Christ do not give the testimony of unity before the world. Unshakable fidelity to truth, opening to others and readiness to listen to them, calm patience on the way, love and sensitivity, are necessary. Compromise does not count; what is important is only that unity which the Lord himself founded: unity in truth and in love.

We often hear it said today that the ecumenical movement of the Churches is at a standstill, that after the spring of the changes brought by the Council, there has followed a period of coolness. In spite of many regrettable difficulties, I cannot agree with this judgment.

Unity, which comes from God, is given to us at the Cross. We must not want to avoid the cross, passing to rapid attempts at harmonizing differences, excluding the question of truth. But neither must we abandon one another, and go on our separate ways, because drawing closer calls for the patient and suffering love of Christ crucified. Let us not be diverted from the laborious way in order to remain where we are, or to choose ways that are apparently shorter and lead astray.

26. Address to Catholic/Methodist International Commission**

You have often remarked in your reports how these attentive (officially delegated Methodist) observers (at the Vatican Council) were struck by the deep affinities between Catholic and Methodist traditions and ideals: between the fervent preaching of personal holiness by the Wesleys and later Methodist leaders, and the work of the spiritual giants of Catholic history. In choosing this affinity as an anchor for your dialogue, you chose wisely; yours has been a truly "holy converse", centred on a shared love of Christ, so that in it the thorny questions which are the legacy of the sad history of modern Christian division (questions which you have not shirked) have been faced with serenity, good will and charity. No one has more need than the ecumenist to remember the words of Saint Paul: "If I speak in the tongues of men and of angels, but have not love, I am a noisy gong or a clanging cymbal" (1 Cor 13: 1).

Your dialogue has ranged wide. Besides discussions of doctrinal differences there has been a strong emphasis on the positive challenges

---

* November 17, 1980, in Fulda, FDR. Extract: SPCU *IS,* 45(1981), p. 9, AAS 73 (1981), p. 85.
** December 5, 1980, Vatican City. With five-year mandates, this Commission between the Roman Catholic Church and the World Methodist Council has been meeting each year since 1967. Cf. its *First Report*, SPCU *IS*, 21 (1973), pp. 22–38; *Second Report*, 34(1977), pp. 8–20. Extract: 44 (1980), p. 12.

which all Christ's witnesses face today—not merely in the social field, trying to state the Christian message effectively in a world bewildered by change, but even more in the delicate inner realm of the Christian conscience, where no man or woman escapes the hard choices, the sacrifices inseparable from holding to Christ.

Do not be upset by the cries of the impatient and the sceptical, but do all in your power to ensure that your search for reconciliation is echoed and reflected wherever Methodists and Catholics meet.

27. Address to Christian Youth of the Taizé Community*

Ecclesial unity, dear friends, is a deep mystery which transcends our conceptions, our efforts, our desires. "Christ bestowed the unity of the one and only Church on his Church from the beginning" (*Decree on Ecumenism*, 4). And at the same time, unity must constantly be sought, reconstructed, for Christians as a whole.

In a certain sense, Christians do not exist before the Church, and they do not continue to exist, as such, independently of the Church. Let us say rather: men and women join the Church to become Christians. "All those who in faith look towards Jesus, the author of salvation and the principle of unity and peace, God has gathered together and established as the Church, that it may be for each and every one the visible sacrament of this saving unity" (*Lumen Gentium*, 9). Unity does not come merely from listening to the same evangelical message, which, moreover, is transmitted to us by the Church; it takes on a mystical depth. We are joined to the very Body of Christ through faith and baptism in the name of the Father, the Son and the Holy Spirit. The Spirit himself justifies us and animates our Christian life: "There is one body and one Spirit, just as you were called to the one hope that belongs to your call, one Lord, one faith, one baptism" (Eph 4:4–5).

Such is the one source that involves and requires, today as at the dawn of the Church, "unity in the teaching of the apostles, and fellowship in the breaking of bread and in prayer" (*L.G.*, 13). The very structure of the Church, with her hierarchy and her sacraments, merely expresses and realizes this essential unity received from Christ the Head. Finally, this unity within the Church of Christ constitutes "a most sure seed of unity, hope and salvation for the whole human race" (*L.G.*, 9). Such is the grace given to the Church from the beginning, such is her vocation.

Unity therefore appears as a fundamental characteristic of the Church. But its realization is difficult, strewn with dangers, at least if we consider the deep unity that Christ wishes. And it is a fact that certain

---

* December 30, 1980, St. Peter's Basilica. The Pope had joined a prayer vigil with over 25,000 Christian youth, from six continents of different confessions, during the annual meeting of the Taizé ecumenical community. Extracts: SPCU *IS,* 45(1981), pp. 12–16.

scissions appeared in this one Church of God right from the beginning. Thereafter the Church experienced more serious disagreements, which our generation inherits and from which it suffers, even if it sometimes provokes new ones. You are particularly sensitive to this suffering, this contradiction. That is a good sign.

Faithfulness to Christ makes it an urgent duty for us to reconstruct full unity. It is true that we share a common heritage in a certain number of things. And there is considerable progress in understanding, charity and common prayer, even if, out of honesty and loyalty to ourselves and to our brothers and sisters, we cannot celebrate the Lord's Eucharist together, for it is the Sacrament of Unity. It is impossible, in fact, to separate eucharistic communion and ecclesial communion in one and the same faith.

This unity of the Church, given by Christ, marred by Christians and therefore ceaselessly to be rebuilt, was especially entrusted to the Apostle Peter, who had come from the shores of Lake Tiberias to the banks of the Tiber and who died as a martyr in this very place in the reign of Nero. It was not to John, the great contemplative, nor to Paul, the incomparable theologian and preacher, that Christ gave the task of strengthening the other Apostles, his brethren (cf. Lk 2:31–32), of feeding the lambs and the sheep (cf. Jn 21:15–17), but to Peter alone. It is always enlightening and moving to meditate on the Gospel texts expressing the unique and irreducible role of Peter in the College of Apostles and in the Church at her beginning. It is even overwhelming, for each of us, to see how much Christ continues to put all his trust in Peter, in spite of his momentary weakness. And Peter took this role seriously, even to the supreme witness of shedding his blood. His First Letter certainly seems to prove that he meditated deeply upon the astonishing words that Jesus had said to him. It reveals the personal spirituality of the one who had received the charge of gathering together the flock of the one Shepherd: "Tend the flock of God that is your charge ... not for shameful gain but eagerly. ... And when the chief Shepherd is manifested you will obtain the unfading crown of glory" (1 Pet 5:2–4; cf. 2:25). Peter remembers that he is the rock but also the shepherd. And when he exhorts the Elders to carry out their pastoral task eagerly, it is because he remembers having received his own pastoral task in response to a threefold protestation of love.

The charism of St Peter passed to his successors. This is why at a very early time the Church of Rome played a leading role. ... At the end of the first century, the Bishop of Rome, St Clement, intervenes with authority in the Church which is in Corinth, precisely in order to re-establish in it internal unity. Towards the year 110, St Ignatius of Antioch, writing to the Church in Rome, greets it as the one which presides over the universal assembly of love. The famous epitaph of Abercius, which can be seen in the Vatican Museum, bears witness to the influence of the Roman Church about the year 180. St Irenaeus, Bishop of Lyons at the end of the second century, proclaims that every Church desiring to preserve the apostolic tradition must for this purpose make sure that it remains in communion with Rome. . . .

Communion in the Church necessarily has a visible countenance, an institutional aspect, thanks in particular to the service of unity which the papal, episcopal and priestly ministry is. This ministry brings about, in the strong sense of the word, communion among Christians because it is in the first place an apostolic ministry, a real link with the origins, with what founded the Church: bishops and priests preside, in fact, over the sacraments and the proclamation of the Word, which make the Lord Jesus our contemporary.

28. Letter concerning Saints Cyril and Methodius*

As a geographical whole Europe is the fruit of two currents of Christian tradition, with two different but deeply complementary forms of culture.

St Benedict's influence embraced not only Europe, first of all Western and central, but through the Benedictine centers his influence also reached other continents. He is at the very center of that current which starts from Rome, the See of St Peter's successors.

The Holy Brothers of Thessalonica highlight first the contribution of ancient Greek culture, and afterwards, the influence of the Church of Constantinople and of the Eastern tradition. This has deeply marked the spirituality and culture of so many peoples and nations in the Eastern part of the European continent.

Today, after centuries of division of the Church between East and West, between Rome and Constantinople, the Second Vatican Council has taken decisive steps in the direction of full communion. Therefore, the proclamation of Saints Cyril and Methodius as Co-Patrons of Europe, alongside St Benedict, seems to correspond fully to the signs of our time. Especially if that happens in the year in which the two Churches, Catholic and Orthodox, have entered the stage of a decisive dialogue, which started on the Island of Patmos, linked with the tradition of St John the Apostle and Evangelist. Thus, this act intends to make this date memorable.

This proclamation also intends for men and women today to testify to the pre-eminence of the proclamation of the Gospel, entrusted by Jesus Christ to the Churches, and for which the two brothers, Apostles of the Slavs, toiled so much. This proclamation is the way and instrument of mutual knowledge and union among the various peoples of the new-born

---

* December 31, 1980. By this Apostolic Letter *Egregriae virtutis* the two blood brothers, born in Thessalonica in the ninth century, were declared Co-Patrons of Europe. Paul VI had already declared St. Benedict Patron of Europe, Oct. 24, 1964. Extract: *Oss. Rom.*, Jan. 1, 1981. TFS trans.

Europe. It ensures the Europe of today a common spiritual and cultural heritage.

I hope that thanks to the mercy of the Holy Trinity, through the intercession of the Mother of God and of all the Saints, what has divided not only the Churches but also peoples and nations may disappear; that instead, the differences of tradition and culture will prove to be the mutual fulfillment of a common richness.

May awareness of these spiritual treasures which have become along different ways the heritage of the individual nations of the European continent help modern generations to persevere in peace and mutual respect for the just rights of every nation, not ceasing to render the services necessary for the common good of the whole of humankind and for man's future on the whole earth.

Chapter Fourteen
RELATIONS WITH
THE JEWS

Introduction

When the Secretariat for Promoting Christian Unity members and consultors met for the very first time, in November 1960, Cardinal Augustin Bea informed them that the SPCU would undertake "the question of treating the Jews not on its own initiative, but at the express command of Pope John XXIII".*

After the Council, Paul VI established the Secretariat for Non-Christians, as well as the Secretariat for Non-Believers. But to the SPCU was confided the religious aspects of Jewish concerns.**

Although the SPCU had then a separate desk for Catholic/Jewish concerns, only on October 22, 1974, was a separate Commission for Religious Relations with the Jews papally established; on December 1, 1974, this Commission issued guidelines for the implementation of the Council's statement. Since 1972, a Liaison Catholic/Jewish Committee has been meeting annually.

I
VATICAN II'S DECLARATION
"NOSTRA AETATE"

Introduction

The SPCU approved its first draft on Jewish relations in November 1961, and included its final version as chapter five of *On Ecumenism*;

---

* As the Cardinal reminded the Council Fathers in November 1963. Cf. *Council Speeches* (New York: Paulist Press, 1964), p. 254.
** " . . . In rebus Iudaeos sub aspectu religioso respicientibus." Cf. *On the Reform of the Roman Curia (Regimini Ecclesiae), AAS* 59 (1967), p. 919.

chapter four treated religious freedom. Only in the second session (1963) did the Council discuss the subject. The Fathers urged that the document stand by itself and include also people of other world faiths, *e.g.*, Islam, Hinduism, Buddhism, African religions, etc. At the third session (1964), the new version was debated, and the Council approved the corrected, final draft at the fourth session, October 28, 1965: 2,221 in favor; 88 opposed. *The Declaration on the Relation of the Church to Non-Christian Religions (Nostra Aetate): AAS* 58 (1966), pp. 740–744. Here, nos. 4–5. English: SPCU translation, with some later changes by TFS.

* * *

As the Council searches into the mystery of the Church, it remembers the spiritual bonds which tie the people of the New Covenant to the offspring of Abraham.

Thus the Church of Christ acknowledges that, according to God's saving design, the beginnings of her faith and her election are found already in the patriarchs, Moses and the prophets. She professes that all who believe in Christ—Abraham's sons according to the faith (cf. Gal. 3, 7)—are included in this patriarch's call, and likewise that the salvation of the Church is symbolically prefigured in the exodus of the chosen people from the land of bondage. The Church, therefore, cannot forget that she received the revelation of the Old Testament through the people with whom God in his inexpressible mercy made the ancient covenant. Nor can she forget that she draws sustenance from the root of that well-cultivated olive tree onto which have been grafted the wild shoots, the Gentiles (cf. Rom. 11, 17–24). Indeed, the Church believes that by his cross Christ, who is our Peace, reconciled Jews and Gentiles, making the two one in himself (cf. Eph. 2, 14–16).

The Church keeps ever in mind the words of the Apostle about his kinsmen: "Theirs is the sonship and the glory and the covenant and the law and the worship and the promises; theirs are the fathers and from them is the Christ according to the flesh" (Rom. 9, 4–5), the Son of the Virgin Mary. She also recalls that the apostles, the Church's foundation-stones and pillars, as well as most of the early disciples who proclaimed the Gospel of Christ to the world, sprang from the Jewish people.

As Holy Scripture testifies, Jerusalem did not recognize the time of her visitation (cf. Luke 19, 44), nor did the Jews, in large number, accept the Gospel; indeed, not a few of them opposed its dissemination (cf. Rom. 11, 28). Nevertheless, now as before, God holds the Jews most dear for the sake of their fathers; he does not repent of the gifts he makes or of the calls he issues—such is the witness of the Apostle (cf. Rom. 11, 28–29; also cf. *Dogmatic Constitution on the Church: AAS* 57 [1965], p. 20). In company with the prophets and the same Apostle, the Church awaits that day, known to God alone, on which all peoples will address the Lord with a single voice and "serve him with one accord" (Soph. 3, 9; cf. Is. 66, 23; Ps. 65, 4; Rom. 11, 11–32).

Since the spiritual patrimony common to Christians and Jews is then so rich, the Council wishes to foster and commend mutual understanding and esteem. This will be the fruit, above all, of biblical and theological studies and of brotherly dialogues.

True, the Jewish authorities and those who followed their lead pressed for the death of Christ (cf. John 19, 6); still, what happened in his passion cannot be charged against all the Jews, without distinction, then alive, nor against the Jews of today. Although the Church is the new People of God, the Jews should not be represented as rejected by God or accursed, as if this followed from Holy Scripture. All should see to it, then, that in catechetical work and in the preaching of the Word of God they teach nothing save what conforms to the truth of the Gospel and the spirit of Christ.

The Church, moreover, rejects every persecution against any person. For this reason and for the sake of the patrimony she shares with the Jews, the Church decries hatreds, persecutions and manifestations of anti-Semitism directed against Jews at any time and by anyone. She does so, not impelled by political reasons, but moved by the spiritual love of the Gospel.

Besides, Christ underwent his passion and death freely and out of infinite love because of the sins of men in order that all might reach salvation. This the Church has always taught and teaches still; it is therefore the duty of the Church to proclaim the cross of Christ as the sign of God's all-embracing love and as the fountain from which every grace flows.

We cannot truly call upon God, the Father of all, if we refuse to treat in a brotherly way any class of people, created as all are in the image of God. Man's relation to God, the Father, and his relation to men, his brothers, are so linked together that Scripture says: "He who does not love does not know God" (1 John 4, 8).

No foundation therefore remains for any theory or practice that leads to discrimination between man and man or people and people insofar as their human dignity and the rights flowing from it are concerned.

The Church reproves, as foreign to the mind of Christ, any discrimination against persons or harassment of them because of their race, color, condition in life or religion. On the contrary, following the footsteps of the holy apostles Peter and Paul, the Council ardently implores the Christian faithful to "maintain good fellowship among the nations" (1 Pet. 2, 12) and, if possible, to live for their part in peace with all men (cf. Rom. 12, 18), so that they may truly be sons of the Father who is in heaven (cf. Matt. 5, 45).

II
GUIDELINES ON RELIGIOUS
RELATIONS WITH THE JEWS*

The Declaration *Nostra Aetate*, issued by the Second Vatican Council on 28 October 1965, "on the relationship of the Church to non-Christian religions" (n. 4), marks an important milestone in the history of Jewish-Christian relations.

Moreover, the step taken by the Council finds its historical setting in circumstances deeply affected by the memory of the persecution and massacre of Jews which took place in Europe just before and during the Second World War.

Although Christianity sprang from Judaism, taking from it certain essential elements of its faith and divine cult, the gap dividing them was deepened more and more, to such an extent that Christian and Jew hardly knew each other.

After two thousand years, too often marked by mutual ignorance and frequent confrontation, the Declaration *Nostra Aetate* provides an opportunity to open or to continue a dialogue with a view to better mutual understanding. Over the past nine years, many steps in this direction have been taken in various countries. As a result, it is easier to distinguish the conditions under which a new relationship between Jews and Christians may be worked out and developed. This seems the right moment to propose, following the guidelines of the Council, some concrete suggestions born of experience, hoping that they will help to bring into actual existence in the life of the Church the intentions expressed in the conciliar document.

While referring the reader back to this document, we may simply restate here that the spiritual bonds and historical links binding the Church to Judaism condemn (as opposed to the very spirit of Christianity) all forms of anti-semitism and discrimination, which in any case the dignity of the human person alone would suffice to condemn. Further still, these links and relationships render obligatory a better mutual understanding and renewed mutual esteem. On the practical level in particular, Christians must therefore strive to acquire a better knowledge of the basic components of the religious tradition of Judaism; they must strive to learn by what essential traits the Jews define themselves in the light of their own religious experience.

With due respect for such matters of principle, we simply propose

---

* Title: *Guidelines and Suggestions for Implementing the Conciliar Nostra Aetate (N. 4) Declaration*: Issued by the Commission for Religious Relations with the Jews, over the signatures of the Commission's president and secretary, John Cardinal Willebrands and Pierre-Marie de Contenson, O.P., December 1, 1974. French Text: *ASS* 67 (1975), p. 73–79. English transl. by the Commission.

some first practical applications in different essential areas of the Church's life, with a view to launching or developing sound relations between Catholics and their Jewish brothers.

1. Dialogue

To tell the truth, such relations as there have been between Jew and Christian have scarcely ever risen above the level of monologue. From now on, real dialogue must be established.

Dialogue presupposes that each side wishes to know the other, and wishes to increase and deepen its knowledge of the other. It constitutes a particularly suitable means of favouring a better mutual knowledge and, especially in the case of dialogue between Jews and Christians, of probing the riches of one's own tradition. Dialogue demands respect for the other as he is; above all, respect for his faith and his religious convictions.

In virtue of her divine mission, and her very nature, the Church must preach Jesus Christ to the world (*Ad Gentes*, 2). Lest the witness of Catholics to Jesus Christ should give offence to Jews, they must take care to live and spread their Christian faith while maintaining the strictest respect for religious liberty in line with the teaching of the Second Vatican Council (Declaration *Dignitatis Humanae*). They will likewise strive to understand the difficulties which arise for the Jewish soul—rightly imbued with an extremely high, pure notion of the divine transcendence—when faced with the mystery of the incarnate Word.

While it is true that a widespread air of suspicion, inspired by an unfortunate past, is still dominant in this particular area, Christians, for their part, will be able to see to what extent the responsibility is theirs and deduce practical conclusions for the future.

In addition to friendly talks, competent people will be encouraged to meet and to study together the many problems deriving from the fundamental convictions of Judaism and of Christianity. In order not to hurt (even involuntarily) those taking part, it will be vital to guarantee, not only tact, but a great openness of spirit and diffidence with respect to one's own prejudices.

In whatever circumstances as shall prove possible and mutually acceptable, one might encourage a common meeting in the presence of God, in prayer and silent meditation, a highly efficacious way of finding that humility, that openness of heart and mind, necessary prerequisites for a deep knowledge of oneself and of others. In particular, that will be done in connection with great causes such as the struggle for peace and justice.

2. Liturgy

The existing links between the Christian liturgy and the Jewish liturgy will be borne in mind. The idea of a living community in the service of God, and in the service of men for the love of God, such as it is realized in the liturgy, is just as characteristic of the Jewish liturgy as it is of the Christian one. To improve Jewish-Christian relations, it is important to take cognizance of those common elements of the liturgical life (formulas, feasts, rites, etc.) in which the Bible holds an essential place.

An effort will be made to acquire a better understanding of whatever in the Old Testament retains its own perpetual value (cf. *Dei Verbum*, 14–15), since that has not been cancelled by the later interpretation of the New Testament. Rather, the New Testament brings out the full meaning of the Old, while both Old and New illumine and explain each other (cf. *ibid.*, 16). This is all the more important since liturgical reform is now bringing the text of the Old Testament ever more frequently to the attention of Christians.

When commenting on biblical texts, emphasis will be laid on the continuity of our faith with that of the earlier Covenant, in the perspective of the promises, without minimizing those elements of Christianity which are original. We believe that those promises were fulfilled with the first coming of Christ. But it is none the less true that we still await their perfect fulfilment in his glorious return at the end of time.

With respect to liturgical readings, care will be taken to see that homilies based on them will not distort their meaning, especially when it is a question of passages which seem to show the Jewish people as such in an unfavourable light. Efforts will be made so to instruct the Christian people that they will understand the true interpretation of all the texts and their meaning for the contemporary believer.

Commissions entrusted with the task of liturgical translation will pay particular attention to the way in which they express those phrases and passages which Christians, if not well informed, might misunderstand because of prejudice. Obviously, one cannot alter the text of the Bible. The point is that, with a version destined for liturgical use, there should be an overriding preoccupation to bring out explicitly the meaning of a text, while taking scriptural studies into account.

The preceding remarks also apply to introductions to biblical readings, to the Prayer of the Faithful, and to commentaries printed in missals used by the laity.

3. Teaching and Education

Although there is still a great deal of work to be done, a better understanding of Judaism itself and its relationship to Christianity has been achieved in recent years thanks to the teaching of the Church, the study and research of scholars, as also to the beginning of dialogue. In this respect, the following facts deserve to be recalled.

——It is the same God, "inspirer and author of the books of both Testaments," (*Dei Verbum*, 16), who speaks both in the old and new Covenants.

——Judaism in the time of Christ and the Apostles was a complex reality, embracing many different trends, many spiritual, religious, social and cultural values.

——The Old Testament and the Jewish tradition founded upon it must not be set against the New Testament in such a way that the former seems to constitute a religion of only justice, fear and legalism, with no appeal to the love of God and neighbour (cf. Deut. 6:5, Lev. 19:18, Matt. 22:34-40).

——Jesus was born of the Jewish people, as were his Apostles and a large number of his first disciples. When he revealed himself as the Messiah and Son of God (cf. Matt. 16:16), the bearer of the new Gospel message, he did so as the fulfilment and perfection of the earlier Revelation. And, although his teaching had a profoundly new character, Christ, nevertheless, in many instances, took his stand on the teaching of the Old Testament. The New Testament is profoundly marked by its relation to the Old. As the Second Vatican Council declared: "God, the inspirer and author of the books of both Testaments, wisely arranged that the New Testament be hidden in the Old and the Old be made manifest in the New" (*Dei Verbum*, 16). Jesus also used teaching methods similar to those employed by the rabbis of his time.

——With regard to the trial and death of Jesus, the Council recalled that "what happened in his passion cannot be blamed upon all the Jews then living, without distinction, nor upon the Jews of today" (*Nostra Aetate*, 4).

——The history of Judaism did not end with the destruction of Jerusalem, but rather went on to develop a religious tradition. And, although we believe that the importance and meaning of that tradition were deeply affected by the coming of Christ, it is still nonetheless rich in religious values.

——With the prophets and the apostle Paul, "the Church awaits the day, known to God alone, on which all peoples will address the Lord in a single voice and 'serve him with one accord' (Soph. 3:9)" (*Nostra Aetate*, 4).

Information concerning these questions is important at all levels of Christian instruction and education. Among sources of information, special attention should be paid to the following:

——catechisms and religious textbooks
——history books
——the mass-media (press, radio, cinema, television).

The effective use of these means presupposes the thorough formation of instructors and educators in training schools, seminaries and universities.

Research into the problems bearing on Judaism and Jewish-Christian relations will be encouraged among specialists, particularly in the fields of exegesis, theology, history and sociology. Higher institutions of Catholic research, in association if possible with other similar Christian institutions and experts, are invited to contribute to the solution of such problems. Wherever possible, chairs of Jewish studies will be created, and collaboration with Jewish scholars encouraged.

4. Joint Social Action

Jewish and Christian tradition, founded on the Word of God, is aware of the value of the human person, the image of God. Love of the same God must show itself in effective action for the good of mankind. In the spirit of the prophets, Jews and Christians will work willingly together, seeking social justice and peace at every level—local, national and international.

At the same time, such collaboration can do much to foster mutual understanding and esteem.

5. Conclusion

The Second Vatican Council has pointed out the path to follow in promoting deep fellowship between Jews and Christians. But there is still a long road ahead.

The problem of Jewish-Christian relations concerns the Church as such, since it is when "pondering her own mystery" that she encounters the mystery of Israel. Therefore, even in areas where no Jewish communities exist, this remains an important problem. There is also an ecumenical aspect to the question: the very return of Christians to the sources and origins of their faith, grafted on to the earlier Covenant, helps the search for unity in Christ, the cornerstone.

In this field, the bishops will know what best to do on the pastoral level, within the general disciplinary framework of the Church and in line with the common teaching of her magisterium. For example, they will create some suitable commissions or secretariats on a national or regional level, or appoint some competent person to promote the implementation of the conciliar directives and the suggestions made above.

On 22 October 1974, the Holy Father instituted for the universal Church this Commission for Religious Relations with the Jews, joined to the Secretariat for Promoting Christian Unity. This special Commission, created to encourage and foster religious relations between Jews and Catholics—and to do so eventually in collaboration with other Christians—will be, within the limits of its competence, at the service of all interested organizations, providing information for them, and helping them to pursue their task in conformity with the instructions of the Holy See.

The Commission wishes to develop this collaboration in order to implement, correctly and effectively, the express intentions of the Council.

III
THE LIAISON
CATHOLIC/JEWISH COMMITTEE

1. Address of Paul VI*

This Text (*Guidelines and Suggestions . . .*) evokes the difficulties and confrontations, with all the regrettable elements involved, which have marked relations between Christians and Jews over the past two thousand years.

While this reminder has been salutary and indispensable, one should not forget that there have also been between us down the centuries elements other than confrontations. There are still many people who can witness to what was done by the Catholic Church during the last war, in Rome itself, under the energetic impulse of Pius XII—as we personally testify—and by numerous bishops, priests and members of the faithful, to save innocent Jews from persecution, often at the peril of their own lives.

Moreover, as we look at history as a whole, we cannot fail to note the connections, often too little remarked upon, between Jewish thought and Christian thought. We may here merely recall the influence exercised at various periods in the most exalted spheres of Christian reflection by the thought of the great Philo of Alexandria, who was considered by Saint Jerome as "the most expert among the Jews," a judgment echoed by, among others, the Franciscan Doctor Bonaventure of Bagnoregio.

But, precisely, since the Catholic Church has just commemorated, at the same time as the seventh centenary of the death of Saint Bonaventure of Bagnoregio, that of the philosopher and theologian Thomas Aquinas, who died, like Bonaventure, in the year 1274, there very naturally come to our mind the numerous references of our angelic doctor to the work of the rabbinic scholar from Cordoba, who died in Egypt at the dawn of the thirteenth century, Moshe ben Maimon, in particular his explanations of the Mosaic Law and the precepts of Judaism.

For his part, the thought of Saint Thomas Aquinas was to expand in

---

* January 10, 1975, in Rome, during the Committee's fourth annual meeting. Excerpts: *AAS* 67 (1975), pp. 95–97, from the French. Dr. Gerhard Riegner, Secretary General of the World Jewish Congress, first addressed the Pope. He said that the Jews "are happy that Christians have been invited to learn by what essential traits the Jews define themselves in the light of their own religious experience. We hope that this effort will lead to a greater appreciation of the essential significance that peoplehood and land hold in the Jewish faith". Cf. *New York Times*, January 11, 1975.

its turn in the scholarly tradition of medieval Judaism. As has been shown for example by the studies of Professor Charles Touati of the School of Higher Studies in Paris, and by Professor Joseph Sermoneta of the Hebrew University in Jerusalem, there existed in the Latin West at the end of the thirteenth and in the fourteenth century, a whole Jewish Thomistic school.

These are merely some examples drawn from many others. They bear witness to the fact that at different periods and at a certain level there has been a real and profound mutual esteem and a conviction that we had something to learn from one another.

We formulate, gentlemen, the sincere wish that, in a manner appropriate to our age and thus in a field that to some extent exceeds the limited domain of merely speculative and rational exchanges, a true dialogue may be established between Judaism and Christianity.

We hope that this dialogue, conducted with great mutual respect, will help us to know one another better and will lead us all to know better the Almighty, the eternal One, to follow more faithfully the ways that have been traced out for us by him who, in the words of the prophet Hosea (11:9), is in our midst as the Holy One, who takes no pleasure in destroying.

We dare to think that the recent solemn reaffirmation of rejection by the Catholic Church of every form of anti-Semitism and the invitation that we have extended to all the faithful of the Catholic Church to pay heed in order "to learn by what essential traits the Jews define themselves in the light of their own religious experience" may, on the Catholic side, provide the conditions for beneficial development. We do not doubt that you on your part will correspond, according to your own perspectives, to our effort, which can only have meaning and fruitfulness in reciprocity.

2. Address of Hon. Philip Klutznick to John Paul II*

With *Nostra Aetate,* promulgated by the Vatican Council in 1965 and the Guidelines of 1975 which amplified the teachings of the Conciliar document, the Church embarked on a profound examination of its relationship to Judaism. The establishment of the Commission for Religious Relations with the Jews and the formation of the International Catholic-Jewish Liaison Committee served to encourage a fraternal dialogue based on mutual respect. The result has been a significant improvement in Catholic-Jewish understanding and friendship, based on the affirmation of a shared reverence for Sacred Scripture, the condemnation of anti-Semitism, support of religious liberty, and joint social action.

Judaism and the Catholic Church share in the belief that authentic

---

* March 12, 1979, as spokesman for the Jewish members of the Liaison Catholic/Jewish Committee meeting in Rome. Excerpts from text distributed by Union of American Hebrew Congregations, March 1979.

faith compels religious people to be vitally concerned for the welfare of individuals and societies. God is not indifferent to man's injustice towards his fellow man. We have noted with admiration that in areas of the world where grave violations of religious liberty and of other human rights exist, the Catholic Church has courageously upheld the values which flow from our common conviction that human beings are not accidental appearances on the cosmic scene but creations of God whose dignity stems from the Divine image implanted by the Creator. As a people that has known suffering, and impelled by the moral teachings of our faith, we are committed to the alleviation of human misery and injustice wherever they may be found.

Your Holiness, Poland, your country of origin, was a great center of Jewish culture for over a thousand years. This great epoch in Jewish history came to a tragic end during World War II when most of European Jewry was destroyed, victims of the most virulent anti-Semitism. Your Holiness experienced first-hand the demonic consequences of religious and racial hatred which resulted in the immense human suffering of World War II and culminated in the Holocaust of European Jewry. Therefore you have a special understanding of the importance of eradicating the spiritual sickness that is anti-Semitism and of combatting prejudice in all its forms.

Anti-Semitism is a disease which can be dormant and then reappear in new and insidious guises. That is why the Jewish community has been so concerned with the *problem of Soviet Jewry.*

We dedicate ourselves again to the struggle for human rights and fundamental freedoms for all persons, and to the cause of religious liberty. Jews will work together with Catholics and others in the common search for social justice and peace.

The Guidelines implementing *Nostra Aetate* invite Christians to learn by what essential traits Jews define themselves in the light of their religious experience. In the Jewish self-understanding, the bond of the people of the covenant to the land is fundamental. In the long history of the Jewish people, few events have been experienced with as much pain as the Exile, the *separation of the people from the land promised by God. Never, during this separation, has the people of Israel lost hope in the fulfillment of the Divine Promise.*

Much progress in the relations of the Catholic Church and the Jewish people has been made since Vatican Council II.

At Liaison Committee meetings we have welcomed the progressive elimination of references unfavorable to Jews and Judaism from Catholic teaching materials, and the removal of unfavorable stereotypes from Jewish teaching materials. We trust that during your Pontificate these principles will be reaffirmed and further progress will be made in advancing mutual esteem between our faith communities.

3. Reply of John Paul II*

As your representative has mentioned, it was the Second Vatican Council with its declaration *Nostra Aetate* (n. 4) that provided the starting point for this new and promising phase in the relationship between the Catholic Church and the Jewish religious community. In effect, the council made very clear that, "while searching into the mystery of the church," it recalled "the spiritual bond linking the people of the new covenant with Abraham's stock" (*Nostra Aetate*, 4). Thus it understood that our two religious communities are connected and closely related at the very level of their respective religious identities. For "the beginning of (the Church's) faith and election are already found among the patriarchs, Moses and the prophets," and "therefore she cannot forget that she received the revelation of the Old Testament through the people with whom God in his inexpressible mercy deigned to establish the Ancient Covenant" (*ibid.*). It is on the basis of all this that we recognize with utmost clarity that the path along which we should proceed with the Jewish religious community is one of fraternal dialogue and fruitful collaboration.

According to this solemn mandate, the Holy See has sought to provide the instruments for such dialogue and collaboration and to foster their realization both here at the center and elsewhere throughout the Church. Thus, the Commission for Religious Relations with the Jews was created in 1974. At the same time, the dialogue began to develop at several levels in the local Churches around the world and with the Holy See itself. I wish to acknowledge here the friendly response and good will, indeed the cordial initiative, that the Church has found and continues to find among your organizations and other large sections of the Jewish community.

I believe that both sides must continue their strong efforts to overcome the difficulties of the past, so as to fulfill God's commandment of love, and to sustain a truly fruitful and fraternal dialogue that contributes to the good of each of the partners involved and to our better service of humanity.

The "Guidelines" you have mentioned, whose value I wish to underline and reaffirm, indicate some ways and means to obtain these aims. You have rightly wished to stress a point of particular importance: "Christians must therefore strive to acquire a better knowledge of the basic components of the religious tradition of Judaism; they must strive to learn by what essential traits the Jews define themselves in the light of their own religious experience" (Prologue, "Guidelines and Suggestions for Jewish-Christian Relations," Vatican Commission for Religious Relations with the Jews, Dec. 1, 1974). Another important reflection is the following: "In

---

* March 12, 1979, in reply to Hon. P. Klutznick's address. Extracts: *AAS* 71 (1979), pp. 435–438.

virtue of her divine mission, and her very nature, the Church must preach Jesus Christ to the world (*Ad Gentes*, 2). Lest the witness of Catholics to Jesus Christ should give offense to Jews, they must take care to live and spread their Christian faith while maintaining the strictest respect for religious liberty in line with the teaching of the Second Vatican Council (Declaration *Dignitatis Humanae*). They will likewise strive to understand the difficulties which arise for the Jewish soul—rightly imbued with an extremely high, pure notion of the divine transcendence—when faced with the mystery of the incarnate Word" (Guidelines, 1).

These recommendations refer, of course, to the Catholic faithful, but I do not think it is superfluous to repeat them here. They help us to have a clear notion of Judaism and Christianity and of their true mutual relationship. You are here, I believe, to help us in our reflections on Judaism. And I am sure that we find in you, and in the communities you represent, a real and deep disposition to understand Christianity and the Catholic Church in its proper identity today, so that we may work from both sides toward our common aim of overcoming every kind of prejudice and discrimination.

In this connection it is useful to refer once more to the Council declaration *Nostra Aetate* and to repeat what the "Guidelines" say about the repudiation of "all forms of anti-Semitism and discrimination," "as opposed to the very spirit of Christianity," but "which in any case the dignity of the human person alone would suffice to condemn" (Guidelines, prologue). The Catholic Church therefore clearly repudiates in principle and in practice all such violations of human rights wherever they may occur throughout the world. I am, moreover, happy to evoke in your presence today the dedicated and effective work of my predecessor Pius XII on behalf of the Jewish people. And on my part I shall continue with divine help in my pastoral ministry in Rome—as I endeavored to do in the See of Cracow—to be of assistance to all who suffer or are oppressed in any way.

Following also in particular in the footsteps of Paul VI, I intend to foster spiritual dialogue and to do everything in my power for the peace of that land which is holy for you as it is for us, with the hope that the City of Jerusalem will be effectively guaranteed as a center of harmony for the followers of the three great monotheistic religions of Judaism, Islam and Christianity, for whom the City is a revered place of devotion.

I am sure that the very fact of this meeting today, which you have so kindly asked to have, is itself an expression of dialogue and a new step toward that fuller mutual understanding which we are called to achieve. By pursuing this goal we are all sure of being faithful and obedient to the will of God, the God of the Patriarchs and Prophets. To God, then, I would like to turn at the end of these reflections. All of us, Jews and

Christians, pray frequently to him with the same prayers, taken from the Book which we both consider to be the Word of God. It is for him to give to both religious communities, so near to each other, that reconciliation and effective love which are at the same time his command and his gift (Cf. *Lev* 19:18; *Mk* 12:30). In this sense, I believe, each time that Jews recite the "Shema' Israel", each time that Christians recall the first and second great commandments, we are, by God's grace, brought nearer to each other.

IV
JOHN PAUL II'S
HOMILY AT AUSCHWITZ*

Can it still be a surprise to anyone that the pope born and brought up in this land, the pope who came to the See of St. Peter from the diocese in whose territory is situated the camp of Oswiecim (Auschwitz), should have begun his first encyclical with the words *"redemptor hominis"* and should have dedicated it as a whole to the cause of man, to the dignity of man, to the threats to him, and finally to his inalienable rights that can so easily be trampled on and annihilated by his fellowmen? Is it enough to put man in a different uniform, arm him with the apparatus of violence? Is it enough to impose on him an ideology in which human rights are subjected to the demands of the system, completely subjected to them, so as in practice not to exist at all?

I have come and I kneel on this Golgotha of the modern world, on these tombs, largely nameless like the great Tomb of the Unknown Soldier. I kneel before all the inscriptions that come one after another bearing the memory of the victims of Oswiecim in the languages: Polish, English, Bulgarian, Romany, Czech, Danish, French, Greek, Hebrew, Yiddish, Spanish, Flemish, Serbo-Croat, German, Norwegian, Russian, Romanian, Hungarian and Italian.

In particular I pause with you, dear participants in this encounter, before the inscription in Hebrew. This inscription awakens the memory of the people whose sons and daughters were intended for total extermination. This people draws its origin from Abraham, our father in faith (cf. Rom. 4:12), as was expressed by Paul of Tarsus. The very people who received from God the commandment "thou shalt not kill" itself experi-

---

* June 7, 1979, in Poland, at an outdoor Mass on the site of the former concentration camp of Brezezinka, near the former larger camp of Ozwiecim (known during World War II by its German name of Auschwitz). At Ozwiecim, the Pope prayed at the death cell of Blessed Maximilian Kolbe. Extract: *Origins*, June 21, 1979, pp. 73–74.

enced in a special measure what is meant by killing. It is not permissible for anyone to pass by this inscription with indifference.

Oswiecim is a testimony of war. War brings with it a disproportionate growth of hatred, destruction and cruelty. It cannot be denied that it also manifests new capabilities of human courage, heroism and patriotism, but the fact remains that it is the reckoning of the losses that prevails. That reckoning prevails more and more, since each day sees an increase in the destructive capacity of the weapons invented by modern technology. Not only those who directly bring wars about are responsible for them, but also those who fail to do all they can to prevent them. Therefore I would like to repeat in this place the words that Paul VI pronounced before the United Nations organization:

"It is enough to remember that the blood of millions of men, numberless and unprecedented sufferings, useless slaughter and frightful ruin are the sanction of the covenant which unites you in a solemn pledge which must change the future history of the world: no more war, war never again. It is peace, peace which must guide the destinies of peoples and of all humankind" (*AAS* 57, 1965, p. 881).

If, however, Oswiecim's great call and the cry of man tortured here is to bear fruit for Europe, and for the world also, the Declaration of Human Rights must have all its just consequences drawn from it, as John XXIII urged in the encyclical *Pacem in Terris*. For the declaration is "a solemn recognition of the personal dignity of every human being, an assertion of everyone's right to be free to seek out the truth, to follow moral principles, discharge the duties imposed by justice, and lead a fully human life. It also recognized other rights connected with these" (*AAS* 55, 1963, pp. 295–296).

V

JOHN PAUL II'S REMARKS AT
BATTERY PARK, NEW YORK CITY*

A few months ago, I met with an international group of Jewish representatives in Rome. On that occasion, recalling the initiatives undertaken following the Second Vatican Council under my predecessor Paul VI, I stated that "our two communities are connected and closely related at the very level of their respective religious identities," and that on this basis "we recognize with utmost clarity that the path along which we

---

* October 3, 1979. With the Statue of Liberty in the background, the Pope concluded his speech on the symbolized freedom and justice with "a special word of greeting to the leaders of the Jewish community, whose presence here honors me greatly". Extract: *AAS* 71(1979), p. 1180.

should proceed is one of fraternal dialogue and fruitful collaboration" (*L'Osservatore Romano*, March 12–13, 1979). I am glad to ascertain that this same path has been followed here, in the United States, by large sections of both communities and their respective authorities and representative bodies. Several common programs of study, mutual knowledge, a common determination to reject all forms of anti-Semitism and discrimination, and various forms of collaboration for human advancement, inspired by our common biblical heritage, have created deep and permanent links between Jews and Catholics. As one who in my homeland has shared the suffering of your brethren, I greet you with the word taken from the Hebrew language: Shalom! Peace be with you.

VI
ADDRESS TO JEWISH REPRESENTATIVES IN FRANCE*

It is a joy for me to receive the representatives of the numerous and vigorous Jewish community of France. This community has, indeed, a long and glorious history. Is it necessary to recall here the theologians, exegetes, philosophers and personages of public life who have distinguished it in the past and still distinguish it? It is true also, and I make a point of mentioning it, that your community suffered a great deal during the dark years of the occupation and the war. I pay homage to these victims, whose sacrifice, we know, has not been fruitless. It was from there that there really began, thanks to the courage and decision of some pioneers, including Jules Isaac, the movement that has led us to the present dialogue and collaboration, inspired and promoted by the Declaration *Nostra Aetate* of the Second Vatican Council.

This dialogue and this collaboration are very much alive and active here in France. This makes me happy. Between Judaism and the Church, there is a relationship, as I said on another occasion to Jewish representatives, a relationship "at the very level of their respective religious identities" (Address of 12 March 1979). This relationship must be further deepened and enriched by study, mutual knowledge, religious education on both sides, and the effort to overcome the difficulties that still exist. That will enable us to work together for a society free of discriminations and prejudices, in which love and not hatred, peace and not war, justice and not oppression, may reign. It is towards this biblical ideal that we should always look, since it unites us so deeply. I take advantage of this happy opportunity to reaffirm it to you again and to express to you my hope of pursuing it together.

* May 31, 1980, in Paris. SPCU *IS*, 44 (1980), pp. 87–88.

VII

ADDRESS TO JEWISH REPRESENTATIVES IN BRAZIL*

The Declaration *Nostra Aetate* of the Second Vatican Council states that "sounding the depths of the mystery which is the Church, this sacred Council remembers the spiritual tie which bonds the people of the New Covenant to the offspring of Abraham." In this way the relationship between the Church and Judaism is not something external to the two religions: it is something based on the religious heritage characteristic of both, in the specific origin of Jesus and the Apostles, and in the environment in which the early Church grew and developed. If, in spite of all this, our respective religious identities divide us, and at times they have divided us painfully through the centuries, this must not prevent us now with respect to these same identities, from desiring to make the most of our common heritage and thus cooperate, in the light of the same heritage, in the solution of the problems that afflict modern society in need of faith in God, obedience to his holy law, and active hope in the coming of his Kingdom.

I am very happy to know that this spirit of cooperation exists here in Brazil especially through the Jewish-Christian Fraternity. Jews and Catholics try in this way to deepen their common biblical heritage, without disguising, however, the differences that separate them, and thus renewed mutual knowledge will be able to lead to a more adequate presentation of each religion in the teaching of the other. On this solid basis it will then be possible to build up, as you are already doing, the activity of cooperation for the benefit of the individual person, for the advancement of his rights, frequently trampled on, and his just participation in the pursuit of the common good without exclusivism or discrimination.

VIII

HOMILY CONCERNING THE MIDDLE EAST TENSIONS**

Harsh conflicts have broken out. The Middle East region is pervaded by tensions and strife, with the ever incumbent risk of the outbreak of new wars. It is painful to note that conflicts have often taken place following the lines of division between different confessional groups, so that it has

---

* July 3, 1980, in Sao Paulo. Extract: SPCU *IS*, 44 (1980), p. 88.

** October 5, 1980, Otranto on Italy's southeasern coast. At the end of a homily on martyrdom, commemorating the 500th anniversay of the slaughter of Antonio Primoldo and 800 companions by Moslem Turks. The Pope refers to those further eastern regions where "the three great monothestic religions had their historical origins—Christianity, Judaism, and Islam," and to the present "particularly delicate situations that have developed there and still exist." Extracts: *AAS* 72 (1980), pp. 1016–1017. TFS trans.

been possible for some people, unfortunately, to feed them artificially by appealing to the religious sentiment.

The terms of the Middle East drama are well known: the Jewish People, after tragic experiences connected with the extermination of so many sons and daughters, driven by the desire for security, set up the State of Israel. At the same time the painful condition of the Palestinian People was created. A large part of them are excluded from their land. These facts are before everyone's eyes. And other countries, such as Lebanon, are suffering as a result of a crisis which threatens to be a chronic one. In these days, finally, a bitter conflict is in progress in a neighbouring region, between Iraq and Iran.

Gathered here today, at the tombs of the Martyrs of Otranto, let us meditate on the words of the liturgy, which proclaim their glory and their power in the Kingdom of God: "They will govern nations and rule over peoples, and the Lord will reign over them for ever." Therefore in union with these Martyrs, we present to the One God, to the Living God, to the Father of all men, the problems of peace in the Middle East. We present also the problem, so dear to us, of the rapport and real dialogue with those with whom we are united—in spite of the differences—by faith in one God, the faith inherited from Abraham. May the spirit of unity, mutual respect and understanding prove to be more powerful than what divides and sets in opposition.

Lebanon, Palestine, Egypt, the Arabian Peninsula, Mesopotamia nourished for millennia the roots of traditions sacred for each of the three religious groups. There again, for centuries, Christian, Jewish, and Islamic communities lived together on the same territories. In those regions, the Catholic Church boasts communities outstanding for their ancient history, vitality, variety of rites, and their own spiritual characteristics.

Towering high over all this world, like an ideal center, a precious jewel-case that keeps the treasures of the most venerable memories, and is itself the first of these treasures, is the Holy City, Jerusalem. Today it is the object of a dispute that seems without a solution, tomorrow—if people only want it!—tomorrow a crossroads of reconciliation and peace.

Yes, we pray that Jerusalem, instead of being today the object of strife and division, may become the meeting point towards which the eyes of Christians, Jews, and Moslems will continue to turn, as to their own common hearth; around which they will feel as brothers, no one superior, no one in the debt of others; towards which pilgrims, followers of Christ, or faithful of Mosaic law, or members of the community of Islam, will continue to direct their steps.

IX
ADDRESS TO JEWISH REPRESENTATIVES IN GERMANY*

If Christians must consider themselves brothers and sisters of all men and women, and behave accordingly, this holy obligation is all the more binding when they find themselves before members of the Jewish people! In the "Declaration on the Relationship of the Church with Judaism" in April of this year, the Bishops of the Federal Republic of Germany put this sentence at the beginning: "Whoever meets Jesus Christ, meets Judaism." I would like to make these words mine too. The faith of the Church in Jesus Christ, the son of David and the son of Abraham (cf. Mt 1:1) actually contains what the Bishops call in that declaration "the spiritual heritage of Israel for the Church" (par. 11), a living heritage, which must be understood and preserved in its depth and richness by us Catholic Christians.

The concrete fraternal relations between Jews and Catholics in Germany assume a quite particular value against the grim background of the persecution and the attempted extermination of Judaism in this country. The innocent victims in Germany and elsewhere, the families destroyed or dispersed, the cultural values or art treasures destroyed forever, are a tragic proof of where discrimination and contempt of human dignity can lead, especially if they are animated by perverse theories on a presumed difference in the value of races or on the division of men into men of "high worth," "worthy of living," and men who are "worthless," "unworthy of living." Before God all men are of the same value and importance.

In this spirit, during the persecution, Christians likewise committed themselves, often at the risk of their lives, to prevent or relieve the sufferings of their Jewish brothers and sisters. I would like to express recognition and gratitude to them at this moment. And also to those people who, as Christians, affirmed they belonged to the Jewish people, travelled along the *via crucis* of their brothers and sisters to the end—like the great Edith Stein, called in her religious institute Teresa Benedikta of the Cross.

I mention also Franz Rosenzweig and Martin Buber; through their creative familiarity with the Jewish and German languages, they constructed a wonderful bridge for a deeper meeting of both cultural areas.

It is not just a question of correcting a false religious view of the Jewish people, which in the course of history was one of the causes that contributed to misunderstanding and persecution, but above all of the dialogue between the two religions which—with Islam—gave the world faith in the one, ineffable God who speaks to us, and which desire to serve him on behalf of the whole world.

* November 17, 1980, Mainz, FDR. Extracts: *AAS* 73 (1981), pp. 78–82. TFS trans.

The first dimension of this dialogue, that is, the meeting between the people of God of the Old Covenant never revoked by God (cf. Rom 11:29), and that of the New Covenant, is at the same time a dialogue within our Church, that is to say, between the first and the second part of its Bible.

Jews and Christians, as children of Abraham, are called to be a blessing for the world (cf. Gen 12:2 ff.), by committing themselves together for peace and justice among all persons and peoples, with the fullness and depth that God himself intended us to have, and with the readiness for sacrifices that this high goal may demand. The more our meeting is imprinted with this sacred duty, the more it becomes a blessing also for ourselves.

In the light of this promise and call of Abraham's, I look with you to the destiny and role of your people among the peoples. I willingly pray with you for the fullness of Shalom for all your brothers and sisters in nationality and in faith, and also for the land to which Jews look with particular veneration.

Our century saw the first pilgrimage of a Pope to the Holy Land. In conclusion, I wish to repeat Paul VI's words on entering Jerusalem: "Implore with us, in your desire and in your prayer, respect and peace upon this unique land visited by God! Let us pray here together for the grace of a real and deep fraternity between all men and women, between all peoples! . . . May they who love you be blessed. Yes, may peace dwell in your walls, prosperity in your palaces. I pray for peace for you. I desire happiness for you (cf. Ps 122:6–9)."

May all peoples in Jerusalem soon be reconciled and blessed in Abraham! May he, the ineffable, of whom his creation speaks to us; he, who does not force humankind to goodness, but guides it: he, who manifests himself in our fate and is silent; he, who chooses all of us as his people; may he guide us along his ways to his future!

Praised be his Name! Amen.

Index